GREGOROVIUS'

HISTORY OF THE CITY OF ROME IN THE MIDDLE AGES.

VOL. I.

James Hyatt, Sr.

Ferdinand Gregorovius

HISTORY
OF
THE CITY OF ROME
IN THE
MIDDLE AGES

BY

FERDINAND GREGOROVIUS

TRANSLATED FROM THE FOURTH
GERMAN EDITION
BY
MRS. GUSTAVUS W. HAMILTON

VOL. I

(A.D. 400–568)

LONDON
GEORGE BELL & SONS
1909

ITALICA PRESS
NEW YORK
2000

FERDINAND GREGOROVIUS'
HISTORY OF THE CITY OF ROME IN THE MIDDLE AGES
VOLUME 1

THE ELECTRONIC EDITION WAS DEVELOPED USING
ADOBE PAGEMAKER 6.5 & ADOBE ACROBAT 4.0
AT ITALICA PRESS, 595 MAIN STREET,
SUITE 605, NEW YORK, NY
10044

THE PRINT EDITION WAS PRINTED
ON 60 LB NATURAL PAPER
BY BOOKMOBILE,
ST. PAUL, MN
U. S. A.

THIS VOLUME WAS COMPLETED ON MARCH 10, 2000.
ADDITIONAL VOLUMES TO BE PUBLISHED QUARTERLY.

Library of Congress Cataloging-in-Publication:
Gregorovius, Ferdinand, 1821-1891.
[Geschichte der Stadt Rom im Mittelalter. English]
History of the city of Rome in the Middle Ages / Ferdinand Gregorovius; translated from the 4th German ed. by Mrs. Gustavus W. Hamilton.
p. cm.
Translation of Geschichte der Stadt Rom im Mittelalter.
Originally published: London: G. Bell, 1894-1902.
Includes bibliographical references and index.
Contents: v. 1. A.D. 400-568 — v. 2. A.D. 568-800 (2nd rev. ed.)
1. Rome (Italy)—History — 476-1420. 2. Rome (Italy) — History — 1420-1798.
1. Hamilton, Annie. II. Title.

DG811 .G8313 2000
945'.63203—dc21

00-046150

Cover Illustration: Christ and Saints Peter and Paul, flanked by Saints Cosma and Damiano. Mosaic, c. 530. SS. Cosma and Damiano, Rome.

FOR FURTHER INFORMATION
AND ADDITIONAL TITLES ON ROME,
THE MIDDLE AGES, AND THE RENAISSANCE,
VISIT:
www.ItalicaPress.com

TRANSLATOR'S PREFACE

I SHALL never forget the pleasure with which, while spending a winter in Rome fourteen years ago, I first made acquaintance with Gregorovius's *History*. The book seemed to open up a whole world of interest, and long centuries that had before been hid in darkness became suddenly peopled and alive with stirring scenes. The desire to translate the work and to make it known to others of my compatriots, who had not the leisure, or perhaps the necessary acquaintance with German to read it in the original, crossed my mind even then. But my friends did not encourage the idea, and circumstances prevented me from following the promptings of ambition. The charm that the book possessed for me fourteen years ago it possesses still, and each successive visit to Italy but deepens my gratitude to the author whose work has revealed a thousand years of its past, and has served to link the memory of almost every town of the kingdom, no less than that of every corner of its capital, with some picture of its history. Nearly four years ago I began the translation, of which the present volume is the first instalment. The work has suffered from many interruptions, and the publication of a fourth edition in

Germany, of the appearance of which I was in the beginning unaware, obliged me to go over a great part of the book a second time. But the pleasure that the work afforded, and the delight of living in thought at least again in Rome—which, in spite of all the changes of recent years, exercises over me a fascination little less than it exercised over the pilgrims of the Middle Ages—made me regardless of hindrances, and overcame every consideration. It is only now, while watching the progress of these volumes through the press, that a sense of my presumption in undertaking so ambitious a task has come home to me. In justice to myself, however, I must remind the reader that Gregorovius's *History* has been allowed to remain untranslated and practically unknown in England for more than thirty years; and, judging from the nature and length of the work, it seemed little likely any accomplished scholar, such as those who have given us Curtius or Mommsen, would come forward to give us the *City of Rome in the Middle Ages.* Two qualifications for the task also I at least possessed— command of the necessary leisure, and an intense interest in the subject dealt with.

The work might well have been undertaken by an abler hand. It could have been undertaken by no one to whom it would more truly have been a labour of love. Mrs Lecky, in her article on Gregorovius's Roman Journal, in the present (October) number of *Longman's Magazine,* tells us that the historian himself admitted that his style in the first chapters of the history was *tendu,* "uncertain and therefore laboured." It is, consequently, scarcely surprising that the opening pages of each volume have baffled all my attempts to make them read smoothly. That the defects of the translation are not, however, greater than they are, is due to the help I have received from my kind friend, Dr Meissner, of the Queen's College, Belfast, who, at various stages of the work, has aided me with his valuable criticism and advice; also to Mr G. F. Hill, of the British Museum, who, with infinite care and patience, has revised the notes. To both these gentlemen and to the other friends who, at different times and in various ways, have given me help, I desire to express my sincere thanks.

A. H.

PREFACE TO THE SECOND EDITION.

THE biographical notice prefixed to the present edition of *Rome in the Middle Ages* is a translation, with some omissions, of the *Vorwort* to Gregorovius's *Römische Tagbücher.* This preface was written and the journals were edited, as the public are aware, by Gregorovius's life-long friend, the late Professor Friedrich Althaus, to whose son, Mr T. F. Althaus, I now wish to convey my thanks for his courtesy in allowing me to translate his father's Essay.

My thanks are also once more due to Mr G. F. Hill, of the British Museum, who has aided me in the revision of the volume from beginning to end. The various mistakes pointed out by critics have, I hope, been corrected in the present edition.

A. H.

October 1900.

CONTENTS

BOOK FIRST.

FROM THE BEGINNING OF THE FIFTH CENTURY TO THE FALL OF THE WESTERN EMPIRE IN 476.

CHAPTER I.

CHAPTER II.

CHAPTER V.

CHAPTER VI.

CHAPTER VII.

BOOK SECOND.

FROM THE BEGINNING OF THE REIGN OF ODOACER TO THE ESTABLISHMENT OF THE EXARCHATE IN RAVENNA, 568.

CHAPTER I.

CHAPTER II.

CHAPTER III.

CHAPTER IV.

CHAPTER VII.

BIOGRAPHICAL NOTICE

By the Late Prof. FRIEDRICH ALTHAUS.[1]

FERDINAND GREGOROVIUS, the youngest of eight brothers and sisters, was born at the little town of Neidenburg, in East Prussia, on January 19, 1821. Neidenburg, which owes its foundation to the Teutonic order, stands close to the Polish frontier, and is situated in a desolate tract of country, broken by pine woods, hills and lakes. The place, insignificant in itself, acquires a historic character from the still-existing castle of the Teutonic knights, a monument of the Middle Ages, that played no unimportant role in the history of the Gregorovius family, and in particular was to exercise a weighty influence on the development of its youngest member. Gregorovius's father was *Justiz-rath* at Neidenburg. He found the old castle—originally one of the finest belonging to the order—in partial ruin, and it was owing to his exertions that its restoration was accomplished by the Burggrave of Marienburg, the Minister von Schön. The offices of the Court of

[1] Translated and abridged from the *Vorwort* to the *Römische Tagebücher* of F. Gregorovius.

Justice were now removed to the Castle, and the family acquired therein a magnificent dwelling. The children grew up amidst the remains of great historic memories. The fortress was their pride, and they soon came to regard it as the property of the family. On the imagination of the boyish Ferdinand, above all, the life which they led in its halls and corridors, its vaults and subterranean rooms, the distant views from its turret widows, made a powerful impression. To the influence of his surroundings he himself attributed the fact of his early and decided bent towards antiquity and mediaevalism. He frequently expressed the opinion that he would probably never have written the history of Rome in the Middle Ages, had not his youth been passed in that old castle of the Teutonic knights.

To this chief circumstance of his childhood was added at the age of nine the impression made by the Polish revolution of 1830. Owing to the proximity of Neidenburg to the scene of the bloody struggles called forth by the rising, he not only heard much concerning the events of the war, but had opportunity of adding to his information by personal observation. Soon after the outbreak of the revolution a regiment of Cossacks, driven across the frontier by the Polish rebels, sought shelter in Neidenburg. And again, after the defeat of Ostrolenka, the boy saw the unfortunate Polish fugitives surrendered by thousands to Russia. These events left a deep impression on his mind. They broke like sharp and disintegrating elements from the modern outer world into the world of his historic dreams, rudely linking the present with the past. For the first time he experienced the feeling of hatred towards the oppressor, of compassion with the oppressed. His interest in the Poles, whose blood-soaked plains he looked on from the Castle of Neidenburg, developed into sympathy, which strengthened from year to year, and afterwards found characteristic expression in the beginning of his literary career.

In other respects no sound from the outer world penetrated the solitude of the remote East Prussian village and the monotonous provincial existence of its inhabitants. Gregorovius's father was an austere and serious man, who lived solely for his work. His mother, a tall and handsome woman, religious to enthusiasm, was a chronic invalid, and died of consumption in 1831. Soon afterwards the boy left home to attend the gymnasium at Gumbinnen, taking up his abode with a younger brother of his father, who also was an officer of justice at the place. His tastes were chiefly centred on history, geography and ancient languages, and even in his boyish years he dreamed much of distant countries and ages. A great impression was made upon him when an army doctor, whom he saw once at Neidenburg, told him that he had spent three weeks in Rome. He gazed at the man in astonishment, and then ran to tell his father of the wondrous fact. His thoughts took another flight to distant lands when, in 1833, one of his brothers joined the Bavarians to fight for the Greeks in their struggle for independence. On returning home for the holidays, he was accustomed to lie for hours on the hill where the castle stood, watching the clouds float overhead, and letting his thoughts, oblivious of time, wander with them over land and sea. Indeed, until the end of his life, next to works of history, accounts of travel in distant quarters of the world formed a favourite entertainment of his leisure hours.

His course at the gymnasium ended, he entered the university of Königsberg in the autumn of 1838, at the age of seventeen. And since his father belonged to a clerical family (his great-grandfather, grandfather and father having each in succession been vicar of the same parish in East Prussia), Ferdinand at his father's wish studied theology. But he did so without inclination, and the fact, that with the exception of Caesar von Lengerke (a poet who had strayed into dogmatics) theology was taught in Königsberg by a set of dull pedants, did not contribute to encourage a taste for a study that had been forced upon him. More than to any of the other professors he felt himself drawn to the philosopher Karl Rosenkranz. An afterglow of the age of Kant still lingered over the university of Königsberg, and Rosenkranz, the highly-cultured imaginative thinker and brilliant orator, commanded the enthusiasm of the younger generation. Gregorovius became one of his foremost pupils. He studied Kant and Hegel and believed himself destined to be a philosopher. Of historians he attended the lectures of Drumann and Voigt, but learning, however vast, which lacked the vital spark of genius, failed to satisfy him. Everywhere, however, he experienced the influence of the free scientific spirit which still reigned at

Königsberg. The university was perhaps already on the decline; but, conscious of standing like a lighthouse of German culture on the confines of Slavic barbarism, the German character in East Prussia and its ancient capital put forward all its strength. The work of culture undertaken by the Teutonic knights, the Reformation, Kant, the Wars of Liberation, the foundation of the State on the principles of humanity, all these were the proudly cherished possessions of the East Prussians, and Gregorovius himself had received sufficient of the impress of this virile race to prize the intellectual training which, through his Alma Mater, it received.

He left the university in the autumn of 1841, after having passed the first theological examination. That theology was not his vocation he had meantime more and more clearly recognised. For some years, first in Neidenburg, then at other places in East and West Prussia, he followed the calling of private tutor. He was daunted by the thought of wearing for life the fetters of an official position. He dreamed occasionally of an academic life; but resolved in any case to break with his theological antecedents, and still believing himself destined to become a philosopher, he took his degree in the philosophic faculty at Königsberg with the Dissertation 'Concerning the Conception of the Beautiful in Plotinus and the Neo-Platonists.' Like his teacher Rosenkranz, he at the same time eagerly engaged in literary pursuits. He wrote several poems, chiefly lyric, and in 1845, at the age of twenty-four, appeared before the public with his first book, the romance of *Werdomar and*

Wladislaw, a work which at every turn reflects the *'Sturm und Drang'* period of intellectual development through which he was then passing. With its Polish German complications, its pre-revolutionary provincialism and prison adventures, its Titanic pessimism and its enthusiastic hopes for the future, the romance was entirely the product of the time, and frequently arouses our surprise by the realism which displays the author's close observation of life. But the tone of the book is, above all, romantic. Echoes of Jean Paul, Hölderlin, Eichendorff and Immermann weave themselves into a wondrous symphony. In this youthful work Gregorovius pays his tribute to modern German romanticism, with the evident foreknowledge, it is true, of alienation from a world which did not in truth satisfy him. We cannot say that he realised in irony or in political and philosophic radicalism the discrepancy between his ideals and actuality, as did Heine and Heine's young German comrades. But his longings went out towards great men and great deeds. 'Epic without action,' he says, in the preface to his books, 'such is our time,' and to him mankind seemed wandering in a wilderness of romanticism, from the labyrinths of which they could only be released by the appearance of some heroic leader.

Werdomar and Wladislaw met with no striking success; but in Königsberg, where the romance appeared in the University press, it received attention, and soon after, in 1846, Gregorovius returned to make a longer sojourn in the capital of East Prussia. Destitute of means as he was, he could not make up his mind to abandon the world of teaching; in fact, he continued it as his chief means of subsistence during the next six years. Königsberg, moreover, offered a stimulating intellectual atmosphere, the means for the continuation of scientific and literary studies, and to these he dedicated the greater part of his leisure. Next to philosophy, history once more exercised its attractions over him, and at Drummann's instigation he undertook a monograph on the Emperor Hadrian, a work doing all honour to the young scholar's industry and learning, which was finished at the beginning of 1848, but which, owing to the storms of the revolution and difficulties with publishers, only appeared in 1851. In a retrospect of Gregorovius's life and intellectual development, this history of the Emperor Hadrian still awakens our interest from a twofold point of view, as having been his first historical work of importance, and as the first evidence of the direction of his thoughts towards Rome.

In the meantime the outbreak of the revolution of 1848 had irresistibly diverted the attention of the historian from the distant past to the tumultuous movement of the present. At this time, owing to the bold political ideas of Johann Jacoby and Walesrode's humorous-satirical utterances, freethinking Königsberg was conspicuous as one of the centres of the revolution. Several of Gregorovius's older and younger fellow-students—among them Wilhelm Jordan and Rudolf Gottschall—appeared before the public as poets of a new period of *Sturm und Drang,* and Gregorovius himself entered with enthusiasm into the agitation of popular meetings and clubs, which served as organs to the hopes and fears, the love and hatred of that excited period. He hoped for the regeneration of the German people, but not for this alone. His sympathies, in accordance with his democratic creed, were essentially cosmopolitan. That which he desired for Germany he also demanded as an inalienable right for the other struggling nationalities. He was more especially saddened by the cruel suppression of the revolt of the Poles, for whose struggles for independence, ever since his boyish years at Neidenburg — when he witnessed the tragic vicissitudes of the revolution of 1830—he had always retained the strongest sympathy. His views on this question he made known in the early summer of 1848, in the historical-political treatise *Die Idee des Polentums.* Somewhat later he published his *Polen und Magyarenlieder.* But in spite of all, his character in the main was not in sympathy with politics, but with culture. In his history of Hadrian he notes with satisfaction that so few wars were made under this Emperor, for what was wanted was a peaceful history of mankind, a history of society. And never even in the midst of political strife did he lose sight of the *Culturideal,* of the importance of which during this very crisis of struggle for national development, Germany was reminded by the first centenary festival of Goethe.

Among the writings that appeared in connection with this festival, Gregorovius's *Wilhelm Meister in seinen socialistischen Elementen* was one of the most remarkable. "As the final aim of Nature and History," he observes in this ingenious work, "is to find man, so all genuine poetry is only directed towards the discovery of man. This is the motive of all true tragedy, all comedy and all epic poetry. Goethe is the Columbus who in his Wilhelm Meister has discovered for us the America of Humanism." In the *Wanderjahre* more especially Gregorovius perceived the foundations and fundamental ideas of a world ordered according to Humanistic principles. In his opinion the *Lehrjahre* reflect the eighteenth century; in the *Wanderjahre* Goethe as a prophet foresees the future of mankind and indicates its chief features. Echoes of the latest revolutionary storms, the current of socialistic ideas from France, are blended together in this analysis of Goethe's social philosophy. In the form, and partly also in the constructive dialectics, of Gregorovius's literary contribution to the festival, the influence of a many years' study of Hegel is unmistakable; but his absorption in Goethe's manner of thought already points to his alienation from the abstract formalism of Hegel, which not long after became an accomplished fact.

In 1851 he appeared once more as poet with the drama, 'The Death of Tiberius,' a work which, if it showed no marked dramatic talent, revealed at least the fine epic and lyric gift of which he was to give frequent proofs in after years. The fact that about the same time he erected literary monuments to two Roman emperors shows his increasing interest in the Roman world. At this period he also entered with zest into the study of Italian literature. Dante especially he read with enthusiasm. Longings for the home of the artist's ideals and of physical beauty grew in him, the narrower and more oppressive became the circumstances ot his life in Königsberg. Some incentive from outside alone was needed to set him free.

One of his Königsberg friends, Ludwig Bornträger, a young and gifted historic painter, was sent by the doctors to Italy on account of some ailment of the chest. Gregorovius determined to follow. His means for this undertaking being scanty, he trusted to his talents, and in the spring of 1852 left Königsberg, confident in a good star which pointed the way to the South.

The *Römische Tagebücher* begin at this date, and to them we may turn for all account of his journey, the early years of his sojourn in Italy, his visit to Corsica, his arrival in Rome, and his later experiences and labours in the Eternal City.[1]

. . . . . .

He felt himself happy in beautiful Italy, in the realisation of his longings through so many years of northern fogs, happy in its nature, its art, its antiquity, and among its people. He looked on Italy and the Italians not merely with the eye of the historian and poet, but with a genial desire for

[1] Dr Althaus goes on to relate the circumstances of his first meeting with our author, and tells us that in the winter of 1852–53 Gregorovius dwelt in the neighbourhood of the Pincio, not far from the Piazza Barberini.—TRANS.

social intercourse and enjoyment of the present. He was equally ready for philosophic conversation and for jesting and naïve talk with the naïve people of the South. He loved especially to associate with children, and here his imagination was always active. The mere names of places involuntarily awoke historic associations, and in a few words uttered at a spot he frequently drew a characteristic picture of the surrounding landscape which made an indelible impression on the mind of his hearers.

Italy was to be to him a second home.... During the following years of his life in Rome appeared the works which have made his name famous: the incomparable book on Corsica, *Die Grabmäler der Päpste,* the classic idyllic epic *Euphorion,* the five volumes of the *Wanderjahre in Italien,* the *Geschichte Rom's im Mittelalter,* the monograph on Lucrezia Borgia. This is not the place to speak of these works at greater length; they have won their rank in literature and would secure the renown of the author, even had he received no other recognition than that of the Romans, who awarded him— (for the first time to a non-Catholic)—the citizenship of the Eternal City, and who, by a resolution of their municipality, ordered the translation into Italian of his principal work, *The History of the City of Rome....*[1] The idea of this work

[1] Writing at Genzano, on Oct. 3, 1854, Gregorovius says in his diary (p. 16, 2nd edition): " I propose to write the *History of the City Rome in the Middle Ages.* It seems to me that this work requires a peculiar gift; yea, a commission from Jupiter Capitolinus himself. I conceived the thought, struck by the view of the city from the bridge leading to the island of S. Bartholomew. I must undertake something

as the mission of his life filled Gregorovius with enthusiasm; the passionate longing to carry out the task and the untiring labour which he dedicated to it were the motives which above all else riveted him to Rome for many years and endowed his sojourn in Italy with a noble consecration. The great task accomplished, the Roman period of his life reached its natural end, and the attractions of his German fatherland reasserted themselves. In 1874 he left Rome, and in common with his brother, Colonel Julius, and his step-sister Ottilie, founded a new home in Munich. Here in the city of the fine arts there was no lack of associations with Italy. The University and the Bavarian Academy of Sciences, of which he was elected a member, afforded him the necessary means for intellectual activity, while the proximity of Italy facilitated intercourse with the beautiful country that had become to him a second fatherland. He, whose twofold relations with Italy and Germany were so firmly fixed and widespreading, could not indeed renounce his connections with Italy. Back and back they drew him across Alps and Apennines to the South. If he spent the summer and autumn in Germany, he generally passed the winter and spring amid the circle of his Italian friends, and usually in Rome. Likewise for many years he drew the material for his literary work in great part from Italy, or the relations between Italy and Germany.

great, something that will lend a purpose to my life. I told Dr Braun, Secretary to the Archaeological Institute, of my idea. He listened attentively, and then said: 'It is an attempt in which anyone must fail.'"

. . . . . .

He also visited Greece, Egypt, Syria, and Asia Minor, and published the results of his travels in studies in the history and on the scenery of Athens, the charming idyll *Corfu* and the monograph *Athenais, Geschichte einer Byzantischen Kaiserin....* His *Geschichte Athen's im Mittelalter* was published in 1889. On November 15, 1890, he delivered a festival oration in the Bavarian Academy of Sciences on "The great Monarchies, or the World Empires of History" which was afterwards printed; a pamphlet insignificant in compass, but in contents and style a grand achievement, in which as historian and philosopher he set up a last noble monument of himself.

Scarcely had he finished this work when his brother Julius fell seriously ill. Tenderly nursed by brother and sister, he recovered, contrary to expectation; but his tedious convalescence was scarcely over when the other brother received the summons of fate. His illness lasted but a few weeks, and on May 1, 1891, Ferdinand Gregorovius passed away soon after the completion of his seventieth year.

Of the impression evoked by his character and personality, his talents and his achievements, the sympathy shown during his illness, and the grief called forth both in Italy and Germany by his death, gave eloquent testimony. The King of Italy and the Prince-Regent of Bavaria, the Burgermeister of Munich and the Syndic of Rome, the German and the Italian press gave public expression to their feeling. Different as may be the opinions concerning him, that he united in a rare degree the spirit of the learned enquirer with the creative power of the artist, that his character was firmly rooted in the noblest humanistic ideals, no one could doubt. To an almost unparalleled degree in the second half of the nineteenth century Ferdinand Gregorovius realised in Germany the ideal of a Humanist. Nothing ignoble dared approach him. Democratic in his convictions, he was aristocratic in the same sense that Goethe and Schiller were aristocratic. Above all he valued that liberty and independence which he had attained by heroic exertions and enduring work. In the consciousness of this he was happy in spite of all else that life may have denied him. And as he remained free from the pedantry and exclusiveness of his craft, as in himself he united the character of the scholar and the man of the world, so his historical studies offered no obstruction to the keenest sympathy with the great movements of the time. In this sense history was to him, as Freeman puts it, "the politics of the past, politics the history of the present."

. . . . . .

F.A.

LONDON, *May* 1892.

FERDINAND GREGOROVIUS, HISTORIAN OF ROME

BY D. S. CHAMBERS

1. GREGOROVIUS AND HIS *HISTORY OF THE CITY OF ROME*

The basic account of the life and personality of Ferdinand Gregorovius (1821–91) remains the preface by Friedrich Althaus to the edition of Gregorovius's diary (1852–74), published soon after his friend's death.[1] An abridged version of this preface was translated by Mrs. Annie Hamilton and published in the second edition of Volume One of her translation of his *History of the City of Rome*, so it is included in the present electronic and print versions; she published a translation of the full text with her translation of the invaluable diary, which combines autobiographical information with a first-hand account of Roman life and events in the mid-nineteenth century.[2] The recent new edition of the original German text of the diary omits Althaus's preface but includes the diary's rather fragmentary continuation after 1874 – from the previously unpublished MS. in Munich (Bayerische Staatsbibliothek, Handschriften- und Inkunabelabteilung, Gregoroviusiana, no. 1) – as well as introductory essays, extensive annotations and

[1] *Römische Tagebücher von Ferdinand Gregorovius* (Stuttgart, 1892; 2nd ed., 1893), *Vorwort*, pp. iii-xvi.

[2] *The Roman Journals of Ferdinand Gregorovius*...translated...by Mrs Gustavus W. Hamilton, (London, 1907; 2nd ed., 1911).

bibliography.[3] A biography which appeared in 1921 is mainly useful for its inclusion of correspondence with his publisher,[4] but there are numerous shorter biographical appreciations[5] and miscellaneous studies which testify to a continuing interest in Gregorovius.[6]

Gregorovius, as readers of Althaus's preface will soon discover, was a romantic Northerner, an East Prussian with boundless literary ambition who spent much of his life in Italy. One of a family of eight, he grew up among Baltic lakes and pinewoods, in a former castle of the Teutonic Knights, at Neidenburg, near the Polish border, where his father was a legal official and Lutheran pastor. It was his sympathy with Polish national aspirations in 1830, he later declared, that first aroused in him a passionate interest in poetry and history.[7] At the university of Königsberg he began by studying theology, but later switched to philosophy, and came under the

[3] Ed. by H. W. Kruft and M. Völkel, F. Gregorovius, *Römische Tagebücher 1852–1889* (Munich, 1991). This edition is cited in the footnotes below for any references to the diary after 1874.

[4] Johannes Hönig, *Ferdinand Gregorovius der Geschichtsschreiber der Stadt Rom* (Stuttgart-Berlin, 1921).

[5] See particularly the rediscovered essay by Robert Davidsohn, published by Steffi Roettgen, "Dal Börsen-Courier di Berlino al 'Genio' di Firenze. Lo storico Robert Davidsohn (1853–1937) e il suo inedito Inserto fiorentino," in Max Seidel, ed., *Storia dell'arte e politica culturale intorno al 1900* (Florence, 1999), pp. 313–38 (at pp. 324–32).

[6] Among them, with reference to much unpublished material, A. Forni, *La questione di Roma medievale. Una polemica tra Gregorovius e Reumont* (Rome, 1985). See also the *Tagebücher,* edited by Kruft, as above, and the volume edited by Esch and Petersen cited below, n. 8. An article by the present author, D. S. Chambers, "Ferdinand Gregorovius and Renaissance Rome" (text of the Annual Lecture for 1999 to the Society for Renaissance Studies) is due to appear (2000 or 2001) in *Renaissance Studies.* I am grateful to the editor for permission to repeat some passages from the same article here.

[7] He claimed to have sixteenth-century Polish ancestors called von Grezgorzweski, according to Robert Davidsohn (see Steffi Roettgen, as above, p. 322).

influence of Karl Rosenkrantz (1805–79), a disciple of Hegel. In the 1840s his literary output was already prolific. Besides his dissertation on the aesthetics of Plotinus, he wrote numerous poems and essays, a romantic novel, a study of the Roman Emperor Hadrian and his times and a drama about the death of the Emperor Tiberius. Meanwhile he earned his living as a private tutor and a radical political journalist, strongly committed to the liberal ideals of the revolutionaries of 1848 and shattered by their failure.

Italy, however, which he first visited in 1852, did most to shape the rest of his life and his writing. In 1991, the centenary of his death was celebrated by the German Historical Institute in Rome with a conference, the papers of which have since been published, on the theme of Gregorovius and Italy.[8] After brief visits to Venice and Florence, he took a boat to Corsica, and only reached Rome, his goal which was to remain his home for over twenty years, in October of the same year. In his diary he recorded his pleasure in exploring the city, then characterised by its peaceful silence.[9] He settled down first to write articles about Corsica for a German newspaper, the Augsburg *Allgemeine Zeitung* – they formed the basis for a highly successful book, which he summarised as his "first work whose material was supplied by the majesty of Nature and by real life." He was soon writing more articles, many of them about Rome or its region, vivid descriptions of places and persons, combining subjective experience with historical and local information.[10] In 1853 Gregorovius travelled south, first to Naples and

[8] Arnold Esch and Jens Petersen, eds., *Ferdinand Gregorovius und Italien. Eine kritische Würdigung* (Tübingen, 1993). Particularly valuable is the study by Arnold Esch, "Gregorovius als Geschichtsschreiber der Stadt Rom: sein Spätmittelalter in heutiger Sicht" (pp. 131–84), even though it is mainly confined to Gregorovius's treatment of the century ca. 1360–1460 (Books xi-xiii of his *History*).

[9] *Journals*, as n. 2, p. 3.

[10] *Ibid.*, pp. 3–4. The *Corsica*, first published in 2 vols. (Stuttgart, 1854), was finished in April 1853 and during the same month Gregorovius sent his

its region, then to Sicily. He evidently saw himself at this stage in his life as a literary free spirit, a new Goethe perhaps, but not necessarily a historian, though he was already reading a lot about medieval and later Rome, and in 1854 he began preparing a book on papal tombs, which came out in 1857.[11] This, he explained in a letter to Friedrich Althaus, an admirer of his writing whom he befriended in Rome in 1853, was intended to link papal biography to works of art, and would be "something between a historical study and an English essay, but without English thoroughness" (*Gediegenheit*).[12] The idea of writing it had come to him in St. Peter's, when he fantasised that the tombs resembled a senate of gods or divine protectors of that great temple.[13] At the time he had been admiring a Renaissance monument in the left-hand corner of the apse, Girolamo della Porta's tomb of Paul III.[14] When describing it he made a typical jump of conjecture – the sort of jump for which some critics derided him – by suggesting that the Farnese pope, who died in 1549, is shown meditating on the new age of persecution into which the Church had entered.[15]

articles on "Roman portraits" and "Jews in Rome" to the *Allgemeine Zeitung*. A first collection of his travel essays was published as *Figuren. Geschichte, Leben und Scenerie aus Italien* (Leipzig, 1856); later editions, with additional essays, appeared under the title *Wanderjahre in Italien*.

[11] *Die Grabmäler der Römischen Päpste* (Leipzig, 1857).

[12] Gregorovius to Althaus, 21 April 1854, in F. Althaus, "Ungedruckte Briefe von Ferdinand Gregorovius," *Deutsche Revue über das gesamte nationale Leben der Gegenwart*, 1.2(1894): 247, quoted by Michael Borgolte, "Zwischen 'englischem Essay' und 'historischer Studie,' Gregorovius' *Grabmäler der Päpste* von 1854/81," in Esch and Petersen, as n. 8, p. 104.

[13] Dedication to Dr Alertz (*Grabmäler*, unpaginated); quoted by Borgolte, as above, p. 103; trans. by R. Seton-Watson, *The Tombs of the Popes. Landmarks in Papal History* (Westminster, 1903), p. x.

[14] Described in *Grabmäler*, pp. 146–51 (trans., pp. 108-11).

[15] Ibid., p. 151 (trans., p. 111).

In October 1854, however, he had another revelation, a Gibbon-like experience convincing him that his destiny was to write the history of the city of Rome in the middle ages. This would not be concerned with "decline of the empire" like Edward Gibbon's great work, but rather with the city's eternal vitality during the centuries through which Gibbon had passed rather quickly. He recorded in his diary that he was gazing from the bridge leading to the Tiber Island and contemplating the view beyond it to the Palatine Hill, thinking about medieval Rome dominated by antiquity.[16] (With hindsight, but without mentioning again the view from the bridge, he wrote many years later, in the conclusion to the final volume, "The idea of the work was suggested by the overwhelming spectacle of the monumental grandeur of the city, and perhaps by the presentiment that the history of the Roman Middle Ages would soon reach its perfect close.")[17] A sketch by himself, made on another occasion, presumably, and from a slightly different viewpoint, gives an idea of the prospect.[18]

Gregorovius at once set himself a rigorous programme of reading, including the whole series of Muratori's *Rerum Italicarum Scriptores*.[19] In the relaxed atmosphere of the 1850s he seems to have had no difficulty gaining access to Roman libraries. The Dominicans welcomed him to read at the Minerva,

[16] *Journals*, as n. 2, p. 16. The conception, development and early reception of the work are discussed by Waldemar Kampf, "Die Entstehungsgeschichte des Werkes," in the edition cited below, n. 41, vol. IV, pp. 15–30.

[17] VIII, p. 705.

[18] Many of Gregorovius's sketches (8 sketchbooks survive in Munich, Bayerische Staatsbibliothek, Handschriften- und Inkunabelabteilung, Gregoroviusiana, nos. 7–14) are reproduced in the *Tagebücher,* edited by Kruft and Völkel, as in n. 3; the one referred to here is fig. 27. These reproductions, however, tend to make Gregorovius's pencil sketches look darker and more emphatic than in the original.

[19] *Journals*, as n. 2, pp. 18–24.

so did the Augustinians at the Biblioteca Angelica; the former physician of Gregory XVI, Dr. Clemens August Alertz, gave him the run of his own extensive library. In May 1859 he was even admitted to the Vatican Library.[20] In 1859 he had visited Monte Cassino – the description in his diary[21] is memorable – and in the great monastic library he caught sight of legendary figures, including the Vatican archivist Augustin Theiner whose printed collection of documents relating to papal temporal power were among Gregorovius's essential reading.

The ideal, stated in 1858 in a letter to his publisher, and to which he remained constant, was to combine scholarly research with imaginative presentation, *Forschung und künstlerische Darstellung*.[22] Just as he went instinctively to sources rather than studies among printed books, he had quickly developed a nose for original documents. In part he just felt the need to see and handle them, just as he had a compelling need to see places and monuments for himself. Already in the mid-1850s he had been curious to get access to the Colonna archives and refused to believe the Colonna historian, Antonio Coppi, who told him they contained nothing relevant; he waited until 1862 to see for himself.[23] In December 1857 the duke of Sermoneta gave him access to the Gaetani archives. In September 1858 in Florence he not only looked at manuscripts in the Magliabecchiana but applied for permission to consult the archives.[24] He was disap-

[20] *Ibid.*, p. 56.

[21] *Ibid.*, pp. 66–72.

[22] Gregorovius to Baron Cotta, 25 August 1858, in Hönig, as n. 4, p. 224; also quoted by Kruft and Völkel in the "Einführung" to their edition of the *Tagebücher*, as n. 3, p. 9; and by Esch, "Gregorovius als Geschichtsschreiber der Stadt Rom: sein Spätmittelalter in heutiger Sicht," as n. 8, pp. 177–78.

[23] *Ibid.*, pp. 59, 156, 158; trans. Hamilton, pp. 24, 172, 174. (See also his letter to Baron Cotta, dated New Year's Eve, 1862, in Hönig, as n. 4, pp. 47–48.)

[24] *Journals*, as n. 2, pp. 47–48.

pointed to find virtually nothing there for the early period, but he met Cesare Guasti, Gaetano Milanesi and the Arabic scholar Michele Amari; he must have been advised how much material from later centuries awaited him. At Monte Cassino the monks had allowed him to inspect early charters. But it was a very random hunt at this stage and, quite apart from the inadequacy of catalogues and inventories, one cannot help wondering whether Gregorovius could properly read or understand what he inspected; he was a good Latinist, but he had had no training in paleography and diplomatic.

In Gregorovius's applications to enter private libraries and archives there was also an element of social ambition; even if his diary is full of ridicule about vainglory of this sort, he exploited the kudos gained by public knowledge of the task he had set himself. Thanks to his connections in the Prussian embassy, invitations piled up and he gained entry into exalted circles, to the diplomatic world, to the palaces of the nobility and generally to international and intellectual society in Rome, whether permanent or transitory. In 1860 he was promised an annual grant from the Prussian government.[25] He moved into a three-room apartment with a breathtaking view over the city from its back windows[26]; it was at no. 13 via Gregoriana, a street which he came to love possessively, not least because its name resembled his own.[27] An inscription was placed there in 1992.[28]

After spending some months organising his notes concerning the thirteenth century, on 24 June 1863 Gregorovius wrote to his publisher Baron Cotta that the six-volume plan had to be

[25] *Ibid.*, pp. 92, 99.

[26] *Ibid.*, pp. 105–6.

[27] *Ibid.*, p. 458.

[28] Reproduced in Esch and Peterson, as n. 8, p. 289.

revised.[29] Volume Five was now giving him so much trouble, there was so much material, that the whole of it, i.e., Books Nine and Ten, would have to be devoted to the thirteenth century, with a break at 1260. Volume Six would now deal with the papacy's absence from Rome from 1305 to 1376, and Volume Seven would cover all the rest up to 1527. In another letter he wrote that the later period was less important than the thirteenth and fourteenth centuries,[30] but later, when he came to write about it, he seems to have revised that opinion, too.

Gregorovius had stressed in a letter to his publisher in June 1863 that the problem of slow delivery was largely owing to the bulk of new material he had collected from archives. This may seem rather an exaggeration for the twelfth and thirteenth centuries, but the problem was bound to grow thereafter. He had become aware of three important points: first, that the best hope of his work's success lay not only in his literary genius and a critical use of printed sources, but the discovery and interpretation of new material; second, that some of the best sources of information were not to be found in Rome itself; third, that new opportunities for research had arisen since the momentous events of 1859–60, which had culminated in the Kingdom of Naples, the Duchy of Tuscany and most of the Papal State joining Piedmont in the new Kingdom of Italy. He had to attend all the more seriously to *Forschung*[31]; in the autumn of 1862 he returned to the Florentine archives, but he soon began to plan a much wider campaign. Some of his experiences were discouraging; in September 1863 he found the archives in Bologna in incredible confusion; so were those at Siena. An even worse mess awaited

[29] Hönig, as n. 4, pp. 255–56.

[30] Gregorovius to Cotta, 8 August 1863, in Hönig, as n. 4, pp. 257–58.

[31] This attention to archives is also discussed by Esch (*ibid.*, pp. 158–61); by Kampf, in his recent edition of Gregorovius's *Geschichte der Stadt Rom*, as below, n. 41, IV, pp. 18–22; and in my own article, as n. 6.

him in Orvieto. Only in Naples, which he reached in August 1864, was he more favourably impressed.[32] Volume Five came out eventually in 1865; Volume Six was finished in 1866 and published the following year.

Volume Seven was the hardest of all to write. Gregorovius complained on 22 November 1868 to his long-suffering publisher that it would still take him nearly two more years.[33] In February 1869 he warned that his archival discoveries, particularly those concerning the Borgias, demanded extra space and that he needed to include four chapters on cultural themes; in April he proposed splitting the volume into two parts and adding an eighth volume to conclude the work.[34] In July 1868 he again set out on his travels, inspecting archives in Spoleto, Foligno, Gubbio, Fano and Urbino.[35] Since the Austrian defeat in 1866 and the annexation to Italy of Eastern Lombardy and the Veneto, he was also able to explore the resources of Venice.[36] A first visit was paid at the end of September 1869 to Modena, sacred soil as the home town of Ludovico Muratori, and the Este archives. The revised Volume Seven extended only to 1503 and was published in 1870; it is by far the longest volume, although it contains only a single book, Book XIII. Regarding the fifteenth and early sixteenth centuries, he was certainly justified in his claim to have found new documentary material far and wide. During a first visit to the Gonzaga archives in Mantua in December 1871,[37] he was astonished by the abundance of

[32] *Journals*, as n. 2, pp. 171, 206–7, 211, 216.

[33] Hönig, as n. 4, p. 277.

[34] *Ibid.*, pp. 280–81.

[35] *Journals*, as n. 2, pp. 312–15.

[36] *Ibid.*, p. 316.

[37] On Gregorovius's visits to Mantua and his special appreciation of the Gonzaga archives there, see, as well as my article cited in n. 6, my additional

correspondence from Rome and read some particularly useful letters relating to the Sack of Rome (although the great historian Leopold von Ranke had warned him that there was nothing to find about it that he himself had not seen).[38] Gregorovius just had enough time to insert some of this into his eighth and final volume. But even after he had laid down his pen he went on updating the footnotes for the later editions, adding more recent bibliography, new documentary references and comments. These marvellous and essential footnotes have, in many later editions, been shamefully omitted, cut down or made more "up to date."[39]

2. THE *HISTORY OF THE CITY OF ROME IN THE MIDDLE AGES*

Gregorovius's *Geschichte der Stadt*, as he usually called it, *The History of the City*,[40] can be a nightmare to consult because of the author's successive revisions and insertion of new footnotes and later editors' further revisions and excisions.[41] The English translation by Mrs. Gustavus W. (Annie) Hamilton,[42] presented here, was based on the 4th German

article "Lo storico Ferdinand Gregorovius e Mantova," in R. Signorini ed., *Carlo D'Arco nel suo tempo* (forthcoming).

[38] *Journals*, as n. 2, p. 414.

[39] See also Esch, as n. 8, pp. 134–35, on vandalistic treatment of the footnotes.

[40] F. Gregorovius, *Die Geschichte der Stadt Rom im Mittelalter vom V. bis zum XVI. Jahrhundert*, 1st ed., 8 vols. (Stuttgart, 1859–72); 4th ed. (the canonical, author's final version), 8 vols. (Stuttgart, 1886–96).

[41] The most recent edition of the German text by Waldemar Kampf, 4 vols., (Darmstadt, 1953–57; Munich, 1978) provides a limited selection from Gregorovius's footnotes in vol. IV together with updated bibliographical notes and references.

[42] *A History of the City of Rome in the Middle Ages*, vols. I-VIII (published in stages: London, 1894–1902; 2nd ed. of vols. I–IV, 1900–1905).

edition and is itself a herculean achievement. Fortunately, Annie Hamilton included the footnotes in her translation, though the reader should be warned that she followed the convention used in the German edition of numbering footnotes within the page, not the chapter or section; obviously, therefore, neither page nor footnote numbers correspond exactly between German and English versions.[43] Her translation has long been out of print, apart from the short selections (without footnotes) published under another title by the University of Chicago Press, nearly thirty years ago.[44] More will be said later about Mrs. Hamilton's translation and about the reception of Gregorovius's work in the English-speaking world.

The *History of the City* was planned originally as a work in six volumes. Gregorovius, with (for him rather uncharacteristic) Prussian discipline and exactness, intended to subdivide each volume into two books and each book, covering roughly a century, was to contain seven chapters. Gregorovius began writing in 1856; and Volume One, which follows the scheme precisely, extending from the early fifth century to the death of the Byzantine commander Narses in 567, was ready and published in 1859. His intention, announced at the outset, (I, p. 2: ii, 1/1) was to focus upon the special link – *die Verbindung* – between the German nation and Rome, from 410 to 1527 (Mrs. Hamilton's translation of *Verbindung* as "ancient alliance" hardly seems quite right in the context) – a link circumscribed, in fact, by two

[43] Citations below consist of volume and page numbers (not volume parts, where divided, since the pagination is continuous), followed by book, chapter and section numbers, e.g., IV, p. 301: vii, 7/5. All except page numbers correspond between English and German editions, so that the latter can be checked relatively easily.

[44] Ferdinand Gregorovius, *Rome and Medieval Culture: Selections from the History of the City of Rome in the Middle Ages*, trans. by Mrs. Gustavus W. Hamilton, edited with an introduction by K. F. Morrison (Chicago 1971).

Germanic sackings of Rome, one by Alaric, the other by the landsknechts. The central theme became the efforts to appropriate the world status and renown of the city by Germanic invaders, kings or emperors, popes and the people of Rome itself, but beside this "world historical" dimension, which makes Rome unique, to explain its local or urban evolution. Rome "is endowed with a twofold nature – municipal and cosmopolitan, neither of which is entirely separable from the other" Gregorovius declared (*ibid.*), a statement fundamental to the whole book. That the local forces which arose in the tenth and eleventh centuries failed to withstand the emperors and popes – except for brief periods – becomes a main theme. He describes how both these supreme authorities exploited the idea of Rome as the seat of world power, and how the Romans themselves also exploited it by means of a supposed right to choose popes and emperors. That the papacy prevailed, for better or for worse, in spite of its own times of trouble, furnishes the ultimate theme.

Gregorovius sometimes succumbed to Hegelian modes of thought and defined his subject in terms of conflict and/or conjunction between abstract ethnic forces, Germanness and Latinity, but he does not pursue this idea constantly, which is just as well since it does not always make sense: many of the ideologues of papal authority and jurisdiction, and even some popes, came from north of the Alps, just as some eloquent later champions of imperial authority were Italian. At one point, when writing of the eleventh-century reform movement, Gregorovius himself admitted the contradiction: "the reforming popes were foreigners as were also the better of the cardinals by whom they were surrounded" (IV, p. 301: vii, 7/5). And the presumption of a Hegelian clash or dialectic throughout the centuries between the Latin and the Germanic is from the start bedevilled by problems of diversity within these categories and of assimilation between them as time progressed. Gregorovius himself makes clear that he regards the Goths as "not altogether barbarians"; "long usage had accustomed Italy to German rule and taught Italians to regard it as inevitable necessity" (I, p. 287: ii, 2/1). Theodoric (king 493–526), in fact, is one of his principal heroes, who "gladdened the hearts of the Romans" when he took up residence on the Palatine Hill in AD 500; in a footnote Gregorovius compares him to Peter the Great of Russia (rather to the latter's disadvantage). He pauses to reflect on the twin significance of Cassiodorus and Theodoric, "the Roman and the German, the last Senator and the first Gothic king of Italy, the representative of the ancient culture and the intelligent northern barbarian." The Romans themselves, "rapacious people," were worse plunderers of Roman building stone and marble than the Goths (I, pp. 294–96: ii, 2/1). Even Totila is praised for clemency during his "bloodless" sack of Rome in 546.[45] The Lombards Gregorovius introduces more disparagingly as "rude people.... Another spirit dwelt in the people of Alboin than in the followers of the great Theodoric; the Goths had protected Latin civilisation; the Lombards destroyed it" (II, pp. 16–17: iii, 1/2). But if they were barbaric when they entered Italy in the sixth century, by the ninth century, if not sooner, Gregorovius presents Lombards as a respectable ingredient of the population. For instance, Leo IV (847–55), who miraculously extinguished the fire in the Borgo and protected Rome against Saracen attack, was "a Roman of Lombard ancestry" (III, p. 91: v, 3/2). Commenting on the downfall of the last Lombard principality in Italy in the eleventh century Gregorovius reflects, "The tenacity of the race was marvellous...this German race, to which belongs the glory of forming an essential and noble ingredient

[45] Gregorovius further claims on the basis of a "calm investigation" that the African Vandals in 455 merely did some pillaging, like the Goths (I, pp. 220–21: i, 6/3).

of the Italian nation, maintained its individuality in Italy for five hundred years...even in late times, Countess Matilda, Gregory VII and Victor III were ornaments of the Lombard race" (IV, pp. 216–17: vii, 5/5). However, "at the time of Frederick II the Latin race had entirely assimilated the German elements and represented south of the Alps a new, peculiar nation – the Italian" (V, pp. 270–71: ix, 6/3).

Gregorovius's sympathies, often incompatible, pull him in opposing directions. Generally he wants to sound as pro-German as he can, but he is also the champion of Roman civic patriotism and not, in spite of what his Catholic critics may have suggested, unremittingly hostile towards the papacy; indeed he calls it at one point "the most venerable of all institutions which history has beheld" (III, p. 4: v, 1/1). Leo I (440–61) was "this illustrious man whose memory is justly sacred to the Romans, not only as a legendary deliverer of the city from Attila but also as the alleviator of its misery in the sack of Genseric...the first great Pope" (I, p. 193: i, 5/3). Gregory the Great (590–604) is introduced as "the most eminent and benevolent citizen and former Prefect of Rome" (II, p. 31: iii, 1/3): mediator against the Lombard Agilulf, "the welfare of the city was his first concern" (p. 38). His Sermon on Ezekiel, in which he surveyed present tribulations, is described by Gregorovius as "the funeral oration pronounced by the bishop beside the grave of Rome. This bishop was her noblest patriot, the last scion of an ancient and illustrious house" (II, p. 44: iii, 2/1). While admitting that Gregory the Great did, or could do, little to restore the fabric of Rome, Gregorovius defends him as best he can against charges that he may have had the Palatine Library burnt and pagan monuments destroyed (II, pp. 92–93: iii: 3/2). Another exceptional pope was Nicholas I (858–67): "in Nicholas the consciousness of the monarchy of Rome found its personal expression...he ruled as king over the beautiful country which stretched from

Ravenna to Terracina...the first of the popes to be crowned with the tiara" (III, p. 153: v, 5/1).[46] For different reasons, the scholarly Sylvester II (999–1003), better known as Gerbert of Aurillac, "is like a solitary torch in the darkness of the night" (III, p. 510: vi, 7/2), while the monk and would-be reformer Leo IX (1049–54), "the fourth German pope...inaugurated a new period" (IV, p. 74: vii, 2/3). His successor, Nicholas II (1058–61), urged on by Hildebrand, enacted a real turning point with the decree of 1059 which empowered only the college of cardinals to elect popes: "the rescue of the papal election from the influence of the Roman nobility and, if possible, also the German crown, was now accomplished...the supplementary consent [of the Roman people] henceforward remained merely a traditional form" (IV, pp. 115–16: vii, 3/3).

Gregorovius seems almost to revere, at the same time as he deplores, the elaborate machinery of papal power being constructed: "the marvellous system of the hierarchy soon resembled a great fortress surrounded by a hundred concentric walls which mutually protected one another" (*ibid.,* p. 118). Above all, he praises the papacy of Hildebrand as Gregory VII (1073–85): "one of the greatest politicians of all nations and all time" (IV, p. 93: vii, 3/1). "In this man of commanding genius the stern and magnificent spirit of the ancient Romans seemed reincarnate.... He was the Caesar of papal Rome" (IV, p. 167: vii, 5/1). He compares Gregory (favourably) to the greatest of military conquerors in his account of Henry IV's submission at Canossa in 1077: "the weaponless victory of the monk has more claim on the admiration of the world than all the victories of an Alexander, a Caesar or a Napoleon. Besides a Gregory, a Napoleon seems merely a barbarian" (IV, p. 232: vii, 6/2). Besieged

[46] Attention is drawn to Gregorovius's approval of Gregory and Nicholas by G. Arnaldi, "Gregorovius als Geschichtsschreiber der Stadt Rom: das Frühmittelalter," in Esch and Petersen, as n. 8, pp. 117–30 (pp. 127–28).

in Rome by the avenging Henry "this wonderful man bid defiance to fate as heroically in the Mausoleum of Hadrian as in the tower of Cencius" (*ibid.*). Much as Gregorovius deplored the hierocratic vision of a pope claiming to be supreme over all other authority, and his disastrous alliance with the Normans who sacked the city in 1084, he again praises the pope at Napoleon's expense in his concluding judgement: "To Gregory belongs a place among the rulers of the earth, men who have moved the world by a violent yet salutary influence. The religious element, however, raises him to a far higher sphere than that which belongs to secular monarchs. Beside Gregory, Napoleon sinks to an utter poverty of ideas" (IV, p. 256: vii, 6/5).

Alexander III (1159–81) was also praised, "one of the mightiest of the popes, the great opponent of the Emperor Barbarossa" (IV, p. 565: viii, 5/3), but it is Innocent III (1198–1216) who wins the laurels as "the true Augustus of the papacy"; a "coolheaded lawyer" who by his astuteness "imparted such a tremendous power to the papacy that it carried states, churches and civic society irresistibly onwards in its mighty current" (V, pp. 101–2: ix, 3/1). Unfortunately Innocent made a bad mistake in 1211 by summoning Frederick of Hohenstaufen from Sicily to claim the imperial crown (*ibid.,* p. 98). Gregorovius deplored, however, some of Innocent's successors: Gregory IX (1227–41) as a persecutor of heretics, Innocent IV (1243–54) as an avaricious persecutor of secular powers: "an unscrupulous priest...shrinking from nothing that his own advantage dictated" (V, p. 306: ix, 7/2). What he says about Boniface VIII (1294–1303) is slightly more cautious, perhaps because Boniface belonged to the Gaetani family who were patrons and friends of Gregorovius.[47] He characterises him as "a highly gifted man of

[47] E.g., the duke of Sermoneta was the dedicatee of Gregorovius's *Lucrezia Borgia*. His friendship with the family, particularly with Donna Ersilia, is evident at many points of his diary. His good use of the Gaetani (Caetani)

a despotic nature...the great-hearted sinner" (*magnanimus peccator*, citing for this a contemporary, Benvenuto of Imola) (V, p. 596: x, 2/4).

Regarding northern emperors from Charlemagne onwards, Gregorovius's judgements were mixed. He was a keen patriot of Bismarck's Prussia but had little enthusiasm for the greater German tradition of imperial ambition beyond Germany itself. "In our century we cannot contemplate the spectacle of these Roman journeys of our ancestors with entire satisfaction, but are forced to commiserate Italy, which, although the cause of the expeditions, had to endure them for upwards of three hundred years" (IV, p. 34: vii, 1/3). Sometimes his criterion for praise or blame was (as with the popes) their acts relating to Rome and the traditions of the city; but this can also be overwhelmed by pride in their wider political or cultural achievements. Thus Charlemagne, Patricius and then papally crowned Emperor in 800, is inevitably a hero for having restored the dignity of Rome, though Gregorovius insists that if the Romans had been opposed, he would never have become emperor (II, p. 507: iv, 7/3). He had reservations about the Frankish dynasty for its hierocratic self-justification and support of papal temporal power in Italy; nevertheless there seemed to him to be a further point to be made, on another high plane: "Charles's coronation sealed the reconciliation of the Germans with Rome, the alliance between ancient and modern, the Latin and the German world" (II, p. 512: iv, 7/3), a typically bold statement and of course highly disputable.

In the lowest points of depravity of the papacy in the tenth and early eleventh centuries, Gregorovius is proud to present the Saxon emperors as protectors and saviours of the city of Rome and of the Church. Otto I (962–75), who removed from

archives is illustrated in many footnotes, e.g., VI, p. 730 n. 1: xii, 7/5; or VIII, p. 39 n. 1: xix, 1/3.

the Roman nobility their control over the papacy, Otto II (973–83) with his Byzantine bride, Theophano, and the young Otto III (983–1002), determined to make Rome his place of residence, all struck Gregorovius forcibly. His picture of the two young world figures in Rome together in the Lateran palace in 996 – the twenty-four-year-old pope Gregory V (the first, but short-lived German pope) and the fifteen-year-old Otto III (III, p. 412: vi, 5/1)[48] – provides one of the most indelible images in the whole book, signifying a few months of harmony in Rome between the two bearers of divine authority. Another high point came with the coronation in 1046 of Henry III (1039–56) "never again was a king of Germany received with such glad acclamations by the Roman people"; first crowned Patricius, "he restored to the city its character of metropolis" (IV, p. 54–63: vii, 2/2). Flattering the Romans into the belief that not only had they chosen him as emperor but also elected the new pope – the candidate he had brought with him (Suidger of Brabant, as Clement II the second German pope) – Henry III is presented in a congratulatory tone by Gregorovius, though at the same time he underlines the dangerous new tyranny to which the Romans had succumbed. He imposes openly censorious verdicts therefore on Henry IV (1056–1106) and Henry V (1106–25), though in each case is unable to restrain a degree of Germanic pride. The former, although "a libertine and a despot," nevertheless "will ever live as a great and tragic champion in the history of the German nation"; he saved it "from the spiritual tyranny of Rome" (IV, pp. 299–300: vii, 7/4). As for the latter, "The Roman expedition of Henry V (1111) was a splendid exhibition of the power to which Germany could attain in spite of tedious civil wars" (IV, p. 329: viii, 1/2). The sequel, however – tumult in Rome after the submission of Pope Paschal II and a hurried imperial coro-

[48] See also Arnaldi, as n. 46, pp. 125–26.

nation, Henry's retreat from Rome taking with him as captives the pope and sixteen cardinals – was "an outrage such as the fourth Henry never committed...the audacity of his coup d'état does not clear him from perjury.... The history of Henry V and Paschalis II furnishes one of the most striking examples of the facility with which in political life treaties are made and broken although provided with all the seals of religion" (IV, pp. 339–57 (347, 353, 357): viii, 1/2,3).

Gregorovius was in a quandary when he reached the earlier Hohenstaufen. Of Conrad III (1138–52) he approves, for at least Conrad replied politely to the presumptuous way the Roman Senate invited him to rule and reside in the city in 1151. "Italian patriots should therefore for once extol a German king that in spite of the urgent entreaties of Italy (they usually forget these entreaties) he did not descend the Alps like some destructive Attila" (IV, p. 517: viii, 4/5). And he could hardly have withheld praise from Conrad's son, Frederick I Barbarossa: "the true imperial Colossus of the Middle Ages lives in German history as an object of national pride, the symbol of the return of glory to the German empire" (IV, p. 624: viii, 6/4). But Gregorovius favoured Italian civic independence, that of Rome above all, and deplored hierocratic ideologies, the imperial as much as the papal, and foreign domination of Italy. So he employed paradoxical arguments in partial justification of Barbarossa, who, unlike his father, treated the envoys of Rome abruptly in 1155: "he may probably have thought that madmen stood before him," Gregorovius suggests (IV, p. 534: viii, 5/1). He concludes, "Had it not been for Frederick's despotic plans and wars, the freedom of the cities would not have obtained such rapid development, nor would these cities have won such speedy recognition of their political rights. Barbarossa, contrary to his intentions, rendered at least this service to Italy which resisted him so valiantly" (IV, pp. 624–25: viii, 6/4).

About the later Hohenstaufen, however, Gregorovius was less enthusiastic. Even Frederick Barbarossa has to take some of the blame: in the first place, for the marriage arranged between his son Henry and Constance, daughter of Roger II of Sicily. "The unity and power of Germany were thus uselessly sacrificed to the domestic policy of the imperial dynasty and were condemned afresh to tedious wars beyond the Alps" (*ibid.*). The Emperor Henry VI (1191–97) showed "unscrupulous want of honour, avarice and the barbarism of a despot" (IV, p. 638: viii, 6/4). Greater allowances have to be made for Frederick II owing to his "profound hatred of the selfish policy of the priests, a hatred which governed his entire life" (V, p. 96: ix, 3/1); "the most complete and gifted character of his century," he was "founder of a political principle of centralised government in Sicily" (V, pp. 268, 271: ix, 6/3).

But even if Gregorovius wrote respectfully of certain strong popes and emperors when their actions enhanced the prestige of Rome, his greatest sympathy lay with the Romans themselves whenever they were at all effective in reasserting an independent identity. He found these episodes, even if doomed, of enormous historical interest, starting with the aristocratic, pope-making clans dominant in the tenth century. "If in the ninth century the history of the city itself is lost in the history of popes and emperors, during the tenth the Romans themselves appear in person before us. With the fall of the Carolingian authority and the papal authority, the history of the mediaeval senate and civic nobility begins to assert its independence" (III, p. 241: vi, 1/1). Alberic "the Senator," who died in 954 (son of the "Senatrix" Marozia of the Tusculan dynasty) – nothwithstanding his son Octavian, who succeeded him as Senator and then became the scandalous Pope John XII – is reckoned to earn "the foremost place among the Roman citizens of the Middle Ages… worthy of the name of Roman" (III, p. 326: vi, 2/4); "scarcely at any other time has the city enjoyed peace and security such as that which it enjoyed during the long reign of Alberic" (III, p. 303: vi, 2/3). Years later, in 1885, Gregorovius published an article about a coin, which he had identified as bearing his hero's name, and managed to insert a reference to it in the fourth edition (III, p. 299n: vi, 2/2). Likewise John Crescentius, who led a rebellion against Otto III and assumed the title of Patricius in 985 (III, p. 400: vi, 4/4), is judged "a brave man…a patriotic Roman" (III, p. 419: vi, 5/2) though Gregorovius seems resigned that Crescentius had earned his fate at the hands of Otto III's "appalling criminal tribunal" (III, pp. 429–31: vi, 5/3).

When in the mid-twelfth century some institutional forms of communal government emerged, giving Rome at least a degree of resemblance to other Italian cities, Gregorovius comments, "At no point of our history do we regret the poverty of our authorities so deeply as here, where the question is one of such a memorable revolution.… Some historians [notably Otto of Freising] casually mention that the indignant Romans hastened to the Capitol, restored the long lost Senate and renewed the war against Tivoli" (IV, p. 451: viii, 3/3); "I have here made the first comparatively scientific attempt to deal with the sources of the civic constitution" (IV, p. 454n: viii, 4/1). He goes on, "The first civic constitution was formed under Jordan Pierleone in 1144 and from him the Senatorial era was reckoned" (IV, p. 489: viii, 4/3), explaining that the Pierleoni were a new rich family, quite distinct from the families who had dominated the city in the previous two centuries. About the part played by the preacher Arnold of Brescia ("the man of the hour"), Gregorovius is somewhat vague, but insists he was not the leader of the revolution "which was due instead to the impulses of the time and to the special conditions of Rome" (IV, p. 478: viii, 4/3). Arnold's polemics against priestly corruption fitted conveniently enough with the civic programme, though in the end he was doomed to undergo "the fate of all prophets – the people whom he had so long held spellbound surrendered him" (IV, p. 528: viii: 5/1).

Nevertheless in Gregorovius's opinion Frederick Barbarossa missed a great opportunity when he came to Rome to be crowned in 1155. "Instead of magnanimously restricting the Roman democracy within reasonable limits, as he might easily have done, and then removing it from the papal influence and placing it under the authority of the empire, he repelled it with blind contempt, made enemies of several other cities, and at length saw all his extravagant schemes fall to ruin" (IV, p. 546: viii, 5/2).

For a few years, Gregorovius declares, "The Roman commune was a respected free state" (he instances its treaty in 1165 with Genoa). In May 1167 it confronted the emperor "with the greatest army Rome had sent into the field for centuries." The Romans' terrible defeat at Monte Porzio was "the Cannae of the Middle Ages…old men and matrons wept in the streets." The sequel was that Barbarossa – in spite of having assumed the authority of Roman Patricius – sacked the district near St. Peter's (the "Leonina" or defensive enclave of Leo IV) before he withdrew (IV, pp. 580–85: viii, 5/5).

At the end of the twelfth century (as at the end of the tenth) Gregorovius perceived another of those brief periods when the balance seemed almost to be right. Under the constitution agreed between Pope Clement III and the Senate in May 1188, in which the pope was recognized as overlord: "The rights of the Emperor in particular were left utterly unheeded…the pope's authority as a temporal ruler consisted…merely in the investiture which he conferred on the freely elected magistrates of the republic, or in the alliance of papal with civic justice in cases of twofold nature" (IV, p. 621: viii, 6/3).

However, according to the terms of final submission to Innocent III in 1205, the elected Senate of fifty-six was replaced by a papally approved single Senator holding executive power. Thus "the Roman people forfeited in succession their three great rights:

the papal election, the imperial election and the election of the Senate" (V, p. 49: ix, 1/4). Even so, "The city…attained her civic autonomy and at brilliant intervals even acquired complete independence as a republic.… Incapable of making good her claim to be regarded as the *Urbs Orbis,* incapable of becoming head of a universal confederation of Italian cities, she restricted her ambition to the aim of ruling the territory of the Roman duchy from the Capitol.… The municipal history of Rome in the thirteenth century contains some honourable passages" (V, pp. 4–5: ix, 1/1).

One of these "honourable passages" came in 1234 when "the city of Rome, at an unfavourable time, made the attempt to throw off papal dominion and to form a free state within her boundaries. Had she succeeded she would have extended her territory nearly to the limits of what she had possessed shortly before the Punic War" (V, pp. 170–71: ix, 4/3). In the end, Senator Luca Savelli's bid to control Tuscany and the Campagna collapsed and the peace signed by the Senator Angelo Malabranca in May 1235, while preserving the city's autonomy, simply restored the arrangements made under Innocent III (V, p. 179: ix, 4/4). Gregorovius conveys his own excitement at these bold, if vain, attempts of the Romans – flaunting red and gold banners inscribed with the letters SPQR – to subjugate other cities, particularly Viterbo: "The attempt made by the Romans to render Latium subject to the Capitol deserves more attention. A new spirit animated the Roman people. As in ancient times, in the days of Camillus and Coriolanus, they undertook conquering expeditions against Tuscany and Latium" (V, p. 164: ix, 4/3). Another high peak was reached during the ascendancy of Brancaleone degli Andalò, a noble from Bologna. As Senator — also styled as Captain of the Roman People — for an unprecedented period of three years (1252–55), later renewed after a short interval of exile, he "suddenly brought the senatorial office in Rome into high esteem, and imparted a transient splendour to the city" (V, p. 285:

ix, 7/1); "Were definite information concerning his government forthcoming, we should find that under him the democracy rose to greater power" (V, p. 310: ix, 7/3). In other words, had there been more source material Gregorovius would have made more of Brancaleone than he did; he complained that "among the city archives no parchment remains to recall its existence" and that no inscriptions of names and armorial bearings survive of office-holders, as found in other cities (V, pp. 296–97: ix, 7/2).[49] Tending to Brancaleone's discredit, Gregorovius mentions the likelihood that in his second term 140 towers were demolished, which meant the ruin of many antiquities (V, p. 323: ix, 7/3); though he points out that "the barbarous destruction of houses was almost as common an occurrence as the issue of some fresh police regulation in the present day" (*ibid.,* p. 325).

The downfall of the Hohenstaufen and ascendancy from 1265 of Charles of Anjou as papally appointed king of Naples, the 'Senator' who ruled Rome for ten years through pro-Senators, is portrayed by Gregorovius (V, pp. 260, 454–56: x, 1/3, 4/1) as "stern and awe-inspiring" but beneficial: the civic tradition stayed relatively intact, and was soon to emerge with a new lease of life on a modified scale. "The transference of the civic authority...to the popes was advantageous to Rome since the system placed some check upon the nobility, reduced the danger of a tyranny and created at least a permanent principle making for civic order...this system of government which had been introduced by Nicholas III [in 1278]...long endured" (VI, pp. 8–9: xi, 1/1).[50] Here Gregorovius confers praise upon that truly Roman pope of the Orsini who prescribed that only Romans, not external princes or nobles, should hold the office or title of "Senator," but he is appreciative in the same context towards

[49] Gregorovius added in a new footnote that a few had been found in the Senatorial Palace but not dating from before the time of Martin V (p. 297, n. 1).

[50] Nicholas's constitutional reform is outlined in V, pp. 485–87: x, 4/3.

Clement V, the first of the popes to reside in southern France (although no one, least of all the Romans, anticipated that this was to be a long-term arrangement).

Henry VII of Luxemburg also gets a measure of praise from Gregorovius, as "a noble but powerless man" (VI, p. 13: xi, 1/1), a thwarted peacemaker, who had to battle his way through Italy in 1310–12 and finally through Rome itself before he received the imperial crown, though the manner of his coronation, in the Lateran Basilica rather than in St. Peter's, in compliance with the wishes of the Romans, did little honour to the idea of world authority (VI, pp. 58–61: xi, 1/3). His death at Buonconvento near Siena in 1313, and his tomb in the Camposanto at Pisa, signify "the last imperial sacrifice offered by the German fatherland to the soil of Italy, with which it was united by centuries of a great though bloody history" (VI, p. 88: xi, 2/2).

Gregorovius narrates without overmuch comment the farcical sequel when Lewis of Bavaria (1314–47), unrecognised and condemned by Pope John XXII, invaded Italy and came to Rome in 1328 ("a caricature of a great tradition") for a ludicrous popular coronation. Sciarra Colonna, who in 1303 had threatened Boniface VIII, presided and "held the crown of empire in St. Peter's to place it on the head of a German king who for the first time in history received the sacred diadem from the hands of a delegate of the people" (VI, p. 147: xi, 3/4). After this Lewis deposed John XXII and a Roman crowd approved his choice of a Minorite friar as pope; "thus an emperor whom they themselves had crowned and a pope whom they themselves had made, sat in sight of the astonished Romans. Both institutions had sunk to their lowest depths." Indeed, in this period Gregorovius writes off all the players – popes, emperors and the city itself: "in poverty and obscurity she withered away, decayed and crushed, a rubbish heap of history" (VI, p. 184: xi, 4/3). (The latter image, dear to twentieth-century demagogues, was not perhaps meant so crudely as Annie Hamilton's translation suggests; Gregorovius used the word *Scherbenberg*, a mound of sherds or ancient fragments, therefore at least implying that Rome was still a site of great archeological value.)

Upon this "rubbish heap," however, emerged Cola di Rienzo, "the knight of the Holy Spirit and Tribune of the Roman People" who receives a very full treatment -- virtually two whole chapters. Gregorovius has been criticised for lavishing disproportionate attention upon this strange figure and it may be that he did so partly because the chronicle and other sources are so much more informative than they are for Brancaleone and his predecessors. Nevertheless, while Cola's programme in 1347 was a final looking back, a farewell "to a past ideal," his "fantastic scheme of once more gathering the peoples in the absence of the pope round the ancient Capitol and of re-erecting the Latin empire of the world awoke for a moment the enthusiastic belief in the idea of universal Roman citizenship" (VI, pp. 373–74: vii, 7/4); hinting at what Gregorovius thought might be the proper destiny for Rome, and still thought so, over five centuries later. "The great and truly ingenious scheme of making Italy into a confederation with Rome as its head was expressed for the first time" even if the outcome was that "a political idea of the highest importance was destroyed by its fantastic alliance with the idea of world monarchy" (VI, pp. 252, 279: xi, 6/1,2). Gregorovius pointed out some striking parallels. Cola's comparison of himself with Christ reminded him of Danton (VI, p. 287 n. 1: xi, 6/3). "Napoleon's outrageous coronation and the theatrical pomp of his imperial court were only separated from the scenes of Cola's tribunate by four and a half centuries" (*ibid.*, p. 277 n. 2). Only Cola's last phase in Rome, after his return in 1352, did not become him, owing to his tyranny and his feeble attempt to escape death from a lynch mob by disguising himself. "Had Cola but stepped with high courage among the raging multitude to receive death at the hands of his Romans on the Capitol, he would have ended his life in a manner worthy of ancient hero" (VI, pp. 369–76 (p. 372): xi, 7/4). As well as these political judgements, Gregorovius could not resist adding one of those Hegelian touches which sometimes intrude upon his historical positivism: "the phenomenon of Cola can only be explained by the poetic force which every age possesses" (VI, p. 374 n.: xi, 7/4).

* * *

New themes develop in the *History of the City* as Gregorovius passes into the fourteenth century and beyond. The old themes – antagonism or association between Latin and Germanic worlds, and the resurgence of the civic identity of Rome, whether independently or in and out of partnership with popes or emperors – were wearing rather thin by then, with the absence of the papacy in Avignon and the weakness of the empire. But he did not altogether loose sight of them. He lingers over the papacy's tightening control of Roman civic autonomy and the latter's final, dying gasps: the popular revolution, crushed by Boniface IX in 1398 (VI, pp. 550–52: xii, 4/1) when "for the first time Rome recognised the full dominion of a pope"; the rising against Eugenius IV in May 1434, brutally avenged by Cardinal Vitelleschi (VII, pp. 43–60: xiii, 1/3); Stefano Porcari's conspiracy to murder Nicholas V and proclaim a republic in January 1453 (VII, pp. 131–34: xiii, 2/3); the disruption caused by the gang of Tiburzio (whose father had been executed with Porcari) in 1460 "when the democratic movement sank to the level of a bandit enterprise" (VII, pp. 188–89: xiii, 3/1). He portrays an increasingly despotic papacy – though benevolent towards the arts and secular learning – gradually suffocating the civic spirit of the Romans and concentrating its efforts upon temporal power in Italy. "The continued existence of the Capitoline Republic would undoubtedly have obliged the popes of the fifteenth century to turn their attention mainly to the spiritual sphere. Having become absolute rulers of Rome, they abandoned their noblest tasks as high priests of Christianity to establish their ecclesiastical states as secular princes" (VII, p. 4: xiii, 1/1). Julius II (1503–13) is rightly seen as the most successful architect of the papal temporal state "without excessive nepotism": proceeding "first to secure a firm footing in Rome, then to lay hands on greater things" (VIII, p. 38: xiv, 1/1).

The new theme of the Renaissance – or 'renascence' as Annie Hamilton rather unnecessarily "translates" it, not thereby making the word Gregorovius uses sound any more English – becomes more and more intrusive in Volumes Seven and Eight, probably playing a much a larger role there than Gregorovius had ever envisaged when he started writing back in the 1850s. It had already been present in Volume Six, with Cola di Rienzo, "the prophet of the Latin renascence" (VI, p. 376: xi, 7/4), who, as collector of inscriptions, is later described as "the actual founder of antiquarian studies" (VI, pp. 683–84: xii, 7/2). The chief herald, however, had to be Petrarch. Gregorovius wrote, "with Petrarch's arrival the city acquires traits of individual life and a completely modern character." The coronation of Petrarch on the Capitol (in 1341, as poet laureate) "inaugurated a new century of culture" (VI, pp. 206, 216: xi, 5/1).

Gregorovius admits to some ambiguity about the term Renaissance. In his long chapter on cultural life in the fifteenth century he declares "the great national deed of the Italians was the Renascence of antiquity" (VII, p. 530: xiii, 6/1) and his long and informative reviews of the arts and learning in the fifteenth century and their continuation under Julius II (1503–13) and Leo X (1513–21) amply illustrate this. He emphasizes how much the papacy embraced the fashion of renewed inspiration from classical antiquity. "On the eve of its fall the Papacy enthroned itself in splendour and majesty; the centre of gravity of all the political relations of Italy and Europe lay in Rome; for only two decades was the city of Rome the classic theatre of this splendid culture" (VIII, p. 120: xiv, 2/1). Julius he praises as a patron: "The greatness of Julius II shines generally by the impetus which he gave to great works" (VIII, p. 119: xiv, 1/6), "a great character who possessed a decided taste for plastic form" (VIII, p. 124: xiv, 2/1). However, he sharply distances himself from rhetoricians who acclaimed Julius II "a genuine Roman" by asking, "What would Leo I and Gregory I have said to this pagan transformation of the Apostolic office?" (VIII, p. 174 n. 1: xiv, 2/2).

Gregorovius also uses extended meanings for the Renaissance. "On one side only it was a revival of antiquity; speaking generally it was the entire reform of western culture. In the Latin world it appeared as the renascence of classical paganism. In the German it became the renascence of evangelical Christianity..." (VII, p. 2: xiii, 1/1). He also refers, rather vaguely, to a sudden and more general transition: "After the Council of Constance mankind experienced a radical change. It passed from the fantastic world of the Middle Ages to the practical conditions of life"; part of the Latin contribution was also to "burst the geographic frontiers of the ancient world. They...discovered the passage to the Indies, and finally a new world – America" (*ibid.,* pp. 2–3).

In addition, there are passages where Gregorovius seems to associate Renaissance with morality, mentality and political behaviour in ways which often seem to have been borrowed, without due acknowledgement, from Jacob Burckhardt's *Civilization of the Renaissance*, first published in 1860. Gregorovius had met Burckhardt in 1853, and together with Friedrich Althaus and another friend they had even gone on a short tour together,[51] visiting the Greek temples of Paestum, but – for whatever reason – they did not keep in touch, and Gregorovius never noted in his diary anything about Burckhardt's book. There are only two footnotes in the *History of the City* which refer to it: one of them simply quoting a piece of information about manuscript book production in Florence, the other a disagreement with Burckhardt's explanation for the artistic "unproductiveness" of late mediaeval Romans (VII, p. 550n: xiii, 6/1; VII, p. 659 n. 1: xiii, 7/1). Perhaps the lack of a general acknowledgment reflects badly on Gregorovius, but it may be taken as another case of his rather cavalier attitude to the work of established scholars: Burckhardt, with his chair in the University of Basel, was just another of them.

In Volume Six there are already traces of Burckhardt; near the beginning Florence is hailed as "the first modern state" (VI, p. 4: xi, 1/1) and in the concluding chapter on culture in the fourteenth century we read: "Released from the bonds of caste, of party and of the scholastic system of thought, man appeared as a personality. He also rent the mystic veil of faith" (VI, p. 671: xii, 7/1). In Volume Seven there are more of these echoes. "The Italian character in general in the last thirty years of the fifteenth century displays a trait of diabolical passion…a criminal selfishness reigns supreme" (VII, p. 297: xiii, 4/4); "crime itself in the hands of the Borgias became a work of art" (VII, p. 431: xiii, 5/2).

Gregorovius makes only too clear his view that the papacy was heading towards a terrible doom in the 1520s. He reverts to a note of almost cosmic solemnity when he mentions the burning by Martin Luther of Leo X's bull of excommunication. "From this day the German people…were called to assume the spiritual leadership of the world. It was the same earnest and

[51] Althaus's Preface, as n. 1, p. xvi; *Journals,* as n. 2, p. 6 (omitted in Annie Hamilton's abridged translation in vol. I of the present edition).

devout nation that had defeated the corrupt Roman empire and erected the German imperium, that had safeguarded the papacy in Rome, that for centuries had shed its blood in Italy in defence of the great ideal of culture of the Christian republic. In its indignation it now burst the strong chains of history which from the time of Charles the Great had bound it to Rome and her degenerate Papacy..." (VIII, p. 270: xiv, 3/5). Leo's anathema against Luther in 1521 signified another momentous turning point: "after 1500 years of the growth and existence of this marvellous creation [the Catholic Church] the German intellect made the discovery that without ceasing to be deeply religious and a Christian, a man might dispense with this vast and formal apparatus for salvation" (VIII, p. 276: xiv, 3/5).

Gregorovius could not resist the temptation to liken the end of his history to the beginning. In one of the last of his over-imaginative verbal flights, he compares the landsknechts to the barbarian followers of Alaric: "In the year 1527 as in the year 410 Rome was an object of contempt to brave warriors, who told one another that this capital of the world was only the lying Sodom and Gomorah of all sins.... Here stood countless churches as temples had stood in the time of the Goths, filled with gold and silver images and vessels" (VIII, p. 566: xiv, 6/3). He declares that the speeches attributed to Bourbon by contemporary historians are "such as Brennus, Alaric or Arnolf might have delivered in sight of Rome; and in truth the different periods of time seemed to close in a strange circle" (ibid., 565–66: xiv, 6/3). Finally, after a graphic account of the sack, "listening to the laments of the Humanists, we might believe ourselves transported back to the times of Jerome, and never did the circumstances of periods so widely severed by time so closely resemble one another as the fall of Rome in 1527 resembled that of 410. In the former period the city was still half pagan, now, owing to the renascence, it had reverted to paganism. Then, as now, every religious man recognised that Rome had met with deserved chastisement, but now, as then, arose the same cry of woe, that glorious Rome, the light of the world, the mother of mankind, had perished" (VIII, pp. 651–52: xiv, 7/3). Sadoleto and Erasmus are quoted in the following pages in the guise of new St. Jeromes.

As the tragic sequence of events unfolded, Clement VII (1523–34) is saddled with much blame. "The still inextricable entanglement of theology in politics demanded the continued existence of the ecclesiastical State, and Clement VII recognised he could only save it by forming a close alliance with the emperor." He emerges as "the most unfortunate of popes. Had this pope of the Downfall ["dieser Papst des Unterganges"] been a greater character he would have stood forth at least as a tragic figure.... For Clement VII was the last pope whom circumstances summoned to defend the liberty of the Italian people against the restored imperial authority and against foreign dominion as his great predecessors had defended it in ancient times. He failed pitiably" (VIII, p. 701: xiv, 3/5). The humiliation of Clement even when reconciled with Charles V is underlined: "As in former days Barbarossa knelt before the great Alexander III, so Charles V knelt in reverence before the miserable Clement VII" (VIII, p. 671: xiv, 7/4). The imperial coronation at Bologna in 1530 was "a humiliation for the pope and a deposition of Rome from her ancient right" (*ibid.,* p. 674).

Gregorovius does not qualify this final recurrence of Germano-Latin conflict and papal "Downfall" by conceding that he might in some ways have overdrawn the catastrophe – not all of northern Europe renounced the papacy for ever, and even within a few years of the Sack of Rome in 1527 there was an amazing resurgence of papal authority – and that the city, too, expanded and prospered as the sixteenth century continued.

Some readers today may find the later volumes thematically rather disjointed, hyperbolic and filled with tendentious value judgements. Maybe Gregorovius would have been wiser to close his story at the beginning of the fourteenth century, which, when he reached that point, he had identified as the end of the Middle Ages (VI, p. 671: xii, 7/1) – though he did not stick to this: he also identified the end of the Middle Ages for Rome with Martin V's return to the city in 1420 after the Council of Constance had put an end to the Great Schism (VII, p. 1: xiii, 1/1), with the Sack of 1527, and even – in his diary – with the events he himself witnessed in Rome in 1870 when he wrote, "Today the Middle Ages have as it were been blown away by a tramontana [north wind]."[52] Volumes Seven and Eight, however, cover much ground that was relatively unfamiliar at the time they were written and are greatly enriched by the fruits of Gregorovius's original research. For his use of unpublished source material from archives and manuscript collections, Gregorovius deserves much credit as a pioneer.[53] The conclusion or "Close of the History" at the end of Volume Eight contains some thoughts about the nebulous "spirit of the middle ages" – but leaves the reader with a clear idea of the author's purpose in his long journey through so many centuries, the reasons why he wished to carry the story no further, and its immediate relevance to events which he had lived through or witnessed in the nineteenth century.

* * *

It is easy to criticize Gregorovius on various grounds, but it is difficult not to admire his overall achievement. Among the faults with which his book was charged by Ranke himself are a certain discontinuity, an unevenness in mastery of source material in the later volumes and – above all – a tendency to

[52] *Journals*, as n. 2, p. 389.

[53] Discussed further in my article, as n. 6.

become more a history of the papacy than of the city.[54] However, had Gregorovius tried to write about medieval and Renaissance Rome without, or with much less of the papacy, it would have made nonsense of his essential idea of the city, its unique mixture of the cosmopolitan and the municipal, mentioned at the beginning of this chapter.[55] Much of the book had, therefore, to be about the papacy and general politics, only in part could it be urban social and economic history. In fact, Gregorovius never loses sight of the local urban dimension, and serves it well, even if there is less of it than many readers today would like to see (and which only recent research has made more possible). He provides bird's-eye views or descriptions at successive periods, or interposes a review of the "condition" (*Zustand*) of the city. For example, at the very beginning is a memorable "general view of Rome in the last period of the Empire" (I, pp. 21–30: i, 1/2), drawing upon Ammianus Marcellinus to illustrate the extraordinary wealth still flaunted by the aristocracy and the vast number of buildings still standing. Later the reader can enjoy "a walk round the city in the time of Otto III" (III, pp. 540–62: vi, 7/5) and a description of Rome in the twelfth century, derived from the "Mirabilia" and other accounts, in which Gregorovius insists that "the forest of towers must have impressed even the mightiest of emperors" (IV, pp. 682–93 (at p. 692): viii, 7/4). There is a comparable "overall picture" of the city in the thirteenth century, when he suggests "the great-

[54] See Forni, as n. 6, p. 57, and the last section of this Introduction for more on the reception of Gregorovius's *History*. Forni notes (pp. 10–11) that in 1877 Alfred von Reumont argued, against Gregorovius's approach, that historians of mediaeval Rome needed to move on an urban and regional, not universal plane.

[55] Esch discusses this point, noting that a history of Rome could hardly be written like a history of Perugia or of Osnabrück (as n. 8, p. 133).

est fortresses of the patrons stood within the ancient city on the hills that sloped to the Forum and the Circus Maximus… the forsaken hills thereby recovered a new life and in spite of the want of water became in part repeopled" (V, pp. 657–80 (p. 663): x, 7/5). Gregorovius then takes us round, identifying the strongholds of the Frangipani and Anibaldi, the Savelli and the rest. When he reaches the early fifteenth century, he draws heavily on Poggio Bracciolini's description of the ruined sites of Rome (VI, pp. 717–27: xii, 7/5), and finally, in the last chapter of Volume Seven, he makes a brilliant attempt at a socio-topographical portrayal of the city in about 1500. He begins (repeating a point made about the twelfth-century city) by observing that a Jubilee pilgrim in 1500 would have noticed far fewer church cupolas than there are today; many towers still, but only the low domes of the Pantheon and of a few Sistine churches. Then he deals with the city district by district, describing in turn each of the fourteen *rioni*, both buildings and social fabric, with lists of the families established in each locality (VII, pp. 726–93: xiii, 7/5).[56]

Another widely expressed criticism is that Gregorovius is too prone to fall back on his imagination for literary effects. An example may be taken from Volume Four. In his evocative account of the renewed importance of the Capitol in the mid-twelfth century, Gregorovius wrote: "Sitting on the prostrate columns of the Temple of Jupiter…among mutilated slabs and inscriptions, the monk of the Capitol, the rapacious Consul or the ignorant Senator might gaze in wonder at the ruins and wonder at the capriciousness of fortune." He even added "that perhaps some well known lines of Vergil might come to his mind" (IV, p. 465: viii, 4/1) – almost a transposition, as Gregorovius admits

[56] On Gregorovius's astonishing knowledge of Roman topography see also Esch, as n.8, pp 155–56.

in a footnote, of Poggio's famous reflections in his *De Varietate Fortunae* three centuries later. Equally fanciful is the portrayal of Conradin on his entry to Rome in 1260 (though Annie Hamilton's translation has a rather strained air to it): "the voices of sirens enticed him to that lovely and fatal land, the historic paradise of German desire, whence his illustrious fathers seemed to cry to him for vengeance" (V, p. 410: x, 2/3). But perhaps the best example of all is Gregorovius's vision in Volume Seven of the decrepit Pius II in August 1464, vainly waiting on the promontory of Ancona for his crusading fleet to depart. "From the windows of the episcopal palace Pius looked across this lovely sea towards the East where lay Byzantium and Jerusalem and the past of the human race; perhaps at the same hour the young Columbus gazed from another shore towards the West in the clouds of which the future of mankind still lay thickly veiled" (VII, p. 215: xiii, 3/2).[57]

None of this seriously mars Gregorovius's extraordinary combination of learned synthesis and inspired presentation, of serious research enlivened by literary skill (the objectives he had stated to his publisher back in 1858). If one consults the footnotes there is plenty of evidence there of a critical approach to sources and avoidance of second-hand judgements; often there are detailed arguments about the dating of manuscripts or information extracted from unpublished documents (e.g., names of civic office holders). As for literary quality, Gregorovius must be read with a sense of period and an awareness, too, of his deliberate distancing of himself from a professional academic style; moreover, readers of Annie Hamilton's English version have to bear in mind that she may not always do justice to his German prose.

Why is it still worth reading Gregorovius's *History of the City of Rome*? Perhaps because no one else has ever attempted

[57] The importance of Pius II for Gregorovius – as for Burckhardt – is discussed by Esch, as n. 8, pp. 143–46.

such a task on so grand a scale and managed to sustain it with such extraordinary vitality, humanity, breadth of learning, vision and perceptiveness. Gregorovius's sense of historical continuities and parallels was excited in many contexts but most of all, on the grand scale, by his awareness that he was writing about a unique city and its long temporal as well as spiritual involvement with the papacy at the very time when this involvement was ending. The events which he lived through had an extraordinary relevance to his subject, as he declares in his conclusion, and few historians have conveyed such a sense of immediacy about remotely distant events. For example, the battle of Civita in 1053, when Leo IX's army was defeated by the Normans, he compares to the battle of Castel Fidardo in 1860 when the Piedmontese overthrew the foreign legions of Pius IX (IV, p. 79: vii, 2/4), or when discussing Paschal II and Henry V concerning lay investiture, he refers to a speech made by Cavour in 1861 (IV, p. 336–37n: viii, 1/2); when discussing the fifteenth-century conspirator Stefano Porcari he mentions a seditious pamphlet which "repeated his political views and bore his name" printed in 1866 (VII, p. 138: xiii, 2/3): "Rome, as we have frequently remarked, is the only place in the world where the ghosts of the past have failed to find repose." There are numerous other instances. When the Italian kingdom finally took over Rome, just as he was nearing the end of his great work, he felt that it was time for him to leave the city. He considered it a travesty for Rome to become the capital of Italy, that it would be appropriate for it to remain the place of papal residence but as a sort of cosmopolitan, republican enclave within Italy[58] – indeed this is the form which he often implies it might have been moving towards in the Middle Ages had it not been for the "retarding

[58] Note, e.g., his reflections towards the end of 1870 (*Journals*, as n. 2, pp. 389–90) and those on 9 June 1875 and 9 June 1876 (*Tagebücher*, as n. 3, pp. 356, 371–72).

principle" of papal temporal power and worldly ambition.[59] He even suggested that such a mini-republican Rome might one day become the federal capital of Europe. Gregorovius of course could not remotely foresee how little antique tradition would count in a so-called European Union over a century later, a union founded on a Treaty of Rome but of which Rome has never stood the remotest chance of becoming the epicentre.

It goes without saying that over a century of new research and changed viewpoints have either expanded, qualified or invalidated many passages of Gregorovius's *History*, but the specialist can go elsewhere for revisions, corrections and subsequent bibliography. No later author's overview of this extraordinary city's history can possibly be compared with it in range, with the possible exception in our own time of the book by Richard Krautheimer,[60] the visual dimension and modern scholarship of which make it a perfect companion, though not a substitute, for Gregorovius.

3. GREGOROVIUS'S LATER CAREER AND WRITINGS, 1872–91

Gregorovius's diary suggests that by the winter of 1870–71 he was thankful to be near the point of finishing his great work,[61] but also dreading the vacuum it would leave. Nevertheless, even at this late stage, he was vastly extending his

[59] For instance, summing up on Charlemagne, he remonstrated: "Who can deny that the idea of a sacred metropolis, a temple of eternal peace in the midst of struggling humanity…is great and admirable?" (III, p. 3: v, 1/1).

[60] R. Krautheimer, *Rome: Profile of a City, 312–1308* (Princeton, 1980). The terminal date (or perhaps 1312) might have done better for Gregorovius, too.

[61] E.g., entries on 13 November 1870, 19 January 1871 (*Journals*, as n. 2, pp. 389, 395).

archival research, accumulating in Modena, Mantua[62] and Rome much additional material, particularly about the period of Alexander VI (Rodrigo Borgia, pope from 1492 to 1503) and his immediate successors. Having reached the end of his great work he needed a fresh purpose, to ward off depression. He wrote in his diary on 9 May 1872 that he had decided to write a book about Lucrezia Borgia, the daughter of Pope Alexander VI whose third husband was Ercole d'Este, duke of Ferrara, brother of Isabella, marchesa of Mantua. Meanwhile he would continue research, both for Lucrezia and for revisions to his *History of the City*. In Rome in the summer of 1872 he gained access to the archives of the confraternity of the Sancta Sanctorum and of the Capitoline notaries, the latter thanks to a practising notary who was their archivist, Filippo Bechetti.[63] In Bechetti's office he began transcribing documents from the register of Camillo Beneimbene, a notary who practised in the Rione Sant'Eustachio from 1467 to 1505, and among whose distinguished clients were the Borgias. Gregorovius used it for his first paper – the first of many – delivered to the Bavarian Academy in November 1872.[64] It was just the sort of documentary subject from the Renaissance period in which his greatest strength lay as a serious historian; it is still a ground-breaking piece. After a discussion of the college of Capitoline notaries, based on its statutes, Gregorovius exemplified the varied information in the notaries' act books from the late fourteenth century onwards. He used extracts from Beneimbene's register referring to wills, marriage contracts, property transactions, deeds of donation and other legal acts, noting how many data about

[62] *Ibid.*, p. 428.

[63] *Ibid.*, p. 429.

[64] *Ibid.*, p. 433.

individuals and families could be derived from this sort of material.[65] He had some qualms about the Lucrezia book: "I have no real interest in it," he wrote in his diary on 30 March 1873,[66] but he thought the money would be useful for the trip to Greece he was still yearning for. Whatever he was feeling at the moment when he wrote that diary entry, the book reads as though he enjoyed writing it, and it was enhanced by an appendix of sixty documents and three facsimiles.[67] Completed in only nine months, it was an instant success. The first German edition, published in March 1874, sold out within two months; a second and third edition followed. Italian and French translations rapidly appeared.

Meanwhile, Gregorovius's thoughts and feelings about Rome were very mixed by the early 1870s, when Italian unification had at last been achieved and the city became the new kingdom's capital. No doubt he enjoyed being fêted as Rome's secular historian, and in July 1872 the municipal authorities even offered to pay for the translation and publication in Italian of his great work. A contract was signed, and somehow reconciled with the earlier contract for a translation, the first volume of which had been published in 1866 by a Venetian firm which subsequently went out of business.[68] As an expert on Italian archives (few can have visited so many collections as he had done in the previous ten or fifteen years) he was invited in April 1872 to discuss the subject

[65] "Das Archiv der Notare des Capitols in Rom und das Protocollbuch des Notars Camillus de Beneimbene von 1467 bis 1505," *Sitzungsberichte der philosophisch-philologischen und historischen Classe der k.b. Akademie der Wissenschaften zu München*, 1872, pp. 491–518.

[66] *Journals*, as n. 2, p. 439.

[67] More about this book and about Gregorovius's later output of historical articles on specialized subjects, mainly with a Roman basis, from the fifteenth to the early seventeenth centuries, is contained in my article cited above, n. 6.

[68] *Journals*, as in n. 2, pp. 430–31.

with the Minister of Education. Two months later he presented a promemoria concerning archives in Rome and its region, proposing the setting up of a Roman "commissione di storia patria"; a periodical, "Archivio storico romano"; and eventually a collection of texts, "Scriptores Urbis Romae."[69] In March 1876 he was made an honorary citizen,[70] on the strength of which he wrote a paper about decrees of honorary citizenship in sixteenth-century Rome, which he delivered to the Accademia dei Lincei, of which he had become a member.[71] His paper was based on a register in the Archivio Capitolino; among previous honorary citizens whose names he had found in it were Christophe de Longueil, Gasparo Contarini, Paolo Giovio, Carlo Sigonio, Pirro Ligorio, Michelangelo and Titian.[72]

These honours in the new Rome were countered, however, by hostility from the Vatican and clerical extremists. In March 1874 the *History of the City* was placed on the Index.[73] Gregorovius consoled himself with the thought that his persecutors were trying to get at the municipal authorities or even at Bismarck rather than himself. He did not waver in his long-standing views on the anomaly of the temporal power and the futility of the new dogmas, but he was understandably shaken by this instance of bigotry. It meant that he was no longer *persona grata*

[69] *Ibid.*, p. 429.

[70] *Tagebücher*, as n.3, p. 363.

[71] He was admitted as an external member in February 1876: the official decree (in Latin) is in Munich, Bayerische Staatsbibliothek, Handschriften- und Inkunabelabteilung, Gregoroviusiana, no. 19, item 12.

[72] *Tagebücher*, as n. 3, pp. 368–69. The article was published as "Alcuni cenni storici sulla cittadinanza romana" in *Rendiconti della reale Accademia dei Lincei*, Memorie della classe di scienze morali, storiche e filologiche, I (1877): 314–46; and as "Römische Bürgerbriefe seit dem Mittelalter" in Gregorovius's *Kleine Schriften zur Geschichte und Cultur*, I (Leipzig, 1887), pp. 265–323.

[73] *Journals*, as n. 2, pp. 449–50.

in ecclesiastical libraries, or even in some social circles. In spite of his honorary citizenship, in 1877 he was not even informed that his proposals for a Rome historical commission and publications had been adopted. He rightly believed there had been a conspiracy against him because his work was on the Index.[74] This humiliation was followed in 1879 by a polemical attack on his early book about papal tombs, an Italian translation of which had appeared the previous year.[75] Stefano Balan, deputy archivist of the Vatican, was responsible for this, and berated Gregorovius for having dared to write: "The time will come when the tombs of the popes will have the same importance as today the busts and statues of Roman emperors." This proved, wrote Balan, his complete failure to understand the supernatural and eternal mission of the papacy.[76] But he also castigated Gregorovius for disparaging remarks about some of the Renaissance popes; for accepting uncritically that Sixtus IV was directly concerned in the Pazzi Conspiracy in Florence in 1478 and for not accepting that Alexander VI and Cesare Borgia were just doing their best to regain the lands of the church from robbers and tyrants or that Julius II was warmongering only to guard the flock of Christ.[77]

Such attacks help to explain why in 1874 Gregorovius decided to leave Rome and return to Germany, but the hostility from ultra-Catholics was not the only reason. Paradoxically, while he detested the policies of Pius IX and for years had ridiculed him as "the mummy in the Vatican," he was nostalgic for

[74] *Tagebücher*, as n. 3, p. 378.

[75] F. Gregorovius, *Le Tombe dei papi: prima traduzione italiana rivista ed accresciuta dall'autore* (Rome, 1879). The publisher's preface indicates that the translator was *avvocato* R. Ambrosi.

[76] S. Balan, *Le tombe dei papi profanate da Ferdinando Gregorovius, vendicate colla storia* (Modena 1879), p. 2.

[77] *Ibid.*, pp. 50–51, 54, 57.

the silent city he had first known in the 1850s. Always an ardent supporter of Italian unity, he had hated the prospect of Rome becoming the capital of Italy and was duly repelled when it happened: speculative building, new road construction, the disastrous cleaning up of ancient monuments, Piedmontese bureaucracy blended with southern corruption, he hated it all. So he decided to make his home in Munich, in spite of Bavarian Catholicism, as the German city from which Italy was most accessible and also because, during the last few years, he had come to feel welcome there. He even made a family home, of a sort, in Munich, sharing an apartment with his brother Julius, his step-sister Ottilie and her son Hermann.

In spite of living in Munich, Gregorovius returned very often to Italy, to find new material to insert into revised editions of his books as well as to do new research for the occasional papers and monographs that he went on producing, many of them relating to Rome and some of them based on research in Munich as well, such as the one about a contemporary German account of the Sack of Rome in a manuscript he had found at the Staatsbibliothek.[78] Meanwhile, his research in Modena and Rome advanced to the seventeenth century, as he had become interested in the diplomatic background to the Thirty Years War and the strained relations of pope Urban VIII with the Empire and with Spain. He read a paper about this to the Bavarian Academy in December 1878 and recorded his surprise that neither Döllinger, who presided, nor any other member of the Academy, had fallen asleep[79]; Henry Simonsfeld, the historian of the German Fondaco in Venice, judged it the best piece of critical

[78] "Gumppenbergs Bericht vom Sacco di Roma" (originally printed, under a longer title, in the *Sitzungsberichte*, 1877, pp. 327–97), reprinted in *Kleine Schriften zur Geschichte und Cultur*, I (Leipzig, 1887): 181–264.

[79] *Tagebücher*, as n. 3, p. 409.

historical writing Gregorovius ever did, and Gregorovius seems to have come to the same conclusion.[80] Gregorovius soon afterwards abandoned the idea of a large project about the Thirty Years War. Something more appealing had turned up. In the spring of 1880 he at last satisfied an old yearning and visited Greece.[81] After returning home, he decided to write about the city of Athens in the Middle Ages, which would enable him to start new archival research, from about 1300 onwards, in Naples, Palermo, Florence and Venice. In planning this sequel to the work which had taken up the central part of his life, he gained a new incentive to continue his travels and researches and to maintain his many friendships in Italy. In March 1889, only two years before his death, the book on Athens was finished[82] (unfortunately it was never translated into English), but he still toiled on the fourth revised edition of the *History of the City of Rome*.[83]

4. RECEPTION AND REPUTATION OF GREGOROVIUS'S *HISTORY OF THE CITY OF ROME*

In 1862, when Volume Three of the *History of the City* appeared, Gregorovius complained that his work had been received

[80] H. Simonsfeld in *Allgemeine Deutsche Biographie*, vol. 49 (Leipzig, 1904), p. 529; cf. *Tagebücher*, as n. 3 (p. 409): "es war der beste Vortrag, den ich gehalten habe" (see also n. 94 on p. 551). It was published as "Urban VIII. im Widerspruch zu Spanien und dem Kaiser. Eine Episode des dreissigjährigen Kriegs" (Stuttgart, 1879), but not, strangely, reprinted in the *Kleine Schriften*. An Italian translation (thanks to the eager publishers, Fratelli Bocca of Rome) quickly followed.

[81] *Tagebücher*, as n. 3, p. 419. His diary for this journey has not survived.

[82] *Geschichte der Stadt Athen im Mittelalter. Von der Zeit Justinians bis zur türkischen Eroberung*, 2 vols. (Stuttgart, 1889); new ed., edited by H.-G. Beck (Munich, 1980).

[83] He had reached the last two volumes before his death in 1891, although they were not published until 1894–96; this is proved by footnotes citing

in silence by the German academic world,[84] but one wonders what he can have expected, as an outsider? In fact, there were various quite encouraging signals; rather it was Gregorovius who did the snubbing. In 1862–63 an attempt to draw him to Munich for several months of each year had been made on behalf of Maximilian II, king of Bavaria,[85] the intermediary being Ranke's former pupil Wilhelm von Giesebrecht (1814–89), then professor at Königsberg. Gregorovius found Giesebrecht, whom he had met when revisiting his own former university in 1860, a self-satisfied "man of order...and of rule," and resented his savage attitude towards Garibaldi.[86] Nor did he greatly admire Giesebrecht's book on the mediaeval German empire, of which so far the first two volumes had appeared.[87] The offer was refused. In August 1865, having turned down another proposal, he declared in his diary that he was "an author who pursued historical studies without uniting them with any practical vocation for teaching – as many English historians do."[88] But he went on feeling unappreciated, at the same time resolutely going his own way, seemingly unconcerned if he offended those in established positions, and preferring whenever possible to cite primary sources rather than acknowledge the judgements

recent publications, e.g., reference to an article published in 1888 in VII, p. 466n: xiii, 5/3.

[84] Gregorovius to F. Althaus, 24 June 1862, in Althaus, "Ungedruckte Briefe," as n. 12, p. 249.

[85] *Journals*, as n. 2, pp. 166, 185.

[86] *Ibid.*, p. 100.

[87] *Geschichte der deutschen Kaiserzeit*, Bd. 1 (1855), Bd. 2 (1858). (The fifth and final volume, which reached the twelfth century, with Henry the Lion, did not appear until 1880. The work has never been translated into English.) In October 1860 Gregorovius shared with J. F. Böhmer at Frankfurt, a respected editor of medieval imperial registers, some disparaging opinions of the work (*ibid.*, p. 103).

[88] *Ibid.*, p. 236.

and disputes of respected contemporaries, or even to name them. Although he occasionally cites Giesebrecht in footnotes, Gregorovius does not align himself with Giesebrecht's and other historians' *grossdeutsch* ardour over German imperial ambitions in Italy, just as he does not underwrite in his later editions the *kleindeutsch* opposition to them of Heinrich von Sybel, Prussian nationalist and founding editor of the *Historische Zeitschrift*.

Nevertheless, Gregorovius did acquire goodwill in Germany, helped by encounters during the summer holidays he customarily took in Bavaria. From 1863 his acquaintance with Giesebrecht warmed, and he also became friendly with the liberal Catholic theologian, Ignaz von Döllinger.[89] Both of them introduced him to professional mediaeval historians,[90] and it must have been thanks to Giesebrecht and Döllinger that he became first a corresponding member in 1865 and then a full member (*Mitglied*) of the Bavarian Academy of Sciences in September 1871[91]; much as he disliked the academic establishment Gregorovius valued this honour deeply. He remained in Munich throughout the autumn of 1871 (his installation at the academy was on 2 November) going for long walks with Döllinger and frequenting Giesebrecht's house, where on one occasion he even met Leopold von Ranke on a visit from Berlin.

[89] Impressions in August 1863 recorded in *Journals*, as n. 2, pp. 185–86; in 1868, *ibid.*, p. 318. See also F. Seebass, "Ignaz von Döllinger und Ferdinand Gregorovius. Unbekannte Dokumente ihrer Freundschaft," *Deutsche Rundschau*, 80 (1954): 150–55.

[90] For instance, at a dinner party given by Döllinger in August 1863, he met two keen *grossdeutsch* exponents, von Höfler (from Prague) and Ficker (from Innsbruck) (*Journals*, as n. 2, p. 186). He does not record any impressions or notes of conversation.

[91] *Journals*, as n. 2, p. 406. Letters and diplomas recording Gregorovius's admission to this and to other learned societies (mainly Italian) are in Munich, Bayerische Staatsbibliothek, Handschriften- und Inkunabelabteilung, Gregoroviusiana, no. 19.

Ranke, then aged seventy-six, turned out to be "One of the most interesting men I ever saw; tiny, lively, with a witty smile." During dinner Ranke told Gregorovius that his *History of the City of Rome* was too "Italianising" (*italienisierend*) – whatever that implied. Gregorovius was not put down easily and replied that an Italian critic had called it too German.[92] Gregorovius still complained in March 1873 that he was despised by the German academic world, but this seems to have been occasioned by an encounter with Theodor Mommsen (1817–1903), the famous historian of ancient Rome (particularly the Republic) and authority on Roman coins and inscriptions, also one of the founders of the *Preussisches Jahrbuch*: "Mommsen came to Rome, and still remains here. Only met him accidentally at dinner. Like Richard Wagner, he is evidently a sufferer from megalomania. The occupants of professors' chairs refuse to recognise me, because I work independently and accept no official post, and even, *horribile dictu*, possess a modicum of poetic talent. The pedants of Germany received the *History of the City of Rome* with silence and shrugs. No notice of it, to my knowledge, has been taken by any of the official organs of criticism."[93]

Of course, Gregorovius cannot be judged on the same plane as the dinosaurs of German "scientific" (*wissenschaftliche*) historiography, Ranke and Mommsen and their disciples. But Ranke himself, if critical on some grounds, expressed respect for Gregorovius's book,[94] and rated it more highly than the rival *History of the City of Rome* by Alfred von Reumont (1808–87), which came out before Gregorovius's final volumes were ready.[95]

[92] *Ibid.*, pp. 412–13.

[93] *Ibid.*, p. 439. A cold encounter with Mommsen is also noted by Forni, as n. 6, p. 36.

[94] Forni, as n. 6, p. 57. On some points of criticism see above, p. xxxiii–xxxvi.

[95] A. von Reumont, *Geschichte der Stadt Rom*, 4 vols. (Berlin 1867–70) (the work has never found an English translator).

Von Reumont was a Catholic aristocrat from the Rhineland, an official at the Prussian Embassy whom Gregorovius knew well, and thanks partly to whom he had gained his pass to the Vatican Library. He was, in fact, more attracted to the history of Florence (and is better known for his works about it) than to Rome; his book had been commissioned by the king of Bavaria and its scope was very different from that of Gregorovius. It extended from the origins of the city to the present day, i.e., the reign of Pius IX, and had no pretensions to be a work of original research. Nevertheless the two books invited comparison and Gregorovius was deeply resentful of von Reumont, alleging that he had taken material from his own earlier volumes; Friedrich Althaus also helped by writing a review article in support of his friend, to which von Reumont responded.[96] Another Catholic German historian whose work overlaps with that of Gregorovius, in spite of being very different in scope and chronological span, is Ludwig Pastor (1854–1928), author of the *History of the Popes from the Close of the Middle Ages*.[97] The overlap comes in Pastor's earlier and Gregorovius's later volumes, for Pastor includes much that has a direct bearing on the city's history; Gregorovius was aware of this and added several references to Pastor's Volume One when revising his own Volume Seven for the fourth edition.[98] Pastor is more often given the credit as the pioneer archival researcher for sources bearing on fifteenth- and early sixteenth-century Rome, although he started work con-

[96] Forni, as n. 6, pp. 9–10. Gregorovius's hostility is expressed in diary entries for 7 April 1867 and March 1873 (*Journals,* as n. 2, pp. 273–74, 330, 439). For comparative discussion of both works seee Forni (*passim*), and Esch, as n. 8, pp. 178–80.

[97] L. Pastor, *Geschichte der Päpste seit dem Ausgang des Mittelalters*. The first edition of vol. 1 was published at Freiburg im Breisgau in 1886; vol. 2 followed in 1889.

[98] E.g., VII, pp. 134, n. 1, 139n: xiii, 2/3.

siderably later (in about 1879) and had much more assistance than Gregorovius.[99] On 6 March 1879, when only twenty-five, he wrote in his diary that on the previous day he had been in the Barberini Library in Rome and sat near Gregorovius, "a man whose historical and political outlook was the furthest conceivable opposite to my own."[100] He also recorded in his diary, in March 1895, a conversation with the aged Jacob Burckhardt who had pronounced Gregorovius too free with his imagination, though he first said that there were some good points about his work.[101] As a trusted Catholic apologist, Pastor had access to the Vatican Archives; he also worked more systematically and in many other archives and libraries, being free to do so over a much longer period. Gregorovius nevertheless achieved an astonishing amount of original research, working against publisher's deadlines, particularly in those four rushed years from 1869 to 1872; and it must be agreed that his approach and style are more striking just as his judgements are often much less biased than Pastor's.

It is hard to deny, finally, that Gregorovius succeeded in his aim to combine serious research with literary art. Even traditionalists among German historians have conceded that point, acknowledging that it has a special quality of its own.[102]

* * *

[99] W. Wühr, ed., *Ludwig von Pastor. Tagebücher – Briefe – Erinnerungen* (Heidelberg, 1950), pp. 122–23.

[100] Ibid., p. 124.

[101] "Gregorovius hat seine Verdienste, aber er lässt der Phantasie zu viel Spielraum" (*ibid.,* p. 276, quoted also by Esch, as n. 8, p. 132).

[102] E.g., Paul Kehr, "Ferdinand Gregorovius und Italien. Ein Nachruf zu seinem 100. Geburtstag," *Deutsche Revue*, 187 (1921): 194–200. See also W. Kampf, "Gregorovius und seine Kunst der Geschichtsschreibung," in vol. IV of his edition, as n. 41, pp. 47–54 (p. 54).

Gregorovius remarked after visiting Paris in 1878 that Athens and London were the two cities he still needed to see in order to feel truly civilised.[103] He made it to Athens but never to London, in spite of invitations, one as early as 1862 from Friedrich Althaus,[104] who had gone to live there in 1853.[105] Gregorovius was (or so he wrote) under the impression that Althaus had gone much further, and that he was living beyond the Ohio or the Mississippi. Joking apart, he may have thought that there was little to choose between Britain and the United States, and have been equally prejudiced against both countries, either on account of their liberal commercial ethos or simply because, in spite of being accomplished in many languages, he was not very strong in English.

He was anxious nevertheless that his work should be appreciated in the English-speaking world. His travel writings had great success there, beginning with the *Corsica*, which appeared immediately in two separate English-language versions.[106] They continued to find translators – among them the tireless Annie Hamilton[107] – and (presumably) appreciative readers. His historical work did less well. The first publication in Germany of the earlier volumes of the *Geschichte der Stadt* does not appear to have aroused much interest, but in 1871 attention was drawn to Volume Seven, the first of the two about Renaissance Rome, in a famous article by Lord Acton, the liberal Catholic, German-speaking guru of late

[103] *Tagebücher*, as n. 3, p. 408.

[104] Letter to Althaus, 24 June 1862, as above n. 12.

[105] Althaus records this in his article of 1882, as n. 12, p. 242.

[106] Translations by R. Martineau (London, 1855) and A. Muir (Edinburgh, 1855).

[107] E.g., *The Island of Capri*, translated by M. D. Fairburn (Boston, 1879; London 1896); *Siciliana. Sketches of Naples and Sicily*, translated from the German by Mrs. Gustavus Hamilton (London, 1914).

Victorian Britain.[108] Acton explained in a letter to Döllinger that because of illness he had not had time to finish this review article properly, and was afraid it might hurt the author,[109] whom he had met several times in Rome and Munich. In fact, he only mentioned Gregorovius once after the first two pages, but at least he conceded that the chapters on the period of Alexander VI were among the best and most solid Gregorovius had written thanks to his use of ambassadors' reports. But Acton objected to the idea that Alexander VI was a weak product of a corrupt environment – which he attributed to Gregorovius without any precise quotation – and most of the article was devoted to his own defence of Alexander's temporal programme as "full of intelligent policy of a worldly sort." Gregorovius, who had certainly been misrepresented, had a rejoinder in a new footnote printed in the second and third editions[110] referring to this article by *"ein Engländer"* which opposed his judgement; it had not shattered him at all, he wrote, but merely excited his wish to see in print the author's long-awaited book on ecclesiastical history — a body-blow, since those who knew Acton probably guessed already that he never would get down to writing his big book. The offensive part of this footnote was discreetly omitted from the fourth edition and the English translation.[111] Acton had the last word in their exchange by not mentioning Gregorovius at all in the article about German historical scholarship with which he introduced the first number of the *English Historical Review* in 1886.[112]

108 "The Borgias and Their Latest Historian," *North British Review*, January 1871, pp. 351–67; reprinted in his *Historical Essays and Studies*, edited by J. N. Figgis and R. V. Laurence (London 1907), pp. 65–84.

109 V. Conzenius, ed., *Ignaz von Döllinger – Lord Acton. Briefwechsel 1850–90*, III (Munich 1964–71), p. 14 (Acton to Döllinger, 7 February 1871).

110 *Geschichte der Stadt*, VII, 3rd ed. (Stuttgart, 1880) (Bk xiii, chap. 5, sect. 5), p. 492.

111 *Ibid.*, VII, p. 526n: xiii, 5/5; cf. 4th ed. (Stuttgart, 1896), VII, p. 499n.

112 Lord Acton, "German Schools of History," *EHR*, 1 (1886): 7–42.

By the 1880s and 1890s the British and American markets for books about early and late mediaeval Rome were becoming rather over-supplied. Among the first had been T. H. Dyer, *The City of Rome: Its Vicissitudes and Monuments from Its Foundation to the End of the Middle Ages* (London, 1865; 2nd ed., New York and London, 1877), who even made an acknowledgment to Gregorovius; for the earlier period Thomas Hodgkin's *Italy and Her Invaders*, vols. 1–4 (Oxford, 1880) had appeared. Relating to the Renaissance period, there were S. G. C. Middlemore's translation of Burckhardt (London, 1878) and the seven volumes of John Addington Symonds's *Renaissance in Italy* (1875–86), as well as two source-based works on papal Rome: Mandell Creighton's *History of the Papacy,* the first edition of which came out in five volumes in 1882–94; and the English translation of Ludwig Pastor's *History of the Popes*, of which the first volume was published in 1891. This point was stressed by Edward Armstrong in a short review of the first volumes of Annie Hamilton's translation of Gregorovius's *History of the City*. It should have come out sixteen years earlier, he wrote in 1896, recording that he himself had unsuccessfully tried to persuade a friend to translate it and that Annie Hamilton had at that time also refused the job.[113] It may have been Armstrong who persuaded R. W. Seton-Watson (later a famous authority on Central and Eastern Europe) to translate Gregorovius's *Tombs of the Popes* with a "Memoir of Gregorovius,"[114] which is largely derived from Althaus's original preface to the diary.[115] Meanwhile, Gregorovius's *Lucrezia Borgia* also took long to reach an English-language readership. A translation, by John

[113] *EHR*, 11 (1896): 136.

[114] Seton-Watson, as n. 13, pp. xvi-xli.

[115] See above, nn. 1–3.

Leslie Garner, at last published in New York in 1903, appeared in London the following year.

One might have expected a greater effort to make Gregorovius known to English-language readers on the part of his old friend Friedrich Althaus (1829–97). Although they exchanged letters for the rest of their lives, after 1853 they did not meet again until the summer of 1878.[116] Althaus was the first translator from English into German of Carlyle's *Frederick the Great*, and wrote mainly on English themes for a German readership.[117] From 1874 until his death in 1894 he was professor of German at University College London. He acted as one of Gregorovius's promoters in German, but not, it appears, in English; as well as writing blurbs in the *Allgemeine Zeitung* for successive volumes of the *History of the City*,[118] he even contributed a biographical piece to a literary review in 1882.[119] Gregorovius bequeathed to him his diaries, and Althaus immediately set about their publication in Germany. He revealed in his preface, dated at London May 1892, that his friend had edited the text heavily before his death. He also testified that Gregorovius had destroyed many of his papers and asked friends to burn his letters, a wish with which Althaus says he complied, destroying forty years of correspondence.[120] He and other friends nevertheless saved some from the flames;

[116] *Tagebücher*, as n. 3, pp. 403–4.

[117] F. Althaus, *Englische Charakterbilder*, 2 vols. (Berlin 1869), was reviewed by Gregorovius himself in the *Allgemeine Zeitung* of 10 June 1870.

[118] Gregorovius wrote to his publishers on 29 November 1867 asking for proofs of vol. VI of the *Geschichte der Stadt* to be sent to Althaus at 5 South Bank, Regent's Park, London (Hönig, as n. 4, p. 268). See also a letter of 7 November 1872 (*ibid.*, p. 328).

[119] F. Althaus, "Ferdinand Gregorovius. Ein Lebensbild," *Nord und Süd*, 23 (1882): 322–37.

[120] Preface, as n. 1, p. iv; *Journals*, as n.2, p. viii (omitted from abridged version in vol. I of the *History* reprinted in the present edition).

Althaus himself published a few in a Berlin periodical in 1894, excusing himself as they were not among those which had contained many indiscretions.[121] Other fragments of Gregorovius's vast correspondence have appeared in print from time to time, but the project for a complete edition of the surviving letters is now uncertain.[122]

Why Friedrich Althaus seems to have done so little for Gregorovius's English readership is one of the many subjects on which the missing correspondence might have enlightened us. At least as early as 1873 Gregorovius had been hoping for an English translation of the *History of the City*.[123] Who was it that Edward Armstrong had in mind for the job? Was it Althaus who finally persuaded Annie Hamilton?[124] Why had so much time been lost? Annie was a woman of private means and abundant free time, an Italophile and a fan of Gregorovius's *History* since about 1880–81, but she did not agree to undertake her heroic labour until the summer of 1890. Unfortunately, as she mentions in her translator's preface to Volume One, she had not been warned about the author's latest revisions and had to do much of her work again when the fourth German edition appeared (I, p. v). She does not say that Althaus helped her with her translation of the *History of the City*, though she thanked others, including George Hill of the British Museum (she does however thank Althaus's son for permitting her to include in the second edition an abridged version of his father's biographical preface to the diaries). There is no doubt about Annie Hamilton's total commitment to translating Gregorovius; she even added

[121] As n. 12.

[122] Forni, as n. 6, p. 2n, mentions this project of Professor W. Kampf. The present uncertainty about it I owe to information from Professor Arnold Esch.

[123] Hönig, as n. 4, p. 330 (letter of 18 January 1873).

[124] See n. 113.

some helpful (if historically not very valuable) addenda to his footnotes. For instance, she corrects his remark that, as in the tenth century the Forum was buried deep in dust, by noting that since recent excavations it was now "kept in a state of exemplary but inartistic neatness" (III, p. 543n: vi, 7:5); and concerning a twelfth-century tower in a house where, according to Gregorovius, "the Jews now slaughter buffaloes," she adds, "Signor Lanciani tells me that...the Jews, having been provided with a new slaughter-house...no longer kill buffaloes here" (IV, p. 370n: viii, 2/1).[125] As the translated volumes appeared, from 1894 onwards, they received briefly appreciative notices in the *English Historical Review*; when the Renaissance volumes, Seven and Eight, finally came out in 1900–1902 Edward Armstrong, again the reviewer, rather condescendingly acknowledged that her skill as translator was improving.[126] The English translation of Gregorovius received no notices at all in the *American Historical Review* (founded in 1895).

So the *fortuna* in English of Gregorovius's *History of the City* has been rather negative; he deserved better. He did not even get an obituary notice written by an English historian in the *English Historical Review* but an appreciation (admittedly quite a long one, though not accurate in all details) by a Viennese journalist with whom he had once been friendly.[127] The opportunity has now come for him to be better appreciated.

[125] For some later examples, see VIII, p. 146, n. 1; p. 167n; p. 398n (xiv, 2/2; 2/3; 4/4).

[126] *EHR*, 17 (1902): 820.

[127] Sigmund Münz, *EHR*, 7 (1892): 697–704. See also Forni, as n. 6, p. 47, on a curious confusion of Münz with F. X. Kraus, a Catholic ecclesiastical historian who also wrote a piece about Gregorovius, in which he stressed his "closed nature" (notwithstanding his known exuberance).

BOOK FIRST.

FROM THE BEGINNING OF THE FIFTH CENTURY TO THE FALL OF THE WESTERN EMPIRE IN 476.

HISTORY OF THE CITY OF ROME IN THE MIDDLE AGES.

CHAPTER I.

1. Plan of the Work—The City of Rome in Ancient Times and in the Middle Ages.

THE aim of these volumes is to present a comprehensive history of the City of Rome in the Middle Ages; a subject which, apart from its connection with the Papacy and the Empire, has not hitherto been dealt with. The Romans themselves, upon whom the task of writing it should more especially have fallen, have been withheld by a variety of causes from making the attempt, and have only contributed a quantity of valuable material towards so truly national a work. Will it therefore be considered presumptuous in one not of the Latin race, but a German, to venture on this arduous undertaking? I do not fear the imputation; not only because the domain of knowledge is free territory, but also because, that next to the Romans and Italians, no other people in the Middle Ages had relations with

Rome so close and so international as the Germans. Since the Goths of Theodoric, who first subjugated Rome and then reverently upheld her; since the Franks of Pepin and Charles, who freed the city from the yoke of the Lombards and Byzantines and again restored her to prosperity, for centuries, through the Germanised Roman Empire, Germany has stood in no ordinary relations to Rome. To the German nation Rome is an imperishable title of glory, and the mediaeval history of the city has become an element inseparable from that of Germany.

When I first conceived the thought of writing this work, my aim was as follows: that, from all extant and accessible material and with the aid of many years' acquaintance with the monuments and topography of the city, I would trace the course of its history from the first fall of imperial Rome under the power of the Visigoths of Alaric in the year 410, down to the last fall of the Papal city into the hands of the troops of Charles V. in 1527, when, at the beginning of the Reformation, the ancient alliance between Germany and Rome was for ever sundered.

Throughout the long space of more than eleven hundred years, Rome is to the historian as a lofty watch-tower, whence he can survey the movements of the medieval world, so far as that world derives from her its impulse or stands in active relation to her. For she is endowed with a twofold nature—municipal and cosmopolitan, neither of which is entirely separable from the other. Thus it was in ancient times, and thus it remained throughout the Middle Ages.

Three cities shine conspicuous in the history of mankind, by reason of the universal influence which they exercised upon it—Jerusalem, Athens, and Rome. In the course of the life of the world, all three are factors working with and through each other for human civilisation. Jerusalem, the capital of the small and impotent Jewish race, was the centre of that enigmatic theocracy from which Christianity emerged, and therefore the metropolis of the religion of the world. Long after its fall it maintained a second historical existence, by the side of, and in relation to Rome. The Romans had destroyed it in ancient times; its people were scattered over the world; its sanctity had passed away to Christian Rome; but in the eleventh century it again revived, and during the period of the Crusades was the goal of Christian pilgrims and the object of the great struggle between the nations of Europe and Asia. Then, together with the ideas of which it had been the symbol, it sank again into silence and obscurity. Jerusalem.

Aside the city of the One Jehovah, polytheistic Athens shines on another summit of historic life, as the first centre of Western genius, of its science, its philosophy and its beautiful ideals. Then arises mighty Rome, the law-giver of the political world. Athens and Rome are indissolubly united and correspond to each other, as mind to will and thought to deed. In them are embodied the classic forms of life. The intellectual power of Athens Athens.

excites the enthusiastic love, the practical greatness of Rome the reverent admiration of mankind. All the creative work of thought and imagination was collected in the capital of Hellenic genius; and the little Republic of Pallas Athene exercised an ideal dominion over the human race which still endures, and will for ever endure, in the universal civilisation of mankind.

Rome. The universal sovereignty of Rome, on the other hand, a unique, incontrovertible fact of history, rests on quite other foundations. Anyone who considers the existence of this wonderful city only from the outside, may assert that with unparalleled military skill, and with no less unparalleled political genius, she subjugated the world, and robbed, or destroyed, the flower of nations nobler than herself. In contrast to free and genial Athens, he sees only slavery and despotism. In Rome he discovers poverty in creative ideas of civilisation; he sees only a great political impulse towards conquest, a great practical intellect with its accompanying wants, and the marvellous and gigantic structure of the political system of justice and of civil law. But everything which tends to raise the intellectual spirit to the higher regions of thought he finds either not cultivated at all, or only acclimatised from other lands. Even the wealth of noble works of art which beautify the city only seems to him the spoils of Tyranny, behind whose triumphal car the captive Muses follow, forced to serve the prosaic Queen of the World.

This fact is undeniably true, but it is not the

whole truth. The origin of Rome from her myth-shrouded germ, her growth, and finally her unrivalled supremacy, will, next to the rise and dominion of Christianity, ever be one of the deepest mysteries of history. And Christianity, which sprang up within the narrow confines of Jewish nationality, though cosmopolitan in its essence, was drawn to Rome, the capital of the world, as to a seat already prepared for it by history, where, from out the ruins of a political monarchy, it was destined to raise up a moral monarchy in the giant form of the Church. The marvellous power by which one city obtained dominion in language, customs, and intellect over so many different nations cannot be explained. Its development can only be followed in a long chain of events, whilst the inner law, which governs the fact and which is called Rome, remains inexplicable to us.

It was not by the educating power of the intellect which emanated from the Acropolis of Athens that the world was conquered and governed, but, through streams of blood, by the all-devouring Jupiter of the Capitol. The city of Romulus, on the banks of the Tiber, inherited the treasure and the work of three parts of the world, in the midst of which she was built in the fairest country on earth. In herself she had no creative genius either for religion or science; she incorporated and made them her own, and she was in the highest degree adapted to spread civilisation abroad, and to give form and language to the spirit by which it was animated.

The Imperium.

Cosmopolitan power makes its appearance with Rome. It becomes a system which embraces in a universal order all that had hitherto been developed and formed in the ancient world, which throws down the narrow confines of nationalities, and unites tribes and peoples under a central government as members of one great family. It is this principle which, when brought to bear on mankind, exalts it above the individualism which was the ideal of Greece. It is, in a word, the idea of the "Imperium," or of the Empire, which originated in Rome and gave its form to the world. It is the idea which has ruled the West as an inherent principle down to our own times. Its power and continuity have only been approached by the Church, and the Church in its visible shape is only the religious form of the ancient idea of the State.

Before the Romans the idea of the "Imperium" does not appear in history. The principle, however, that the moral world is by the law of its being a unity (a monarchy) is involved in monotheistic Judaism. In the "chosen people" of Israel, and in their prophets, lies the first consciousness of a universal mission, and there the cosmopolitan idea of Christianity had its origin.

Among the Greeks no religious ideas of the kind are to be found. The Greek ideal rests in the universal culture of the free, all-searching intellect. The Kosmos of the spirit was created by the Greeks, but politically it was only represented in a scattered colonial system, whilst the Hellenic State is an individual State or confederation. Beyond Hellas there was only the despised barbarian, just as beyond the Mosaic theocracy there was only the despised heathen. Even to Aristotle the non-Hellenic races were outside the law and destined by nature to servitude. If Alexander, who, in opposition to Greek ideas, wished to realise the idea of a universal Hellenic kingdom embracing the barbarian races, had turned his plans to the West, the course of the world's political system would have suffered no other change than that which followed in the Hellenised East. For, with the death of this enlightened ruler fell to pieces the universal Hellenic Empire which he had founded.

Rome at length achieved what Greece, fortunately for the complete development of her own genius, did not achieve; in the form of the Empire she embraced civilisation in a universal organism. The Empire was the civilised world of an epoch, for which Greece had created intellectual culture, Rome had constructed civic laws, and Judaism had provided the universal religion. Virgil has expressed the full consciousness of the mission of the Romans in the imperishable verses:—

"Tu regere imperio populos, Romane, memento:
Hae tibi erunt artes, pacisque imponere morem,
Parcere subiectis, et debellare superbos."

The dogma of the sovereignty of Rome.

This high-sounding dictum, which so completely expresses the character and mission of Rome, impressed itself deeply on mankind; and the motto of the mediaeval Empire, *"Roma Caput Mundi*

Regit Orbis Frena Rotundi," is nothing more than its echo. From Augustus downwards the belief was firmly rooted that the Romans were the nation elected to universal supremacy, and that the Roman Empire was the Empire of the world, even as among the Jews the belief remained, that their nation was a divine nation, and their religion the religion of the world.

The line of demarcation which Greece and her greatest thinkers had drawn between herself and the barbarians, as Israel had done between herself and the heathen, disappeared in the cosmopolitan Empire of the Romans, under which all forms of civilisation were accepted, all religions enjoyed freedom of worship, and all nations rights of citizenship. Thus, in the Roman Republic was represented the unity of civilized mankind, of which the elected head was the Emperor, and the capital "Rome, the Eternal," the miracle of the inhabited earth, the product and monument of the history of the world.

Gradual ruin of the city.

The majestic city grew, waxed old, and sank side by side with the Empire, and its dissolution is a process as remarkable as was its growth; as vast an effort of time being necessary to destroy and lay low this colossus of laws and administration, of political institutions, of traditions and monuments of past centuries, as had been required to build it up. There is no spectacle in human history so tragic and so thrilling as the fall and final extinction of mighty Rome. Seven years before the incursion of the Western Goths, the last poet of the Romans stood on the Palatine; thence he surveyed the still unconquered city, and filled with enthusiasm, he celebrated the indescribable splendour of ancient imperial Rome, her golden-roofed temples, her triumphal arches, her columns, her monuments, and the gigantic buildings in whose colossal foundations human art outrivalled nature.[1] Scarcely two hundred years after Claudian, Bishop Gregory stood in the pulpit of S. Peter's, and in his gloomy sermon likened the once immeasurable city to a broken earthen vessel, and the once sovereign people to an eagle, which, bereft of its plumage and enfeebled with age, droops dying on the Tiber's shore. Eight centuries after Gregory, Poggio Bracciolini stood amidst the ruins of the Capitol. Of ancient Rome he saw nothing but the remains of ruined temples, overthrown architraves, rent arches, and fragments of the splendours of the Forum, where cattle now grazed. He wrote his book on *The Changes of Fortune,* the doom which all that is great must inevitably undergo.[2] The same sight three hundred years later inspired the English Gibbon with the idea of writing the history of Rome's ruin, an idea which he subsequently developed in his immortal work, *The Decline and Fall of the Roman Empire.* Though actuated by similar feelings, it is needless to say that

[1] Claudian, *Panegyric on the Sixth Consulate of Honorius,* vv. 39-52. The poet apostrophises the universal character of Roman supremacy in pompous terms: *De cons. Stilichonis,* iii., v. 130, &c.

[2] *Historiae de Varietate Fortunae libri quatuor.* Poggio wrote this book shortly before the death of Martin the Fifth; and from this melancholy survey of the ruins of the city dates the rise of Roman archaeology.

I do not for a moment aspire to rival such men as these. Deeply stirred by the sight of Rome, I resolved not only to depict the ruin of the city, but to follow it on in its reawakening to a new world-governing power. Rome alone amongst all the cities of the world has been honoured with the divine title of "Eternal," and the prophecy of the poet, *"Imperium sine fine dedi,"* in her attains reality.[1]

Rome rises to a new life

The Roman Empire, sunk in the decrepitude of age, fell under the onslaughts of the vigorous German tribes. The majestic city of the Caesars fell of itself when the Roman State and its ancient worship perished. The Christian religion destroyed and transformed the Pagan city of the ancient Romans, but she rose again from out the catacombs, her subterranean arsenal, a new Rome, veiled again in myth. For as Romulus and Remus had been the founders of ancient Rome, so now were two holy Apostles, Peter and Paul, the legendary creators of the new city. This also grew slowly and amidst terrible changes, until, under a system unrivalled in history, it once more became the capital of the world. And since it was Rome that

[1] Rome is called *"Urbs aeterna"* as early as the time of Hadrian; see coins in Cohen, vol. ii. n. 1299 *seqq.,* n. 1303. The idea is expressed in the official title given to Rome in the Cod. Theodosianus. Edict A. 364 of the Emperors Valentinian and Valens to the Prefect Symmachus: *Intra urbem Romam aeternam* (lib. xv. tit. i. n. 11). In other Edicts Rome is spoken of as *venerabilis* and *inclyta. Aurea Roma,* a very common phrase in the Middle Ages, is used by Prudentius:—

Agnoscat Judaea legens, et Graecia norit,
Et venerata Deum percenseat aurea Roma.
—*Apotheos.,* v. 385, ed. Dressel, 1860.

gave form to that great period in the life of the human race which we call the Middle Ages, just as she had already given form to Antiquity, we shall do well to investigate the elements which combined to invest this one city, after so great a fall, with a second supremacy. Unlike the origin of her ancient dominion, this new birth of Rome presents no difficult enigma, being fully explained by the idea of the Empire, which, firmly rooted in the West, now became bound up with Christianity and produced the Roman Church.

through the instrumentality of the Empire and the Church.

That the Christian religion arose simultaneously with the foundation of the Empire of the Caesars, is one of those great historic facts which we are accustomed to call providential. It permeated the ancient Empire and blended with it, the cosmopolitan idea of Christianity being in perfect accord with the theory of a universal monarchy. Constantine recognised this. The new Church adopted the administrative organisation of the Empire; she extended over the bishoprics and districts a network of administration which corresponded to the constitution of dioceses as fixed by Constantine.[1]

[1] From the time of Constantine onwards the Imperial Church was divided into the three great Apostolic Patriarchates of Rome, Alexandria and Antioch; this was confirmed by the Sixth Canon of Nicea. By the side of these were formed the later (non-apostolic) Patriarchates of Jerusalem and Constantinople, and the Second Oecumenical Council had already (381) acknowledged the rank of the Bishop of Constantinople as second only to that of the Bishop of Rome. The latter soon claimed spiritual authority not only over the Prefecture of Italy (the political dioceses of Rome, Italy, Illyricum Occidentale, and Africa), but also over the Praefectura Galliarum, that is, over the entire West. The ecclesiastical Patriarchates therefore corresponded, according to

She was in her outward form a Latin creation, having the Empire for her type. Gradually she developed into a spiritual power, but remained enclosed within the State, and was preserved by the Empire so long as it endured. From the time of Constantine onward, the universal Emperor was also the head of the Universal (Catholic) Church, in which no bishop had precedence over another, whilst the Oecumenical Councils, summoned under the Imperial authority, gave it unity.

As soon as the Germans had overthrown the Western Empire, the Roman Church, in her essence a still purely spiritual phenomenon, and, as such, unsusceptible of injury at barbarian hands, cast aside her wrappings and appeared as the universal authority in the West. She here usurped the place of the Imperial power, the principle of which she preserved as a law in her Ark of the Covenant. Latinity and the ancient civilisation which had passed over to her—or rather, the remnant of which she had taken into her keeping—were both saved. And here she stood—the only bulwark against which broke the surging deluge of Barbarism. That she was already an immovable organisation when the ancient Empire fell, is one of the most important facts in history, for on the firm foundation-stone of the Church the whole life of Europe was established anew.

The Church therefore, which had arisen from the

the Imperial hierarchy in the time of Constantine, to the Praefecti Praetorio, the Bishops of the dioceses to the Vicarii and Rectores of the provinces.—Plank, *Gesch. der christl. kirchl. Gesesellschafts-verfassung,* Band l; and Gieseler, *Kirchengeschichte,* Band 1.

union of Christianity with the Roman Empire, drew from the Empire the system of her centralisation and the treasures of an ancient language and culture. The degenerate ancient races, however, could not provide her with the vivifying material necessary to her development; on the contrary, they it was who perverted Christianity, inoculating the new system with the ancient Paganism. By means of historic ties the Church allied herself with youthful Germanism, and the union forms her second epoch in universal history. The primitive races of Germany possessed only a religion of nature, which offered no resistance to the Christian religion, such as that presented by the Paganism of the classic nations deeply-rooted as this was in the dominion of a thousand years, in literature and art, in ritual and the state. The Germans were, for the most part, already Christians when they gained possession of the Roman West. While actually overthrowing the Empire, they yet bowed in reverence before the Roman Church as before the Roman imperial ideal; the tradition of which had become the political dogma of the world. The Church herself, in her essence the guardian of the theory of the unity of the human race, or the Christian republic, inculcated in them this Latin idea. She strove to Romanise them. The ecclesiastical creed of the Germans, their hierarchy, the language and rituals of their faith, their festivals, their apostles, and saints were all Roman or grouped around a Roman centre. It eventually came to pass that the Germans, the rulers of the Latin races with which they had become intermingled on

The Church and the Germans.

The Germano-Roman Empire.

the ancient classic soil, themselves restored the Empire they had previously destroyed. The restoration, however, was essentially the work of the Roman Church, which of necessity demanded the Empire, her own prototype, as supplying a guarantee of the universal religion.

For this great achievement, the alliance of the old with the new, of the Latin with the German, world, the continued existence of the City of Rome was essential. Rome, in truth, towered like an Ararat of human civilisation amid the universal deluge of barbarism which followed on the overthrow of the Western Empire. The ancient capital of the world remained, or became, the moral centre of the transformation of the West. But after the power and splendour of the political Empire had fallen from her, she could no longer have retained this position, had not the bishops, who had taken up their seat within her, acquired for the Church in the Roman City supremacy over every other episcopate. They attained to the high priesthood of Christianity. They made Rome the Delphi or Jerusalem of the new Confederation of the peoples and united to the original imperial idea of the Capital of the World the Jewish conception of a City of God. The supremacy to which, with Roman arrogance, they laid claim, could find no basis in the unpolitical teaching of the Saviour, nor in the face of the equality which originally existed in all the apostles, all priests and all congregations nor yet in the antiquity of the Roman bishopric, since the Churches of Jerusalem, Ephesus, Corinth and Antioch were all older than that of Rome. But the ancient tradition of the foundation of the bishopric of Rome by Peter soon endowed the claims of the Roman Church with a victorious power, and already in the first century this Apostle was esteemed Head of the Church, and the immediate vassal and vicar of Christ himself.[1] For to him the Saviour had said, "Thou art Peter, and on this rock will I build my Church." On these words, which are to be found in only one of the four Evangelists, rests the origin of Papal domination. They are still to be read in huge letters round the frieze of the great cupola of S. Peter's, and they have been to the Roman Church what those of Virgil were to the Empire.[2]

Rome and S. Peter.

Not only was the doubtful, because unauthenticated, foundation of the Church by Peter disputed by the jealous East, but the consequences of her suprem-

[1] It is scarcely possible to believe in the actual foundation of the Roman Church by Peter. Even did the Apostle teach and meet his death in the city, yet he had found there, on his arrival, a Christian community already in existence, and, like S. Paul, worked in it as an apostle, without, however, being invested with any episcopal office. The Roman Church cannot point with certainty to any definite founder. It arose out of the numerous body of Jews established in the city, reinforced by converts from Paganism.—Karl Hase, *Kirchengesch.,* 1885, i. 168.

[2] *"Tu est Petras, et super hanc Petram aedificabo Ecclesiam meam, et portae Inferi non praevalebunt adversus eam,"* Matth. xvi. 18. The East contested the conclusions drawn from these phrases, and Origen remarks with reference to the subject: Πέτρα γὰρ πᾶς ὁ Χριστοῦ μαθητὴς—καὶ ἐπὶ πᾶσαν τὴν τοιαύτην πέτραν οἰκοδομεῖται ὁ ἐκκλησιαστικὸς, πᾶς λόγος, καὶ ἡ κατ' αὐτὸν πολιτεία.—Εἰ δὲ ἐπι τὸν ἕνα ἐκεῖνον Πέτρον νομίξεις ὑπὸ τοῦ Θεοῦ οἰκοδομεῖσθαι τὴν πᾶσαν ἐκκλησίαν μόνον, τί ἂν φήσαις περὶ Ἰωάννου τοῦ τῆς βροντῆς υἱοῦ ἢ ἑκάστου τῶν Ἀποστόλων (Ad Matth. xvi. 18; Comment., T. xii. 275 et Huet, in Gieseler I. i. 209).

acy, which followed on the acceptance of the legend, were also contested. In the West the tradition grew with time firm as an article of faith, and the Bishops of Rome called themselves the successors of Peter, the Vicars of Christ, and therefore the Heads of the Catholic Church.[1] If the power of a venerable tradition resting on the conviction of centuries appears strange, we must remember that, in every successful form of religion, tradition and myth constitute the basis of practical operations, and, so soon as the latter have been recognised by the world, are accepted as facts. This particular tradition would, however, have remained ineffectual with regard to any other city. Neither the sanctity of Jerusalem, where Christ lived and died, nor the undoubted foundation of the Church of Antioch by Peter gave these cities any claim to ecclesiastical precedence. But the Bishops in the Lateran, who did not recognise the political importance of Constantinople as a measure of the position of the patriarchs there, successfully asserted the claims which the ancient capital of the world possessed to the reverence and

[1] In the absence of any contemporary information, such as places S. Paul's sojourn in the city beyond a doubt, the foundation of the Roman See by Peter has been the subject of passionate dispute since the time of the Reformation. The statements of Irenaeus, Tertullian and Caius only point to an ancient tradition. Jerome estimated the duration of S. Peter's tenure of office in Rome at twenty-five years. (F. Pagi, *Breviarium Gestor. Pontif. Rom.* on S. Peter.) During the Reformation, Ulrich Velenus wrote his *Tractatus quod Petrus Apost. nunq. Romae fuerit* (vol. iii. of the *Monarchia* of Goldast). After him, this was shown by Flacius and Fr. Spanheim (*De ficta profectione Petri Ap. in urbem Romam*). An instructive treatment of the question may be found in Archibald Bower's *History of the Popes from the*

obedience of nations.[1] The nimbus of Eternal Rome reappeared, this time surrounding her priestly heads; they were the heirs of the Spirit, the discipline and ambitious instincts of ancient Rome reincarnate; and although the Empire fell, its great, if lifeless, machinery still lived on. The provinces still bear the deep impress of the government and administration of Rome, and the rule of the ecclesiastical city soon began to flow through the provisions in the channels which Pagan Rome had traced.

The Papacy.

The Roman Church gradually changed into the Papacy the Imperialism within which she had attained her development as a hierarchical creation. The organization of the Empire was transformed into

Foundation of the See of Rome to the present time, n. 1. The Roman legend concerning S. Peter is fully treated from a Roman standpoint by Gregory Cortesius, *De Romano itinere gestisque principis Apostolorum,* libri ii., Rome, 1770. The question has been revived in our own time. M. Viennet, *Hist. de la Puissance Pontificale,* Paris 1866, vol. i. p. 5 *ff.*; R. Lipsius, *Chronologie der röm. Bisch. bis zur Mitte des 4 Jahrh.,* Kiel, 1869; *Die Quellen der röm. Petrussage,* Kiel, 1872; E. Renan, *L'Antichrist,* Paris, 1873, 2. Cap. and App., holds the presence of Peter in Rome to be probable, and believes that the Apostle here suffered martyrdom shortly after his arrival (A.D. 64). The question was again considered in Rome itself, evidently with the sanction of Pius IX., without a solution being arrived at in favour of either party. *Resoconto autentico della disputa avvenuta in Roma, 9. e 10. Feb. 1872, fra Sacerdoti Cattolici e Ministri Evangelici intorno alla venuta di S. Pietro in Roma.*

[1] The primacy of the Roman Church was founded by the promulgation of the dogma of the supreme Apostleship of S. Peter by Leo I.; a dogma incessantly disputed by the Easterns, who, in the Synod of Chalcedon, succeeded in obtaining a decree which conceded to the Church of Constantinople (New Rome) the same privileges as were possessed by that of Old Rome, and which thus ordained that the political importance of the city should decide the rank of the Churches.

an ecclesiastical system, with the Pope as its centre. The old Imperial Senate, in the form of Cardinals and Bishops, surrounded this elective spiritual monarch, in whose case, as in the case of the Emperors, race and nationality were indifferent; but the constitutional principle which the Caesars had never recognised, was, on the score of the democratic theory of the equality of the priesthood, introduced in Councils and Synods, to which the provinces sent representatives to the universal Senate-house, the Lateran. The governors of these ecclesiastical provinces were the bishops consecrated and controlled by the Pope. The monasteries, scattered over all countries, resembled the ancient Roman colonies, and were strongholds or stations of the spiritual dominion of Rome, as well as of civilization; and, after the heathen or heretic barbarians in Britain and Germany, in Gaul and Spain, had been overcome by the bloodless weapons of Rome, the Eternal City again ruled and gave laws to the fairest portion of the ancient world. However we may regard the new centralisation which emanated from Rome, it was based on the historic requirement of mankind; and the supremacy of Rome was necessary for rude and lawless centuries, since it alone upheld the unity of Christendom. Without an absolute Church, without the Roman spirit of the Bishops, who, in the provinces suppressed, with the power of a Scipio or a Marius, every rebellious tendency to fall away from the orthodox faith, national imagination and traditions would have given birth to a hundred forms of faith. History repeated itself in the fate of Rome and the world; and in the end it was again the Germans, who, a thousand years after the fall of the ancient Empire, destroyed the universal supremacy of the second Rome, and by a great and creative revolution, won freedom of faith and knowledge for mankind.

Sanctity and importance of Rome in the Middle Ages.

During the Middle Ages the reverence of the nations for the city was unbounded.[1] In her, as in the great Ark of the Covenant of ancient as of Christian culture, they saw united the laws, the charters, the symbols of Christianity. In the city of the Martyrs and of the Princes among the Apostles, they beheld the treasure-house of supernatural graces. Here was the centre of the divine administration of the human family; here was enthroned the high priest of the new covenant which claimed to represent Christ on earth. All the chief spiritual and temporal powers received their consecration in Rome; the sources of the priestly power, the power to bind and to loose, the fount of Imperial Majesty, finally, civilization itself, seemed to spring from the hills of Rome, and, like the streams of Paradise, flow to fertilize the four quarters of the world. All the institutions of mankind had originally sprung from this single city. Bishoprics, monasteries, missions, schools, libraries were all colonies of Rome. Like the praetors and consuls of former days, her monks and priests had been sent forth to the provinces and had converted

[1] Arturo Graf, *Roma nella memoria e nelle immaginazioni del medio evo* (Turin, 1882), vol. i. c. 1.

them to faith in the spiritual power of Rome. The remains of Roman martyrs were reverently brought over sea and land to be buried as sacred relics under the distant altars of Britain and Germany. The language of the faith, the schools of the barbarians, were derived from Rome, as were all literature, sacred or profane, music, mathematics, grammar, the arts of painting and architecture. Men in the obscurest borders of the north and west had all heard of Rome, and when her name, which had already thrilled mankind through so many centuries, fell upon their ears, they were seized with a mystic longing, and their excited imagination pictured, in the form of the Eternal City, an Eden of beauty where the gates of Heaven opened or closed. There were long centuries in the Middle Ages in which Rome was truly the law-giver, the instructress, and the mother of nations, encircling her children with a threefold ring of unity—spiritual in the Papacy, temporal in the Empire, the crown of which German kings came to receive in S. Peter's, and the unity of that general civilisation which the ancient Romans had bequeathed to the world.

This should be sufficient to show the stature to which Rome had attained in the Middle Ages, as the dominating power in the Christian Commonwealth of nations. The recollection of the mighty task, which, for the second time in the world's history, Rome took upon herself, should serve to soften the bitterness of the memory of those long centuries of suffering, during which the human race struggled to free itself from subjection to Rome, opposing to her discipline the light of that knowledge to which it had attained. The sins of the ancient despot must be weighed against the great ideas of universal citizenship which she represented, and by which she rescued Europe from the chaos of barbarism and made it capable of receiving a common freedom and culture.

2. GENERAL VIEW OF ROME IN THE LATEST PERIOD OF THE EMPIRE.

We have attempted to give an idea of Rome in ancient and mediaeval times. Let us now sketch an outline of the most characteristic features of Imperial Rome as she appeared shortly before the conquest of the Visigoths, such a picture being necessary to a correct understanding of the Middle Ages.

Topographical outline of the city in Imperial times.

Under the Republic, Rome, in her unassuming majesty, was adorned less by her public monuments of religion and the state than by the virtues of her strong and simple citizens; but when freedom declined, an era of outward splendour set in, accompanied by inward decay. When Augustus took possession of the city, it was a narrow and closely-built chaos of houses and streets, which covered some hills and their intermediate valleys. He first had it divided into fourteen regions, and in conjunction with Agrippa he so adorned these regions that he was able to say he had found a city of bricks and left one of marble. Rome steadily increased during the first three centuries of Imperial rule, and became filled with temples, porticoes, baths, palaces, places of amusement of every kind, and with such an infinite number of statues that it seemed to contain a second population in marble. In the time of Honorius the city covered almost the same area as it does to-day, and was surrounded by almost the same lines of walls. The Tiber flowed through it in a twofold bend, so that on the left, or Latin, side lay thirteen of the divisions of the city, while on the right, or Tuscan, side was the fourteenth division, which comprised the Vatican, Janiculum, and Trastevere. The city proper stretched north, east, and south over eight hills, on which marble temples, fortresses, palaces, gardens, and villas formed a scene of surpassing beauty. It embraced the Hill of the Gardens, the Quirinal, Viminal, Esquiline, and Coelian, which, branching from one common root, stretched towards the centre of the city, with intervening valleys. It further embraced the isolated heights of the Aventine, Palatine, and Capitol which had been inhabited from the remotest times. Skirting the Tiber stretched a broad, low plain divided by the Via Flaminia, with its triumphal arches, and the continuation of the Flaminia, the Via Lata. Here stood many splendid buildings of the Emperors, but the plain, the chief part of which was called the Campus Martius, served the populace rather for pleasure than for habitation, though in later times under the Papacy, after some of the ancient hills had been forsaken, the native population crowded into it.

The city had organically developed from a centre. Even in the time of the Republic, this centre was the Forum and the Capitol which towered above it. If, drawing an irregular line round both, we embrace the Palatine, Coelian, Esquiline, and Quirinal, we find enclosed a by no means wide territory on the left side of the Tiber, in which, during Republican, as well as in Imperial, times, lay the heart of Rome. All the above-mentioned hills inclined from different directions towards the Forum. This Forum itself had formerly been the dwelling of the free population, and the seat of the life of the republican state; the Capitol above it was the fortress of the city, the abode of its gods and the home of its laws. Public amusements had also their consecrated site in the neighbourhood, for the Circus Maximus, containing in itself the most solemn games, lay under the Palatine. Hence the Forum, the Capitol, and the Circus were the three characteristic marks of the state under the Republic.

The Emperors added a fourth monument, their own residence, the fortress of the Caesars on the Palatine. Although Augustus and his successors jealously cared for and beautified the old sanctuaries of the state, they added few new buildings. They adorned the Capitol with statues, and surrounded its base towards the Forum with monuments, columns, and triumphal arches. The Forum became completely transformed by these magnificent buildings, and as it lost its political importance under the Empire, it remained merely a "piazza" of the people, a monument hallowed by tradition of the republican past, the Caesars meanwhile adding other "piazze" magnificently laid out by its side. These were the Imperial Forums of Caesar, of Augustus, of Nerva, of Domitian, and lastly, the Forum of Trajan. In this the Imperial city attained the summit of her magnificence, never afterwards producing anything more perfect. Trajan, under whom the Empire of the Caesars reached its zenith, completed the Circus Maximus; and Vespasian and Titus before him had erected a huge amphitheatre, that Colosseum which is the most expressive monument of the world-subduing, war-like, and cruel character of the Roman people. Passing along the Via Sacra, under the Arch of Titus, past the Palatine, through the Forum of the People, beyond the Capitol, through the adjacent Imperial Forums, the traveller has an entire and almost overpowering view of the chief features of Imperial Rome. After Hadrian had erected the greatest temple of the city, that of Venus and Rome, on the Via Sacra, scarcely a spot available for building remained in the heart of the ancient city. There rose a thickly packed mass of temples, basilicas, and colonnades, of triumphal arches and statues; and above this labyrinth of buildings towered here the Flavian Amphitheatre, there the Imperial fortress, further on the Capitol, and at a greater distance a second Capitol, the Temple of Quirinus on the Quirinal.

Beyond this central district Imperial Rome grew north-east and south over the long hills; north-west over the plain of the Tiber, and in the Vatican and Trasteverine quarter on the other side of the river.

The hills, such as the Aventine, already much built over during the Republic, offered great opportunities for the passion for building which set in with Augustus. The Esquiline, Viminal, and Quirinal were soon covered with palatial streets and pleasure-gardens, as well as provision markets and baths. Further along the hollow which stretched from the Capitol by the river rose new buildings, such as the Theatre of Marcellus, the Flaminian Circus, the Theatre of Pompey, with its vast and varied pleasure-grounds; the stately Pantheon of Agrippa, with its baths; the grand pile of buildings of the Antonines, with the columns of Marcus Aurelius; the great Stadium of Domitian; and lastly, a huge tomb beautified with trees, the dwelling of the dead Emperors—the Mausoleum of Augustus. Answering to this on the other side of the Tiber rose a second tomb of the Caesars, the wondrous work of Hadrian, leading to the Vatican district, and finally, to the less beautiful quarter of the Trastevere, over which towered the ancient stronghold of the Janiculum.

The walls of Aurelian.

Rome, the embodiment in stone and metal of the world's history, was surrounded by walls worthy of her majesty, the work of Aurelian. When the sea of houses had far overflowed the Servian fortifications, Aurelian set in these walls a boundary to her growth, which formed at the same time a defence against the constant inroads of the barbarians. To these celebrated walls Rome owed her preservation during centuries of terror long after the fall of the Empire. Without them the history of the Church and Papacy would have assumed an altogether different form. With the exception of a part of the Trastevere and of the Vatican territory, these walls, guarded by round or square towers, encompassed the entire city with grim and warlike solemnity, " beautifying," as Claudian expressed it, "her venerable countenance." Their dark and time-worn masses, so often stormed, overthrown and restored, yet continuing substantially on the same lines, still inspire the beholder with awe and admiration. Centuries have engraved upon them the names of consuls, of emperors, of popes, and associated them with a thousand memories. Arcadius and Honorius restored them in fear of the Goths in 402, and seven years later, according to the reckoning of a geometer, their circumference was 21 Roman miles.[1]

Sixteen gates led through these walls into the country,[2] and twenty-eight broad roads, paved with

[1] Ammon, at the time of the Visigothic siege, as Olympiodorus (*apud* Photium, 198) says: Εἴκοσι καὶ ἑνὸς μιλίου. In opposition to this is the account of Vopiscus, which estimates them at 50 miles in circumference. Piale. (*Delle mura Aureliane di Roma*) places their utmost limits at 13 miles. Nibby, *Le Mura di Roma*; Canina, *Indicazione Topografica di Roma antica,* p. 19, &c.; Platner's and Bunsen's *Stadtbeschreibung,* i. 646, &c.; Jordan, *Topogr. der Stade Rom.,* I., i. 340 f. Inscriptions over the Tiburtine, Praenestine, and Portuensian Gates inform us of the restoration of the walls under Arcadius and Honorius. *Corp. Inscr. Latin.,* vi. 1188–1190; where we find: *Suggestione V.C. Et Inlustris Comitis et Magistri Utriusq. Militae Stilichonis.*

[2] Porta Flaminia, Pinciana, Salara, Nomentana, Tiburtina, Praenestina, Labicana, Asinaria, Metronis or Metronia, Latina, Appia, Ostiensis, Portuensis, Janiculensis (Aurelia), Septimiana, Aurelia opposite Hadrian's Bridge. Two of these, the Metronia and Latina, are now walled up, the Aurelia opposite the Bridge of S. Angelo has

polygonal blocks of basalt (not reckoning the smaller connecting roads), united Rome with the provinces. In traversing the environs, these roads were lined with tombs in the various forms of temples, round towers, pyramids, and lofty sarcophagi. The Campagna, here bright with verdure, there parched by the sun, surrounded the city—a plain of sublime majesty unrivalled by anything the world could show. Upon it stood countless monuments, tombs, temples, chapels, country-houses of emperors and senators; and intersecting it were the marvellous aqueducts, a sight of impressive grandeur, as their existing ruins still testify. Stretching for miles and miles across the plains until they reached the city, they bore on their mighty arches those imprisoned waters, which, discharging themselves within the walls, supplied the populace through innumerable fountains of marble and bronze, provided the *naumachiae,* served the gardens and villas, and finally, filled the luxurious baths.[1]

perished. The *Breviarium* enumerates thirty-seven gates. The surplus is made up by the gates in the Servian walls and other exits.

[1] According to Procopius, there were fourteen aqueducts (*De bello Goth.,* i. 19). There is no doubt as to the nine quoted by Frontinus: the *Appia, Anio vetus, Marcia, Tepula, Julia, Alsietina, Virgo, Claudia, Anio novus.* In addition to these were the *Trajana* and the *Alexandrina* of Alex. Severus. These aqueducts, eleven in number, were the aqueducts of the city, properly speaking. Besides these, Augustus reinforced the *Marcia* by the *Augusta,* the *Antoniniana* had been added by Caracalla, the *Jovia,* as a branch of the *Marcia,* by Diocletian. The summary of the Notitia, therefore, enumerates nineteen aqueducts. At the present day, Rome possesses but four, the *Acqua di Trevi,* a wretched restoration of the *A. Virgo,*

Such was the city in the zenith of her outward completeness, at the beginning of the fourth century; but, on reaching that period of maturity when stagnation and old age begin, she remained, on account of her greatness, for nearly two hundred years in a condition of scarcely perceptible decline. This period began under Constantine, and, as a matter of fact, with that of the building of the new capital on the shores of the Bosphorus, to adorn and populate which the Emperor robbed Rome of many works of art, as well as of many patrician families. Christianity, now the declared public religion, dealt another blow to the pagan splendour of Rome, and as her monumental history is brought to a close with the Arch of Constantine, the history of her ruin is ushered in with the building of the Basilica of S. Peter, which rose out of the material of the ruined Circus of Caligula, and probably out of that of other monuments as well. Yet, although she had been deserted by the Caesars, and her splendour dimmed by advancing Christianity, Rome remained so awe-inspiring that, even about 384, in the time of Gratian, the rhetorician Themistius exclaimed, "Rome, the noble and world-famed Rome, is immeasurable, a sea of beauty baffling all descrip-

the *A. Felice,* the *A. Paola,* to supply which Paul the Fifth employed the waters of the Trajana, and the *A. Marcia,* the restoration of which was begun in 1866. With regard to the ancient aqueducts, see: R. Lanciani, *I. commentarii di Frontino intorno le acque e gli acquedotti; Atti della R. A. dei Lincei,* ser. iii. vol. 4, 1880. With respect to the more modern: Cavallieri, *Sulle acque della moderna Roma,* Rome, 1859; Blumenstihl, *Brevi notizie sull' acqua Pia,* Rome, 1872.

tion."[1] Her splendour and the number of her monuments were extolled by Ammianus Marcellinus, Claudian, Rutilius, and Olympiodorus with the greatest enthusiasm.

The fourteen regions of Augustus.

According to the system of Augustus, Rome remained for centuries divided into fourteen civic regions, with their quarters or "Vici," their divisional magistrates, and their cohorts of guards. They were as follows:—1, Porta Capena; 2, Caelimontium; 3, Isis and Serapis; 4, Templum Pacis; 5, Esquilinae; 6, Alta Semita; 7, Via Lata; 8, Forum Romanum Magnum; 9, Circus Flaminius; 10, Palatium; 11, Circus Maximus; 12, Piscina Publica; 13, Aventinus; 14, Transtiberim. These are the names, which, as it appears, were derived not from official but from popular custom, and which are handed down to us through the so-called *Curiosum Urbis* and the *Notitia.* These are two topographic registers taken from the archives of the City Prefecture, one belonging to the time of Constantine, the other to that of Honorius, or Theodosius the Younger. They describe the fourteen regions of Rome, and, as a rule, define the extent of the buildings to be found within their limits; while at the end they give a short survey of the libraries, obelisks, bridges, hills, fields, forums, basilicas, baths, aqueducts, and roads of Rome, to which in general a short statistic is

[1] *Inclyta ac celebris Roma immensum est, atque omni oratione majus pelagus pulchritudinis*: Themist., *Orat.* 13 *amat. in Gratian.,* p. 177. See Carlo Fea's *Dissert. sulle Rovine di Roma,* the first fundamental attempt at a history of the ruins of Rome up to the time of Sixtus the Fifth. (In the third vol. of his translation of Winckelmann's *Geschichte der Kunst,* Rome, 1784.)

appended. Their statements, although often doubtful and obscure, are invaluable as the only authentic information we possess regarding the outward aspect of Rome in the fourth and fifth centuries. And here the reader may follow them in brief, in order that he may understand the most important points in the topography and monuments of Rome at every period of the Middle Ages.[1]

3. THE FOURTEEN REGIONS OF ROME.

I. Region Porta Capena.

The first region of Rome, the Porta Capena, stretched from the ancient Servian gate either to the Aurelian wall, or beyond it to the Porta Appia, now S. Sebastian; divided by the Appian and Latin Way, it turned citywards until it reached the Coelian. In this district lay the celebrated Vale of Egeria, with its grove, its sanctuary of the Camenae, and the sacred Temple of Mars; and in its neighbourhood was the brook Almo, to which these registers give especial prominence, and the recollection of which was preserved by the worship of Cybele. Three triumphal arches spanned the Appian Way within

[1] On the *Curiosum Urbis* and the *Notitia,* Sarti, Bunsen and Preller have been the first to throw light. I have followed the text of the last-named authority (*Die Regionen der Stadt Rom,* Jena, 1846), and am acquainted with the texts of Panciroli, Labbe, Bianchini, and Muratori. The oldest official document on which the *Curiosum* is based belongs, in Preller's opinion, to the time of Constantine, and to a date earlier than that of the erection of his triumphal arch. The *Curiosum* he holds to have been compiled between the reigns of Constantine and Theodosius the Younger, the *Notitia* in that of the latter. The latest researches are those of H. Jordan, *Topographie der Stadt Rom im Altertum,* Berlin, 1871, Band ii.

the walls, and were dedicated to Drusus, Verus, and Trajan. An arch which still remains half destroyed in front of the gate of S. Sebastian, and which formed part of an aqueduct, has erroneously been held to be that of Drusus. On the further side of the wall were found the Circus of Maxentius and the Tomb of Cecilia Metella. Both buildings stood intact at the time of Honorius; the circus, the last building of its kind apparently, no longer in use; the tomb still entire, faced with its squared stones, and ornamented with its frieze, and as yet far removed from the period which transformed it into a fortress. In this district the dead of Pagan and Christian Rome rested side by side, for in the midst of the tombs of the Via Appia was, and still exists, the entrance to the catacombs of S. Calixtus, where, in long and narrow corridors, and in layers of from three to five stages, Christianity long undermined Rome, until the edict of Constantine summoned the now perfected form of the Church from the dark cells of martyrdom into the light of day. As early as the sixth century a district on the Via Appia was named "Ad Catacumbas."[1] The numerous Jews in Rome had also one of their subterranean burial-places

[1] S. Gregory, E. III. 30, 568: *ad secundum urbis milliarium in loco, qui dicitur ad Catacumbas.* This word, which does not appear before the end of the third century, was used to denote a particular Christian burial-ground, that of S. Sebastian, and was later also applied to other Christian cemeteries. It is to be explained, with Ducange, from the word κύμβος (depth or excavation), or better, with De Rossi, from *cubare*; in which case *cata cumbas* would be equivalent to *cata accubitoria*; that is to say, *ad coemeteria christianorum.—Roma sotterranea cristiana,* iii. p. 427.

along the same road, and in the immediate neighbourhood of the Christian catacombs. The *Notitia* finally conducts us in the same region to the Baths of Severus and Commodus, and to the mysterious Mutatorium Caesaris.[1]

II. Region Coelimontium.

Coelimontium was the second region. It embraced the whole Coelian Hill. The *Notitia* there mentions the Temple of Claudius, the Macellum Magnum or Great Market, the station of the Fifth Cohort of Guards, the Castra Peregrina, where in later times the foreign legions were quartered, the Caput Africae, a street which will be frequently mentioned in the latest Middle Ages.[2]

III. Region Isis and Serpais.

The Amphitheatre of Titus, not yet called Colisaeus, is noticed in the third region of Isis and Serapis. The Emperor Philip celebrated in it the 1000th anniversary of the Foundation of Rome with the most magnificent secular games, shortly after it had been restored by Alexander Severus. In the time of Honorius this wonderful building stood unimpaired with all its columns, its wealth of

[1] The ancient Porta Capena lay below the present Villa Mattei. (Canina's *Roma Antica,* on this Region.) The boundaries of Region I. are not exactly ascertained. The name of the Almo (now Acquataccio), has given rise to the opinion that it extended beyond the wall of Aurelian. The ancient Temple of Mars, the most celebrated sanctuary of this region, undoubtedly stood *extra portam Capenam.*

[2] The Anonymus of Einsiedeln of the eighth century says: *Arcus Constantini. Meta sudante. Caput Africae. Quatuor Coronati.* The *Caput Africae* is mentioned in inscriptions of Imperial times, the most ancient of which belongs to the year 198, C. I. L. VI. 1052. The *vicus Capitis Africae* received its name from an immense building, apparently the Paedagogium of the Imperial pages. Giuseppe Gatti, *Del Caput Africae,* Annal. dell' Instit., 1882.

statues, and its seats, the latter, according to our lists, numbering no less than 87,000. The region received its name of Isis and Serapis from its most important temple,[1] of which, however, there remained no more trace than of the Moneta, the Imperial mint in the same quarter, the Ludus Magnus and Ludus Dacicus, gymnasia of the gladiators, the Camp of the Marines from Misenum (*Castra Misenatum*), and the Portico of Livia.[2] We only recognise from their ruins the Baths of Titus and Trajan, which the registers place close by. It is, however, uncertain whether these magnificent baths, first built by Titus over a part of the Golden House of Nero and afterwards continued by Trajan, were still in use in the time of Honorius, when people were accustomed to frequent the Baths of Diocletian, Constantine, and Caracalla. Meanwhile, the Roman could wander in the most luxurious apartments, he could admire the group of the Laocoon in its original position, and enjoy the exquisite paintings which relieved the gloomy severity of the halls and corridors with the cheerful light of poetry.[3]

IV. Region Templum Pacis.

The fourth region adjoined the amphitheatre, and stretched as far as the Roman Forum, and behind it,

[1] An attempt has been made to discover the site of the temple by the present church of S. Pietro e Marcellino, Preller, *Die Regionen Rom's,* v. 124; Fea, *Miscell.,* i. 222,

[2] A further fragment of marble belonging to the celebrated Capitoline plan of the city, bearing the words PORTICUS. LIVIAE, was discovered beside S. Cosma and Damiano in the summer of 1867.

[3] The Thermae Titianae et Traianae occupy the space extending from the Colosseum to S. Martino ai Monti, and to them also belonged the huge ruin named "Sette Sale."

to the Forum of the Emperors, then across the street Suburra, to the Carinae. This region first took its name from the Via Sacra, then from the Temple of Peace; but the plans no longer mention this celebrated building of Vespasian. Burnt by lightning in 240, it ever afterwards remained in ruins. Close to the amphitheatre rose Domitian's fountain, the Meta Sudans, the brick base of which still stands erect in the form of a cone; also the renowned Colossus of Zenodorus, once dedicated to Nero, and placed by Hadrian beneath his great twofold Temple of Roma and Venus. This sumptuous building, with its immense Corinthian pillars and gilt roof, was ever counted one of the chief ornaments of Rome. The fourth region was distinguished by the many magnificent buildings which stood on the Via Sacra. Conspicuous above all in the freshness of its splendour was the Basilica Nova, built by Maxentius, but inaugurated by Constantine, the mighty ruins of which were long erroneously supposed to be those of the Temple of Peace. The registers name the Temple of Jupiter Stator, the Temple of Faustina, the Basilica of Paul, the Forum Transitorium. Of this last-named Forum, the beautiful remains of one of the halls dedicated to Minerva are still standing.[1]

[1] Vespasian had dedicated the Templum Pacis after the Jewish War. In the time of Procopius its remains were still to be seen beside the Basilica of Maxentius. The surrounding space was known as Forum pacis: ἣν φόρον Εἰρήνης καλοῦσι Ῥωμαῖοι ἐνταῦθα γάρ πη ὁ τῆς Εἰρήνης ναὸς κεραυνόβλητος γενόμενος ἐκ παλαιοῦ κεῖται—*De Bello Goth.*, iv. 21, 570 (Bonner's edition). The *Notitia* cites in good order: Aedem Jovis Statoris, Viam Sacram, Basilicam Constantinianam, Templum Faustinae, Basilicam Pauli, Forum Transitorium.

The registers also speak of the Temple of Tellus, the street of the Suburra, even the Tigillum Sororium on the Vicus Cyprius, that monument to the memory of Horatius and the sister whom he murdered, which the Romans then guarded as jealously as they did the sacred House of Romulus on the Palatine, and the fabulous Boat of Aeneas on the bank of the river by the Aventine.

V. Region Esquiliae.

In the fifth region we are led to the Esquiline and part of the Viminal hill. The Registers speak here of the Lake Orphei, a reservoir of water adorned with the statue of Orpheus;[1] the Macellum Livianum, a great provision market for the necessaries of the people laid out by Augustus;[2] and the Nymphaeum of Alexander, a huge fountain with a magnificent façade erected by Alexander Severus.[3] Beyond the station of the Second Cohort of Guards, the Gardens of Pallas, the well-known freedman of Claudius; the Sullan Temple of Hercules, the Castrensian Amphitheatre, the Campus Viminalis, the Temple of Minerva Medica, and a sanctuary to Isis Patricia. This last must have stood on the most beautiful street of the quarter, the Vicus Patricius, where also were situated the Thermae of Novatus, mentioned in the history of the first century of Christian Rome.

[1] From the fact that S. Lucia in Selce also bore the surname in Orfeo, we may infer that the fountain stood in the neighbourhood of the church.

[2] Where S. Maria Maggiore and S. Vito now stand.

[3] The Nympheum Alexandri stood, as it appears, in the neighbourhood of the Trofei di Mario. (Pump-room of the Aqua Julia). The Anon. of Einsiedeln says: *Sanctus Vitus. Nympheum. Sancta Biviana.*

The whole district of the Esquiline, Viminal, and part of the Quirinal was mainly inhabited by a population of the lowest class, for whom the Emperors in later times provided pleasure-grounds and baths. The registers do not mention the Thermae of Olympias on the Viminal over the Subura, but the martyrologies transfer to them the death of S. Lawrence, and tradition asserts that on their site the ancient church of S. Lorenzo in Panisperna was erected.

VI. Region Alta Semita.

The last baths of Rome are found in the sixth region, Alta Semita. They bore the name of a street supposed to have led from the Quirinal to the Porta Nomentana. In this region the registers also give the ancient and beautiful Temple of Salus on the Quirinal, and the Temple of Flora near the Capitolium Antiquum. This was the first of the Capitols, namely, the renowned temple ascribed to Numa on the summit of the hill, in the triple cellae of which stood the statues of Jupiter, Juno, and Minerva. That this, the original prototype of the later Tarpeian Capitol, remained standing in the fifth century, is one of the most remarkable facts recorded in the *Notitia.* The Temple of Quirinus is further represented as intact. This was one of the most beautiful sanctuaries of the city, magnificently restored by Augustus. Doubtless the Colonnade of Quirinus was still in use, as there is an epigram of Martial in its honour, and the leaden statue of Mamurus Veturius seems to have been preserved not far from the temple which was the work of this metal-smith, the artist of the

Ancilian shields.[1] The registers then lead us between the Temple of Quirinus and the Thermae of Constantine. These immense baths were, however, the last which arose in Pagan Rome—the last great building in the spirit of antiquity—and with it closes the long list of works dedicated by the Emperors to the use of the populace. In the time of Honorius, and long afterwards, the celebrated twin Colossi of Horse-tamers stood in front of these baths. The building itself must have been in a ruinous condition,[2] damaged probably in 367, during the revolt against the Prefect Lampadius, whose palace was close by. It was, however, restored by Perpenna in 443.

In the same region, on a still larger scale, were the Thermae of Diocletian on the Viminal, the most extensive of any baths in Rome, and, except those of Caracalla, the most frequented. They were standing in undisturbed splendour in the time of Honorius, but even then were regarded by the Christians of Rome with pious aversion, from the fact that Diocletian had employed many thousands of Christian prisoners in their construction. On account of their lavish

[1] The *Liber Pontificalis,* "Vita Innocenti," n. 58, speaks of a *Balneum juxta templum Mamuri* and *clivum Mamuri* (probably beside S. Susanna, near the Gardens of Sallust); whence Becker and Preller conclude that there the *Statua Marmuri* must have also stood.

[2] The reader will find in the third vol. of the present history the legend of the *Equi,* or *Caballi Marmorei,* which gave their name to a district. The church of S. Agatha was also known as in *Equo Marmoreo.*

decoration in marble and painting, their costly colonnades and halls adorned with mosaics, they called forth greater admiration than any other building of the kind. Olympiodorus reckons about 2400 places for baths in the chambers.[1]

No less celebrated were the Gardens of Sallust, which extended from the Quirinal to the grounds of the Pincio, and to the Salarian Gate. These gardens were a favourite resort of the Emperors Nerva and Aurelian, and contained not only lovely pleasure-grounds, but a circus, baths, temples, and colonnades. The *Notitia* speaks of them: they were the first buildings of Rome which were destroyed five years after the triumph of Honorius. In the neighbourhood of these gardens stood the Malum Punicum and the so-called Gens Flavia. The name of this quarter, "Pomegranate," may have been taken from some statue or tree, and here Domitian transformed his house into a temple and a mausoleum for the Flavian family.[2]

As the Gardens of Sallust formed the boundary of the sixth region towards the Pincian Gate, so

[1] According to Olympiodorus (*apud* Photium, 198), the Antonine Baths possessed 1200 marble seats, those of Diocletian almost double the number. The topographers place the latter baths now on the Viminal, now on the Esquiline, or Quirinal. The truth is that all three hills joined each other on the spot on which these baths were built. A church to S. Ciriacus had early been constructed within them; Ciriacus and Sisinnius having been among the number of Christians who laboured in their construction. Since the pontificate of Pius the Fourth, the beautiful church of S. Maria degli Angeli has stood within the Baths.

[2] The site of the Temple of the Gens Flavia was that on which stands the present palace of the Ministry of Finance.

the Castra Pretoria marks its confines towards the Porta Salaria and Porta Nomentana. The *Curiosum* does not mention the Camp of the Praetorians on the Tiber, for it had already been destroyed by Constantine.[1]

With the seventh region we descend into the valley towards the Field of Mars. It was called the Via Lata from the street which corresponds to the lower part of the present Corso. The *Notitia* here mentions a triumphal arch, "Arcus Novus," which appears to have been erected by Diocletian, and to have stood at the point where the Via Lata changes into the Flaminian Way. But the greatest ornament of this region was Aurelian's Temple of the Sun, on the slope of the Quirinal hill, a gigantic building of oriental magnificence, which must then have been intact, but which was destroyed as early as the sixth century.[2] Beneath it lay the Field of Agrippa, a space adorned with halls and pleasure-grounds. Other porticos (Gypsiani and Constantini), the Forum Suarium, the Pig Market, and Gardens (the Horti Largiani) show that this low-lying quarter must have been an animated resort of the populace.

VII. Region Via Lata.

[1] The *Notitia* only mentions this camp as a landmark.

[2] To this building belong the colossal ruins in the Colonna Gardens. Fea, *Sulle Rovine di Roma,* p. 302, remarks that this temple was in ruins as early as the sixth century, that eight of its porphyry columns had fallen by inheritance to a widow, who presented them to the Emperor Justinian for the new church of S. Sophia in Constantinople. Codinus, *De orig. Const.,* p. 65; and Anon., "De structura temp. magnae Dei Eccl. S. Sophiae" in P. Combefis, *Origin. rerumq. Constantin.,* p. 244.

VIII. Region Forum Romanum.

The eighth and most famous region, called the Forum Romanum Magnum, represents the true centre of Roman history; in it the greatness of the Empire is reflected in innumerable monuments, temples, columns, statues, triumphal arches, rostra, and basilicas.

Upon the Capitol, the buildings of which the *Notitia* does not mention by name, but only collectively under the head "Capitolium," stood enthroned the sanctuary of Rome, namely, the Temple of Jupiter. It is this building that confers upon the Capitol its title of "the golden," and from which is apparently derived the appellation, "Aurea Urbs," still in use in the Middle Ages. Its roof was covered with gilt metal tiles, the bases and capitals of its columns were gilt, and it was adorned with gilt statues and monuments. The gates also were of gilt bronze. That the temple was still perfect in the time of Honorius, Claudian himself informs us, and Procopius conclusively establishes the fact.[1] The Capitol, the hoary head of Rome, however, must already have worn a bare

[1] Zosimus, v. c. 38, relates that when the doors were stripped by Stilicho of their metal plates, the inscription, *Misero regi servantur,* was disclosed to sight, and that the violator of the temple hence came to a miserable end. The theft could not have taken place until after the triumph of Honorius, for at that time Claudian still speaks of the reliefs on the doors:—

juvat infra tecta Tonantis
cernere Tarpeia pendentes rupe gigantes,
caelatasque fores. —*De VI. Cons. Hon.,* v. 44.

That Stilicho had not destroyed the Sibylline books previous to the and neglected aspect after Christianity had proscribed the temples and sanctuaries of her religion.

Descending by the Clivus Capitolinus, the path of the Triumphators towards the Forum—we are dealing with the time of Honorius—we find in perfect preservation those temples, the ruins of which are still to be seen, namely, the Temple of Concord, the Temple of Saturn, and those of Vespasian and Titus. All these are enumerated in the register, which also mentions the "Golden Genius" of the Roman people, that is to say, the temple erected to it, together with the equestrian statue of Constantine, which must long have remained on the Arch of Severus.[1] The Milliarium Aureum or Golden Milestone of Augustus at the same arch is specified and distinguished from the Umbilicus Romae. Three Rostra are designated, a fact which has occasioned no little perplexity. The most ancient of these tribunes, which was adorned by the beaks of the vessels taken at Antium, stood in ancient times in front of the

year 403 is also evident from Claudian, *De bello Goth.,* v. 230, where he thus speaks of them as still in existence:—

> *quid carmine poscat*
> *Fatidico custos Romani carbasus aevi.*

[1] Fea, p. 410, observes that the equestrian statue of Marcus Aurelius had been held to be that of Constantine, and that to this error the statue owed its preservation throughout the Middle Ages. Such an error is intelligible during barbarous times, but it is scarcely credible that at the date of the *Notitia* the figure of M. Aurelius could be mistaken for that of Constantine. I assume, however, that long after the equestrian statue of Constantine had perished, that of M. Aurelius was christened by the name of the later Emperor, as the fabulous Caballus Constantini of the later *Mirabilia.*

Curia. It was, however, removed by Julius Caesar to another site apparently below the Capitol, but which can no longer be precisely ascertained. Augustus must therefore have erected the Rostra Julia opposite the Temple of Caesar. The Arch of Severus, which still remains standing, is not, however, mentioned by the registers, nor is that of Tiberius below the Temple of Saturn, which in the fifth century must have also been in existence.

The list of the remaining buildings in the Forum given by the *Notitia* is not exhaustive, although the most conspicuous are enumerated. The Senatus is the first specified; it was apparently the building recently erected by Domitian for the Senate, not far from the Arch of Severus as this side of the Forum long remained animated. Perhaps at that time the Curia Julia on the slope of the Palatine may still have been preserved. It is not indeed specified in the *Notitia,* but a Curia Vetus which is mentioned in the tenth region, that of the Palatine, may quite possibly have been intended to designate it, a distinction being thus formed between the old Curia, that of Julius Caesar, and the new Curia, or the Senatus. An inscription found in S. Martina speaks of a Secretarium of the Senate, built by Flavianus and restored by the Prefect Epiphanius.[1] It appears from this that

[1] *Salvis Dominis Nostris Honorio et Theodosio Victoriosissimis Principibus Segretarium Amplissimi Senatus Quod Vir Inlustris Flavianus Instituerat et Fatalis Ignis Absumpsit Flavius Annius Eucharius Epifanius V.C. Praef. Vice Sacra Jud. Reparavit et Ad Pristinam Faciem Reduxit.* Gruter, 170; Canina, *R. Ant.,* p. 167;

this building of the Senate must still have been in use in the time of Honorius.

In the same neighbourhood also stood the celebrated Temple of Janus Geminus. It is not mentioned by the *Notitia,* but Procopius speaks of it with minuteness, and in the Middle Ages we again find it as the Templum Fatale. The *Notitia* cites also the Basilica Argentaria, which stood on the Clivus Argentarius, now the Salita di Marforio, but it does not show in this region the Basilica of Aemilius Paulus, which it represents instead in the neighbouring fourth region. This splendid building of the Aemilian family, ornamented with columns of Phrygian marble, stood near the present church of S. Adriano, and corresponding with it was the Basilica Julia on the other side of the Forum, the position of which has now been decided by means of excavations. On the southern side the register shows the Vicus Jugarius, the Graecostadium, the Basilica Julia, the Temple of Castor and Pollux, and finally the Sanctuary of Vesta.[1] We thus see, that in the time of Honorius the ancient splendour of the Forum still existed, but that the paltry rem-

Nardini, ii. p. 230; *C.I.L.,* vi, 1718. Epiphanius was Prefect of the city, A.D. 412. The Curia Hostilia, the ancient Senate House destroyed by fire at the obsequies of Clodius, was never restored, the Curia Julia, completed by Augustus, serving in its stead.

[1] The Regia or Atrium of Vesta, with the dwellings of the Vestals and of the Pontifex Maximus, and the temple itself occupied the space in front of and beside the present church of S. Maria Liberatrice. Excavations which have taken place since 1871 have brought to light the circular foundations of the temple, and in 1883 were discovered the remains of the atrium of the Vestal Virgins.

nant of political life which yet survived had migrated to the neighbourhood of the Arch of Severus.

From here the Imperial Forums were entered. According to the statement of the *Notitia,* there were four, close to one another—the Forums of Julius Caesar, of Augustus, of Nerva, of Trajan. They remained in undiminished splendour, the first with the Temple of Venus and the equestrian statue of Caesar standing before it; the second with the great Temple of Mars Ultor, of which three splendid Corinthian pillars still remain; the third with the Temple of Pallas; and the fourth with its column of Trajan, which, as a sacred monument of the greatness of Rome, was preserved even through the barbarous Middle Ages, and still bids defiance to Time.[1] Both the libraries and the equestrian statue of the great Emperor remained to astonish the beholder. His Triumphal Arch also probably remained erect, and, since several triumphal arches had been dedicated to the memory of Trajan, the assumption that it was from one in his Forum that the sculptures were taken to decorate the Arch of Constantine, is very doubtful. Ammianus Marcellinus still speaks with enthusiasm of this Forum. It was forty-eight years before the entry of Honorius that the Persian prince, Hormisdas, visited Rome in company with the Emperor Constantius. "As the Emperor," says the historian, "reviewed the vast city and its environs, spreading along the slopes, in the valleys and between the

[1] Plan of all the Forums, by Ferd, Dutert; *Le For. Rom. et les Forums de J. César,* &c., Paris, 1876.

summits of the Seven Hills, he declared that the spectacle that first met his eyes surpassed everything he had yet beheld. Now his gaze rested on the Temple of the Tarpeian Jupiter—now on baths so magnificent as to resemble entire provinces—now on the vast pile of the amphitheatre, massively compact, of Tivoli stone, the summit of which seemed almost beyond the range of human sight; now on the Pantheon, rising like a fairy dome, and its sublime columns with their gently inclined staircases, adorned with statues of departed Emperors; not to mention the Temple of the City, the Forum of Peace, the Theatre of Pompey, the Odeum, the Stadium, and all the other architectural wonders of Eternal Rome. When, however, he came to the Forum of Trajan, a structure unequalled by any other of its kind throughout the world, so exquisite, indeed, that the gods themselves would find it hard to refuse their admiration, he stood as if in a trance, surveying with a dazed air the stupendous fabric, which neither words can picture, nor mortal ever again aspire to rear. Then, realising the futility of attempting any similar masterpiece, he exclaimed despairingly, that the horse which Trajan bestrode in the midst of the Atrium was all that he would, or could, imitate! Prince Hormisdas, who stood close beside him, thereupon rejoined with admirable adroitness, 'In order, most august Emperor, that the horse you propose to set up may have a stable worthy of him, at once command one to be erected as magnificent as this!' Being asked what he thought of Rome, the Prince replied, that in one respect he was disappointed, namely, to find that, even here, men were only mortal![1] After inspecting everything with the profoundest amazement, the Emperor admitted that fame, which exaggerated all, had not adequately described the glories of Rome. Finally, as a contribution to her splendours, he caused an obelisk to be erected in the Circus Maximus."

In the time of Trajan the statues of the great philosophers, poets, and rhetoricians still stood in the Forum; and to these were added new statues: Claudian and, later, even Sidonius Apollinaris received statues,[2] and as late as the beginning of the seventh century, the poetry of Virgil and the sterile verses of living poets were recited in the halls of Trajan's library.

IX. Region Circus Flaminius.

The Circus Flaminius, in the ninth region, was situated in what is now the most densely populated part of the city; namely, in that wide plain which stretches from the Capitol along the river to the present Piazza del Popolo, and as far as the bridge of Hadrian. It embraces also the Campus Martius, the splendours of which Strabo described as so magnificent as to render the rest of Rome merely an appendage. But the fire under Nero, and the changes effected by his successors, each of whom

[1] Ammianus Marcellinus, xvi. 14 *seq. Id tantum sibi placuisse aiebat, quod didicisset, ibi quoque homines mori.* Gibbon reads *"displicuisse,"* and the expression is more appropriate to the fulsome tone of the foreign monarch.

[2] Claudian speaks of this statue in the *Praef. de bell. Goth.*:—

Sed prior effigiem tribuit successus ahenam,
Oraque patricius nostra dicavit honos.

outdid his predecessor in his mania for building, completely transformed the aspect of this extensive region. It developed into a new Imperial town of such wealth that its earlier magnificence may well have been forgotten. The *Notitia* does not speak of the Circus Flaminius itself, a great part of which remained standing during the later Middle Ages, but mentions the adjacent stables of the four factions of the Circus. It also passes over the Amphitheatre of Statilius Taurus, but shows three theatres, namely, that of Balbus, with 11,510 seats, that of Marcellus, the gigantic fragments of which serve to remind us in some degree of its ancient magnificence, with its 17,580 seats, and the Theatre of Pompey, with its 22,888 seats. It is silent concerning the Hekatostylon, or Portico of Pompey, yet this pleasure resort was doubtless in perfect preservation. Of other porticos, however, the register mentions that of Philip, the stepfather of Augustus, but not the adjacent portico of Octavia, the superb ruins of which are still to be seen in the present Ghetto not far from S. Angelo in Pescaria.

A short way from this was the double portico of Minucius (Minucia Vetus and Frumentaria), where in later Imperial times distributions of corn were made to the citizens. Close by stood the Crypta of Balbus, probably a covered hall, in the rear of his theatre.[1] We must add to these halls the colonnade of Cneius Octavius, which brought the wayfarer from

[1] The Theatre of L. Cornelius Balbus, a friend of Augustus, stood on the spot now occupied by the Palazzo Cenci. The site of the Amphitheatre of Statilius Taurus has not been ascertained.

the Flaminian Circus to the Theatre of Pompeius, where we find a magnificent covered pleasure-ground, extending from the present Palazzo Mattei to the Palazzo Farnese. Further towards the river, Theodosius, Gratian, and Valentinian had erected colonnades (*porticus maximae*), and built in front of Hadrian's Bridge a triumphal arch which lasted down to the latest Middle Ages.

On the right stood the Portico of Europa, but the *Notitia* mentions neither this building nor the Hall of Octavius, although it speaks of the Porticos of the Argonauts and of Meleager.

The Campus Martius, the smaller part of the hollow outside the Flaminian and Teverine fields, follows. As the ancient Field of Mars stretched from the Altar of the god (by the present Palazzo Doria) beyond the Mausoleum of Augustus, its boundaries were fixed by the Aurelian Wall with the Flaminian Gate. The walls extended with their towers along the river as far as the Bridge of the Janiculum (Ponte Sisto). Within the Campus Martius, between the walls on the one side, and the Via Lata and Flaminia on the other, stood the buildings enumerated by the *Notitia.* The list does not, however, include those in the neighbourhood of the Mausoleum of Augustus.

Here was the great Stadium of Domitian, with 33,080 seats, an admirable building, out of which the beautiful Piazza Navona has arisen; beyond were the Trigarium, a smaller circus, and the Odeum for musical competitions, which was reckoned amongst the most admired of the works of Constantius, and must therefore have been of surpassing beauty. The Pantheon of Agrippa could not have been especially prominent, although this greatest monument of the great benefactor of Rome is now considered one of the principal ornaments of the city. The baths, however, to which it originally belonged, have long since disappeared. The Baths of Nero, enlarged by Alexander Severus, and situated near the Piazza Navona, have likewise entirely disappeared. Both buildings are enumerated by the *Notitia.*

On the other side of the Pantheon rose the Temple of Minerva, where the church of S. Maria Sopra Minerva now stands, and close by a Temple of Isis and Serapis. The Antonines, emulating Trajan and Hadrian, had raised beside the Via Lata basilicas or temples to Marciana and Matidia, a temple to Hadrian, and a column in honour of Antoninus, and the Senate had erected a temple and a lofty column to Marcus Aurelius, which, with that of Trajan, survived the fall of Rome. Two renowned monuments of Augustus, however, of which one at least existed until the fifth century and even longer, are not named by the *Notitia*; these are the Gnomon or Sun-dial, of which the Obelisk still stands on Monte Citorio, and the beautiful Mausoleum, built by the Emperor for himself and his family. Neither does the *Notitia* mention the outer side of the Field of Mars towards the Aurelian Wall, where several tombs of distinguished men were situated. Here was the tomb of Agrippa, somewhere about the present Piazza del Popolo, and that of the Domitian family, where Nero was buried, below the gardens of Domitian and Lucullus. These gardens extended over the Pincio, and in the time of Belisarius the palace of the Pincii on this hill still remained in habitable condition.

X. Region Palatium.

The tenth region embraced the Palatine, and from the Imperial Palaces was named Palatium. These colossal dwellings of the Caesars remained habitable in the days of Honorius, and, though in places fallen to decay and robbed of their ornament, even down to those of the Byzantine Exarchs. Until the time of Alexander Severus, many Emperors continued to build on the Palatine, but to Augustus and Tiberius were due its two principal buildings, the Domus Augustiana and Tiberiana, of which the *Notitia* speaks by name. Domitian had contributed some additions, and Septimus Severus had erected the Septizonium, a large and beautiful entrance towards the Coelian and Circus Maximus, which survived as a ruin until the days of Sixtus V., and which is frequently mentioned in the history of the mediaeval city. The *Notitia* speaks of it under the title of Septizonium Divi Severi. Amongst the other renowned temples of the Palatine, it describes the Temple of Jupiter Victor, and the Temple of Apollo, built by Augustus, where the Palatine library was situated.[1] It also mentions the House of Romulus and the mythic Lupercal. Other ancient sanctuaries of the city of Romulus reposed here on

[1] Since the purchase of the Farnese Gardens by Napoleon III., new light has been thrown on the topography of the Palatine, thanks to the exertions of Pietro Rosa and his successors.—*Guida del Palatino,* by C. L. Visconti and R. A. Lanciani, Rome, 1873.

the slopes of the Palatine, where now stand the churches of S. Anastasia, S. Teodoro, and S. Giorgio in Velabro, and their sanctity was preserved by tradition down to the latest times of the Empire. Here too, where the Lupercalian festival in honour of Pan was celebrated even as late as the end of the fifth century, Christianity had to fight its hardest battle against the memories of Paganism.[1]

XI. Region Circus Maximus.

The eleventh region included the Circus Maximus between the Palatine and the Aventine, and spread from the end of the latter hill to the Velabrum and the Janus Quadrifons. This Circus, the spina of which had been adorned by Constantius with a second Obelisk, contained no fewer than 385,000 seats, and was the largest building of its kind. Here races and games were constantly celebrated, the Circus remaining in its full splendour until the overthrow of the Gothic kingdom. Near it stood the ancient sanctuaries of Sol and Luna, that of the Magna Mater, and those of Ceres and Dispater. The Clivus Publicus led from the Circus to the Aventine. This region, finally, extended as far as the Forum Boarium under the Palatine.[2]

[1] On the Palatine hill itself stood the *Casa Romuli,* the *tugurium Faustuli,* the *Roma quadrata*; lower down on the declivity called Germalus stood the traditional cavern of Lupercus, where Romulus and Remus were said to have been suckled by the she-wolf; and in its neighbourhood the Ruminalian fig tree.

[2] The *Curiosum* places the Arcus Constantini in Regio XI. Since it is impossible that it can be the Triumphal Arch of Constantine, which the registers must have spoken of in Regio X., Bunsen (iii. 1, 663) holds it to be the Janus Quadrifons in the Velabrum. This view is favoured by the juxtaposition of names in the *Curiosum: Herculem olivarium, Velabrum, Areum Constantini.*

XII. Region Piscina Publica.

The two following regions which bounded the city on this side of the river at present form the most deserted district of Rome. They became depopulated in the Middle Ages, earlier than any other part of the city. The twelfth region was called Piscina Publica from an old public bathing-place of Republican times, of which not a trace remains. The Antonine Thermae, or the Baths of Caracalla, are its only celebrated buildings of any antiquity. Their ruins—the grave of many magnificent statues, such as the Flora of Naples, the Farnese Hercules and the Farnese Bull—testify more than any other of this period to the Oriental luxury, extravagance, and colossal scale of Imperial buildings.

XIII. Region Aventinus.

The thirteenth region comprises the Aventine and the valley close to the river. There stood the ancient Temple of Diana, built by Servius as the sanctuary of the Latin Confederation, and the Temple of Minerva; and although they are not mentioned in the registers, probably also the Temple of Juno Regina and Dea Bona. There were situated the Baths of Sura and of Decius; and on the shore the Emporium, where vessels discharged their cargoes, the Horrea or granary —on the present Marmorata—and other establishments connected with harbour traffic.[1]

[1] Piale, "Degli antichi arsenali detti Navalia" (*Pont. Accad. di Arch.*, 1st April 1830), shows that the Emporium was situated under the Aventine, while the Navalia are to be looked for on the Ripa Grande. The latter view is opposed by Becker, who holds that the Navalia occupied a site (not yet ascertained) on the Field of Mars—*Handbuch,* i. 158, &c. Excavations which have taken place on the banks of the river behind the Marmorata (since January 1868) have

XIV. Region Transtiberim

The fourteenth and last region of Rome comprised all the territory on the other side of the river, the Janiculum which Aurelian had enclosed within his walls and the Vatican hill, which was not surrounded by walls until the ninth century. The following bridges led to this quarter:—

The Bridges

1. Sublicius, which was made of wood, the oldest bridge of Rome. The date of its ruin is uncertain, but it is scarcely probable that the bridge which was first destroyed by Sixtus IV. in 1484, and the remains of which we still see rising out of the water near S. Michele, can be identified as the Sublician.

2. Aemilius, now known as the Ponte Rotto; the latter name it received in 1598. It was also called the Pons Lepidi—perhaps after M. Aemilius Lepidus, its probable restorer—Lapideus in the dialect of the people, and also Palatinus. In the thirteenth century it was known as Ponte di S. Maria and also the Pons Senatorius or Senatorum.

3 and 4. Fabricius and Cestius are the bridges which still lead to the island. The first, called "de Quattro Capi" from a four-headed Herm, leads into the city; the second, called also Pons Gratiani, from its restorers, Valentinian, Valens and Gratian, but now known as S. Bartolommeo, united the island with the Trastevere.

5. Janiculensis, later Ponte Sisto, on account of

revealed the Site of the ancient Emporium. The blocks of marble from the Imperial quarries found there, none of later date than 206 A.D., were clearly brought thither from Greece, Asia, and Africa. P. Luigi Bruzza, "Iscrizioni dei marmi grezzi" (*Ann. dell' Inst.,* 1870, p. 106 *seq.*).

its restoration under Sixtus IV. in 1475, is called in the *Notitia* "Aurelius." In the *Acts of the Martyrs,* however, it is known as "Antoninus," apparently because it had been previously built by Caracalla, or M. Aurelius Antoninus. The bridge was called Ponte Rotto in the Middle Ages until the time of Sixtus IV.

6. Next follows the Vaticanus, called also the Pons Neronianus and later Triumphalis, which was planned by Caligula to reach the Gardens of Domitian. Having fallen into decay before the year 403 (the erection of Hadrian's Bridge probably rendered it superfluous), the *Notitia* passes it over in silence. Its ruins, however, still exist close to Sto. Spirito.

7. Pons Theodosii and Valentiniani, called "in Ripa Romaea," and also Marmoreus, a short distance from the Marmorata, was entirely destroyed in the year 1484 by Sixtus IV.[1]

8. The Aelian Bridge. The splendid work of Hadrian was replaced by that of the Vatican. Even in the eighth century this bridge was named S. Peter's, leading, as it did, directly to the Vatican Basilica.[2]

[1] Not mentioned in the *Notitia,* because belonging to a later date than this compilation. Jordan, *Topographie der S. Rom.,* i. 1, 421.

[2] The opinions held by archaeologists, with regard to the bridges of ancient Rome, are as utterly at variance as clocks and philosophers, to speak with Seneca. Piale, *Degli antichi ponti di Roma al tempo del secolo v.,* Roma, 1834; Preller and Becker, i. 692; Jordan, i., section "Brücken"; Mayerhöfer, *Die Brücken in alten Rom.,* Erlangen, 1883. The Regionaries give: *Pontes VIII. Aelius, Aemilius, Aurelius, Mulvius, Sublicius, Fabricius, Cestius et*

The Caesars had beautified the Trasteverine quarter with extensive pleasure-grounds. Gardens, such as those of Agrippina, later those of Nero, and the famous gardens of Domitian rendered the neighbourhood of the Janiculum and the Vatican a favourite place of resort with the Emperors, who frequently retired to their villas in this quarter. The *Notitia* mentions the *Horti Domities,* but its statements are somewhat vague. While summing up the district of the Vatican under "Vaticanum," it appears under the Circus of Caius (Gaianum)[1] to indicate the Circus of Caligula, which was rendered conspicuous by the lofty obelisk now adorning the Piazza of S. Peter's; the only obelisk in Rome which has not at some time or other been levelled with the ground. It towered over the spina of the Circus, which, however, even in the time of Honorius, was already overshadowed by the Basilica of the Prince of the Apostles. This Circus was called in the Middle Ages *Palatium Neronis.* The *Notitia* speaks of Naumachiae in the Vatican territory, but not of the Tomb of Hadrian, which, at the beginning of the fifth century, stood undisturbed, not having as yet

Probi. The Pons Mulvius already so named by Livy, is called by the *Notitia,* Molvius or Mulvius by Procopius, Μόλβιος; by Prudentius (*Contra Symmach,* i. v. 452) Mulvius, corrupted into Molle in the Middle Ages. The derivation of the name itself is unknown. The Pons Probi, the eighth bridge of the *Notitia* and *Curiosum,* is difficult to ascertain.

[1] *Gaianum et Frigianum,* "Gaianum" from Caius Caligula to whom the Circus owed its origin; "Frigianum," according to Preller from the Phrygian goddess, whose worship had its seat in the locality. The Basilica of S. Peter was erected close to the sanctuary of Cybele, or Magna Mater.

been plundered by the Visigoths of Alaric, or the Greeks of Belisarius.[1]

The *Notitia* names the Janiculum, but we do not know in what condition the old fortress on the hill then stood. A large population had its quarters in Trastevere proper, also on the slopes of the Janiculum, and through all succeeding ages this district has remained densely inhabited. Mills, baths, streets, fields and temples are here named in the *Notitia.* Here stood the gardens of Geta, which had been apparently laid out by Septimius Severus, and which may have reached to the Porta Septimiana. This gate, or rather the surrounding district, is mentioned in the *Notitia* by name, and having originally belonged to the Fortress of Aurelian, and being united to the Janiculum by two long lines of wall parallel with the river, it apparently received its name from the grounds of Septimius.

The island in the Tiber

It is uncertain whether the island in the Tiber was reckoned in the fourteenth region. The *Notitia* neither mentions the island in general, nor yet the Temple of Aesculapius, nor those of Jupiter or Faunus. In the time of Honorius, a palace belonging to the powerful family of the Anicii seems to have stood there. The island itself bore in the Middle Ages, for some unknown reason, the name Lycaonia.[2]

[1] The station of the seventh cohort of the watchmen was situated in Trastevere, close to the present S. Crisogono, where it was excavated in 1867.

[2] With reference to the names of the island, see Visconti, "Città e famiglie nobili e celebri dello stato pontificio," *Monum.*

Tables of statistics from the last period of the Imperial city have preserved to us some lists of the multitudinous houses, of the public buildings, and even of the statues of Rome.[1] They enumerate two Capitols, two great Race-courses (besides smaller ones), two great Meat Markets (Macella), three Theatres, two Amphitheatres, four splendid Gymnasia for gladiators (Ludi), five Naumachiae for naval combats, fifteen Nymphaea, or Palaces of Fountains, 586 Public Baths, eleven Great Thermae, 1352 Water-basins and Fountains. Of public works of other kinds, they enumerate two Great Columns, thirty-six Triumphal Arches, six Obelisks, 423 Temples, twenty-eight Libraries, eleven Flora, ten

Antichi Sezione, ii. 25. Claudian, in *Prob. et Olyb. Cons.,* v. 226, says:—

Est in Romuleo procumbens insula Tibri,
Qua medius geminas interfluit alveus urbes
Discretus subeunte freto, pariterque minantes
Ardua turrigerae surgunt in culmina ripae.

This passage seems to prove that the walls of Aurelian were continued on the inner side of the river as far as the Fabrician Bridge, the Septimian Wall corresponding to them on the side of the Trastevere.

[1] The summaries of the *Curiosum* and the *Notitia*; the *Enarratio fabricar. urbis* of Polemius Silvius, compiled about 448, according to the appendices of the *Curiosum,* printed by Mommsen in *Abh. d. Sächs. Ges. d. W.,* iii. 269 f.; the summary, relating to the *Notitia,* incorporated by Zacharias, rhetorician and Bishop of Mitylene, in his ecclesiastical history (in the sixth century); two manuscripts in the Syrian tongue in London and the Vatican, The first edition of the text is by A. Mai, with a Latin translation (*Script. Vet. Nov. Coll.,* x., praef. xii.-xiv.). See also Preller, *Regionen,* p. 237; Urlichs, *Cod. urbis, R. Topogr.,* p. 49 f; Jordan, *Topogr.,* ii. 575 f. The most correct edition of text and Latin translation is by Ignazio Guidi (*Bull. della Comm. Arch. di Roma,* 1884).

Chief Basilicas, 423 Quarters of the City, 1797 Palaces or "Domus," and 46,602 houses or "Insulae."[1]

[1] Mercati (*Degli obelischi di Roma*) maintains that forty-eight ancient Obelisks had been brought to Rome. The summaries enumerate only six, naturally the largest, two in the Circus Maximus, one of 88, the other of 222, feet in height, one in the Vatican (75 feet), one in the Campus Martius (75 feet), two in the Mausoleum of Augustus (each 42 feet). All these obelisks still adorn Rome. Parker, *The twelve obelisks in Rome,* Oxford, 1879, 2nd Ed.

CHAPTER II.

1. Condition of the Buildings in the Fifth Century—Exaggerated Zeal of the Fathers in Overthrowing the Statues—Claudian's Description of Rome—Imperial Edicts of Protection—Attempts of Julian to restore the Ancient Faith and their Consequences.

WHILE the registers of the regions give us an idea of the outward aspect of the city in the fifth century, they tell us nothing of the condition of those splendid buildings which had so long sheltered the ancient faith. Had the temples of Rome been only deserted? Had the gods been merely banished to the solitude of their cells, behind the closed doors of the Temples? Had the triumphant hatred of long-persecuted Christianity disfigured or destroyed them? Or, finally, was the new religion, complying with practical shrewdness and its necessity, already taking possession of this or that temple of Paganism, seizing it for its own, and, after complete purification by holy water and prayer, transforming it into a dwelling for the Cross?

The Fathers of the Church derived from the Jews their hatred of Rome, which they named Sodom or Babylon, when speaking of the heathen of the city, but likened to Jerusalem, when referring to the number of monks and nuns which it contained. If we accept literally some of their utterances, we are forced to believe that even before the invasion of Alaric the temples and the images of the gods had been overthrown. After the fall of Rome, S. Augustine wrote that all the gods of the city had been previously destroyed. He delivered a sermon on the Gospel of S. Luke, disproving the reproach of the heathen that Rome had been destroyed not by the barbarian enemy but by Christ, who, they asserted, had overthrown the honoured and ancient gods. "It is not true," he cried, "that after the fall of the gods Rome was taken and plunged in misery; for the idols had previously been overturned, and nevertheless the Goths under Rhadagaisus were defeated. Remember this, brethren! it is not long since this took place, only a few years ago. After all the images had been overthrown in Rome, the Gothic King Rhadagaisus came with an army, much more powerful than that led by Alaric, and although he sacrificed to Zeus he was vanquished and annihilated."[1]

At the same time Jerome rejoiced while he apostrophised Rome: "Mighty city! ruler of the universe, city praised by the voices of the Apostles, thy name of Rome the Greeks translate by 'Power,' but the Jews by 'Eminence'! Because thou art called a

[1] Sermon cv. de verb. evang. Luc xi. n. 13 (t. v. 1, 546): *mementote fratres, mementote: non est longum, pauci anni sunt, recordamini. Eversis in urbe Roma omnibus simulacris, Rhadagaysus rex Gothorum cum ingenti exercitu—*

slave be exalted by virtue, not debased by indulgence. Mindful of the example of Nineveh, thou mayest escape by penance the curse with which the Redeemer threatened thee in the Apocalypse. Beware of Jovinian's name, which is derived from the name of an idol! The Capitol is filled with filth, and the temples of Zeus and its ceremonies are utterly neglected." In another treatise, of the year 403, the same Father says, "The golden Capitol is filled with mire, all the temples of Rome are defiled with dirt and cobwebs! The city rises up from her seats, and the people passing by the half-destroyed temples hasten to the graves of the martyrs. He who is not impelled to the faith by reason is constrained thereto by shame."[1] He reflects with pride on Gracchus, a prefect of the city, to whose cousin, the pious Laeta, he writes how Gracchus had destroyed the caves consecrated to Mithras, and broken all the idols dedicated to the stars, Korax, Nymphe Miles, Leo, Perses, Helios, Dromo

[1] Lib .ii. ada. Jovinianum ad fin: *squalet Capitolium, templa Jovis et caerimoniae conciderunt.* Nardini, *R. Ant.* ii. 332, concludes from this too hastily that in the time of Jerome the Temple of Jupiter was already in ruins. Its destruction he ascribed to the Goths; the passage which he wrongly cites is, however, merely a figure of speech like another in Jerome, Ep. cvii. *ad Laetam,* belonging to the year 403 (Ed. Verona, i. 672): *auratum squalet capitolium. Squalere* is also found in Claudian, *De VI. Cons. Honor.,* v. 410, used in a similar sense with regard to the Palatium, because it was forsaken by the Emperor:—

Cur mea quae cunctis tribuere Palatio nomen
Neglecto squalent senio?

Also in Proemium, lib. ii. of the *Commentary on the Epistle to the Galatians.* Jerome says: *vacua idolorum templa quatiuntur.*

and Pater, in order to enable himself to be baptised; and full of joy, he exclaims, "Paganism is banished from the city into the wilderness, those who were once the gods of the nations abide with the bats and the owls among the desolate house-tops. The banners of the soldiers are blazoned with the Cross, the purple of kings and their jewelled diadems are adorned with the likeness of that gibbet which has wrought for us salvation."[1]

But a single passage of Claudian suffices to prove the foregoing picture of the devastation of Rome a gross exaggeration. The passage is that which describes the poet as he stands in 403, in the Palace of the Emperors, showing to the newly-entered Honorius the same temples and gods which his father Theodosius first showed to him as a boy.[2]

"The lofty palace, tow'ring to the sky,
Beholds below the courts of justice lie;
The num'rous temples round, and ramparts strong,
That to th' immortal deities belong;
The Thund'rer's domes; suspended giant-race
Upon the summit of Tarpeian space;
The sculptured doors; in air the banners spread;
The num'rous tow'rs that hide in brass their head;
The columns girt with naval prows of brass;
The various buildings raised on terreous mass;

[1] Ep. cvii. *ad Laetam de institutione filiae,* t. i. 642. This rhetorical letter instructs a noble Roman lady how to educate her daughter.

[2] *De VI. Cons. Honor.,* v. 42 *seq.*:—

Attollens apicem subjectis regia rostris.

The Regia is here the Palace of the Caesars, and by "the rostra" the poet evidently means the locality of the Forum itself. It is *pars pro toto.*

The works of nature joining human toils;
And arcs of triumph decked with splendid spoils.
The glare of metal strikes upon the sight,
And sparkling gold o'erpow'rs with dazzling light."
—*Hawkins' Translation.*

The warfare, however, which existed between Christianity and Paganism had already produced many changes. In the eastern province many temples had been ruthlessly destroyed, and even in Rome, during the popular risings, several had been devastated. Through the hatred of the Christians, hundreds of statues must also have been broken and defaced. The complete destruction of works of art in Rome was only prevented by the edicts of the Emperors, by the reverence in which the city and its associations were held, and by the influence of the Pagan aristocracy, an aristocracy numerously represented in the Senate. Jealous for the preservation of the monuments, the Romans guarded them with such affection as to win the praise of the Greek historian Procopius, who, a hundred and fifty years after Honorius, wrote as follows: "Although the Romans have long endured barbarian rule, they have preserved as far as possible the buildings of their city, and the greater part of its adornments, which, owing to their own intrinsic greatness and excellence, will defy time and neglect."[1] The Christians of Rome could by no means have shared the passion for destruction possessed by Augustine or Jerome. To the credit of their patriotism it may be assumed

Edicts of the Emperors for the protection of the Monuments.

[1] *De bello Goth.*, iv. 22.

that their horror of idolatry extended only so far as to deprive Rome of those wonders with which their renowned ancestors had endowed her, and which centuries had served to consecrate.

It was, moreover, the duty of the city prefect to watch over the public buildings, the statues and triumphal arches, in short, over everything that beautified Rome. Out of funds assigned to him, he had to defray the cost of restoring buildings, and in the year 331, or 332, the Roman Senate restored the Temple of Concord on the Capitol.[1] Neither Constantine nor his sons were sincerely hostile to the ancient Gods, whom they had abjured mainly from motives of statecraft, and the series of edicts issued by succeeding Emperors proves that the Imperial guardianship was extended to all the monuments of Rome without distinction, whether belonging to the cult of Paganism, or to the civil requirements of the populace. There were enactments which prohibited the prefect and the other officials from erecting new buildings in Rome, their duties being confined to the preservation of the old. They also prohibited the public from robbing ancient monuments of their stone, from destroying their foundations, from breaking their marbles, and carrying off their materials for the construction of new buildings.[2] The same edicts also applied to

[1] Gruter, p. 100, 6. Beugnot, *Histoire de la destruction du paganisme en occident,* i. 106.

[2] Cod. Theod., lib. xv. tit. i., de operib. publicis; tit. i. n. 11, Impp. Valentinianus et Valens ad Symmachum P. U. n. 19; Impp. Valens, Gratianus et Valentinianus ad Senatum, n. 15; Impp. Valentinianus, Theodosius, et Arcadius Proculo P. U. Constant. Other edicts of

the temples. Far from the Emperors lay the slightest thought of their destruction; they simply ordered the temples to be closed, and imposed the penalties of the law on those who resorted thither, or who sacrificed to Pagan deities.[1] As soon, however, as the Christians seized on temples, which they did with greater security beyond the walls and on the Campagna, edicts were issued to prevent a repetition of such occurrences. "Although," says the Emperor Constantine in 343, "every superstition is to be completely uprooted, yet we desire that all buildings of temples which are situated without the walls shall remain untouched and undisturbed. For since from some of them have been derived the games, or the amusements of the Circus and the Agonalia, it is not fitting to destroy that from which sprung the ancient diversions of the Roman people."[2]

Restoration of the Pagan Religion under Julian.

Julian, a belated Greek philosopher, young and impetuous, filled with an enthusiasm for the great figures of antiquity and with hatred of the fanatical priests, who, by their pedantry and arrogance, had made Christianity repulsive to him, inspired, to, with an ardent longing to revive the ideals of ancient Greece, strove to restore the worship of the ancient

Honorius and Arcadius: Cod. Justin., viii, t. x., de aedific. privatis; tit. xii., de operib. publicis; tit. xvii., de sepulchris violatis.

[1] Honorius commanded in the year 399: *Sicut sacrificia prohibemus, ita volumus publicorum operum ornamenta servari* (Cod. Theod., xvi. 10, 15 and 18). De Rossi, *Bull. d. Arch. cristiana,* iv. n. 4: "I templi pagani sotto gli imperatori cristiani."

[2] *De Paganis sacrificiis et templis,* lib. xvi. tit. x. Imp. Constantinus ad Catullinum P. U.

Gods. The believers in the old order were now the persecuted and oppressed, for whose rights he did battle. In the revolution of life produced by the new teaching, with the fall of the gods of Greece he saw the overthrow of learning, art and literature—the greatest treasures of the human race. From the pagan philosophers of Athens and Asia, he had imbibed the aristocratic teachings of the ancient wisdom; but they remained a sterile possession without life-giving power. Neither the Homeric heroes nor the philosophers could arise at the Emperor's summons. At his command, it is true, the ancient temples were re-opened or restored, and the aged priests, whom he reinstated in their privileges and immunities, sacrificed once more to Mithras, Pallas and Jupiter; this reaction, however, could produce nothing more than a transient fanaticism. In vain the apostate Emperor turned away from the newly arisen Sun of Humanity, with whimsical defiance, to worship the sinking Helios of the Greeks. Julian died, it is said, with the cry, "Thou hast conquered, O Galilean!" His obstinate struggle against the great Christian revolution could not stem its progress. With himself fell, as unjustified and unreasonable, his scheme of a restoration, and the new doctrines of Christianity thereby acquired increased influence. The Christians now rose in revenge throughout the entire Empire. Headed by fanatical monks, they waged a crusade against the temples and statues of the heathen. In the course of a few decades fell the magnificent sanctuaries in Damascus and Ephesus, Carthage and Alexandria, where the Serapeum, the wonder of the East, with all its wealth of art, was burnt in 391. Contrary to the expectations of the Egyptians, however, the world did not perish in consequence. The pagans were in despair. The authorities, still in part pagan, took refuge in a curious means of defence; namely, in appointing Christian soldiers to guard the threatened temples. But in his edict, issued from Milan to Symmachus, prefect of the city, in 365, Valentinian forbade the practice, as an abuse of the Christian religion. The veto, however, was issued not so much out of enmity towards paganism as from complaisance to the Christian bishops, Valentinian as well as Valens holding fast to the Roman principles of religious toleration.[1]

2. GRATIAN'S ATTITUDE TOWARDS PAGANISM—DISPUTE CONCERNING THE ALTAR OF VICTORY—ZEAL OF THE EMPEROR THEODOSIUS AGAINST THE PAGAN CULT—THE STILL PAGAN CHARACTER OF THE CITY—DOWNFALL OF THE OLD RELIGION IN THE TIME OF HONORIUS—THE TEMPLES AND THE STATUES—ACCOUNTS OF THEIR NUMBERS.

Suppression of Paganism.

Gratian, son of Valentian, was the first Roman Emperor who, disdaining the traditional dignity of Pontifex Maximus and of the insignia that belonged to it, made a resolute stand against Paganism.[2]

[1] Marangoni, *Cose gentilesche,* &c., p. 227.

[2] The custom, so offensive to Christians, of adoring the images of the Caesars, was abandoned at an early date. Cod. Theod., *De imaginib. imperialib.,* lib. xv, tit, iv, A. 425.

While the poor and the middle classes readily exchanged the ancient religion of their forefathers for the new teaching, which was the solace of the oppressed, a strong minority of the Roman aristocracy obstinately adhered to their ancestral faith.[1] Amidst this minority were many wealthy men, members of illustrious families, who had rendered important services to the State and were actuated by motives of patriotic enthusiasm. The pride of many of the Senators was wounded by the notion of having a God in common with the Plebs; and the democratic and communistic principles of Christianity—the ideas of equality and brotherhood, which threw down the barrier between masters and slaves—were at variance with the legitimate institutions of the aristocracy. In Christianity they rightly foresaw a social revolution, which would involve the ruin of the State itself. Rhetoricians and authors, educated in the ancient literature and philosophy, out of reverence to the genius of antiquity remained zealous adherents of the pagan cult; as for example in the East, Libanius and Zosimus; and in Rome, Symmachus, Ammianus, Eutropius, Ausonius, Claudian, Macrobius, and others.

The Altar of Victory—struggle concerning it.

In 382, however, Gratian commanded that the

[1] About the year 400, Prudentius reckons 600 noble families who had become converts to Christianity, among them the Probi, Anicii, Olybriaci, Paulini, Bassi, Gracchi:—

Sexcentas numerare domus de sanguine prisco
Nobilium licet ad Christi signacula versas,
Turpis ab idolii vasto emersisse profundo.
—*Contra Symmach.*, i. v. 566.

celebrated statue of Victory should be removed from the Senate House, and in connection with this religious and political symbol of the greatness of Rome, arose that memorable struggle, which is one of the most affecting scenes in the tragedy of dying Paganism. "Victory" was the brazen statue of a winged maiden, a figure of exalted beauty, surmounting the globe, with a laurel wreath in her hand. Caesar had once placed this masterpiece of Tarentum over the altar in his Curia Julia; Augustus had adorned it with the spoils of Egypt, and henceforward no congress of the Senate was opened without sacrificial rites in honour of this national divinity, "the maiden guardian of the State."[1] Her altar had been removed by Constantius, but was replaced by Julian. When, by Gratian's edict, it was now a second time removed, the patriotic grief of the Pagan Senators knew no bounds. They sent the prefect and pontifex, Quintus Aurelius Symmachus, the head of the Pagan party, and a man of honoured character and distinguished descent, on several missions to the court of Milan, to implore the restoration of the goddess of Victory. The stirring speech which Symmachus composed on his second embassy in 384, but did not deliver, represents the last official protest of expiring Paganism. "It appears to me," says the illustrious Roman to the Emperors Gratian and Valentinian II., "as if Rome herself stood before you, and spoke to you in this wise: 'Most excellent Princes, Fathers of

[1] Preller, *Röm. Mythologie*, ii³. 246, is of the opinion that the statue of Victory was placed by Domitian in his new Curia.

your country, respect, I entreat you, the years to which holy religion has allowed me to attain. Let me be permitted to follow the faith of my fathers, and you will not repent it. Let me live in conformity with my customs, for I am free. This faith has placed the universe in subjection to my laws, these mysteries have repulsed Hannibal from the walls and the Semnones from the Capitol. Have I lived so long, only to be turned adrift in my old age? That were too insulting a chastisement.'"[1]

But the new spirit of the age and the eloquence of S. Ambrosius, the great Bishop of Milan, prevailed against the despairing appeal of the august priest of now powerless Jupiter.[2] And later, Prudentius, taking the opposite side of the controversy, foretold in an inspired apostrophe, supposed to be addressed by ageing Rome to the Emperors Arcadius and Honorius, that the Christian faith would invest Rome with a new life and a second immortality.[3] A third

[1] *Relatio Symmachi,* 1. x Ep. 54. Beugnot has an excellent chapter on this tragic dispute, liv. viii. 6. See also Gibbon, chap. 28; O. Gerhard, *Der Streit um den Altar der Victoria,* 1860; Sievers, *Studien zur Geschichte der Röm. Kaiser,* 1870, p. 469 f.

[2] Ambrosius replied to this report of Symmachus by his letter to Valentinian (A. 384). Both documents are found in Prudentius, Parma, 1788, T. i. Ambrosius said: *Quid mihi veterum exempla proferitis? odi ritus Neronum. Non annorum canities est laundanda, sed morum.* Ennodius of Pavia, as late as the sixth century, made the following epigram on the subject :—

Dicendi palmam Victoria tollit Amico:
Transit ad Ambrosium; plus favet ira deae.

[3] *O clari salvete duces, generosa propago*
principis invicti, sub quo senium omne renascens
desposui, vidique meam flavescere rursus

appeal from the old Roman party to the Emperor Theodosius met with no better success. But, after the Senate had appeared in vain before four Emperors in as many as seven embassies, aided by an unexpected event, namely, the murder of Valentinian II. by the Frank Arbogast in 392, it ultimately secured its object. The rhetorician Eugenius, whom that powerful minister and general had raised to the throne, hastened to invoke support from the followers of Paganism. He himself was a Christian, but the head of the party which had raised him to power, the respected Senator Nicomachus Flavianus, a zealous follower of Paganism, undertook the restoration of the ancient religion. The old faith was again sanctioned; the overthrown statue of Zeus again stood erect, and the altar of Victory was once more placed in the Curia. The ancient ceremonies were again celebrated in Rome; and Eugenius was forced to look on while Flavianus, Consul in 394, publicly attended the festivals of Isis, the Magna Mater and the Lustration of the city. Not daring, however, to restore the property of the temples, appropriated by Gratian in 383, he bestowed it instead on Flavianus and other senators who still adhered to the ancient religion. But this was the last effort of Paganism, and the struggle between

canitiem; nam cum mortalia cuncta vetustas
inminuat, mihi longa dies aliud parit aevum.
quae vivendo diu didici contempnere finem.
—*Contra Symmach.,* ii. v. 665 *seq.*

Prudentius answered the Report of Symmachus again in the year 403 in the two poetic books which are his most successful productions.

the followers of Eugenius and Theodosius its death struggle.[1] Theodosius, in early life a Pagan, afterwards a Christian fanatic, from 378 co-regent with Gratian in the East, was now the man of the future. He had a brother-in-law to avenge in the person of the murdered Valentinian, and his triumph was rapid and complete. With the aid of the saints he triumphed over the gods and crushed the aristocracy and the usurpers. Fortified by a prophecy of the anchorite, John of Lycopolis, brought to him by an Egyptian eunuch, foretelling that he would win a bloody victory, he departed from the East with an army for Italy. In vain Flavianus appealed to the golden statue of Zeus against the approaching enemy, who was already crossing the Julian Alps. The god hurled his thunderbolts no longer. The battle in the neighbourhood of Aquileia, in September 304, sealed the overthrow of Paganism. Eugenius was taken prisoner and beheaded. Arbogast fell by his own hand. Flavianus, whose life Theodosius wished to spare, died on the field of battle.

The bigoted victim made his entry into Rome, where Paganism, which had been restored by force, was immediately extinguished. The priests of the ancient religion were banished, the recently opened temples were again and for ever closed. The statues of Flavianus were overthrown, and not until 431, by

[1] A poem discovered by Delisle in Paris, containing the invective of a Christian contemporary against Flavianus, throws light upon these events. Morel, *Revue Arch.,* June and July 1868; De Rossi, *Bull. d. arch. crist.,* 1868, n. 4: "Il culto idolatrico in Roma," nel 394 and n. 5; "Il trionfo del Cristianesimo in Occidente," nel. 394.

command of Theodosius II. and Valentinian III., was the memory of the celebrated senator honoured by the restoration of his column in the Forum Trajanum.[1] The Christians triumphed in Rome. So far did their insolence go, complained the pagan Zosimus, that Serena, the wife of Stilicho, entering the Temple of Rhea, took from the neck of the goddess the costly necklace and transferred it to her own.[2] The last vestal witnessed with tears of despair this act of sacrilege, and pronounced the curse of the goddess on Serena and her entire race, a curse which was destined to be fulfilled. The sacred flame of Vesta was extinguished;[3] the voices of the Sibyls and the Delphic Oracle were heard no more; scarcely an orator dared to defend openly the condemned faith. Can the zealous Theodosius have left the altar and statue of Victory in the Curia? It is just possible that he may have permitted a now harmless symbol of national associations to remain, since the poet Claudian at a later date speaks of the Victory, as though the goddess were present at the triumph of Stilicho and Honorius.[4] The altar was

[1] The Imperial diploma, discovered in the Forum Trajanum in 1849, has been printed and explained by De Rossi, *Annal. d. Inst.,* 1849, p. 283 f., c. i. 1. vi. n. 1783.

[2] Zosimus, v. c. 38.

[3] From this time onwards, until the excavations in 1883, the sanctuary and rites of Vesta remained veiled in deep obscurity.

[4] Claudian, *De Cons. Stilich.,* iii. v. 205:—

O palma viridi gaudens et amicta trophaeis,
custos imperii virgo;

and *De VI. Cons. Honor.,* v. 597:—

Adfuit ipsa suis ales Victoria templis
Romana tutela togae.

doubtlessly overthrown and removed, but the Emperors continued to impress the image of the ancient goddess on their coins.

The character of Rome remains Pagan.

So much is quite certain that, in the days of the same Theodosius who forcibly proclaimed Christianity the religion of the State, notwithstanding all edicts, and in spite of the closing of the temple, the public character of Rome was still Pagan. At the same time that monks—disciples of Antony, the Egyptian anchorite—who made their way to Rome about 341, wandered about the well-preserved temples of the gods, to visit the newly-founded basilica of S. Peter, or to kneel at the graves of the martyrs, the Pagans still celebrated their ancient festivals. For, in contradiction to the edict of the State which prohibited Pagan sacrifices, sacrificial priests (*sacerdotes*) were appointed in the fifth century, whose function it was to provide the people with games in the circus and the amphitheatre.[1] The chapels of the Compitalian Lares still stood at the corners of the streets, and the Christian poet Prudentius complained that Rome had not one, but several thousand genii, whose portraits and symbols are to be found over doors of houses and baths, and in every corner of the city. S. Jerome, too, was incensed by the cunning of the Romans, who, under the pretext that it was for the

[1] As I shall presently show, these games survived as late as the sixth century. About 403, a short time previous to the Visigothic invasion, nothing had as yet been changed in the manner of their celebration. Prudentius (*contra Symmach.,* ii. v. 948) says: *Quis venit esuriens Magni ad spectacula Circi?* and *ibid.,* v. 862:—

Jamque Lupercales ferulae undique petuntur
Discursus juvenum.

safety of their houses, hung wax candles and lanterns before the ancient tutelary deities.[1]

So far, then, the drastic laws of Theodosius had not been able to suppress either the cult of the old gods or the Pagan party in Rome, as represented by the generated Symmachus and his august friend Praetextus, the latter of whom was the especial favourite of the people. Repeated edicts, commanding the temples to be closed and the altars and images to be removed, show clearly enough, that even in the provinces the Pagan shrines and their observances still obstinately lived on. Honorius and Arcadius, the sons of Theodosius, continued to issue edicts for the protection of public monuments, and it was only with the beginning of the fifth century that the Pagan religion, like a moth-eaten robe of state, fell from the shoulders of ancient Rome. The important law of secularization in 408 appropriated —to use a modern and intelligible expression—all the Church lands. The revenues (*annonae*) which, by means of taxes, tributes and estates, had accrued to the temples from time immemorial, and by which the services and the public festivals were defrayed fell to the Fiscus, but the same edict that entirely robbed the Pagan religion of all means of support, commanding altars and idols to be destroyed, declared the temple itself to be the property of the

[1] Prudentius, *contra Symmach.,* ii. v. 455 *seq.,* and v. 850 *seq. Quamquam cur Genium Romae mihi fingitis unum?* S. Jerome in Isaiam, iv. 672. Beugnot, ii. 139: "On a donc raison de dire, que pendant le jour comme pendant la nuit l'aspect de Rome devait etre celui d'une cité ou l'ancien culte dominait." Lamps to the Madonna later took the place of the lights before the images of the Lares.

State, and thus saved it as a public building from destruction.[1] Seventeen years afterwards followed the edict of Theodosius and Valentinian III., dated from Constantinople, which enacted that "All chapels, temples and sanctuaries—if such still remained standing—should be destroyed at the order of the magistrates, and be purified by the sign of the holy Christian religion." That the expression "destroyed" (*destrui*), however, was not taken literally, is shown by the significant appendix, immediately following, which commands that the temples be converted into Christian sanctuaries.[2] In every case where this happened the ancient inscriptions and even the pagan reliefs were allowed to remain untouched. Prudentius could now sing:—

[1] As early as 399 Arcadius and Honorius had issued the following edict concerning Africa *Aedes inlicitis rebus vacuas nostrarum beneficio sanctionum ne quis conetur evertere, decernimus enim, ut aedificiorum quidem sit integer status—De Pagan sacrif. et templis,* lib. xvii. tit. x. n. 18; in n. 19 succeeds the important edict of Honorius and Theodosius II. of 15th Nov. 408: *Templorum detrahantur annonae—simulacra suis sedibus evellantur—aedificia ipsa templorum—ad usum publicum vindicentur.* As in present times, the monasteries of Italy since their dissolution. For there is nothing new under the sun.

[2] Edict: *Omnibus sceleratae mentis paganae exsecrandis,* and commentary of Gotofredus on the word *destrui.* Henceforward the temples were transformed into churches, and the Christians began to place on them inscriptions to the effect that the dwelling of the demons had been converted into the House of God: θεοῦ γέγονεν οἶκος τὸ τῶν δαιμόνων καταγώγιον—φῶς σωτήριον ἔλαμψεν, ὅπου σκότος ἐκάλυπτεν — *Corp. In. Graec.,* iv. (1877) n. 8627; De Rossi, "I templi pagani in Roma sotto gl' imperatori cristiani," *Bullettino Archeol.,* 1866, n. 4, p. 55.

"Rejoice, ye nations all, rejoice,
Roman and Greek and Jew,
Egypt and Scythia, Persia, Thrace,
One king is lord of all."[1]

Paganism in its public character had thus practically disappeared; the remnant of such of its votaries as remained followed the forbidden flame of their ceremonials in secret meetings, either amidst the deserted solitude of the Campagna, or in the remote recesses of the mountains. The temples, meanwhile, remained standing in Rome, all those at least which, by their greatness and splendour as works of art, appealed to national pride and sentiment; and although some of the less important sanctuaries may have been destroyed, there is evidence to show that a great number of them remained intact in the fifth century. The traveller in Rome still views with admiration the small circular temple attributed to Vesta, and its neighbour, the Temple of Fortuna Virilis, and noting their admirable preservation, laments the error of time which has permitted these insignificant temples of antiquity to survive, whilst the Capitol, the Temple of Venus and Rome, and all the other monuments of ancient splendour, have either been swept from the face of the earth, or only suffered to exist as forlorn ruins over which ignorance, legend and erudition have alike contributed to spread a moss-like pall. The temples were closed, and falling

The Temples.

[1] *Gaudete, quidquid gentium est,*
Judaea, Roma et Graecia,
Aegypte, Thrax, Persa, Scytha,
Rex unus omnes possidet.
—Prud. *Cathemerinon, Hymn.* xii. v. 201.

victims to the ever-decreasing taste for restoration, became, with the baths and theatres, a prey to all the destructive influences of nature and life. One of the Fathers of the Church, living in Jerusalem, pictures the deserted city as it appeared at this time, its magnificent temples befouled with dirt, and spiders shrouding, with the grey threads of fate, the radiant heads of the forsaken gods.

The Statues.

But far more easily injured than the temples and palaces, were the beautiful works of Greek and Roman sculpture, which in countless numbers adorned the buildings, the squares, the halls and baths, the streets and bridges. Such was the fate of that multitude of sculptured gods and heroes in bronze and stone, which had gradually been erected in the immense city: an assemblage which represented, in every form and guise, the activity of genius, the regular beauty as well as the misformed offspring of the fancy of centuries. Constantine, who had plundered the cities of Europe and Asia in order to decorate the new Rome on the Bosphorus with images of the faith and works of art of every kind, was the first to take away statues from Rome. In his Hippodrome alone he placed sixty statues, doubtless of remarkable beauty, amongst them one of Augustus.[1] It is known that he caused a monolith, 100 feet high, of Egyptian porphyry, to be brought from Rome to Constantinople, the removal of which occupied three years. This splendid colossus was erected in the

[1] *Incerti Tempor. demonstrationes, seu originum Constant.* in Combefis, *Orig.*, p. 29; Codinus, *De Origin.*, p. 51, relates that he carried away the statue of Fortuna from the Palatium at Rome.

Forum of Byzantium, and it was asserted that the Palladium, which Constantine had secretly abstracted from the Temple of Vesta in Rome, was inclosed within the base of the column. But the multitude of works of art was so inexhaustible that Constantine's robbery was scarcely appreciable, and if under his successors many valuable representations of the gods fell a sacrifice to the fanaticism of the Christians, nevertheless the Emperors in general sought to protect the public statues, and the poet Prudentius makes Theodosius thus address the pagan senate:

Cleanse, O Princes, the marbles from the traces of decay,
Let the statues that great artists have wrought
Stand spotless. May they be the noblest ornaments
Of our fatherland. And may no degenerate abuse
Transform to the purposes of vice the monuments of art.[1]

Even the orthodox and zealous conquerors of the pagan faction of Eugenius ordered that the statues of the ancient gods, after they had ceased to be objects of veneration, should be preserved as public monuments, and we have evidence to show that, towards the end of the fifth century, defaced statues of

[1] *Marmora tabenti respergine tincta lavate,*
O Proceres; liceat statuas consistere puras,
Artificum magnorum opera. Haec pulcherrima nostrae
Ornamenta fuant patriae, nec decolor usus
In vitium versae monumenta coinquinet artis.
—*Contra Symmach.,* i. v. 591.

Fea, *Sulle rovine,* p. 279, appeals also to the authority of S. Ambros., Epist. 18, n. 31, t. iii. 886 B., where he says to the Emperor Valentinian: *Non illis satis sunt lavacra, non porticus, non plateae occupatae simulacris.*

the gods were restored by order of the city prefect.[1] Writers of the fourth and fifth centuries speak of the squares, baths and colonnades as being filled with statues. The outward aspect of Rome remained Pagan, as did that of Constantinople; for even in this the Christian capital of the East, the Imperial Palace, the Hippodrome, the Baths of Zeuxippus, the Palace of Lausus, that of the Senate, and the Forums were filled with ancient figures of gods and heroes in the fifth and sixth centuries.[2] After the overthrow of the ancient religion, both cities became by degrees transformed into museums of art. The Roman palaces also contained valuable collections of sculpture and paintings. Even in the state-chambers of Bassus, Probus Olybrius, Gracchus and Paulinus—all converts to Christianity—the nude deities of the old mythology continued for some time a source of pleasure to the guests who assembled there.[3] The time, however, was near when noble Romans, out of fear of Christ, or of Alaric, buried many of their favorite metal or marble gods like treasures in the earth, from which they were only recovered after long centuries.[4] Now

[1] Inscription of the Prefect Anicius Acilius Aginatius Faustus (prefect before the year 483), who had a *simulacrum Minerbae* restored after the sack of Rome by Ricimer. *Annal. d. Inst.,* 1849, p. 342; *C.I.L.,* vi. n. 526 and 1664.

[2] See my work, *Athenaïs,* c. x.

[3] The palace of Symmachus stood on the Coelian, on the site of the present Villa Casali. De Rossi, *Anal. dell' Inst.,* xxi. 283.

[4] The bronze Hercules in the Vatican was found buried and carefully walled up underground in the Theatre of Pompey, the Venus of the Capitol in the Subura. The latter was dug up between the Viminal and Quirinal. Friedrichs, *Bausteine zur Gesch. der griech.-röm.*

that the Gods of Greece remained imprisoned in their temples, the workshops of sculptors and painters were also forsaken. Artists had no longer any mission. A few Christian masters depicted Biblical subjects on sarcophagi; but Pagan sculptors no longer created a Venus or Apollo, nor did they produce artistic friezes or columns of classic style for temples. The ruin of their workshops and their art was the consequence of the fall of the ancient religion. Countless blocks of marble from the State quarries of Greece, Asia and Africa remained unused on the Marmorata by the Tiber; and the fact that ancient blocks are still sometimes excavated in this locality seems to point to some disaster having befallen the workshops for which the costly material had originally been destined.

Number of Statues.

Finally, do we wish to learn, from the short enumeration at the end of the *Notitia,* how numerous the more prominent statues were in Rome at the time of Honorius, we are informed that there were in the city two Colossi, twenty-two great equestrian statues, eighty gilt and seventy-four ivory statues of the gods; and though we are not told how many statues adorned the triumphal arches, the fountains, theatres, porticoes and baths, we learn, from a later computation made in the time of Justinian, that at the period at which the author wrote, or if not then, at all events in the fifth century,

Plastik, Nr. 585. Two of the finest bronzes of antiquity were found buried in like manner, namely, the statue of Victory at Brescia, and the little figure of Mercury in the British Museum. Leake, *Topography of Athens,* 1841, p. 59, note 1.

3785 bronze statues of emperors and distinguished men existed in the city.[1] We shall see, moreover, that Rome, even in the time of Gregory the Great, although strewn with ruins of that magnificance with which Augustus, Agrippa, Claudius, Domitian, Hadrian, and Alexander Severus had endowed the mistress of the world, and notwithstanding the ravages of Goths and Vandals, was yet richer than all the modern capitals of Europe combined.

3. TRANSFORMATION OF ROME BY CHRISTIANITY—THE SEVEN ECCLESIASTICAL REGIONS—THE OLDEST CHURCHES BEFORE THE TIME OF CONSTANTINE—ARCHITECTURAL FORM OF THE CHURCHES.

Changes worked by Christianity.

Whilst Christianity thrust its roots deeper and deeper into Imperial Rome, and, enveloping the city in its mysteries, effected in her a metamorphosis which ranks among the most extraordinary phenomena in history, it exerted a threefold influence, destructive, creative and transforming, on the outward form of the city. All these three processes can, in general, be conceived as being active at one and the same time. But as soon as a new element is

[1] *Narratio de ornatu Romae,* by Zacharias, based upon more ancient authorities, and also upon the summary of the Regionaries. Comparing the estimates with passages of Cassiodorus, the number of statues does not seem incredible. Zacharias enumerates *fontes aquam eructantes MCCCLII,* and *signa aenea MMMDCCLXXXV imperatorum aliorumque ducum*; further, XXV bronze statues representing Abraham and the Kings of the House of David, which had been brought to Rome by Vespasian. Text and translation in the already cited editions by Mai and Guidi.

cast like a seed into the midst of an ancient system, the laws of life demand that it should develop its own forms before it can change or supersede the existing status. It is an important fact that the Christian Church, even in the first period of its existence, took possession of the city of Rome, and, disregarding the fourteen municipal regions, divided it, in accordance with its own system of administration, into seven ecclesiastical districts. These must have been seven parishes for the notaries, or recorders of the martyr-histories, and for the seven deacons, or guardians of Church doctrine and discipline. The distribution is attributed to Clement, the fourth Bishop of Rome, who lived in the time of Domitian; and the assignation of districts to the deacons is attributed to Evaristus, the sixth bishop, in the time of Trajan, who is also supposed to have allotted the titular, *i.e.*, the parish, churches of the city to the presbyters.[1]

The seven ecclesiastical regions.

Attempts have been made to connect the number of these ecclesiastical regions either with the fourteen imperial divisions (each of the former being regarded as a combination of two of the latter), or with the seven cohorts of the watch. According to

[1] *Liber Pont.*, "Vita S. Clementis": *hic fecit 7 regiones dividi notariis fidelibus ecclesiae, qui gesta martyrum sollicite, et curiose unusquisque per regionem suam diligenter perquirerent.* "Vita S. Evaristi": *hic titulos in urbe Roma divisit presbyteris, et 7 diaconos constituit, qui custodirent episcopum predicantem propter stylum veritatis.* About the year 238 Fabianus added seven sub-deacons, and after the increase in the number of deacons, which began in the time of Bishop Caius, seven cardinal-deacons were appointed over the entire body of deacons and sub-deacons by Sylvester. Martinelli, *Roma ex ethnica sacra,* c. 4.

the most recent investigation, they were as follows:—The First Ecclesiastical region embraced the Twelfth and Thirteenth Civic Regions (Piscina Publica and Aventinus); the Second, roughly speaking, covered the Second and Eighth (Coelimontium and Forum Romanum); the Third, the Third and Fifth Civic Regions (Isis and Serapis and the Esquiline); the Fourth comprised the Sixth and perhaps the Fourth (Alta Semita and Templum Pacis); the Fifth almost corresponded to the Seventh (Via Lata), and embraced a part of the Ninth (Circus Flaminius); the Sixth represented the rest of the Ninth Region as far as the Vatican; and lastly, the Seventh corresponded to the Fourteenth Civic Region (Trastevere).[1]

Oldest churches.

Our information regarding the oldest churches in Rome assigned by Bishop Clement to these regions is, at least, equally imperfect. As early as the time of Honorius, at the beginning of the fifth century, there were already several important churches. Of such churches, some had been built before Constantine, others founded in the time of this Emperor, and not a few erected under his successors, by bishops possessing entire freedom in the choice of

[1] Nardini (*Roma Ant.,* i. 125) has attempted to restore the seven ecclesiastical regions, the boundaries of which he believes to have been assigned to them by Sylvester. Bianchini, *De regionibus urbis Romae* (edition of Anastasius, vol. ii. pp. 137–140), tries to discover them from the important passage in the life of Simplicius (about the year 464), from which I only record: *Reg. III. ad S. Laurentium, I. ad S. Paulum, VI. et VII. ad S. Petrum.* The latest explanations of this difficult subject are due to De Rossi, *Roma sotterranea cristiana* (1877), iii. 515 *seq.*

a site. These, the oldest temples of Christianity, were built at first, and even in the time of Constantine, only at the extremities of the city, being, in nearly every case, cemetery or catacomb churches, but, as the new faith advanced by degrees into the centre of the pagan city, churches rose side by side with the temples of the ancient gods, and finally even within them.

S. Pudenziana.

Tradition designates, as the first and oldest church of Rome, the Basilica of S. Pudenziana. According to legend, S. Peter lived on the Esquiline hill, in the Vicus Patritius, being an inmate of the palace of the Senator Pudens and his wife Priscilla, in which he established a house of prayer. The sons of Pudens, Novatus and Timotheus, who are mentioned by name in the epistles of S. Paul, there owned baths, and here the Bishop, Pius I., is said to have founded a church at the request of the Virgin Praxedis about 143. In the Pre-Constantinian period, and during the era of persecutions, Christians did not openly possess any churches, but were accustomed to meet together in houses, lent for the purpose, by private individuals—their owners. After the edict of Constantine, which proclaimed freedom of worship, these houses of prayer were recognised as churches; they retained the names of the pious owners by whom they had been founded, and many retain them even now. S. Pudenziana is the first of the churches of Rome recognised by the *Liber Pontificalis.*[1] Its tribune

[1] "Vita S. Pii." The notes of the editors of the *Liber Pontificalis,* Franceso and Giuseppe Bianchini, are also of value with respect to

still retains ancient mosaics representing Christ between the twelve Apostles, and Praxedis and Pudenziana, the two daughters of Pudens. These, undoubtedly the finest of all the Roman mosaics, were begun under Pope Siricius (384–398) and finished under Innocent I. (402-417). In the course, however, of many restorations, much of their original character had unfortunately been sacrificed.[1] With this church was united that of the "Holy Pastor," the brother of Pius I.[2]

S. Maria in Trastevere

To Bishop Calixtus I. (217-222), whose name is still borne by the celebrated catacombs, are attri-

the topography of the city (second edition, Rome, 1731). A more correct edltion is due to Giov. Vignoli, Rome, 1724, 3 vols. To the Abbé L. Duchesne belongs the merit of a new edition which embodies all the light thrown by the critical researches of recent times upon the subject: *Le Liber Pontificalis, Texte, Introduction et Commentaire,* Paris, 1884.

[1] In the restoration of this church by Cardinal Enrico Gaetani (in 1588), the representations of two Apostles perished in the cutting away of the apse. The ancient inscription of the apse recorded the names of the presbyters Ilicius, Leopardus and Maximus as restorers of the church in the time of Siricius. The picture represents the church and houses in the Vicus Patricius, the preservation of which was due to the Prefect Valerius Messala (396–403), as is evidenced by the inscription: SPLENDOREM PUBLICUM IN VICO PATRICIO....ET FIERI ET ORNARI PROCURABIT. De Rossi, *Bullet. Arch.,* 1867, n. 4. With regard to the Mosaics, see the same writer in the text with reference to the illustrations (*Mosaici Cristiani*).

[2] Davanzati (*Notizie della bas. di S. Prassede,* Roma, 1725) holds the house of Pudens to have been the earliest abode of S. Peter in the city, and that the Apostle there founded the titular church of Pudens, which, however, is to be looked for in the present S. Prassede; S. Pudenziana being first built by Pius I on the site of the Baths of Novatus. Martinelli (*Primo Trofeo della Croce*), on the other hand, maintains that the first church founded by S. Peter is that of S. Maria in Via Lata.

buted, though without any ground whatever, the first foundations of S. Maria in Trastevere; and to his successor, the building of S. Cecilia in the same quarter. The foundations of the oldest churches on the Aventine, those of S. Alexius and S. Prisca, are supposed to belong to the beginning of the fourth century. But all basilicas before the time of Constantine are doubtful.[1]

As soon as Constantine had given full freedom to Christianity, larger, and to some extent more sumptuous, basilicas arose in Rome. Their architectural form, which, like the worship of the Church, had long before been developed in the catacombs, appeared as a completed actuality, and remained a precedent for succeeding centuries. We can imagine the Roman, who still sacrificed to his gods in splendid columned temples, regarding with contempt these churches of Christianity, their pillars hidden like the spoils of plunder in the interior of the building, and the façade of the temple itself concealed behind a walled vestibule, in the midst of which a "cantharus" or fountain was also hidden. At this period, the creative art, like the poetry and learning of the ancients, was taking its leave of mankind, the date of its disappearance being manifested in the Triumphal Arch of Constantine, the border of two epochs. This arch the Roman Senate adorned with sculptures robbed from another arch dedicated to Trajan. As these were not sufficient,

[1] I have adopted in this enumeration the statements of the *Liber Pontificalis,* and consulted the writings of Ugonio, Martinelli, Marangoni, Severano, Panciroli, Panvinius, De Rossi, &c.

the artists of the time, to whom some of the reliefs were entrusted, were obliged to confess that the ideals of their forefathers had vanished, and that the day of the barbarians had dawned. The Triumphal Arch of Constantine may thus be described as the gravestone of the arts of Greece and Rome.

Painting, as a rule, shared the fate of sculpture, though, in individual cases, it was more fortunate. Exhausted art, which had outlived its inspirations, seemed to follow Constantine to Byzantium, there submissively to enter the service of Christianity. In Rome, after the fifth century, painting forsook the lively ideals of antiquity which had reappeared in graceful ornamentation in the catacombs, and, resting on technical methods inherited from Imperial times, turned to mosaic as its most fitting medium. Mosaic is essentially the art of decadence—the gilt flower of barbarism—and, in its character, corresponds to the period of hierarchical despotism, when, after the loss of free institutions, Officialism, robed in gold brocade, penetrated alike Church and State. Nevertheless, to mosaic belongs the faculty of expressing with marvelous power the deep mystic earnestness, the dreadful loneliness of religious passions, with their wild fanatic energy leaping forth in the midst of centuries where the light of knowledge had become extinct.

With sculpture and painting the architecture of the ancients also perished. In architecture, the character and genius which had originally animated the Romans had found its most fitting expression, until, with the ruin of political life, its activity also disappeared. To its last great achievements in Rome belong the Temple of the Sun, the Walls of Aurelian, the Baths of Diocletian, the Circus of Maxentius, the Basilica Nova, and the Baths of Constantine. After these nothing more was built in Rome of a truly Roman character; which shows that, with the disappearance of the ideal impulse, the executive, or technical, faculty also disappeared. When architecture, passing beyond the limits of ancient culture, the ideal of which it had forsaken, was compelled to build churches instead of temples, it found itself in a curious dilemma. Being obliged to avoid everything belonging to the Pagan religion, to forsake the perfected styles of antiquity, with a happy instinct it borrowed the form of its churches from the purely civil halls of justice or basilicas, which answered the organization and liturgical requirements of the Christian community at the same time that it adopted the structural arrangements of the chapels in the catacombs.[1] Buildings were thus erected for which not only the sculptural ornament, but even the rough material, was appropriated from Pagan monuments, and architecture, adopting essentially antique features, such as the columned temple, infused into them the primitive character of the new faith. The attractiveness of this archi-

The Basilica-form.

[1] The word originally used to designate a church was *Dominicum,* or House of the Lord; not until the time of Constantine did the expression basilica become customary. Du Cange, *ad voc. Dominicum*; and De Rossi, *Bulettino di Archeol. Cristiana,* 1863, Part i. 26, and in the section dealing with Basilicas in his *Roma sotteranea,* t. iii. x.; Kraus, *Die Cristliche Kunst in ihren frühesten Anfängen,* Leipzig, 1873.

tectural system consisted in the unpretending, but solemn simplicity of an harmoniously blended whole, to which only mosaic ornament and the adoption of ancient pillars imparted grace. The churches were continually subjected to additions and changes, which the simple mathematical perfection of the old temples would not have tolerated. They expanded with the worship, and became so disguised by irregular additions of chapels and oratories that, through the increased number of altars, and even of tombs, one might have imagined them transformed again into catacombs. In the course of this history we shall not encounter in Rome a single basilica that has not been altered several times.

4. CHURCHES OF CONSTANTINE— THE LATERAN BASILICA— THE ORIGINAL CHURCH OF S. PETER.

Churches of Constantine.

Tradition ascribes the foundation of the following basilicas in Rome to the Emperor Constantine: S. John Lateran, S. Peter in the Vatican, S. Paul without the Walls, S. Croce in Jerusalem, S. Agnes beyond the Porta Nomentana, S. Lorenzo without the Walls, and SS. Marcellinus and Peter beyond the Porta Maggiore; but we can ascertain nothing definite of these buildings, and perhaps S. John Lateran alone owes its origin to the Emperor.

Palace and Basilica of the Lateran.

His wife Fausta owned the houses of the Lateran family, an ancient Roman race whose name has become immortal not through deeds, but owing to the possession of a spacious palace.[1] The date at which the Aedes Laterani had become the property of the Emperor is not known. Constantine, however, gave that part of the Lateran which is called the Domus Faustae to the Roman Bishop as a residence, and the successors of Sylvester dwelt there for nearly a thousand years.[2] Near the Lateran palace stood the ancient basilica erected by Constantine, a building by no means large, and consisting probably of three rather than five aisles, the columns of which had been taken from Pagan temples; but we are without any real knowledge of the original structures, the only clear account that has come down to us being in respect to the later building erected under Sergius III.[3] in the beginning of the tenth century. The earlier basilica was dedicated to Christ,

[1] Plautus Lateranus, consul-designate, was executed by Nero as a participator in the conspiracy of Piso. Tacitus, *Annal.,* xv. c. 49 and 60; Juvenal, *Satire,* x. 17, speaks of *egregias Lateranorum ades.* In 1595 leaden tubes were found at the Lateran, with the inscription, *Sexti Laterani.—Sexti Laterani M. Torquati et Laterani.* Marangoni, *Storia della capella Sancta Sanctor. di Roma,* c. i.; Stevenson, "Scoperte di antichi edifizi al Laterano," *Annal. d. Inst.,* 1877, p. 332 f.

[2] Baronius (on the year 312) asserts that the Roman Bishop was in possession of the Lateran immediately after the recognition of Christianity, because the Council of Miliziades was held *in domo Faustae in Laterano* on the 2nd Oct. 313.

[3] In 1756 a relief was discovered (now attached to the wall of a corridor in the Lateran) representing the Porta Asinaria, and a basilica, which must be that of Constantine. It is illustrated in Adinolfi, *Roma nell' età di mezzo* (1881), i. 185. According to the *Liber Pontifcalis,* "Vita S. Silvestri," Sylvester dedicated the church on Nov. 9. With regard to the history of all the so-called buildings of Constantine, see Ciampini, *De sacris aedificiis a Constantino M. constructis*; Rasponi, *De Basilica et patriarchio Lateranensi,* Roma, 1656; Valentini, *Basilica Lateranesnse descritta ed. illustrata,* Roma, 1839.

under the title of the Saviour, and it was only in the sixth century that it received the name of S. John the Baptist. But it was called, as well, the "Basilica of Constantine" after its founder, and also the *Basilica aurea*, from the rich ornaments which adorned it. The *Liber Pontificalis* specified the numerous gifts with which Constantine had endowed it—gold and silver images of great weight, cups, vases, candelabra, and other vessels decorated with opals and amethysts; but evidently the writer of the life of Sylvester enumerated in the catalogue all the treasures which were accumulated during succeeding centuries. The basilica of Constantine maintained, as the mother church of Christendom, *Omnium Urbis et Orbis Ecclesiarum Mater et Caput,* supremacy over all other churches in the world, and even claimed to have inherited the sanctity of the temple at Jerusalem, the Ark of the Covenant of the Jews being preserved beneath its altar. But although each successive Pope inaugurated his reign by the solemn act of taking possession of the Lateran, this episcopal church was soon destined to be eclipsed by that of the Prince of the Apostles.[1]

Basilica of S. Peter.

It is entirely unknown under what Pope and Emperor the church of S. Peter was founded, but besides the unanimous voice of tradition, all that can be gathered on the subject from the Acts of the Church, added to the testimony of the oldest chroniclers, lead us to the conclusion that it dated from the

[1] *History of the Lateran Basilica in the Middle Ages,* in G. Rohault de Fleury, *Le Latran au Moyen Age,* 1877, to which is attached an atlas with drawings.

time of Constantine. The *Liber Pontificalis* states that at the request of Bishop Sylvester the Emperor erected a basilica to S. Peter in the Temple of Apollo and enclosed the body of the Apostle in an irremovable coffin of bronze of Cyprus. The Temple of Apollo in Vatican territory is certainly only known to legend, but later excavations have shown that the church of S. Peter was founded near a sanctuary dedicated to the service of Cybele, whose rites were long celebrated in Rome, and survived even after the time when Theodosius knelt at the grave of the Apostle.[1] Legend relates that Constantine himself inaugurated the foundation by turning the first spadeful of soil, of which moreover he carried twelve basketfuls, in honour of the twelve Apostles. Whether the Circus of Caligula was already destroyed, or whether this occurred during the construction, we do not know; it is at least certain that the basilica was built on one side of the Circus and out of its materials. This site was especially chosen for the church of the Prince of the Apostles as having, according to tradition, been the scene of his crucifixion, and the spot being further sanctified to Christianity by the martyrdoms which it had witnessed under Nero.

The original form of the basilica was preserved

[1] Inscriptions relative to the Taurobolia and Kriobolia, connected with this worship, were discovered at the beginning of the seventeenth century, in the rebuilding of the basilica. The last of these inscriptions belongs to the year 390. Beugnot, &c, i. 159; *C. I. L.,* vi. p. 497-504. Prudentius at the same date describes this bloody sacrifice in his Hymn to S. Romanus. It is undoubted that at the end of the fourth century the mysteries of the Taurobolia survived in this district (the Vatican) side by side with the mysteries of Christ.

for a long time, and although widened by additions during the Middle Ages, it was never entirely rebuilt until the beginning of the sixteenth century, under Julius II.[1] The ancient church, which was over 500 palms long and 170 palms high, had five naves and a transept, and ended in a semi-circular tribune or apse.[2] In front of its entrance stood an atrium or "paradisus" 255 palms long and about 250 palms broad, which was encircled within by a colonnade. A broad flight of marble steps led up to the atrium, upon which was the platform where S. Peter's successors received the successors of Constantine, when the latter came to pray at the grave of the Apostle, and at the later date to receive the Imperial crown at the hands of the Pope.

The great church was erected in haste. The execution and the workmanship were bad, and the style from the first barbarous; the apse and outer walls were built from materials collected at random; the architrave, which rested upon the columns within, was pieced out of antique fragments, and even the ancient pillars of marble or granite, ninety-six in

[1] The most ancient description of S. Peter's is given in the Vatican Codex 3627, of Petrus Mallius (dating from the latter half of the twelfth century); *Historia Basilicae Antiquae S. Petri,* edited by De Angelis, Rome, 1646; and better in the *Acta Sanctor.,* t. vii., Junii, pp. 37–56. The latter was followed by Maphaeus Vegius († 1457), *De rebus antiquis memorabil. Basil. S. Petri*, in four books, in the same vol. of the Bollandists.

[2] Plan and measurements of the ancient basilica in Bonanni, p. 12, according to the estimates of Alpharanus, Severanus, Oldini, &c. Length of the present church, 829 1/2 palms; its height to the point of the cross, 593 palms.

number, did not correspond either in capitals or bases. Slabs of marble from the Circus, on which the original inscriptions or Pagan sculptures still remained, served for the threshold.[1] We are surprised to find in the earliest basilica of S. Peter the characteristic peculiar to so many of the present churches of Rome, namely, the presence of Pagan relics in the shape of fragments and patchwork of ancient marbles. The interior, which was entered by five doors opening into five naves, was large and of imposing dimensions. The light descended into the lofty central nave through small arched windows disclosing the rough rafters of the roof, and flickered, now on a pavement formed of a patchwork of antique marbles, now on high walls as yet unrelieved by mosaics. The principal nave, ending in a wide arch, may not improbably have recorded the fact that the arch of the saint who had gloriously triumphed in the bloody fight of faith replaced that of a Pagan Emperor. Here the glance of the pious Christian rested on the altar over the shrine or grave of the Apostle, where a little temple on six porphyry columns rose over the body of S. Peter. The re-

[1] *Antiquae Vatican. Basil.—facies exterior, apsis, et muri extremi—e laterum, tophorumque fragmentis, circo, adjacentibusque aedificiis eversis, celeri opera rudique arte aedificati fuerunt.* Extract from Grimaldi in Martinelli, p. 345, and Nardini, iii. 355. Severanus quotes an inscription to Trajan found on the epistyle of a column of the Triumphal Arch; and Torrigius, *Le sacre grotte Vat.,* p. 111, maintains that the base of the great cross on the gable bore the Greek name of Agrippina. Even Leo IV. in the ninth century converted a little column, on which was the Greek dedication to Serapis, transcribed by Torrigius, p. 110, to the adornment of a window in the bell tower.

mains themselves were said to lie below in a golden vault in the coffin of gilt bronze in which Constantine had had them enclosed, beneath lamps which were never extinguished, and the biographer of S. Sylvester informs us in the *Liber Pontifcalis* that over the coffin stood a massive cross of gold as high as the coffin was long, on which the following words appeared in niello work:—

"Constantine the Emperor, and Helena the Empress."
"This royal house surrounds a hall that gleams with equal splendour."[1]

The central nave ended with the apse or semi-circular tribune, an imitation of the niche in the civil basilicas of Rome, where were situated the chair of the praetor and the seats of the judges. The tribune of the ancient church of S. Peter was decorated with symbolic mosaics, representing Constantine exhibiting to the Saviour and S. Peter the model of the church; and some original lines stood below which were still extant in the Middle Ages.

"Quod duce te mundus surrexit in astra triumphans
Hanc Constantinus Victor tibi condidit aulam."[2]

About the year 366 Bishop Damasus added a Font or Baptistery to the Atrium of S. Peter's, the

[1] *Lib. Pont.* (Duchesne), n. xvii.:—

Constantinus Augustus et Helena Augusta
Hanc domum regalem simili fulgure coruscans aula circumdat.

De Rossi, *Inscript. Christ.*, ii., p. 200, supplies, after the word *regalem, auro decorant quam.*

[2] It is uncertain whether this epigram belongs to the original mosaic, or to that due to the restoration by Adrian I. It was transcribed by Andreas Fulvius (iii. 84), on the destruction of the ancient tribune.

splendid mosaics of which were celebrated by Prudentius in some verses which,[1] together with a short description of S. Paulinus, form the only description we have of the basilica at the time of Honorius. The celebrated Bishop of Nola, of the family of the Anicii, a gifted poet, like Prudentius, sacrificed the artistic taste of the Paganism in which he had been brought up to the sincere enthusiasm of the Christian. After having attended the banquet in the courtyard of the basilica, which the rich Senator Alethius, according to the somewhat boisterous custom of the time, gave to the poor on the occasion of the funeral of his wife Rufina, he described the impression which the church had made upon him in the following words:—"To what joy hast thou raised even the Apostle as thou fillest his whole basilica with a multitude of the poor; whether it be under the vast central roof, in the long broad aisle, where from out the distance the Apostolic chair dazzles the eyes and rejoices the heart; or where two lateral roofs spread out their arms in double colonnades; or where the atrium expands into an entrance hall, adorned by the fountain which, refreshing our hands and lips with its welcome flow, gurgles under the shadow of the massive bronze cupola with its four pillars forming a mystic circle round the gushing waters. Could there be any ornament more befitting the entrance to the church? preparing, as it does, all who come in for the sacred mysteries that await them."[2]

[1] *Peristeph.*, xii.; *Passio Beator. Apostolor. Petri et Pauli*; v. 31–44.

[2] S. Paulin, Epist. XXXIII. ad Alethium (Antwerp Edition, p. 289).

Bishop Damasus placed in the Baptistery the chair which tradition, from the second century onwards, had alleged to have been the actual chair of Peter. This remarkable seat, the most ancient throne in the world, first occupied by simple unpretending bishops, then by ambitious Popes ruling nations and peoples, still survives. In the seventeenth century, Alexander VII. had it inclosed within a bronze chair which, bearing the metal images of the Four Doctors of the Church, stands in the tribune of the cathedral. On the feast of the Apostle in 1867 the chair was uncovered for the first time for two hundred years, and exposed to public view in a chapel. It is in reality an ancient sedan chair (*sella gestatoria*), to the now worm-eaten oak of which additions have from time to time been made in acacia wood. The front is decorated with ivory bands, on which fighting animals, centaurs and men are represented in diminutive arabesque figures; it also contains a row of ivory panels engraved with the labours of Hercules, an appropriate symbol for the Herculean work of the early Papacy in the history of the world. These panels did not originally belong to the chair, but were evidently affixed as ornaments in later times, occasionally with such carelessness that some are even fastened on upside down. Beyond doubt, this celebrated chair, if not belonging to apostolic times, is of very great antiquity, though the suggestion that it may be the *sella curulis* of the Senator Pudens is altogether untrustworthy.[1]

[1] I saw the chair in June 1867. De Rossi, who has made it the

The Middle Ages surrounded S. Peter's with a circle of chapels, churches, cloisters, dwellings for the clergy, and houses for the pilgrims, so that the Vatican grew into the holy city of Christendom; though, in the time of Honorius, there were as yet but few buildings in the neighbourhood of the basilica. Amongst them, the oldest was that built near to the Tribune, the Templum Probi, the sepulchral chapel of the celebrated senatorial family, which had embraced Christianity earlier than any other in Rome.

The family of the Anicii had been conspicuous from the time of Constantine. Their fame, beyond that of any other senatorial family, filled the annals of the city in the last days of the Roman Empire, and even down to the late Middle Ages their name enlisted a traditional homage in the city. It was the Anicii who exercised the greatest influence on the Christian transformation of Rome. Possessed of vast estates in Italy, and in many other provinces of the Empire, they occupied, for more than two centuries, the highest offices of the State. The family was divided into several branches, such as the Amnii, the Auchenii, the Pincii, the Petronii. The Maximi, Fausti, Boetii, the Probi, Bassi and Olybrii also all belonged to the Anicii. In the

subject of careful investigation (*Bulletino Arch.,* 1867, n. 3), believes the arabesques a *rilievo* to be of later date than the fifth century, and the labours of Hercules, although of earlier origin, to be considerably later than the time of Augustus and Claudius. These arabesques cover the most modern portion of the chair. The festival of the Cathedra was originally celebrated on Feb. 22nd; since the days of Paul the Fourth, however, on Jan. 18th.

fourth century, the head of the family was Sextus Anicius Petronius Probus, a man of boundless wealth, and laden with the highest honours of the State. He had shared the consulship with the Emperor Gratian in 371, had been four times invested with the dignity of prefect, and was the last great Maecenas of Rome.[1] In connection with his gifted wife, Faltonia Proba, Probus, who was a friend of Bishop Ambrosius, acknowledged Christianity, accepting it by baptism shortly before his death.

His family buried the great Senator in the chapel which he had previously built (the Templum Probi), and his sarcophagus is still preserved, as, too, is another more ancient and beautiful sarcophagus, that of Junius Bassus, which belongs to the year 358.[2]

The Imperial family also erected their mausoleum near S. Peter's. This mausoleum was apparently

[1] Ammian Marcellin., xxvii. c. II, gives an interesting description of the character of Probus: *claritudine generis et potentia et opum amplitudine cognitus orbi Romano; per quem universum paene patrimionia sparsa possedit, juste an secus non judicioli est nostri*— and: *marcebat absque praefecturis*. With regard to him and his family, see Broglie, *L'Eglise et L'Empire Romain au IV. siecle,* iii. i. 25 *seq.*; Joseph Aschbach, *Die Anicier und die römische Dichterin Proba,* Vienna, 1870. Aschbach believes Faltonia Proba to have been the authoress of the *Cento Virgilianus,* a poem dedicated to the Emperor Honorius in which Biblical scenes are strung together. First edition, Venice, 1472.

[2] The celebrated sarcophagus of J. Bassus stands in the crypt of the Vatican, that of Probus (who died previous to the year 395) in the Capella della Pietà in the basilica itself. Maphaeus Vegius saw the Templum Probi before its destruction by Nicholas V., and preserved the sepulchral inscriptions of Probus and Proba. *Histor, Basil Antiq. S. Petri,* iv. 109, 110.

built by Honorius, and in it were interred his two wives, Maria and Thermantia, the daughters of Stilicho. The mausoleum disappeared, but on its site were discovered in later times the sarcophagus and the remains of the Empress Maria.

In the time of Honorius the ancient basilica of S. Peter was a large and elongated brick building, the gable of which, surmounted by the cross, rose over the pillared, cloister-like vestibule. We can imagine the Pagan Romans who gazed on this unlovely building being inclined to scoff when they thought of the remains of the Jewish fisherman which were there worshipped in a golden chamber, and then turning their gaze to the adjacent mausoleum of the Emperor Hadrian, a splendid rotunda, consisting of two stories of pillars resting on a cube of magnificent marble and ornamented with statues which seemed to look down scornfully on the strange sepulchral church beside it. The adjoining Circus was destroyed; its ruins presented the appearance of a quarry, but the great obelisk of Caligula still rose from above the broken spina, by the side of the Christian church. S. Peter's, standing beside the deserted Circus, must certainly have looked strange enough, but to the Christian it would seem emblematic of the victory of his faith, which triumphantly established itself on the demolished ruins of Paganism. And even in the time of the elder Theodosius troops of pilgrims journeyed to S. Peter's, especially at his festival in June, which was also the festival of S. Paul, and wended, as they still do, their way over the Bridge of Hadrian, a bridge which has borne a longer and more varied train of wanderers than any other in the world.[1] A century had scarcely passed before the splendours of Pagan Rome sank into such oblivion, that the descendants of those men who had looked with hatred and contempt on the rising basilica ascended its steps on their knees as pilgrims, and fell prostrate before the gorgeously gilt tomb of the Galilean fisherman, in that new Capitol of Rome, the Vatican, which, more powerful than that of the ancient Zeus, was beginning to rule the world.

5. THE ANCIENT BASILICA OF S. PAUL—THE WORSHIP OF THE SAINTS—S. LAURENTIUS EXTRA MUROS AND IN LUCINA—S. AGNES—S. CRUX IN HIERUSALEM—S. PETRUS AND MARCELLINUS—S. MARCUS—S. MARIA MAGGIORE—S. MARIA IN TRASTEVERE—S. CLEMENS—ASPECT OF ROME IN THE FIFTH CENTURY—CONTRASTS IN THE CITY.

Basilica of S. Paul.

At the request of Sylvester, Constantine is said to have also erected a basilica to S. Paul, a mile distant from the city, on the Ostian Way; and on the spot where, according to legend, the Apostle had suffered death, or where his body had been conveyed by the pious matron, Lucina. The first church probably only consisted of a chapel over his grave, and this chapel was not founded by Constantine. In the year 383, the Emperors Valentinian II., Theodosius and Arcadius commanded Sallust, the

[1] Prudent., Hymn xii.:—

Ibimus ulterius, qua fert via pontis Hadriani
Laevam deinde fluminis petemus.

Prefect of the city, to build a larger and more splendid basilica on the site of the old.[1] This church was begun by Theodosius and finished by Honorius. As the Goths under Alaric found the basilica of S. Paul a beautiful temple and spared it during the sack of the city, we may assume that it was completed by Honorius as early as 404.[2]

This celebrated church, which surpassed the basilica of S. Peter in beauty, resembled it in general plan, but it was larger in dimensions, being 477 feet in length and 258 in width.[3] On first entering, the spectator must have been lost in admiration of the five majestic naves, divided by four rows of pillars. These pillars, of which there were twenty in each row, had been taken from ancient buildings, and their dissimilarity, caused by some of the immense Corinthian capitals being of stucco, and of barbaric design, was to some extent atoned for by their number, their size, and the value of the stone. In the central nave alone there were twenty-four monoliths of the finest Phrygian marble (Pavonazetto) about forty palms high. The architect had thrown arches from column to column, above which rose a high wall, decorated with mosaics in the sections over the pillars, but lacking as yet the portrait busts of the successors of S. Peter, which belong to a later date. The ceiling of the nave was resplendent with

[1] Baronius, *Annal. Eccl.,* a. 386, contains the Rescript taken from a codex of the Vatican.

[2] The inscription over the mosaic of the Triumphal Arch runs:—

Theodosius cepit perfecit Honorius aulam
Doctoris mundi sacratam corpore Pauli.

[3] Ugonio, p. 235.

gilt bronze, and the floor and the walls were of panelled marble. The central nave, as in S. Peter's, ended in a gigantic Arch of Triumph, which rested on two massive Ionic columns, and this arch Galla Placidia, the sister of Honorius, decorated with mosaics in the time of Leo I.[1] In the centre stands a colossal half-length effigy of Christ, who, with the staff in His hand, looks down on His followers with awe-inspiring severity, as though He would have them bow their faces in the dust before Him, the Medusa-like countenance seeming to forbid any less submissive mode of approach. At the sides are the Apocalyptic symbols of the four Evangelists, below the twenty-four Elders, and at the extremities SS. Peter and Paul. In these rude mosaics the style afterwards known as Byzantine was first introduced into Rome. It is a mistake, however, to trace to Byzantium a style which was essentially Roman in its traditions, which had found its models for the technical treatment of larger figures in the thermae and palaces of Rome, and which finally, as regarded the Christian ideal of art, merely gave expression to the unpleasing and gloomy character of Rome itself. The Arch of Triumph in S. Paul's spanned the high altar and the shrine under which the body of the Apostle lay in a bronze coffin, permitting the tribune (separated from it by the wide transept) to be so placed as to be visible with its mosaics.

[1] The inscription on the Arch announces:—

Placidiae Pia Mens Operis Decus Homn....
Gaudet Pontificis Studio Splendore Leonis.

The wealth of S. Paul very nearly equalled that of S. Peter. Gold, silver and precious stones in fabulous splendour and profusion dazzled the worshipping Christians, and in later times only too effectually the Eastern barbarians. The poet Prudentius, on beholding the basilica in its pristine splendour in the time of Honorius, wrote the following lines:—

Parte alia titulum Pauli via servat Ostiensis,
Qua stringit amnis caespitem sinistrum.
Regia pompa loci est: princeps bonus has sacravit arces
Lusitque magnis ambitum talentis.
Bracteolas trabibus sublevit, ut omnis aurulenta
Lux esset intus, ceu iubar sub ortu.
Subdidit et parias fulvis laquearibus columnas
Distinguit illic quas quaternus ordo.
Tum camuros hyalo insigni varie cucurrit arcus:
Sic prata vernis floribus renident.[1]

Saints to whom the first churches were dedicated.

Such were the three chief basilicas of Rome which form the historical starting point of all the other churches which subsequently came into existence. It is, however, important to note to whom these early churches were dedicated. Christ, SS. Peter and Paul were, in the middle of the fourth century, the

[1] *Peristephan.,* Hymn xii. v. 45-54. With regard to the basilica in general, see N. M. Nicolai, *Della Basilica di S. Paolo,* Roma, 1815; and Barbier de Montault, *Descript. de la Bas. de S. Paul hors les murs à Rome,* Rome, 1866. The church retained all its ancient beauty until destroyed by fire on July 17, 1823. Its restoration, begun by Leo XII., was continued by his successors, the interior decorations of the roof having only been completed during our own days. Although subject to various modifications, the original plan of the building has been adhered to. Its splendour is cold and prosaic as the age itself, but the effect of the columnar perspective is one of unparalleled beauty.

heads of the Roman religion, the two Apostles being moreover patrons of the Roman Church, the one as her traditional founder and first bishop, the other as the Apostle of the heathen, S. Peter representing the hierarchical, S. Paul the dogmatic, power of Christian Rome. The cult of the Virgin was as yet not officially recognised in the fourth century, and the saints had no public churches. The places of worship were, as a rule, named after those by whom they had been built or founded.[1] But the ever-increasing respect paid to the graves of the martyrs soon had the effect of transferring the site of their worship from the catacombs to the churches of the city. The dead were borne back again from the fields to rest within the walls and receive the altars that were their due. It also became necessary to combat the many vivid recollections that still existed of Paganism and its temples, by the erection of numerous churches in every district of the huge city; a process out of which a new mythology soon arose and completely superseded the old.

S. Laurentius

Laurence was one of the first martyrs who was honoured with the tribute of a basilica. According to a legend, this archdeacon, a Spaniard by birth, suffered death on a burning gridiron in the Baths of Olympias during the reign of Decius. His grave, which was shown on the road to Tibur (Tivoli), in the Catacombs of the Ager Veranus, was visited by pilgrims from Tuscany and Campania, and was celebrated in verse by the Spanish poet Pruden-

[1] Even the burial places were named after their founders, Priscillae, Praetextati, Pontiani, Calixti, Domitillae, &c.

tius.[1] After the persecutions of the Christians had come to an end a basilica was erected to the famous martyr; this made the third basilica beyond the gates of Rome, S. Peter's being at that time also outside the city. The biographies of Sylvester ascribe this basilica to Constantine. The first building, amounting only to a chapel over the martyr's grave, was in later times embellished at the cost of Galla Placidia, under Sixtus III. and Leo I.

The great veneration in which S. Laurence was held is testified by the fact that two other churches had already been consecrated to him in the Campus Martius. Moreover, not far from the Theatre of Pompey, Bishop Damasus, a Portuguese who was related to the saint, founded a basilica in his honour, that of S. Lorenzo in Damaso, between the years 366 and 384. This church apparently stood near the Curia or Atrium, the place of Caesar's murder, and with its building the destruction of the Curia probably began. The ancient church of Damasus was entirely demolished at the end of the fifteenth century, and replaced by the new building within the palace of the Vice-Chancellor.[2]

S. Lorenzo in Lucina is of earlier date than the reign of Honorius, and since such adjuncts as *in Lucina, in Damaso,* &c., were usually given in

[1] Perstiphan., Hymn xi. v. 195, &c.

[2] *Lib. Pont.* on Damasus: *Hic fecit basilicas duas, unam juxta theatrum sancto Laurentio.* Lorenzo Fonseca, *De Basilica S. Laur. in Damaso,* Fani, 1745 This church was also called in Prasino, probably from the fact that the stables of the faction of the Greens were situated close by. Duchesne, *Lib. Pontif.*, p. 213, note 7.

memory of the founder, the erection of this building has been ascribed to Lucina, a Roman matron. Others believe, however, that it received its name from a temple dedicated to Juno Lucina, although no building of the kind is known to have stood on the Campus Martius. The basilica was situated in the neighbourhood of the sun-dial placed by Augustus beside the obelisk which served as its gnomon.[1]

S. Agnes.

In the time of Honorius the catacomb church of S. Agnes, beyond the Nomentan Gate, also stood over the grave of the martyr, beside an already ancient cemetery, and near the round mausoleum which still survives. This mausoleum, on the strength of its mosaics representing the vintage, was long held to have been a temple of Bacchus; it was, however, in reality the mortuary chapel of the two daughters of Constantine, Helena and Constantina.[2] Helena was married to Julian, Constantina first to Aniballianus, and secondly to Caesar Gallus. The latter princess is described

[1] A third church, dedicated to S. Laurence in Panisperna, also named *ad Formosum* or *in Formonso*, stands on the Viminal. The date of its erection is unknown. The word *Panisperna* is believed to have been derived from *panis* and *perna* (bread and ham), an explanation suggestive of the sacrifice of swine in honour of Jupiter Fagutalis. Other authorities hold it to have been derived from the name of the Prefect Perperna Quadratus, who restored the Baths of Constantine. I myself discovered amid fragments of marble in the gardens belonging to the church the remains of an inscription bearing clearly the name PERPERNA. Unfortunately, the fragment has been lost.

[2] Joh. Ciampini, *De sacr. aedif. a Constant. exstructis,* c. 10, believes the rotunda to have been a temple to Bacchus, transformed by Constantine into a chapel; an opinion which Laderchi in his history of the Basilica of S. Marcellinus and Peter seeks to refute.

by Ammianus Marcellinus as wicked and wanton, although the *Acts of S. Agnes*—a foolish bungling work, which even Baronius treats as a forgery—represent her on the contrary as a holy virgin. At all events, she has been honoured as S. Constanza from the thirteenth century downwards.[1] A great porphyry sarcophagus, which was found in the round church, now stands close to a similar sarcophagus of the mother of Constantine in the Vatican. The celebrated Empress Helena was buried on the Via Labicana, three miles beyond the Praenestine Gate (Porta Maggiore), in a magnificent round chapel, the ruins of which are now recognised in the Torre Pignatarra (tower of the earthen vases).[2]

The first building of S. Croce in Gerusalemme is ascribed by legend to the pious Helena, and in it she is said to have laid a part of the true Cross, which she herself had found. The date of the foundation of this ancient church is unknown. It was built in a deserted spot, at the north-eastern corner of the walls near the Castrensian Amphitheatre, and beside the Baths of Helena. The *Liber Pontificalis* places it in a fabulous Palace Sessorium, from which the Porta Maggiore was called Sessoriana.[3] The S. Croce

[1] Bottari (*Pitture e Sculture Sagre,* tom. iii. init.) has destroyed the nimbus surrounding the head of this Megaera, representing, with some show of probability, that the sanctity of a pious matron named Constantina, to whom an inscription attributes the building of S. Agnese, has erroneously been transferred to the wife of Gallus. See the inscription, which was to be read on the apse of the church previous to its restoration by Pope Honorius (625–638), in De Rossi, *Inscr. Christ.,* ii. 44. Also Duchesne, note 80, p. 196, of his *Liber Pontificalis.*

[2] Bosio, *Roma sotterr.,* p. 323.

[3] *Palatium Sessorianum* or *quod appellatur Sessorium*: hence the

church itself also went by this name, though it was originally called *Basilica Heleniana* and *Hierosalem,* a title which it bore in 433 under Sixtus III., and by which it must consequently have been already known in the time of Honorius.[1]

S. Petrus and Marcellinus.

The last church attributed to Constantine was dedicated to two saints, Peter the Exorcist, and Marcellinus. It stood at the third milestone of the Via Labicana at a spot called *ad duas Lauros,* beside an imperial villa and not far from the so-called Mausoleum of Helena. It was a catacomb church, and the tradition that it had been built by Constantine is due to its being in the neighbourhood of the mausoleum.[2]

All these ancient basilicas, for the most part catacomb churches, stood either beyond the gates or at

church in *Sessorio* or *Sessoriano.* The palace is thus spoken of for the first time in the Excerpt. Valesiana, where it is related that Theodoric while in Rome caused one of his nobles to be beheaded *in palatio, quod appellatur Sessorium* (Ammian. Marcellin., ed. Eyssenhardt, p. 541). In the Itinerary of the Anonymus of Einsiedeln, it is designated as *palatium juxta Hierusalem.* Adinolfi, *Roma—di mezzo,* i. 272, conjectures this palace to have been the Castrensian Amphitheatre, but throughout the Einsiedeln Itinerary the amphitheatre is invariably spoken of apart from the palace.

[1] Nibby on Nardini, ii. 12, and Raimondo Besozzi, *Storia della Basil. di S. Croce in Ger.* The latter derives the name from the earth which Helena had brought from Calvary and laid down there. That the designation *Hierusalem* is of very ancient date is proved by an Inscription which stood below the mosaics in the apse as late as the fifteenth century. *Sanctae Ecclesiae Hierusalem Valentinianus, Placidia et Honoria Augusti votum, solverunt.* Duchesne, *Lib. Pont.,* note 75, p. 196.

[2] Jacobi Laderchii *de Sacris Basil. SS. Martyr. Marcellini Presb. et Petri Exorcistae Diss. Hist.* Rom., 1705. The church also seems to have borne the name of S. Tiburtius.

the very extremities of the city. Christianity, however, described an ever-narrowing circle round the city, and in the last years of Constantine had already settled under the Capitol; that is, if we may rely on the statement that Bishop Marcus there founded a basilica to the Evangelist whose name he bore. In the council of Symmachus in 499 this church appears as a titular.[1]

S. Maria Maggiore.

Undoubtedly one of the most beautiful basilicas of Rome, that of S. Maria Maggiore near the Macellum of Livia on the Esquiline, is of early date, having been built by Bishop Liberius between 352 and 366. Legend associates a vision with the foundation of this church. It is related that one August night, John, a rich patrician, saw in a dream the Mother of God, who commanded him to build her a basilica on the spot where in the morning he should find fresh fallen snow. On hastening to Liberius to inform him of the apparition he found that the bishop had had a similar vision. The miracle indeed had taken place, and Liberius had the plan of the basilica traced in the snows of August, the liberality of the patrician providing the expenses of the building. The legend is explained by history. The building of the now basilica was a monument of the creed of Nicaea and of the orthodox teaching of Athanasius, for which Liberius himself had suffered two years of exile.[2] But the Virgin Mary had in the fourth

[1] *Lib. Pont.* (Duchesne, p. 202) " Vita Marci": *hic fecit duas basilicas, unam via Ardeatina ubi requiescit, et aliam in urbe Roma juxta Pallacinis.*

[2] Liberius, in the hope of attaining his return to Rome, weakly

century no recognised cult in Rome, and was only accorded worship for the first time after the year 432, when Sixtus III. rebuilt the Basilica Liberiana, decorating it with mosaics, and consecrating it especially to the "Mother of God."[1]

S. Maria Trastevere.

The beautiful basilica of S. Maria in Trastevere, although named after Bishop Calixtus I., was either founded or rebuilt by Julius I. between 337 and 354. The date of its dedication to Mary is uncertain, but it received its present form from Innocent II.[2]

S. Clemente.

Yet more worthy of attention is the church of S. Clement, an ancient basilica between the Lateran and the Colosseum, mentioned by Jerome at the end of the fourth century. It was dedicated to the celebrated bishop, who is held to have been the second or third successor of the Apostle in the see of Rome, but the idea that it originated in the house where the Consul Clement was accustomed to assemble the believers is

joined the semi-Arian party. He was on this account later regarded as a heretic by the Church. "Liberius and Felix" in Döllinger's *Papstfabeln des Mittelalters.* We may assume that the basilica was founded on his return to Rome in expiation for the errors of the past.

[1] *Liber Pontif.* in the life of Liberius: *hic fecit basilicam nomini suo juxta macellum Liviae*; "Vita Sixti III.": *hic fecit basilicam S. Marie quae ab antiquis Liberii cognominabatur juxta macellum Liviae.* From a palace in the neighbourhood it was also called the Basilica Sicinini.

[2] *Lib. Pontif.,* "Calixtus": *hic fecit Basilicam trans Tiberim.* The adjunct *S. Mariae,* read by Vignoli, is absent from the best MSS. Martinelli, *Roma ex eth.,* s. p. 247, denies that the basilica was built by Calixtus. Ugonio asserts it, though without foundation, and says that it is the oldest church dedicated to Mary in Rome. The *Liber Pont.,* in the life of Julius I., says: *fecit—basilicam Juliam juxta forum divi Trajani, basilicam Transtiberina regione XIIII. juxta Callistum.*

a supposition incapable of proof.[1] Displaying, as it does, monuments belonging to various periods of early history, S. Clemente in its site and origin more deserves our attention than any church in Rome. For below the floor of the basilica are found huge blocks of tufa, the remains of some building, belonging, if not to the time of the Kings, at least to that of the Republic. Above stand other remains of Imperial times. Modern excavation further shows that the earliest church of S. Clement was erected on the site of a temple dedicated to Mithras. When, in the course of time, this basilica, with which S. Jerome was acquainted, had fallen to decay, it gave place to the mediaeval church, and notwithstanding the many alterations which this later building has suffered, it still remains the most authentic type we possess of the ancient Roman basilica.[2]

The fifth century saw the churches still steadily increasing, and though we have so far been unable to discover whether any belonging to this period were built within, or on, the ruins of ancient temples, several after the middle of the century can be proved to have had such an origin.[3] Paganism was now

[1] Hieron, *De vir. ill.* c. 15: *obiit tertio Trajani anno, et nominis ejus memoriam usque hodie Romae extructa ecclesia custodit.* Rondininus, *De S. Clemente papa et martyre, ejusque basil. in urbe R.,* Roma, 1706.

[2] Jos. Mullooly deserves our gratitude for the light which his excavations have thrown on the history of this church. See his work: *S. Clement, Pope and Martyr, and his Basilica in Rome,* Rome, 1869. De Rossi, *Prime origini della bas. di S. Clemente, Bull. di Arch. Christ.,* 1863, n. 4, 1870, p. 125 f.

[2] Even were any enumeration of the churches in Rome ever compiled before the year 540, no information with regard to the number

completely extinct in Rome; the city was Christian, imbued with the new faith and governed by the perfectly developed system of ecclesiastical administration at the head of which stood the venerated bishop. But its outward aspect was still completely Pagan. Its ancient form endured while the unassuming basilicas of Christianity, the greatest of them distant from the walls, or in the outer districts of the city, were scarcely noticed amidst the countless monuments of Pagan splendour.

Twofold character of the city.

But at the beginning of the fifth century all these splendid buildings of past ages, closed, deserted, despised, dishonoured, had become mere lifeless monuments of bygone pomp. Christianity had acquired possession of the immense city, but remained utterly powerless to invest its inheritance with fresh vitality. The mighty emblems of the civilisation of antiquity, the beauty and wealth of its art, the work and pastimes of centuries, were allowed to perish, and all the use that Christianity made of them was to adopt, here and there, a solitary temple, a group of columns, or a few blocks of marble. Never in all history has the human race so deliberately renounced a perfectly developed civilisation. Nevertheless, the Rome of antiquity was not completely severed from the new Rome. The Christian city rose within its ancient predecessor and

existing in the beginning of the fifth century has come down to us. De Rossi, *Roma Sotterr.*, i. 129. In the Breviarium of Zacharias we are told: *Sunt in ea ecclesiae apostolor. beator., ecclesiae catholicae XXIV.* But since this account was compiled in the sixth, the insignificant number twenty-four must have been borrowed from some authority of much earlier date.

harmonised with it, Pagan and Christian elements blending together. Thus the mediaeval city, by its union of past and present, by the coalition of the ancient forms of Paganism with the new forms of Christianity, acquired that impress of a twofold nature, such as has never been repeated elsewhere.

The ruins of antiquity survived, and have their place in this History, as well as the Church and the Papacy, which, in the overthrow of Caesarism, absorbed within itself the political genius of Roman Empire. We shall see the shades of the ancient Romans still wander among the citizens even in the later Middle Ages. The state fabric, the religion, the cosmopolitan civilisation of Paganism had attained too powerful a form to make it possible that it should be completely overthrown. Not only its monumental, but its moral, ruins still endured, and through all succeeding centuries the Romans continued to possess a remnant of their ancient character. We may even assert that, long after Christianity had gained the victory, it was this remnant of the ancient spirit that contributed to found the universal sovereignty of the Papacy, since in the Papacy was embodied the ancient majesty of Rome.

The genius of Antiquity itself survived in the Church and its gorgeous ritual. In every period, even in the times of its lowest degradation, it breathes upon us from the history of the past, though it be but as the visionary longings of the unfortunate Roman for a return of an ancient dominion. It inspires, too, the inextinguishable reverence for the greatness of his ancestors and the ever-recurring delusion of a possible restoration of the Roman Empire. At the close of the Middle Ages this pagan genius suddenly appeared victorious over Christianity in the splendid form of the Renascence.

Having traced the outward aspect of the city in the time of Honorius, let us, with the fifth century, enter upon the history of the long and in part dark centuries which follow.

CHAPTER III.

1. Entry of Honorius into Rome at the End of the Year 403—His Residence in the Palace of the Caesars —The Last Gladiatorial Contests in the Amphitheatre—Departure of Honorius for Ravenna—Incursion and Defeat of the Barbarians under Radagaisus—Fall of Stilicho.

The reader will have learnt the condition of the Roman Empire in the beginning of the fifth century. Since it had been divided into an Eastern and Western Empire, and the continued pressure of the nomadic hordes had broken down the frontiers and the feeble legions who defended them, the great structure fell gradually to pieces. The city of Rome itself was no longer the seat of the Emperors of the West, who had long before deserted her, to take up their abode in Milan. The Romans, trembling before the invasions of Sarmatians and Germans, and deprived, through the absence of the Imperial court, of the most fertile sources of their prosperity, besieged their feeble Emperor with entreaties for his return to their deserted city, just as, nearly a thousand years after, their descendants implored the Popes to leave Avignon and return to declining Rome.

The young Honorius yielded to the universal

appeal, and, at the end of 403, made his solemn entry into Rome. Italy was now free from the Goths, who, marching from Illyria under the leadership of the dreaded Alaric, had made their appearance in the country in the winter of 400. For through their defeat by Stilicho, the minister, general, and father-in-law of Honorius, in the bloody battle-fields of Pollentia and Verona in 402, Rome was spared the horrors of a Gothic conquest. The Emperor could therefore now leave Ravenna to celebrate his Decennalia, his sixth consulate, and the triumphs which he owed to his great general. Stilicho, a man of Vandal descent, had risen to power at the court of Theodosius, had married Serena, the niece of the Emperor, and was the first German who, by his energy and power, attained an influential position in Rome.[1]

This was the first sight of the kind that the city had witnessed since the triumphal processions of Diocletian and Maximian in 303. Where she had once, in the consciousness of universal dominion, celebrated her victories over the distant peoples of Persia, Africa, Britain and Germany, she now inaugurated the less proud, but happier festival of deliverance from the immediate dread of enemies. It was indeed the last spectacle of an Imperial triumph that Rome ever saw. The poet Claudian has left us an attractive picture of the journey of Honorius, of his entry, and of the festivities which were given in his honour.[2] It seemed as if affrighted

[1] Claudian frequently extols his genius and heroic beauty.

[2] *De VI. Cons. Honor.,* Prudentius also, after the victory over the

Rome had decked herself as a bride to meet her long-expected wooer; but the bride was old, and the wooer feeble.

Honorius approached by the Milvian Bridge, Stilicho seated beside him on the Car of Victory. He passed slowly along through the triumphal gates erected in his honour, amidst the acclamations of the people who filled the streets as far as the Capitol and Palatine and even covered the roofs of the houses, now shouting for the young Augustus, now for the great hero. They gazed with childish admiration on the unaccustomed sight of troops of warriors, for the most part barbarian, with their flowing banners, steel armour, and helmets adorned with peacock's feathers. All the public bodies were marshalled in order for the reception of Honorius, who, however, condescended to excuse the Senate from the servile ceremony heretofore observed of accompanying his carriage on foot. We can easily picture with what grief such senators as were still Pagan must have recalled the past, when the Emperor proceeded by the Triumphal Way to the Capitol of Jupiter, and with what indignation they must have denounced the Christian priests, who, with crosses and banners, and with the Bishop Innocent at their head, had gone to meet the Emperor.

Innocent the First, 417.

Although the Roman bishop, in virtue of his office,

Goths, which in his opinion the Emperor and Stilicho owed to Christ, summons Honorius to ascend the triumphal car:

Scande triumphalem currum, spoliisque receptis
Huc Christo comitante veni.

—*Contra Symmach.,* ii. v. 731.

had already become a person of considerable importance, he was as yet merely a priest, the nominee and submissive subject of the Emperor. The distinction between Church and Empire, between spiritual and temporal power, was so far unknown. A great part of the Roman people was still Pagan. Even around the person of the Emperor, amongst the highest officials of the court, believers in the old and new religions, Pagan and Christian, mixed indiscriminately. There were, moreover, Arians in Rome, the Germans in the Imperial service belonging almost without exception to the Arian faith.

It would be a great mistake to imagine that this cosmopolitan city, although forsaken by the Imperial court, and permeated by Christianity, bore everywhere the appearance of decay. Though its temples were deserted, its theatres and racecourses were still frequented, and its sumptuous palaces, at any rate, were inhabited by a nobility who revelled in princely luxury.

The Emperor inhabits the palace of the Caesars.

Honorius took up his abode in the Palace of the Caesars, and the various swarms of imperial attendants again filled the deserted halls of the Palatine. For more than a hundred years the huge fortress had remained forsaken, having during this long period only twice served as a resting place for the Emperors, when they came from their distant court to visit Rome. Robbed by Constantine of some of its finest ornaments, this vast palace resembled a lordly dwelling-place, the splendour of which is beginning to fade, because its inhabitants are impoverished or dying out. "But now" (we quote the flatteries of the still Pagan court-poet Claudian) "the ancestral palace of the Caesars rejoiced at being again inhabited by its deity, resumes its traditional aspect, giving to the expectant people weightier oracles than ever issued from Delphi, and allowing the statues to be crowned with fresh laurels."

Honorius remained a year in Rome. He gave the people games in the Circus Maximus, races, hunts of wild animals, and Pyrrhic war dances. But the Romans were deluded in their expectations of a revival of the secular sports of old, and murmured also at the suppression of the gladiatorial combats, prohibited by the Emperor shortly before his triumph at the earnest entreaty of the Christian poet Prudentius.[1] Although, in his Edict of 325, Constantine had condemned these cruel spectacles, he had only succeeded in restricting them. Under his followers they had been revived,[2] and, according to the testimony of an ancient ecclesiastical writer, it was at length owing to the self-sacrifice of a brave monk that these horrors were brought to an

End of the gladiatorial contests.

[1] At the close of his poem against Symmachus:—

Quod genus ut sceleris jam nesciat aurea Roma,
Te precor, Ausonii dux augustissime regni,
Et tam triste sacrum jubeas, ut caetera tolli.

For the task of putting an end to this custom had been bequeathed to him by his father Theodosius:—

Ille urbem vetuit taurorum sanguine tingi,
Tu mortes miserorum hominum prohibeto litari.

[2] Cod. Theodos., xv. tit. 12, n. 1. *Cruentia spectacula in otio civili et domestica quiete non placent, &c.* The opinion of Baronius, that Honorius had restored the gladiatorial games, is opposed by Muratori and Pagi, *ad ann.* 404. With regard to the sacrifice of Telemachus and the suppression of the games, see Theodoret, *Eccl. Hist.,* v. c. 26.

end. Telemachus threw himself one day into the midst of the excited and astonished gladiators in the amphitheatre, and, carried away by a noble enthusiasm, sought to hinder them in their murderous struggle, whereupon the enraged spectators stoned him to death. Honorius, however, commanded that the victim should be placed in the list of martyrs, and thenceforward prohibited the gladiatorial fights. The legend is beautiful and deserves to be true, for amongst all the games of antiquity, to which Christianity put an end, there were none, the suppression of which redounded more to the honour of humanity. No definite information of the date of the complete cessation of this pagan amusement has come down to us. We hear no more of gladiatorial combats in the amphitheatre of Titus, but only know that wrestling and combats with wild animals continued more than a hundred years longer.

Honorius establishes his court in Ravenna, A.D. 404.

Honorius did not feel himself at ease in Rome. The deserted splendour of the city oppressed and bored him, and apparently the news of the approach of fresh hordes of barbarians at the end of the year 404 drove him hurriedly back to the security of marsh-encompassed Ravenna. Here he took up his abode, remaining in safety, whilst an incursion of over 200,000 Celts and Germans, under the leadership of Radagaisus, descended from beyond the Alps and laid waste North Italy. Stilicho overcame these hordes near Florence, whither they had advanced, after spreading destruction everywhere along their march. He speedily routed them, and once more freed Rome from the ruin which had menaced her.

The grateful people erected a statue of bronze and silver to the hero in the Rostra;[1] and a triumphal arch to the Emperors Arcadius, Honorius, and Theodosius.[2] This was the last honour bestowed on the great Stilicho, for, in August of the year 408, he fell a victim to the intrigues of the palace and to his own negotiations with Alaric, King of the Visigoths. Concerning the character of these negotiations, history gives very doubtful information. Alaric, a bold Gothic leader of illustrious descent, in his youth had acquired Roman customs and learnt the arts of war. His valiant deeds had won him the honourable title of "Balthe," a title also enjoyed by his family, which, next to that of the Amals, was the most renowned of the Gothic tribes.[3] Called by his restless people in the last days of Theodosius to the kingly office, he had invaded and laid waste the provinces of the Empire below the Danube, advanced

Statue erected in honour of Stilichio.

Alaric's early life.

[1] The cippus on which stood the statue of Stilicho was excavated near the Temple of Concord, and now stands in the Villa Medici. For the inscription, see *Corp. In. Lat.,* vi. 1731. An inscription in honour of Stilicho and his army (the name of the general was erased after his fall), POST CONFECTVM GOTHICVM BELLVM, was discovered by the Arch of Severus in 1880. Henzen, *Bull. dell' Inst.,* 1880, p. 169; *Bull. d. Comm. Archeol. Com.,* viii. 135.

[2] The inscription is in the Anon. of Einsiedeln, nr. 7, emended by De Rossi, *Le prime raccotte d'antiche iscrizione compilate in Roma,* 1852, p. 121; and *Corp. In. Lat.,* vi. 1196. De Rossi holds that this triumphal arch, of the situation of which no information remains, stood in the neighbourhood of Hadrian's bridge. A triumphal arch to the Emperors Gratian, Valentinian and Theodosius also stood in this part of the city. The words: *Ad Perenne Indicium Triumphorum Quib. Getarum Nationem In Omne Aevum Docuere Extingui* soon became ridiculous.

[3] Joseph Aschbach, *Gesch. der Westgothen*, Frkf. a M., 1827, p. 66.

even into the Peloponnesus, and reduced unhappy Greece to a desert. Many of the cities and honoured temples of Hellas were destroyed. Athens, however, according to a beautiful legend, was defended by the shades of Pallas and Achilles. Almost overthrown by Stilicho in the narrow passes of Arcadia, Alaric had nevertheless extricated himself from his desperate position, and through the intrigues of the enemies of Stilicho at the Byzantine court, the devastator of Greece was declared General of Illyria and ally of the Eastern Empire.[1] Alaric had finally led his rapacious people against Italy, but defeated at Pollentia and Verona in 402 and 403, he was driven back to the shores of the Danube. Negotiations with Stilicho had prevailed on him to forego the alliance with the Eastern Empire and to enter the service of Rome. According to the treaty, he had remained in Illyria, which province the Roman general hoped to wrest from the Byzantine Empire, but now suddenly reappeared on the frontiers of Italy. With barbarian cunning, he demanded from Honorius compensation for his march and his inaction in Epirus. The Emperor was, however, at the time in Rome, and Stilicho hastened thence from Ravenna to deal with the difficult business. The Senate, which the ambitious general had restored to power with the view of strengthening his own designs, was summoned to the Palace.[2] After he had laid before it the demands of Alaric and urged their acceptance, a sum of 4000 pounds of

[1] These circumstances are skilfully treated by H. Richter, *De Stilichone et Rufino,* Halle, 1860.

[2] Claudian, *De Cons. Stilichonis,* lib. iii., extols him for this act.

gold was voted to the Gothic King. Lampadius, the most respected man in the Senate, hereupon rose and shouted in scornful indignation, "This is no peace, but a purchase of servitude,"[1] then, alarmed at his own audacity, the noble Senator rushed out to seek an asylum in the nearest Christian church. The incident however became an event, and the enemies of Stilicho gained their point. The national party, whose endeavour it was to prevent the advance of barbarians at the Roman court, at last brought about the ruin of the great general.[2] The Emperor was told that Stilicho had sworn with Alaric to deprive him of the throne, in order to secure the crown for himself or his son Eucherius. The death of Stilicho was accordingly decreed and executed. The last hero of Rome clung for protection to the altar of a church in Ravenna, and, treacherously enticed thence, calmly offered his neck to the headsman's sword. The murder took place in 408.[3]

Fall of Stilicho, A.D. 408.

The Romans received the news of the fall of the great general to whom they owed their deliverance from the Goths with satisfaction. They reminded themselves that he had been a German barbarian. The Pagans execrated him as a Christian

[1] *Non est ista pax, sed pactio servitutis.* Zosimus, v. c. 29.

[2] Reinhold Pallmann, *Gesch. der Völkerwanderung von der Gothenbekehrung bis zum Tode Alarichs*, Gotha, 1863, p. 292, &c. Although Stilicho was a Roman, at least by birth, his father having been an officer of German cavalry under Valens, he was nevertheless a barbarian in the eyes of the Romans.

[3] Gibbon describes the circumstances of his fall with the talent of a tragedian, but his sympathy for the fallen hero does not allow him to take a wholly impartial view.

who had burnt the Sibylline books, and the Christians in their turn reproached him with his and his son's secret partiality for the idolaters.[1] Stilicho's monuments were overthrown, but whilst the eunuchs of the palace displayed the bloody head of his son to the Romans, they already felt the presentiment of their own doom.

2. ALARIC ADVANCES AGAINST ROME, 408—HIS DEMON—PRESENTIMENTS OF THE FALL OF ROME— FIRST SIEGE—THE EMBASSY OF THE ROMANS—TUSCAN HEATHENISM IN ROME—THE SIEGE IS AVERTED—HONORIUS REJECTS THE PEACE—ALARIC APPEARS FOR THE SECOND TIME BEFORE ROME, 409—THE ANTI-EMPEROR ATTALUS—ALARIC LEAVES FOR RAVENNA—BESIEGES ROME FOR THE THIRD TIME.

Invasion of Alaric.

Even had the Gothic King hoped to divide the East and West with his former enemy, he nevertheless had but little cause to regret his shameful death. The only rival from whom he had anything to fear, the opponent who had driven him forth out of Italy and condemned him to five years of inactivity, was no more, and his death left Alaric for the time being ruler of the destinies of Rome. He now resolved to try his fortune once again, and left Illyria for the north of Italy, invited thither by the friends of the murdered Stilicho, and by the call of the Arians, whilst the refusal of the tribute offered a sufficient pretext for

[1] The Pagan Rutilius exclaims in indignation, v. 41:—

Quo magis est facinis diri Stilichonis acerbum,
Proditor arcani quod fuit imperii.

his breach of faith. Legend relates that the ruthless conqueror, who had already devastated the beautiful Hellas, was incessantly goaded onwards by a demon, urging him to march against Rome. A pious monk had hastened to him, imploring him to spare the city and to refrain from the monstrous deed he had undertaken, on which the Goth answered: "I do not act of my own will, but am incessantly tormented by one who urges me on, saying, 'Up, up, destroy Rome.'"[1] Jerome and Augustine recognise in this demon a celestial voice, and in Alaric an instrument sent of heaven to inflict on the corrupt city the chastisement due to the fulness of her sins. The force of the historic current was, however, the demon that urged the Gothic King to venture on so unparalleled an act. The thought of taking Rome, the hitherto unconquered mistress of the world, must always have appeared to human imagination as something stupendous, whilst at the same time it exercised an irresistible charm over the mind of an ambitious barbarian. With the expedition of Alaric began the conquest of enervated Italy by the German race; then, first forsaking the restless, aimless life of a nomad tribe, the Germans entered upon the first stage in the process of civilisation, but in so doing they dealt the death-blow to the Roman Empire. Alaric may have hoped, with the possession of Rome, the more

[1] Sozomen., ix. c. 6; Socrates, *Hist. Eccl.,* vii. c. 10: ἄπιθι τὴν Ῥωμαίων πόρθησον πόλιν; Claudian, *De Bello Pollentino* (Getico), v. 544:—

Non somnia nobis,
Nec volucres, sed clara palam vox edita luco est:
Rumpe omnes Alarice moras.

effectually to embarrass the political relations of Italy, but could scarcely have expected to make himself master of the city for any length of time, lacking, as he did, not only the support of a state or a nation, but the auxiliaries and alliances which had supplied strength to Pyrrhus and Hannibal.

Presenting documents concerning the fall of the city.

The city was still the embodiment of all civilisation, the Palladium of mankind. Even although she had ceased to be the seat of the Emperor and of the highest officials of state, she remained the ideal centre of the Empire. Her very name was to her a power. The ideas, "Rome" and "Roman," were impressed on the system of the universe. Although, by means of long and bloody wars, she had brought so many nations into subjection, she had never inspired hatred; for all, even the barbarians, were proud to call themselves Roman citizens. It was only fanatical Christians who regarded her with horror as the seat of idolatry. The Apocalypse prophesied the fall of this great Babylon which had made all nations drunk with the wine of her pleasure. The Sibylline books, which had been found in Alexandria in the time of the Antonines, had announced the downfall of the city after the speedy appearance of Antichrist, who was expected to return from the ends of the earth in the form of the inhuman monster, the persecutor of the Christians, the matricide Nero.[1] The Palladium of Rome would then have lost its power, if the might of the city and of the glorious Latin race had not arisen again through Christianity. In opposition to Virgil, the Fathers of

[1] Sibyllinor, iv. 119 *seq.*; v 93 *seq.*, ed. C. Alexandre, Paris, 1869.

the Church, Tertullian and Cyprian, asserted that the Empire of the Romans, like the dominion of the Persians, Medes, Egyptians and Macedonians, which had preceded it, so far from being imperishable, was hastening to its end, and legend relates that even Constantine, summoned by an oracle, had built the new Rome by the Bosphorus because ancient Rome was inevitably doomed to destruction.[1]

The pressure of Sarmatian and German tribes against the boundaries of the Empire in the fourth century lent more probability to the prophecy, and universal terror was manifested lest the city should fall into the hands of the barbarians, by whom, according to Christian belief, it was destined, like Nineveh or Jerusalem, to be destroyed with fire. It was no wonder that, even in the time of Constantine, a voice had been heard, announcing that with the fall of Rome would take place the dissolution of the world. "When the Capital of the Universe," so spoke the orator Lactantius, "shall have fallen and gone up in flames, as the Sibyls prophesy, who can doubt that there will have come the end of the world and of all human things? For this is the city which still sustains the universe, and we must fervently pray the God of Heaven that His will may be postponed, and that the accursed tyrant who is to commit this outrage may not appear sooner than we expect, and put out this light, with the extinction of which the world itself will pass away."[2]

[1] Lasaulx, *Der Untergang des Hellenismus,* Munich, 1854, p. 42.

[2] Lactanctius, *Divinar. Institut.,* vii. c. 25. *At vero cum caput illud orbis ceciderit, et* πῦρ *esse coeperit, quod Sibyllae fore ajunt, quis dubitet,*

With the first appearance of the Goths in Italy, this fear had taken definite shape. It lends to the poem of Claudian on the Gothic war that tone of deep and supernatural dejection which the dread of the inevitable fall had aroused. "Arise, O venerable Mother," says the poet, "free thyself from the ignoble fears of old age! O city, coeval with the earth! When the Don shall water the plains of Egypt, and the Nile the Maeotian Marshes, then only shall iron Lachesis lay on thee her doom." These bold apostrophes, however, were only the signs of overpowering fear. As soon as Alaric moved, Rome was seized by panic, which has been well described by Claudian himself. Scarcely had the King of the Goths advanced to the Po in 402, than the Romans imagined they heard the neighing of his horses, and immediately prepared for flight to Corsica, Sardinia and the Greek islands. They gazed with superstitious terror at the eclipsed moon, telling each other of fearful comets, of visions, and of dreadful portents, whilst the old interpretation of the twelve vultures of Romulus, signifying the continuance of the city for twelve centuries, seemed likely to be fulfilled.[1] Stilicho, the recent saviour of Rome, was dead, and the generals of Honorius, Turpilio, Varanes and Vigilantius were not able to fill his place. The court of Ravenna refused Alaric's

venisse jam finem rebus humanis, orbi terrarum. Lactanctius, the pupil of Arnobius, studied rhetoric in Nicomedia in the time of Diocletian. Late in life he became the tutor of Crispus, the unfortunate son of Constantine.

[1] Claudian, *De Bello Pollent.*, v. 265 :—

Tunc reputant annos, interceptoque volatu
Vulturis incidunt properatis saecula metis.

proposals of peace and his moderate demands for money in the proud consciousness of Imperial majesty, but unsupported by Imperial power. Feeling itself secure in the Adriatic marshes, it left Rome to its fate. The city, however, being no longer the seat of Imperial authority, could not in one sense be affected by its own subjugation, since "where the Emperor was, there was Rome."[1]

The King of the Goths had already crossed the Po at Cremona, and, laying waste the length and breadth of the land, advanced by Bologna to Rimini, and, meeting no resistance, proceeded southwards by the Flaminian Way. He encircled the walls of Rome with swarms of his Scythian horsemen and with the bulk of his Gothic infantry, all alike covetous of the spoils of Rome.

Alaric lays siege to Rome, 408.

Alaric did not attempt an attack, he surrounded the city, placed his troops at each of the principal gates, cut off all supplies both by land and sea, and awaited the inevitable result of his measures. The Romans remained behind their newly-strengthened walls of Aurelian; they sought to terrify the enemy by the sight of the bloody head of an illustrious woman, Serena, the unfortunate widow of Stilicho and niece of the Emperor Theodosius (the daughter of his brother Honorius), dwelt in her palace in Rome, whither eunuchs had restored her daughter Thermantia, the repudiated wife of the Emperor, to her keeping. For on the death of his first wife,

[1] *Ubi Imperator, ibi Roma.* Ὅτου ἂν ὁ βασιλεὺς ᾖ, ἐκεῖ ἡ Ῥώμη, in Herodian; see Bryce, *The Holy Roman Empire,* p. 26. In later days it was also said by the Popes in Avignon: *ubi Papa, ibi Roma.*

Maria, the elder daughter of Stilicho, Honorius had sought her sister Thermantia in marriage, although at the time she was little more than a child. The Senate suspected that Serena, in revenge, had summoned the Goths to Rome and had an understanding with them. They consequently ordered her to be executed. The Princess Placidia, sister of Honorius, and through Theodosius cousin of Serena, at the time a girl of one and twenty, gave her consent to this shameful deed. Placidia lived in her dower house in the Palatium, as did two other women of princely rank, namely, Laeta, formerly wife of the Emperor Gratian, and her aged mother, Pisamena. The Senate, however, was deceived in the expectation that after the death of Serena, the Goths, losing all hope of entering the city, would abandon the project and withdraw. Famine and pestilence raged within, and the noble princesses sold their jewels to minister to the wants of the people.

The Senate, reduced to despair, at last sent the Spaniard Basilius, and John, the tribune of the Imperial clerks, to the Gothic camp to negotiate a friendly treaty. When the messengers came into Alaric's presence, they told him, as they had been commissioned to do, that the great Roman people, accustomed to war, were ready for a decisive battle if, by rejecting all reasonable conditions, he drove them to extremities. "The thicker the grass, the more easily mown," was the contemptuous answer of the barbarian King to the miserable comedians, who appeared before him in the soiled senatorial purple. He required, as the terms for his withdrawal, the surrender of all valuables and of all the slaves of barbarian descent within the city, and when the ambassadors asked what, in that case, he contemplated leaving to the Romans, he replied "Only their lives."

Activity of Paganism in Rome.

Reduced to despair, the old Roman party summoned to their aid the mysteries of their proscribed religion. Old men from Tuscany, experienced in the ancient arts of augury, invited, perhaps, by Pompeianus, the Pagan Prefect of the city, undertook to call fire from heaven to free Rome from the enemy, if the Senate would celebrate the solemn sacrifice to the gods on the Capitol and in all remaining temples, according to ancient custom. The Pagan historian, Zosimus, who is our informant, maintains that even the Bishop Innocent permitted, though he did not approve, the design; but the historian is honest enough to admit that Paganism proved itself extinct in Rome, for no one dared be present at the sacrifice; the soothsayers were sent home, and the Romans resorted to more efficacious means.[1]

The Romans purchase the withdrawal of the enemy.

After a second embassy, Alaric declared himself satisfied with a ransom of 5000 pounds of gold and 30,000 pounds of silver; he required in addition 3000 pieces of skins dyed in purple, 4000 silken doublets, and 3000 pounds of pepper, a demand which shows the luxurious requirements of the barbarians. A forced tax did not suffice to raise the huge sum of money; and the ornaments of the closed temples

[1] Zosimus, v. c. 41; Sozomenus (a Greek and a Novatian), v. c. 7.

were seized; the images of gold and silver were melted down, a fact which proves that costly statues of the gods still remained in Rome. Amongst the sacrifices which fell to the crucible, Zosimus laments, above all others, the national statue of Virtus, with which, as he expresses it, the last remains of bravery and honour perished in Rome.

No sooner had Alaric received the ransom than he allowed the famished Romans an egress by some of the gates, a market every three days, and intercourse with the ports. He himself withdrew to Tuscany, taking with him no fewer than 40,000 barbarian slaves, who had by degrees escaped to him from the city and from the palaces of their masters. He awaited an answer from the court of Ravenna, where messengers from the Senate had gone, to lay before the Emperor, in Alaric's name, overtures of peace and alliance. But Honorius, or his minister Olympius, rejected these proposals, although the demands of Alaric were by no means unreasonable, since he promised to be satisfied with a yearly sum of gold and corn, with Noricum, Dalmatia, the two Venetias, and the dignity of a general of the Imperial army.

Among the messengers sent by Rome to the Emperor was Bishop Innocent, but neither his exhortations, nor the entreaties and representations of the remaining members, who depicted the hardships suffered by Rome in the darkest colours, made any impression on Honorius, and Alaric soon learnt in Rimini, whither the new minister Jovius had invited him, of the contemptuous refusal of the Emperor to bestow on him the title of General of the Empire.

Alaric now advanced a second time against Rome, but before doing so, he sent Italian bishops to Honorius, to inform the monarch that he was resolved, should the Emperor insist on war, to abandon to flames and the ravages of the barbarians that venerable city which, with all its splendid monuments, had already been for more than a thousand years the mistress of the world. He even reduced his own claims and gave up his demand for any title or dignity; he would be satisfied, he declared, with Noricum alone, with a yearly tribute of corn, and with a treaty of friendship, which should accord him permission to turn his arms against the enemies of the Empire. The minister, however, explained that the court had determined never to make peace with Alaric, they had sworn it by the head of Honorius, and rather would they be guilty of perjury to God than to the Emperor.[1]

The moderation of the Gothic King is not sufficiently explained by the respect for the authority of the Empire, common to all, even the boldest barbarian. A conqueror is never daunted by respect, only by fear, and Alaric may have imagined that, thrown entirely on the resources of his isolated, badly-equipped army, his dominion over the city would prove a very fleeting one, and that it would be wise, therefore, to prefer to it the possession of a province of the Empire, limited, indeed, in size, but guaranteed by treaty. When he again appeared before Rome, he recognised that it would be a desperate enterprise for his unskilled soldiery to attempt to lay siege to, or storm the walls of

Second siege of Rome.

[1] Zosimus, v. 50.

Aurelian. He resolved rather to surround the city, and to starve it out. With this aim, he made himself master of Portus, the important harbour of Rome, on the right side of the mouth of the Tiber, and by means of it became possessed of all the sources of supplies to the city.

Attalus elected Emperor.

Alaric's next idea was to bring about a political revolution in Rome, not so much that be really desired to dethrone Honorius, as because he needed a puppet emperor to give a show of legitimate authority to his own movements. The trembling Romans agreed to the proposal of the Gothic agents to desert Honorius and to recognise Alaric as Protector of the city. An uproar forced the Senate to treat with the Gothic King. On his motion, the Emperor was declared deposed, and Attalus, the Prefect of the city, raised to the Imperial throne.

Far from Alaric lay the thought of occupying the throne himself; he was satisfied with overthrowing the lawful dynasty and setting up as Emperor, with the consent of the Senate and people, a Roman to whom he himself did homage. He forthwith received from Attalus the dignity of Generalissimo of the Empire whilst the Goth Athaulf, his sister's husband, was named Prefect of the Cavalry.[1]

The Roman populace congratulated Attalus, applauded the appointment of Tertullus to the Consulship, and looked forward to games in the Circus and

[1]Wietersheim, *Gesch. der Völkerwanderung,* Leipz., 1859, Bd. I, p. 232, attributes Alaric's moderation to his respect for Rome. This respect was shared by all barbarian monarchs, as the history of the succeeding times will show.

distributions of gifts. The family of the Anicii alone held aloof from the tumultuous proceedings, and their neutrality was unfavourably noticed by the people. This powerful family, the head of the Christian aristocracy in Rome, feared with reason a reaction of Paganism. For Attalus himself was a Pagan, and although to please the Goths he had acknowledged Arian Christianity, and allowed himself to be baptised by an Arian bishop, he not only caused the ancient temples to be reopened, but the Labarum, with the monogram of Christ, to be omitted from his coins, where he placed instead of the sign of the Cross, the lance and the figure of the Roman Victory.[1]

The Gothic army, joined by the troops of Attalus, left Rome to besiege Ravenna, Alaric bringing the rival Emperor with him, and scarcely did the Goths show themselves before the walls of the town than Honorius lost courage. He proposed negotiations, and even offered himself as co-regent with Attalus. The offer, however, was refused. His rival would have achieved success had he supported the aims of Alaric with power and insight, but the former prefect of Rome would not listen to the proposals of his creator; he despised the barbarians; neither, although the Gothic King offered him troops for the conquest of Africa, did he make any attempt to wrest this

[1] Vaillant, *Numismata,* iii. 154, and Cohen, *Médailles Impériales,* vi. 496; gold and silver coins of Attalus bearing the inscription, *Invicta Roma Aeterna.* Rome, seated on the lion seat, in her right hand the Victory, in her left the inverted spear, On the coins of Gratian Rome is also represented without the Labarum, but with the victory and the spear.

province from the imperialists. He was altogether a useless puppet, neither statesman nor general. The defection of his minister Jovius strengthened in Honorius the idea of flight to Constantinople, until the sudden appearance of six cohorts in the harbour of Ravenna restored his courage. The strength of this city rendered all the efforts of Alaric vain; he continued, moreover, to treat with the Emperor. As for his creature Attalus, he simply utilised him as an effective bugbear, until finally he divested him of the purple and diadem at Rimini, sent the Imperial insignia to Ravenna, and kept the ex-Emperor and his son Ampelius prisoners in his camp. In the meanwhile, negotiations for peace still dragged on in Ravenna.

The appearance of Sarus, a bold leader of the Goths and a deadly foe of Alaric, his sudden attack on Athaulf, upon whose troops he fell, finally, his friendly reception within the walls of Ravenna, convinced Alaric that he was being deliberately deceived. He broke up his camp and withdrew towards Rome. Whatever may have been the reasons which had induced him hitherto to spare the capital, he now resolved to capture and treat it as the spoils of war. Honorius left it to its fate, contented that the enemy had withdrawn from Ravenna.

Alaric appears for the third time before Rome.

Goths and Huns now lay encamped on the heights before Rome, the sack of which had been promised them by the King. From the Vatican territory the rude warriors looked upon the basilica of S. Peter and beyond it to that of S. Paul, lying on the bank of the Tiber. Their leaders told them that they must turn their thoughts from these richly dowered sanctuaries, but that all the other splendours inclosed within the walls of Aurelian should be theirs when they had entered the city. Their eager gaze surveyed the wonders of architecture, in a world of palaces and streets of bygone centuries, from the midst of which rose obelisks and columns, crowned with gilded statues. They saw temples ranged in long majestic lines along the squares; theatres and circuses rising in ponderous curves; baths with shady halls, or with low and broad cupolas glittering in the sun, and the gigantic palaces of the nobles looking like so many wealthy towns within the town, where their imagination pictured sumptuous chambers filled with jewels, and inhabited by the beautiful and luxurious women of Rome. Their barbarian fancy had been nourished on fables of the inexhaustible treasures of the city, told them by their fathers on the banks of the Ister and beside the Maeotian Swamp, and to their brutal greed the fact that this was the city of the Scipios, of Cato, of Caesar and of Trajan, the city which had given mankind the laws of civilization, added no higher charm. They only knew that Rome had subjected the world by the force of arms, and that in her all its riches were gathered; that treasures which, as yet, no enemy had plundered, would fall to them as the spoils of war. And these treasures were so numerous that they hoped to mete out pearls and precious stones like corn, and to load carriages with vases of gold and embroidered vestments. The rugged Sarmatians in Alaric's army, covered with the skins of beasts and armed with bows and quivers, and the sturdy Goths clad in coats of mail, rough children of nature and of a wandering, warring life, could not grasp the indescribable luxury of Roman arts. They only dimly felt that in Rome they would plunge, as it were, into a bath of sensual pleasure, and merely looked upon the Romans as either despicable gluttons or monkish ascetics.

3. THE NOBILITY AND PEOPLE OF ROME AT THIS DATE ACCORDING TO THE ACCOUNTS OF AMMIANUS MARCELLUS AND S. JEROME—PAGAN AND CHRISTIAN SOCIETY—POPULATION OF THE CITY.

Condition of Roman society.

To depict the city and people over which the army of the Goths was hovering, we can scarcely do better than employ the colours used by the historian Ammianus Marcellinus in painting the manners and customs of his day. His picture, it is true, belongs to the time of Constantius and Gratian, but it no less suits the year 410; for during a space of thirty or fifty years these colours had not time to fade, but only to acquire a greater depth.[1] Ammianus represents the aristocracy as well as the populace of Rome: he brings out all the glaring lights, but groups together all the lower strata into one common mass of shade. Many of his traits resemble those of the old satirists; the remainder show us the Roman nobles as they were in the time of Nero or Domitian, but in

The Pagan aristocracy.

[1] Ammian. Marc., xiv. vi. 4, &c., and xxviii. iv. 6, &c.

an Oriental or Byzantine setting. Ammianus depicts the Roman patrician in his house, his bath, his journey to the city, or to his estates in the Campagna. He describes him in his rooms adorned with splendid sculptures and mosaics, at his meal amidst the flatterers and gamblers who constitute his society, who praise the arrangement of his halls, the beauty of his statues, the weight of his pheasants, fish, and dormice, whilst notaries, with important mien, enter these particulars in a register. He places a book in his hand, as Parini does in that of his noble Milanese, but it is only a volume of Juvenal, or possibly Marius Maximus, out of which, reclining on his silken cushion, he enjoys in retrospect the gallant excesses of his ancestors. For the libraries, like graves, are for ever closed, and the jester, with insidious art, has displaced the philosopher, and the orator supplanted the teacher. If the noble gentleman, who bears the whimsical name of Reburrus or Tarrasius or the like, is tired, he is lulled by the music of flutes or the voices of eunuchs, whilst lyres and water-organs of the size of two-wheeled carriages arouse his enervated spirits. Is he inclined for the theatre? Three thousand female singers and as many ballet dancers, representing some ancient myth, with voluptuous grace are ready to arouse his jaded senses. Thence he goes, like a pasha in a litter, or in a luxurious carriage, to the baths, accompanied by a troop of domestic slaves, ordered and preceded by an overseer; first, the servants of the wardrobe, then the cooks, behind them a mixed collection of slaves and plebeian idlers from his quarter, until the procession ends with a swarm of ashen-coloured and hideous eunuchs of every age, a satire on nature. Thus Fabunius rattles over the uneven pavement of the broad streets of Rome. Perhaps he wishes to alight at the baths of Caracalla, not because the public baths are more sumptuous than the private baths of his own palace, but in order that the great man may there display his magnificence, and allow his hands and knees to be kissed by his dependents. If he gives audience to a stranger, he raises him to the highest pinnacle of happiness when he deigns to ask him which bath or mineral spring he uses, or in what palace he has taken up his lodging.

When, continues Ammianus, any of these magnates undertake a journey, they seem to consider it like a march of Alexander the Great. Do they attend the chase to boast of game which they have not killed, or venture forth in a painted gondola, under the summer sun, from the lake Avernus to Puteoli or Gaeta? As soon as a fly alights on the silken tip of their gilded fans, or the slightest ray of sun pierces through a rift of the broad umbrella, they lament that fate had not caused them to be born among the Cimmerians!

We have no space for further details of the lives of the licentious Roman aristocracy, Christian as well as Pagan; but some remarks of Olympiodorus may serve to show the boundless wealth of the nobles. In order to describe the size and splendour of the Roman palaces, this historian and eye-witness says that each comprised everything contained within a moderate sized town, namely, a hippodrome, forum, temple, fountains and baths, so that we could say:—"A single house is a city, and the city contains innumerable cities."[1]

According, to his assertion, many Roman families drew from their estates a yearly rental of 4000 pounds of gold, without reckoning the natural products, which, had they been exchanged for gold, would have added a third more to this sum. He informs us that Probus, the son of Alypius, by way of celebrating his praetorship, distributed 1200 pounds of gold; that the orator Symmachus, who was a senator of only moderate means, spent, before the fall of the city, on the celebration of his son's praetorship, 2000, and Maximus the almost incredible sum of 4000 pounds, the games lasting only seven days.

The populace were compensated for their poverty by the games in the circus or the theatre, and by the pleasures of the baths, whilst, at the same time, they were fed by the customary distributions of bread, fat, oil, and wine. Ammianus, commenting on some of the most celebrated names amongst the plebeians, such as Cimessores, Statarii, Semicupae, Serapini, Pordaca and others, remarks that they only thought of wine, dice and theatres, and that to them the Circus Maximus was at the same time temple, dwelling, curia, and the palace of all their desires. They might be seen in the squares and on the cross-ways, standing in groups, engaged in eager conversation, whilst the old swore by their grey hairs that the State must

[1] Εἷς δόμος ἄστυ πέλει πόλις ἄστεα μυρία τεύχει. Olympiodorus wrote shortly after the sack of Rome by Alaric. Photius gives an extract from his twenty-two volumes of histories, which extend from the seventh consulate of Honorius to the reign of Valentinian (p. 198, &c.).

perish if, at the coming races, this or that horse or this or that colour won. When the longed-for day appeared, eager crowds gathered at sunrise at the doors of the circus. The same frenzied excitement was shown at every spectacle, whether it was the drama, the chase, chariot race or pantomime. This rage for spectacles, born in the Romans and fostered by idleness, appears to have become an essential part of their nature, and S. Augustine even relates that after the sack of Rome, the fugitives who had escaped to Carthage daily resorted to the theatre, and there formed factions which gave rise to furious rivalry.[1]

The Christian population.

In the midst of the overthrow of Paganism, Christianity worked with a weakening effect upon the dying people. The religion of Christ made moral freedom and equality the principles of the new society, within which mankind was to form a brotherhood of love. These ideas warred against the Roman State as against a pagan and aristocratic institution; but political distinctions crept into the new society in the form of a hierarchical church, which stood in opposition to the Pagan State the foundations of which rested upon slavery. The State, with its despotism, its incurable corruption and its hopelessness, its old age, as opposed to the youthful aspiring Church, provoked men to flee from civic life and its duties. The Romans who had once displayed the highest political energy of which any people could be capable, relapsed into a condition of absolute indifference towards everything that concerned the State, and their apathy was

[1] *De Civitate Dei,* i. c. 32.

the ruin of Rome. If Stoic philosophy, once the refuge of nobler minds in the midst of the evils of Imperial rule, had summoned the citizens to the active fulfilment of their duties, Christian philosophy now drove them instead to a rejection of all that concerned the State. Men only needed to compare the practical precepts of Epictetus and of Marcus Aurelius with those of Jerome or of Paulinus of Nola in order to recognise the contrast. The ideal of life had already become that of mystic contemplation in a cloistered cell. Repelled by a world grown ineffably corrupt, the Christian threw aside the State, descended into the depths of his own personality, and cultivated the inner world of moral freedom which Roman Paganism had neglected. The remains of the civic and political spirit were thus completely submerged in monasticism, and the last gleam of Roman virtue perished in the darkness of the cowl. Noble senators sought shelter in the cloister, and the sons of consuls no longer blushed to show themselves to their companions in the habit of the monk. "In our time, Rome possesses what the world did not know before"; joyously says Jerome, "before, among the wise, mighty and noble, there were found but few Christians, now there are many wise, mighty and noble monks."[1]

The city had become penetrated throughout by spiritual influences, but we can scarcely believe that these were of a nature entirely pure; on the contrary, Christianity had degenerated with extraordinary rapidity; the soil on which the new learning had

[1] Baronius' *Annals,* on this year.

fallen having been less calculated to receive it than any other throughout the world.

From the numerous letters of Jerome, which read like a satire, and, as a companion to the record of Ammianus, should not remain unnoticed, we are able to form a picture of the manners of the period. And even Ammianus, a historian, who was by no means hostile to Christianity, had aleady censured the luxury and ambition of the Roman bishops. We find the following passage on the occasion of the bloody contest between Damasus and Ursicinus concerning the episcopal chair in Rome:—"When I consider the splendour of civic life, I can understand these men, in the desire to attain their object, striving with all the strength of their party; since, could they attain their end, they might be sure of becoming rich through the presents of matrons, of driving in lofty carriages, of dressing in splendid garments, of having such sumptuous meals that their tables surpass those of princes. And yet they might esteem themselves blessed, if despising the splendours of the city, under which they shelter their vices, they imitated the manner of life of some of the country clergy, since these by their moderation in eating and drinking, by their simplicity in dress, and by their humble bearing commend themselves to the true believer in the Eternal God, as men pure and of good repute."[1]

Jerome, formerly a private secretary of Bishop Damasus, describes from personal knowledge worldly as well as spiritual Christians, men as well as women,

[1] Ammian. Marc., xxvii. c. 3. *Sordidae vestes candidae mentis indicia sunt,* says Jerome, filled with monkish zeal (ad Rusticum, ep. 125, c. 7).

but especially such as had an influence on the manners of the time. He depicts the sanctimonious hypocrite, the cunning seekers after legacies amongst the pastors, the haughty devotee, the stupid, proud monk, and the gallant deacon who combines Christianity with Roman pride of birth.

Here is a scene that he gives us in the house of a noble lady: "The descendant of the Decii or Maximii is in the grief of early widowhood; with rouged cheeks she reclines upon a luxurious couch, the gospels bound in purple and gold in her hand.[1] Her room is filled with parasites who entertain the lady with scandal concerning worldly and spiritual things; but she is especially proud of being the patroness of priests. Clergy enter to pay the noble matron a visit, kiss her on the head, and with outstretched hand receive her gracious alms. If they pocket her bounty with, perhaps, a certain polite bashfulness, the monk, who, barefoot and in a black and dirty habit, is dismissed by the servants on the threshold, shows no such hesitation. But see, the motley eunuchs are flinging wide open the doors for the deacon who drives up in a fashionable carriage, with such fiery horses that one might suppose him to be brother to the King of Thrace! His silken garments breathe of perfumed waters, his hair is curled by the barber with the highest skill, and with jewelled fingers foppishly raising his dress, he skips into the palace, his dainty

[1] The sacred volume was customarily bound in Babylonian leather, ornamented with sumptuous inlaid work. Hieron. ad Laetam, ep. 107, n. 12: *Codices amet, in quibus non auri et pellis Babylonicae vermiculata pictura placeat.*

feet clad by the skill of the shoemaker in shoes of the softest and glossiest morocco leather. Any one seeing this man," says Jerome, "would take him rather for a bridegroom than a clergyman"; and we may add that any one seeing him to-day, might deem him one of the silk-bedizened clerical Don Juans of modern Rome. "He is known through the whole town under the nickname of 'Town Coachman,' or the street boys call after him 'Pippizo and Geranopepa.'[1] He is everywhere and nowhere to be met with; nothing happens which he is not the first to know, and there is no gossip of the town which he has not discovered or magnified. His career is in short this: He has become a priest in order to have freer access to beautiful women; his way of life is briefly as follows: He rises early, and having planned the visits of the day, sets forth on his wanderings. Where he finds anything beautiful in a house, be it a cushion, or a fine cloth, or any kind of furniture, he persistently admires it until it is presented to him, for the sharp tongue of the 'town coachman' is feared by all women."

If the matron has to celebrate any Christian ceremony, she does not do it in silence. Like her cousin Fabunius or Reburrus (and we see that, in Christian clothing, it is one and the same aristocracy as that of

[1] *Veredarius urbis...et altili geranopepa, quae vulgo pippizo nominatur.* Words belonging to the slang of the period and now unintelligible. Ep. 22, ad Eustochium, c. 28. The deacons played a conspicuous part in Rome, and administering, as they did, the ecclesiastical property, mixed largely with the world. On this account the archdeacon, next to the bishop, was the most important person in the church.

Ammianus), she has herself carried in a litter to the basilica of S. Peter, preceded by a swarm of eunuchs. There, to appear the more pious, she distributes alms to the beggars with her own hands, and as she celebrates the Agapae, or so-called feasts of love, allows the fact to be simultaneously proclaimed by a herald.

These two characters may suffice to represent their class. Of the other abuses that existed within the Church we learn from a thousand passages in the Fathers. With the order of precedence amongst the clergy, aristocratic arrogance had entered. The deteriorated nature of the Romans remained as it was. Baptism did not change the spirit of the time, and the Christian society within the city shared, with the Pagan, all the elements of culture and taste and the common requirements of life. The greater part at no time laid hold of the teaching of Christ, and if individual Romans, like Pammachius, Marcella and Paula, had fled to the self-renunciation of the cloister, there were thousands who only exchanged Mithras for Christ for the sake of worldly interest, or from fashion or curiosity. All vices flourished in the numerous company of ambitious priests, the unchastity of both sexes forming a grievous satire on the monkish vow of celibacy.

Jerome cites a scarcely credible instance of Roman marriage, which characterizes the moral condition of the time more forcibly than whole volumes would have been able to do. "For several years," he says, "while I was secretary to the Roman Bishop Damasus, I knew of an excellently matched married pair of the lower class. The man had already buried twenty wives, the wife had, however, had twenty-two husbands, and they had united themselves, as they believed, in their last marriage. The expectation of all was strained to the utmost as to which, after so many achievements, would bury the other. The man conquered, and, accompanied by the whole of Rome, wreathed and with a palm branch in his hand, stepped proudly before the bier of his oft-married wife, whilst the people shouted to him from time to time that he deserved a reward!"[1] Such public mockery of marriage is horrible, but the union of such a pair was in no wise more dangerous to morality than were the spiritual relations of the so-called Agapeti and Synisacti, under covering of which Christian women associated with their adopted sons and brothers.[2]

We have quoted only a few passages from a celebrated Father of the Church, and may now calm the sensitive reader with the assurance that to these dark pictures of Roman society there can be opposed some lighter sketches drawn from the same authorities.[3]

Before concluding this chapter, it would have been important to be able to state the population of Rome

[1] Ep. 123, c. 10, ad Ageruchium.

[2] I have pieced together several letters of S. Jerome, such, for instance, as *Ep.* 22, *ad Eustochium,* the most interesting; *Ep.* 123, *ad Ageruchium*; *Ep.* 125, *ad Rusticum*; *Ep.* 147, *ad Sabinianum* (an ecclesiastical Don Juan), &c.

[3] John Chrysostom gives a quite similar description of the manners of Greek society at the same period. Chrysostom's Homilies formed the source whence P. E. Müller derived the material for his *Commentatio Historica de Genio, Moribus et Luxi aevi Theodosiani,* Havniae, 1797.

at the period of Alaric's invasion, but we are entirely without information on this point. According to the *Notitia,* Rome numbered altogether in her fourteen regions 46,602 blocks of dwellings and 1797 palaces;[1] but owing to efflux and the ever-increasing poverty of the city as of the provinces, her population must have considerably decreased after the time of Constantine, and at the date in question it could scarcely have amounted to more than 300,000 inhabitants; indeed, even this computation is probably too high for the Rome of that period.[2]

[1] The summary of the *Curiosum Urbis* gives *Insulae per totam urbem XLVIDCII. Domos MDCCXC.* The summary of the *Notitia*: *Insulae XLVI. milia sexcentae duae, and domos mille septaingentae nonaginta VII.* Zacharias enumerates dom. 46,603, palat. 1797.

[2] Dureau de la Malle, comparing the proportions of Athens, Paris and Rome, estimates the population of the capital of the world under the Empire, up to the time of Aurelian, to have amounted, at the highest, to 576,738 souls, rejecting, as utterly fabulous, the reckonings of Vossius, Lipsius, Gibbon, &c. (*Economine politique des Romains,* Paris, 1840, i. liv. 2. c. x., &c.). According to the latest researches, on the other hand, it has been estimated that under Trajan the Roman population must have numbered about a million and a half. Wietersheim, *Völkerwand.,* i. 242; Ludwig Friedländer, *Darstellung aus der Sittengeschichte Rom's.,* i.

CHAPTER IV.

1. Alaric takes Possession of Rome, 24th August 410—Sack of the City—Triumph of the Christian Religion—Forbearance of the Goths—Alaric Withdraws in Three Days.

Capture of Rome by Alaric, Aug. 24, 410.

The Goths, as they had previously done, laid siege to the city at every gate, Alaric directing his attention to the Porta Salaria adjoining Monte Pincio, before which, apparently because of the greater weakness of the walls, he took up his headquarters. These he fixed at Antemnae on the hill above the Salarian bridge. The ancient place must, even at this time, have been in ruins, and, apparently, during the siege of the Goths it fell into yet deeper decay. We have no exact information either of the preparation for defence on the part of the Romans, or of the duration of the siege. It would appear, however, that Alaric, instead of ordering an assault, calmly awaited the effects of famine and of his secret understanding with the Arians and Pagans within the city, and the great number of slaves who had deserted to his camp must have considerably aided the fulfilment of his ends. Rome undoubtedly fell through treachery, but in the course of a century, so completely had the circumstances of Alaric's conquest faded from memory that the Greek historian Procopius relates the most improbable legend concerning it. He asserts that Alaric, feigning the intention of raising the siege, sent three hundred boys as pages to the Senate, with the request that the Fathers would keep these Gothic youths as a lasting remembrance of his respect for the august body and its fidelity to the Emperor. He further asserts that Alaric had given the youths secret orders to slay the guard at the Porta Salaria on a certain day at noon and to storm the gate, all of which instructions were duly carried out.[1] At the same time Procopius states that another version of the taking of Rome reported how the noble Faltonia Proba (widow of the celebrated Sextus Anicius Probus), seeing the sufferings of the people and the prospect of their being degraded into cannibals, in despair had given admission to the Goths. This latter fable probably arose from the fact that the rich and influential matron had carried on negotiations with Alaric, whereby she succeeded in inducing the King not only to spare the lives of the Romans, but to refrain from inflicting any injury on the churches.

The very year of the city's fall remains doubtful, the statements of historians wavering between 409 and 410, and the precise date being lost amid the confusion of the time. Chroniclers of later date, however, fix the 24th August 410 as the day of the final catastrophe, and it is best to abide by their decision.[2]

[1] Procopius, *De bello Vandal.,* 1, 2. Hence we may assume that in the time of Procopius the number of senators amounted to 300.

[2] According to Prosper and Marcellinus, the fall of Rome took

It was night when the Goths gained admission by the Porta Salaria.[1] No sooner had the foremost entered, than they threw firebrands on the houses in the neighbourhood of the gate, and the flames, quickly spreading in the narrow streets, caught the adjacent buildings of Sallust.[2] The beautiful palaces of the historian of the Jugurthine war and the conspiracy of Cataline, and that in which the Emperor Nerva had breathed his last, served as the first torches for the sack of Rome.

The heroic fall of Carthage, of Jerusalem and of

place during the period that Flavius Varanes ruled as sole consul, therefore in the year 410. The *Hist. Miscella.: captaque est Roma IX. Kal. Septemb. a MCLVIV. conditionis suae.* Theophanes, *Chronogr.*, p. 70: πρὸ θ΄ καλανδῶν Σεπτεμβρίου. Cedrenus, p. 335 D: ἔπαθε δὲ τὴν τοιαύτνην ἅλωσιν μηνὶ Αὐγούστῳ κς΄, ἰνδίκτῳ Θ΄. The ninth Indiction began on September 1, six days after the fall of the city. Clinton, *Fasti Romani,* i.; Pagi, and after him Muratori, hold it instead to have been in 409. On the other hand, Baronius, Gothofredus, Sigonius, Tillemont, Gibbon, and recent authorities (compare Köpke, *Die Anfänge des Königtums bei den Gothen,* Berlin, 1859, p. 127) are unanimously agreed in favour of the later date. To the statements of Sig. de Rossi I owe additional reasons for holding the same opinion. From his materials for the Corpus of Christian inscriptions we discover that from the time of Constantine onwards, down to 409, there were consular inscriptions for each successive year. Thus 405 supplies 18; 406, 11; 407, 9; 408, 7; 409, 6. For the year 410, none is forthcoming. Later consular inscriptions testify to the restoration of order: 411, 1; 412, 1; 413 and 414, none; 415, 1; 416, none; 417, 1 perhaps; 418, 1; 419, 3; 420, 2; 421, none; 422, 3; 423, 4; 424, 5; 425, 4; 426, 6; 427, 4; 428, 4.

[1] Hieron., Ep. 127, ad Princip., p. 953: *Nocte Moab capta est, nocte cecidit murus ejus.*

[2] *Cf.* Tacitus, *Hist.,* c. 82 the passage describing the struggle between the soldiers of Vespasian and the partisans of Vitellius: *qui in partem sinistram Urbis ad Sallustianos hortos per angusta et lubrica viarum flexerant.*

Syracuse had been fully worthy of the tradition of their great past; but the ignominious capture of Rome, under the sword of Alaric, shocks us by exhibiting the utter demoralisation of the once greatest and most heroic nation upon earth. There was no attempt at resistance—flight, murder, plunder and frightful disorder alone prevailed, forming a scene such as no eyewitness has ventured to describe.

The sack of Rome.

The barbarians burst like a tornado through every quarter of Rome, driving before them crowds of fugitives only to hew them down, then rushing with brutal fury to sack the city. In the first universal thirst for gold they seized and ransacked palaces, baths, churches, temples, quickly emptying the city as thieves a treasure house. The drunken Hun wasted no time in contemplating the works of art which Alexandrian masters had created for the refined luxury of the women of Rome, nor did he understand the use or meanings of the priceless masterpieces dating, perhaps, from Hellenic times, or the valuables which the ancestors of the now plundered Romans had, with the same covetous instinct captured of old in far away Palmyra, Assyria, or Persia. The plunderers seized these treasures, cutting down the trembling glutton Fabunius or Reburrus, or stifling the fair possessor in their brutal embrace. Many of the inhabitants had concealed their valuables during the siege, and the knowledge of the fact gave rise to various legends concerning buried treasures in Rome; but the greater number of the wealthy, under the threats of their escaped slaves, now turned into revengeful informers, were forced to surrender their possessions.[1] In scarcely any other city in the world could a richer booty have fallen into the hands of the enemy; it was, as Olympiodorus, a contemporary, says, illimitable, incredible.[2] Four years later, the Princess Placidia, when the bride of Athaulf, must have blushed when fifty Gothic youths, clad in silken garments, stood before her and smilingly presented, as a wedding gift, a hundred cups, half of which were filled with gold pieces, the other half with jewels; one and all the spoils of her native city.

Recognized sanctuaries.

Alaric had given his soldiers full leave to plunder, but had commanded them to spare the lives of the inhabitants and to respect the churches as sanctuaries, more especially the basilicas of S. Peter and S. Paul.[3] The Goths obeyed, as far as their savage longing for plunder allowed. In their search for spoil there was scarcely a house into which they did not force an entrance, and the humble dress of the terrified inhabitant seemed in their eyes merely a device for concealing secret wealth. Jerome sighed over the scourging which his pious friend Marcella had endured when the wild swarms of the enemy burst into her house on the Aventine. The first nun of noble Roman

[1] The first trace of such legends is found as early as the *Curiosum Urbis,* Region XIV, where it speaks of a *Herculem cubatem; sub quem plurimum aurum positum est.* I was present when, in 1864, the bronze Hercules, now in the Vatican, was unearthed from its grave in the Palazzo Pio, the site of the ancient theatre of Pompey. This colossal figure had evidently, in dread either of the Christians or of the barbarians, been carefully hidden underground and protected by a roof formed of stones.

[2] See Photius, p. 180.

[3] Orosius, v. c. 39.

family exhibited her humble penitential dress; under the raging blows of her tormentors she clasped their knees and simply besought them to spare the virtue of her adopted daughter Principia. The hearts of the barbarians were softened, and they led the pious women to the sanctuary of S. Paul.[1] Others, however, heathens or zealous Arians, had no scruple in breaking into the convents, and forcibly releasing the unhappy nuns from their vow of virginity. A historian significantly tells us that they only respected the sacred vessels belonging to S. Peter's, all other churches being plundered indiscriminately.[2] Bishop Innocent, then a fugitive in Ravenna, had been obliged to resign to the Prince of the Apostles the custody of his basilica, and the safety which it owed to the magnanimity of Alaric and his respect for Christianity, the bishop, from a safe distance, preferred to attribute to the miraculous interposition of the martyrs.

From a background of horrors such as we have pictured shines the more conspicuous an instance of humanity on which the historian, owing, perhaps, to

[1] Hieron. ad Principiam, Ep. 127, n. 12: *caesam fustibus flagellisque ajunt non senisse tormenta: sed hoc lacrymis, hoc pedibus eorum prostratam egisse, ne te a suo consortio separarent.* Marcella died a few days after the sack. Previously, however, there escaped from Jerome's lips the lines of Virgil :—

Quis cladem illius noctis, quis funera fando
Explicet, aut posset lacrymis aequare dolorem?
Urbs antiqua ruit, multos dominata per annos;
Plurima perque vias sparguntur inertia passim
Corpora, perque domos; et plurima mortis imago.

[2] Nicephorus, *Eccl. Hist.*, xiii. c. 35.

the strangeness of the contrast, or from motives of piety, dwells at greater length than on the description of devastated Rome. A Goth forced his way into the house of a pious maiden, who, fearless and alone, stood guarding a pile of costly vessels. As the barbarian was about to fling himself on the precious booty, he was daunted by the calm words of the maiden, who told him that he might do as he willed, that these treasures were, however, the property of the Apostle Peter, who would assuredly punish the act of sacrilege. Rather would the barbarian have plunged his hand amid burning coal; he withdrew, and, informing Alaric of the incident, received orders to convey not only the consecrated vessels, but their pious guardian, under a safe escort to S. Peter's. As the singular company advanced, bearing, with reverent hands, chalices, cups, lamps, crosses sparkling with emeralds and amethysts, it suddenly assumed the character of a procession. Christian fugitives, women holding their children by the hand, old men trembling and defenceless, terror-stricken Pagans, and, mixing peacefully among them, barbarians whose weapons and clothes dripped with blood, and on whose countenances passion struggled with the sudden reverence of faith, all mingling in one train advanced to S. Peter's; and, as through the wild tumult of the plundering host burst the solemn strains of a hymn, the procession presented a picture of contrasts which pious fathers of the Church have, not without justice, glorified as a triumphal progress of the faith.[1]

[1] Orosius, v. c. 39. Augustinus (*De Civitate Dei,* in the earlier

Rome plundered and spared.

The instance of self-control here exhibited was not an isolated one. The Goths, abhorred by the Romans as Arian heretics and as formerly-vanquished foes, gave, it is true, as the avengers of their nation, full vent to their anger against a city, the slavish and degenerate population of which they despised. Under their swords and those of the heathen Huns, the Skyrri, the Alani and the liberated slaves, thousands, both in and outside the city, were cut down; so that, according to the lamentation of S. Augustine, there were not hands sufficient to bury the dead.[1] Rome, nevertheless, sunk in utter dejection, and awaiting the wholesale destruction which had befallen Nineveh and Jerusalem, had reason to extol the forbearance of the enemy. Even among such historians as shudder over the bloodshed, some recount with joy the insignificant number of senators slain, and recall, as an alleviation of the horrors of the time, the far more terrible evils which the city had endured under the unsparing Gauls of Brennus.[2]

chapters) bestows all praise on the Goths, and rejoices in the triumph of Christianity. The incident is also mentioned by Cassiodorus, *Variar.,* lib. xii. ep. 20. Baronius defends the weak and bigoted Honorius against responsibility for the fall of the city, and takes the opportunity of inveighing against the long-buried idolaters.

[1] Procopius, *De Bello Vandal.,* i. 2: Ῥωμαίων τοὺς πλείστους διαφθείραντες, somewhat exaggerated. Isidorus, *Chronic. Gothor.: sicque Roma irruptione atque impetu magnae cladis eversa est.* Philostogius, *Hist. Eccl.,* xii. c. 3, speaks of fire, sword and captivity. Also Hieron. ad Principiam; Augustinus, *De Civitate Dei,* i. c. 3, 12, 13.

[2] Augustinus, *De Civ. Dei,* iii. c. 19; Orosius, ii. c. 19. The Spaniard, writing his history by the advice of Augustine, alludes to the *de Civitate Dei,* and follows the aim of that work. Socrates alone,

The shortness of the period granted by Alaric to satisfy the rapacity of his army also contributed to mitigate the distress; the plunderers spending the allotted period exclusively in collecting spoils. The King, who had previously spared Athens, may have been impelled to expedition by motives of respect for the greatness and sanctity of Rome, and if the majesty of the city had once so deeply impressed the mind of the Persian Hormisdas, how much more powerfully must it have worked on the soul of a hero! At the sight of the capital of the world, with all its majestic columns surmounted by the heroic figures of the past, lying violated at his feet, Alaric must have turned in thought to the great Stilicho, by whom he had been driven out of Greece, been twice defeated in Italy, and during whose lifetime he never could have hoped to enter Rome. Some such feeling, or some political motive, such as the fear of staining his reputation through acts of barbarism, must have been the cause that induced the conqueror to order the withdrawal of the Goths at the end of three days. Alaric left for Campania accompanied by a long procession of waggons, laden with spoils of inestimable value, and a great number of prisoners, amongst them Placidia, the sister of Honorius.[1]

Hist. Eccl. vii. c. 10, speaks of senators having been tortured and put to death "in large numbers," and the *Historia Miscella,* on his authority, reiterates the statement.

[1] Isidorus, *Chron. Gothor.: post tertium diem quo Romam ingressi sunt, nullo hoste cogente, sponte discedunt.* Orosius, ii. c. 19, and vii. c. 39; *Histor. Misc.,* Marcellinus alone, *Chron. apud Sirmond.,* ii. p. 356, speaks of six days: *Alaricus trepidam urbem Romam invasit—sextoque die quam ingressus fuerat depraedata urbe egressus est.* With

2. FORBEARANCE OF THE GOTHS TOWARDS THE MONUMENTS— VIEWS OF AUTHORS ON THIS QUESTION.

Proofs that the Goths did not destroy Rome.

After the Goths had thus voluntarily left the city the Romans had leisure to contemplate their misery undisturbed. The appalling event, the result of a combination of circumstances unparalleled in the annals of history, neither left behind it any military occupation by the conqueror, nor any political change. Since, however, no enemy remained within the walls, and yet everything bore the traces of the ruthless foe, it seemed as if some frightful natural disaster had laid waste the city We may easily imagine the dreadful aspect which it presented after the withdrawal of the Goths, although no historian had the power to depict it, nor have any particulars of the destruction survived. But since the history of the monuments forms a part of our subject, the question as to the nature and extent of the injury now inflicted is important; for although the ruin of the public buildings had already set in under Constantine, the sack of Alaric is usually regarded as inaugurating the period of decay.

Rome, which Honorius and the Romans had so shamefully abandoned, strove to avenge herself by holding up the Goths to the national hatred of the

regard to the Romans led away captive by Alaric, I quote the epitaph on the deacon and physician Dionysius (see Gruter, 1173, n. 3) :—

Hic Levita jacet Dionysius artis honestae
Functus et officio quod medicina dedit...
Postquam romana captus discessit ab urbe
Mox sibi jam Dñs subdidit arte getas.

Italians as destroyers of the most beautiful monuments of antiquity, thereby attaching an everlasting stigma to their name. But investigation, and that, too, on the part of Italians themselves, has reduced these calumnies to silence; and if still occasionally heard, they are nor received as evidences of gross ignorance. The historian may spare himself the trouble of demonstrating the absurdity of representing Goths, Vandals, or any other German race, as endowed with a peculiar spite against temples and statues, or as, during their short sojourn in Rome, not engaged in plunder, but wandering about, hammer in hand breaking statues to pieces, or climbing over theatres with levers to try their strength in the useless work of dividing the gigantic blocks of stone.

The Goths refrained from all mischief in Rome save that inseparably connected with pillage; they injured the buildings of the city so far as the abstraction of what is portable entails injury; what was immovable they spared. Breaking into temples, baths and palaces, they ruthlessly snatched at everything of beauty and value, and under the impulse of wantonness, many beautiful statues were destroyed in the squares. Fire must also have caused a certain amount of devastation, and we have already remarked that, at the very beginning of the sack, the palace of Sallust perished by fire. Its smoke-blackened ruins, a fragment of which still remains, bore witness to those ravages of the Visigoths of which the historian Procopius wrote a hundred and forty years later.[1]

[1] Procopius, *De bello Vanda.*, i. 2: ἐν αἷς ἦν καὶ ἡ Σαλουστίου—ἧς δὴ τὰ πλεῖστα ἡμίκαυτα καὶ ἐς ἐμὲ ἕστηκε.

This, however, is the only celebrated building known to have perished in the capture of the city, and the rhetorical exaggeration of such writers as speak of the destruction of the city by fire can be disproved by the accounts of others. The Byzantine Socrates says that the greater part of the most admirable works in Rome were destroyed by fire under the Goths; Philostorgius relates that Alaric withdrew to Campania and left the city, the splendours of which had already been destroyed by fire and sword under its barbarian captors. Jerome exclaims, "Woe! the world perishes and our sins remain. The illustrious city, the capital of the Roman empire, is destroyed by a single fire!" and Augustine frequently speaks in his works of the burning of Rome.[1] In spite, therefore, of the assertion of the historian Jordanes, who says that "by Alaric's command the Goths were restricted to pillage and did not, as barbarians are accustomed to do, set fire to anything," it must be assumed that Rome had, in some places, been injured by fire.[2]

[1] Socrates, *Hist. Eccl.*, vii. c. 10: τὰ μὲν πολλὰ τῶν θαυμαστῶν ἐκείνων θεαμάτων κατέκαυσαν. The *Histor. Miscella.* and Cassiodorus, *Hist. Eccl.*, tripart. ii. c. 9 (t. i. 368 Opera), repeat the statement. Philostorgius, *Hist. Eccl.*, xii. c. 3: ἐν ἐρειπίοις δὲ τῆς πόλεως κειμένης. S. Hieron, Ep. xviii. ad Gaudent., p. 949 (Verona edition): *Urbs inclyta, et Romani imperii caput, uno hausta est incendio.* The letter belongs to the year 413.

[2] Jordanes, *De reb. Get.*, c. 30. *Alarico jubente spoliant tantum: non autem, ut solent gentes, ignem supponunt.* The passage in Marcellinus *Sirmond.*, t. ii. p. 356, is a correct and precise expression: *Alaricus trepidam urbem Romam invasit, partemque ejus cremavit incendio.* The opinion of Baptista Ignatius, expressed at the end of Zosimus; *intromissus Gothus majori ignominia quam damno urbem omnem depopulatur,* is still milder.

Orosius, a contemporary, relates how, in his anger God had worked more havoc in Rome than man could have done, since it would have been beyond human power to ignite the beams of brass and to overthrow the huge masses of stone, but a flash of lightning had overturned the images of the false gods in the Forum, and fire sent from heaven had destroyed all these abominations of superstition which the fires of the enemy had left unharmed.[1] This account is deserving of notice, not only because it seems to prove that fire had worked a certain amount of damage, but also because it immediately brings before us the tradition of the Christians, who, according to the prophecy of the Sibyls, expected the destruction of Rome through fire. When they now heard of the taking of the city, they believed that the prophecy had been fulfilled, and that Rome, like Sodom, had perished in flames. Orosius, who candidly praises the forbearance of the Goths, and is forced to acknowledge that they had withdrawn voluntarily three days after their entrance, admits that fire had certainly caused some damage to houses, yet not so much as had been inflicted by accident in the seven hundredth year of the city's foundation. He asserts, moreover, that the Romans had acknowledged they would care little for the misfortunes they had suffered in the sack were only the Circensian games restored.[2]

[1] Orosius, *Hist.,* ii. c. 19, p. 143. Garzetti again (*Storia d'Italia sotto il governo degli imperatori Romani,* Capolago, 1843, vol. ii. c. 8) exaggerates the fire, saying: *Roma si potè dire arsa d'un solo incendio e seppellita nelle sue ceneri.*

[2] *Facto quidem aliquantarum aedium incendio, sed ne tanto quidem,* &c. Last book of Orosius, c. 39. The *Liber Pontificalis,* in the Vita

All this testimony of contemporaries has given rise to the belief that the later accounts of the devastation of Rome by the Visigoths are exaggerated. That destruction did take place is undeniable, but taking into consideration the length of their stay, the immense size of Rome, and the vast number of buildings, the ruin inflicted must have been inconsiderable.[1] The monuments were surrounded three days by the rapacious enemy, but were left untouched. The barbarian looked with passing astonishment at the obelisks of Egypt and the triumphal arches of Emperors without having time to conceive the absurd thought of their destruction. When they found statues of gold or silver they broke them up or carried them away, but the gigantic equestrian statues of gilt bronze, as well as those of marble, had no attraction for them, and the sacrilege of robbing the city of its works of art in bronze was reserved for a Byzantine Emperor in the seventh century, when Rome was already completely impoverished, and when her wealth lay solely in the decoration of her churches. Only two years after the conquest of

Caelestini (422–432) records of this Pope: *Hic dedicavit basilicam Juli* (S. Maria in Trastevere) *in qua optulit post ignem Geticum patenam,* &c.

[1] In 1656 Petrus Barga wrote the treatise: *De Privatorum publicorumque aedificiorum urbis Romae evasoribus,* in which he attempts to refute the accusations heaped on the barbarians. With regard to art, however, he is in general more barbarous than the Vandals themselves. Tiraboschi, *Storia della Lett.,* t. iii., is a no less zealous defender of the guiltlessness of the barbarians, and Fea a more able advocate than either. *"Può ben provarsi,"* says he, *"che non s'abbiano portata quella devastazione, che crede il volgo"* (p. 268).

Alaric, the plundered city was visited by a historian and a poet, and so little did she resemble a ruin (whatever S. Jerome may assert as to destruction by fire) that both extol her beauty and splendour. Olympiodorus at this time conceived that picture of her yet unimpaired baths and palaces which is already known to us, and the prefect Rutilius Namatianus, in his farewell poem, instead of speaking of the devastated aspect of the city, turns back from his boat on the Tiber, and dedicates a last longing look to "the most beautiful Queen of the World, whose temples approach the skies."[1]

3. LAMENTATIONS OVER THE FALL OF ROME—S. JEROME —S. AUGUSTINE—CONSEQUENCES OF THE CAPTURE OF THE CITY.

Lamentation over the fall of Rome.

There was one universal cry of horror and anguish when, through a thousand exaggerated voices, the civilised world heard of the fall of Rome. The provinces of the Empire, accustomed through long centuries to regard Rome as the Acropolis of culture, the historic symbol of the existence of all civic law, and even of the world itself, saw this sanctuary suddenly violated and destroyed, and while the belief in the continuance of civilisation was completely shaken, the

[1] Rutilii Claudii Namatiani *de reditu suo,* libri ii., ed. Lucian Müller, Leipzig, 1870. The poet had resigned the prefecture of the city (417) and was about to return to his home in Gaul:—

Exaudi, regina tui pulcherrima mundi,
Inter sidereos Roma recepta polos,
Exaudi, genitrix hominum, genitrixque deorurn,
Non procul a coelo per tua templa sumus.

ruin of the world, as foretold by prophets and sibyls, seemed to have begun.

S. Jerome.

The fall of Rome startled even Jerome in his lonely meditations on the prophets of Israel in distant Bethlehem, and in his grief he writes to Eustochium, "I had finished the explanation of the eighteen books of Isaiah and was about to go on to Ezekiel, which I had promised thee and thy holy mother Paula, and I wished (so to speak) to lay the last touch on the prophets, when I suddenly learnt the death of Pammachius and Marcella, the capture of Rome, and the death of so many brothers and sisters; I then lost recollection and voice, becoming so engrossed day and night with this single thought, how should all this misery be remedied, that I believed myself imprisoned with the saints in their captivity. When, however, I found that the clearest light of the universe was extinguished, that the head of the Roman Empire was separated from the body, or, the better to express it, since with one city the whole world had perished, I became dumb and dejected and had no further power for good, my grief was renewed, my heart was hot within me, and in my thoughts there burnt as it were a fire."[1]

Further he says, "Who could believe that Rome, which was built of the spoils of the whole earth, would fall, that the city could, at the same time, be the cradle and grave of her people, that all the coasts of Asia, Egypt and Africa should be filled with the slaves and maidens of Rome? that holy Bethlehem should

[1] Hieron., t. v., *Op. ad Eustochium,* as the introduction to his Commentary on Ezekiel.

daily receive as beggars, men and women who formerly were conspicuous for their wealth and luxury?"

The sympathetic lament for the fate of ancient Rome, and his outcry, "My voice is choked and my sobs interrupt the words which I write; the city is subdued which subdued the world," fill the reader of to-day with sadness for the nothingness of all earthly grandeur.[1] But the voices of the Romans themselves are silent; and it is therefore doubly touching to hear the lament from the mouth of an aged Father of the Church, a hermit in Bethlehem, addressing his sighs to a weak maiden, a nun, and associating with the fate of the great and illustrious city the Biblical traditions of Moab, Sodom and Nineveh. We are here reminded of the foreboding of the celebrated Scipio, who wept for the future fall of Rome amidst the ruins of Carthage; and whose prophecy had now received a terrible fulfilment. Instead of a despairing hero, however, legend shows us the pitiful spectacle of the Emperor, who, surrounded by eunuchs and shut up amidst the marshes of Ravenna, mistook the loss of his capital for that of a favourite hen, to which he had given the name of the capital of the universe.[2]

Jerome, in the passion of his grief, shows to advan-

[1] *Haeret vox et singultus intercipiunt verba dictantis. Capitur Urbs quae totum cepit orbem*—Ep. 127, ad Princip., i. 953. In his flights of enthusiasm he mingles quotations from Isaiah with Virgil's description of the fall of Troy. Ep. 130, ad Demetriadem, p. 973, &c.: *Urbs tua, quondam orbis caput, Romani populi sepulchrum est;* and p. 974 he speaks rhetorically of *Romanae urbis cineres.* Prosper Tiro, a contemporary, says: *Roma, orbis quondam victrix, a Gothis Halarico duce, capta* (in *Canis,* i).

[2] Procopius, *De bello Vand.,* i. 2.

tage beside his contemporary Augustine. If the laments of the former express the consciousness of the ancient political greatness of Rome, the heart of the African Augustine is touched by no such considerations. The greatest genius among the theologians of the Roman Church was only intoxicated with enthusiasm at the victory of Christianity; but we have no right to blame a character such as his because he regarded the fall of Rome with equanimity. He considered the Empire of the Romans, with all its imperious majesty, its laws, literature and philosophy, only as the accursed work of devils. He saw in Rome only Babylon, the stronghold of Paganism, and bewailed in its ruin, only the external disorder in which it involved the Church, the flight and death of so many Christian brethren. He wrote a consolatory treatise in which he cries, "Why did not God spare the city? Were there not fifty righteous amongst so many faithful? fifty virtuous monks amongst so many servants of God?" While drawing a parallel with Sodom, he rejoices in recognising that God, who had entirely annihilated one city, only chastised the other, since from Sodom none were saved, whilst many escaped from Rome eventually to return there again, and many remained to find an asylum in the churches. He even consoles the abject descendants of the Scipios with the far greater sorrows of Job, representing to them that all pain is only temporary, and seeks to alleviate their misfortune by dwelling on the sufferings of the damned in Gehenna.[1] His treatise *Of the Fall of*

S. Augustine.

[1] *De urbis excidio,* Opera v. pp. 622-628, Venice, 1731.

the City, and his celebrated work, *The City of God,* were written as the defence of Christendom against the constantly repeated reproaches of the exasperated Pagan, who, unjustly laying the blame of the inevitable catastrophe on Christianity, found only too much justification in the passionate declarations of the bishops, which were full of malicious triumph over the approaching ruin of the city. The priests so little dissembled their hatred against this "Sodom and Babylon," that Orosius allows himself to be carried away by regret that Rome was not taken by the barbarians under Radagaisus. With the overthrow of the ancient gods, with the fall of the Victoria and the Virtus, asserted these Pagans, Roman virtue had disappeared, and the cross of Christ had allied itself with the sword of the barbarian to overthrow the city and Empire. To disarm accusations such as these Augustine framed those writings in which the fall of Rome offers a welcome text for an emphatic sermon or reprimand, and for high moral reflections on the divine government of the human race. He tells the Pagans that among those who shamelessly accuse the servants of Christ, many were to be found who would not have escaped death had they not disguised themselves as Christians. For such forbearance as Rome experienced came to her through the grace of Christ, and whatever outrages of any kind were committed during the sack, were only the usual consequences of war.[1]

[1] S. Augustine, *De Civit. Dei,* i. c. 7, and *Sermo* 107 *de verb Ev. Luc.,* 10 n. 13, 11 n. 12.

The Romans reduced to utter ruin.

The fate of the Romans was hard and grievous. The political nimbus which glorified the Eternal City had forever disappeared. After having suffered a first fall, she was bound, according to the laws of nature, to sink ever deeper, and the philosopher of those days was able to foresee the total darkness of the coming centuries, when Rome, seated amidst her own decay, was no more than a name of the past, a mysterious abode of the dead, in which, amid the overthrown statues of Caesars, stood, instead of the Imperial throne, the chair of the bishop. The aristocracy, associated with the ancient institutions of public life, the hereditary support of the city and State, had been uprooted and dispersed over the provinces of the Empire. Suddenly reduced from the possession of vast wealth to absolute beggary, the descendants of ancient and noble houses were to be found in the most distant parts of the Empire, startling the inhabitants by the piteous sight of their hopeless misery.

"There is no place," says Jerome, "which does not shelter Roman fugitives." Many wandered over the sea, seeking refuge in the distant East, many set sail for Africa, where they had family property, and where the governor, Count Heraclian, the hangman of Stilicho, received noble maidens belonging to ancient senatorial families, in order to dispose of them to Syrian slave dealers. Happier than these were the fugitives who had escaped to the loneliness of the islands of the Tyrrhene Sea, Corsica, Sardinia, or even little Igilium (the island rock now known as Giglio), on which Rutilius Namatianus, in passing, bestowed a grateful greeting, because it had so hospitably sheltered such Romans as had fled to it for refuge "So near Rome, yet so far from the Goths."[1]

[1] *Unum, mira fides, vario discrimine portum*
Tam prope Romanis, tam procul esse Getis.
—v. 335.

CHAPTER V.

1. Death of Alaric in 410—Athaulf becomes King of the Visigoths—He leaves Italy— Count Heraclian's Enterprise against Rome— Honorius comes to Rome in 417—Restoration of the City—Departure of Rutilius.

As long as the Visigoths remained in Italy, the depopulated city stood in dread of their return and of a renewed sack, and in its alarm found neither quiet nor energy to repair the damage it had suffered. Alaric, meanwhile, died in the autumn of 410, branded with the stigma of having laid waste beautiful Greece, but at the same time covered with the imperishable glory of having, at the close of his destructive career, conquered and spared mighty Rome. He was buried by his warriors in the river Busento, and his brother-in-law Athaulf elected King in his stead. Alaric, perhaps, had not been endowed with the capacity of rising above the level of an errant barbarian leader; the calculating and equally bold Athaulf, however, seemed in every way fitted for the task of founding a Gothic Kingdom in Italy. He undoubtedly cherished the scheme, but was unable

Death of Alaric, 410.

to carry it into execution, almost a century of tumult and convulsion being required to elapse before the Germans, gradually awaking to ideas of political life, advanced from the position of rapacious allies in the service of the Roman Empire to become the actual rulers of Italy.

We do not know with certainty how long the Visigoths remained in the southern provinces. More fortunate than the soldiers of Pyrrhus or Hannibal, they revelled undisturbed in the Elysian fields of Campania from the fertile banks of the Liris as far as Reggio. No blast of an enemy's trumpet startled them from their encampments; and not the celebrated enchanted statue which stood there, but a storm alone, prevented their further advance into Sicily.

Retreat of the Goths under Athaulf.

Finally Athaulf himself gave the call to arms. A peace with the Empire was concluded; and after prolonged negotiation with Honorius, the Gothic King declared himself ready to leave Italy, and withdraw beyond the Alps to Gaul; there, under the pay of the Empire, to fight against the usurper Jovinus. The pledge of peace was the Princess Placidia, the most precious of the spoils of Rome, at first a prisoner of Alaric in South Italy, and now the betrothed of the bold barbarian King. The marriage seems to symbolise the union of Germany with Rome, the union, that is to say, of the German race and character with those of the Roman; an alliance out of which, in the slow progress of centuries, rose and developed the Italian nation.

The pride of Honorius must indeed have fallen low

when he could give his own noble sister as bride to a barbarian and the devastator of Rome, but Athaulf, entering the service of the Emperor, renounced the ambitious purpose which he had cherished of making himself Caesar. A historian of the time credited the manly King with the following avowal, which forcibly characterises the attitude of the barbarians, as yet unqualified for political life, towards the Empire. "I was," says Athaulf, "first eager to extinguish the name of the Romans, and to make the entire Roman Empire a Gothic Empire, so that what had hitherto been Roman should be Gothic, and Athaulf should be what Caesar Augustus had been. But since experience has taught me that neither the Goths in their unbridled barbarism can obey laws, nor a State subsist without laws, since I was incapable of transforming the Roman Empire, I preferred the glory of re-establishing it through Gothic valour, and of becoming known to posterity as the restorer of the State. On this account I avoid war and strive for peace." In this remarkable sentence appears for the first time above the ruins of the Roman world the idea of a German Empire, such as later times were to see realised.[1] When Athaulf in 411 or 412 led his followers out of Italy, although the passage of the Goths may have again filled Rome with dread, the city remained unharmed owing to the alliance with Honorius.[2]

[1] Orosius, vii. 43. See also R. Köpke, *Die Anfänge des Königthums bei den Gothen,* p. 130, and Bryce, *The Holy Roman Empire,* London, 1866, p. 21.

[2] The statement of Jordanes, *De reb. Geticis,* c. 31: *Qui suscepto*

Rome was threatened with yet another disaster which, however, was averted. In 413, during the universal confusion and powerlessness of the Empire, Count Heraclian, who had been appointed Consul in Africa, revolted, and after having detained the fleet, laden with grain intended for the provision of the city, came himself, with a number of vessels, to the entrance of the Tiber, hoping to overpower Rome, which he believed to be defenceless and without a master. But Marinus, the captain of the Imperial troops, of whom we shall again hear, completely overthrew the usurper on the coast, and Heraclian was forced to return a fugitive to Africa, where he was beheaded.[1]

Gradual return for the dispersed Romans.

The anxiety felt by the court of Ravenna for the tranquillisation of Italy was lessened by the withdrawal of the Goths. The unhappy fugitives returned, though in fewer numbers, from every province. Olympiodorus says that in one day 14,000 arrived in Rome, and that Albinus, prefect of the city in 414, informed the Emperor that the population of Rome had already increased to such an extent that the fixed allowance of corn no longer sufficed.[2] The first panic caused by the fall of the illustrious

regno revertens iterum ad Romam, si quid primum remanserat, more locustarum erasit, is isolated and unworthy of credit.

[1] Orosius, vii. c. 42, recounts with some exaggeration the history of Heraclian's landing and defeat. See also the *Chronicle* of Idatius in Sirmondi, and Marcellinus Comes. Statues were erected on the Arch of Severus in honour of the Emperors Arcadius and Honorius: *Imp. Invict. felicq. dd. nn. Arcadio et Honorio fratrib. S. P. Q. R. vindicata rebellione et Africae restitutione laetus,* Corp. I. L., vi. 1187. They refer, however, to the rebellion of Gildo, A.D. 398.

[2] Olympiodorus in Photius, p. 187.

city was forgotten in dull apathy, yet the belief in the eternal continuance of the Empire remained undisturbed. To the prophecy of Virgil, *"Imperium sine fine dedi,"* was associated the sentence of Daniel in his exposition of Nebuchadnezzar's dream, "And the God of Heaven shall set up a kingdom which shall never be destroyed; and the kingdom shall not be left to other people, but it shall break in pieces and consume all these kingdoms, and it shall stand for ever."[1] Far into the Middle Ages this belief in the eternity of the Empire endured, and even when the ecclesiastical historian thought of Roman dominion as approaching its end, he associated with it the end of the world.

Honorius returns to Rome, A.D. 417.

Honorius did not come to Rome until 417. Never was the entrance of an Emperor more sad or humiliating. Before his carriage, it is true, Attalus walked in chains, but the shame which covered him was reflected back on the Emperor.[2] The Romans themselves, oppressed with the consciousness of their humiliation, received their ruler with slavish acclamations and with mute reproaches. Honorius was no longer able to obtain any reflected glory from the laurels of Stilicho, or to borrow from the muse of Claudian the conqueror's praise. He encouraged the Romans, however, to restore their ruined city, and, if we may believe the testimony of some authors, Rome before long recovered so completely from the Gothic pillage that she stood "more splendid than ever." The

[1] Daniel, ii. 44.

[2] Prosperi, *Aquit. Chron.: Honorius triumphans Romam ingreditur, praeeunte currum ejus Attalo, quem Lyparae vivere exulem jussit.*

insincere verdict of flatterers accordingly bestowed on the wretched Emperor the glorious title of restorer.[1] That Rome, a few years after the Gothic conquest, did certainly still appear magnificent, is shown by Olympiodorus, and also Rutilius, who, returning to Gaul in 417, seeks to comfort her in the inspired verses in which he calls upon the city again to lift up her honoured head, to deck herself with laurels and her towered diadem, and to seize again her radiant shield. "The amnesty," he exclaims, "may cause the terrible sufferings of the sack to be forgotten, and the heavenward glance appease the pain, for even the stars set to rise again. In spite of his victory on the Allia, Brennus had suffered the chastisement due to his presumption. The Samnites had been punished by slavery; even the conquests of Pyrrhus and Hannibal eventually ended in their flight and overthrow. Rome would therefore rise again as the

[1] See the *Descriptio urbis Romae: quae aliquando desolata nunc gloriosior piissimo Imperatore restaurata,* in Labbé and Panciroli. Philostorgius, xii. nr. 5: Μετὰταῦτα καὶ ἡ Ῥώμη τῶν πολλῶν κακῶν ἀνασχοῦσα συνοικίζεται καὶ ὁ βασιλεὺς αὐτῇ παραγεγονὼς χειρὶ καὶ γλώττῃ τὸν συνοικισμὸν ἐπεκρότει. Nicephorus, *Eccl. Hist.*, xiii c. 35; Orosius, vii. c. 40: *irruptio urbis per Alaricum facta est: cujus rei quamvis recens memoria sit, tum si quis ipsius populi Romani et multitudinem videat, et vocem audiat, nihil factum, sicut etiam ipsi fatentur, arbitrabitur, nisi aliquantis adhuc existentibus ex incendio ruinis forte docentur.* A very significant passage. Among other restorations effected by Honorius was that of the Theatre of Pompey: *Corp. Inscr., Lat.* vi. n. 1191: n. 1193, he is called *Romani Orbis Libertatisque Custos.* (Inscription dedicated to him by the prefect of the city, Aurel. Anicius Symmachus, who filled the office of *praef. urbi* between from 418 to 420. Nr. 1195 records that the Roman people had placed a statue of gold and silver delicated to the Emperor Honorius in the Rostra, *pro singulari ejus circa se amore et providentia.*

lawgiver of the ages; she alone need not fear the web of the Fates; to her all countries would again pay tribute, her harbours would once more be filled by the spoils of the barbarian; for her the Rhineland would ever be tilled, and the Nile overflow; Africa would provide her with abundant harvests, and even the Tiber, crowned as a conqueror with bulrushes, would bear Roman fleets upon his waves."

Such are the blessings invoked upon the city by the Pagan poet, whilst with tears he bids her farewell[1]—but his words did not prove prophetic. The city of the Caesars, happily for the western nations, never again raised her wreath of laurel from the dust where it had fallen. But from out the ashes of antiquity she arose again, through the long and terrible struggles of a second birth, to rule the moral universe for centuries by the crucifix, after having previously governed half the earth by the sword.[2]

[1] Rutilius, v. 115–165. He closes this moving apostrophe with the touching lines:—

Hic dictis iter arripimus, comitantur amici,
Non possum sicca dicere luce: vale!

[2] *Sedes Roma Petri; quae pastoralis honoris*
Facta caput mundo, quidquid non possidet armis,
Relligione tenet.

Lines written by Prosper of Aquitaine, *Bibl. Max.,* viii. 106. Beugnot, ii. 115, note.

2. GROWTH OF THE ROMAN CHURCH—SCHISM ON ACCOUNT OF THE EPISCOPAL ELECTION—BONIFACE POPE—DEATH OF HONORIUS, 423—VALENTINIAN III. EMPEROR UNDER THE GUARDIANSHIP OF PLACIDIA—THE VANDALS CONQUER AFRICA—SIXTUS III. POPE, 432—REBUILDS BASILICA OF S. MARIA MAGGIORE—ITS MOSAICS AND CONSECRATED GIFTS—SPLENDOUR OF THE SACRED VESSELS.

Rise of the Roman Church.

While the political and civil institutions of antiquity fell to decay, and through the ever-increasing pressure of the Germans, the Empire lost one province after another, and threatened itself to disappear, one institution alone remained unshaken, one which the very barbarians, although perhaps not until later times, regarded not only as their protector, but as their instrument in the work of acquiring dominion over Rome and many beautiful provinces of Italy. In the midst of the changes of nearly four centuries under the rule of the Caesars a hierarchy of elected priests had occupied the episcopal chair of Rome, almost as old as the Empire itself, and from the time of Peter, the legendary founder, until the entrance of the Goths, five-and-forty bishops had succeeded one another. These Roman priests, whose actions are hidden in the obscurity of legend until late in the fourth century, lived and worked unostentatiously under the shadow of the Empire, and even until the time of Leo I. in the fifth century the chair of Peter had not been occupied by a single bishop of historic importance. The development of the Church went on surely and silently, side by side with the fate of Rome and of the Empire. At first nothing more than a secret society of believers, heroic martyrs had won for her the right of independent existence; then, rising out of her subject position, she attacked Paganism, and triumphed not only over the gods of the ancient religion, but also over the heretic teachings of the Hellenised East. In the time of Imperial despotism, the Church had collected in herself the higher spiritual elements, and had upheld freedom in the sphere of moral life after it had perished in the political world. Her vigorous stand against the despotism of the Caesars was salutary and honourable, but the spiritual institution gradually became corrupted by its unavoidable contact with the material world and by the impulses of avarice and love of power innate in all men. If we deplore the materialisation of the idea of Christianity, we must not at the same time forget that in this world all principles tend to be presented in a material form, which they can only find in the matter afforded by the time in which they exist. The religion of Jesus, embodied in the Church, sought some secular form which was indispensible to its existence amidst the incoming tide of barbarism.

Great wealth of every kind, consisting of voluntary donations, especially in landed property, which was called "patrimony," streamed into the coffers of the Church.[1] The treasures of Pagan temples passed in

[1] The word "patrimony," as applied to the property of the Roman Church, is found for the first time in a letter of Pelagius I., in the sixth century. G. Tomassetti, "Della Campagna Romana," *Archiv. della Società Roman.* vol. ii. 10 (1879).

great part over to her and laid the foundation of her temporal estates. The piety of rich Romans, of women more especially, further increased her wealth; other property was acquired by purchase.[1] The State, even as early as the time of Constantine, recognised the numerous clergy as a privileged caste, exempted it from taxation, transferred the order of precedence of the Imperial hierarchy to the priesthood, who took into their hands the ecclesiastical management of the dioceses and provinces. The followers of Peter were at pains to win for the episcopal chair on which they sat in the Lateran the pre-eminence due to its Apostolic origin, and supremacy for their church over all other churches in Christendom. The fact that theirs was the only church in the West of Apostolic foundation stood the Bishop of Rome in good stead, and on this account pre-eminence was early claimed for, and accorded to it.[2] The Bishop of Rome, the greatest landowner in the Empire, yet without political position, and restricted to ecclesiastical administration, began, even in the fifth century, to exercise a great influence in the city itself, not of a spiritual and moral nature alone, but in innumerable practical ways bearing on the whole tenor of civic life. The removal of the Emperor from Rome enhanced the respect already inspired by faith for the person of the chief priest,

[1] Constantine permitted the bequest of whatever portion of his property the testator willed to the Church, and as early as the fourth century the clergy had succeeded in appropriating a tenth part of all real property throughout the provinces.

[2] Passages of Tertullian and Irenaeus, quoted by Gieseler, *Kirchengesch.*, i. 135, &c.

and the ever-increasing distress soon caused him to appear as the only protector and father of the city. And Rome, politically ruled by a prefect and senate, spiritually directed by a bishop, almost severed from the life of the Empire, the centre of which she had ceased to be, sank by degrees into the position of an isolated municipality, the influence of which was only manifested in the peculiar respect accorded to its bishop. After the Gothic conquest, political matters gradually faded from the range of popular sympathy, to give place to interests of an entirely ecclesiastical nature.

Quarrel concerning the Episcopal Election.

Soon after the year 417 the interest of the city was centred in the contest against the Pelagians, the spirited defenders of the Freedom of the Will against the fatalistic dogma of Augustinian predestination and an all-saving Church, a struggle with which was associated a violent electoral contest for the episcopal chair. The Greek Zosimus, successor to Innocent I., had died in December 418,[1] and while a faction of the clergy and people forcibly elected the archdeacon Eulalius, the majority raised the presbyter Boniface to the Papal chair. The people were in favour of Boniface; the Pagan prefect, Aurelius Anicius Symmachus, however, upholding Eulalius sent letters to Honorius at Ravenna, in which he expressed himself as opposed to Boniface, and the Emperor—in whose hands lay the nomination of the bishops—commanded the election of the prefect's candidate. A schism (the third of the kind

[1] The precise date is uncertain: P. Jaffé, *Reg. Pont. Romanor.,* Edit. 2, p. 51.

in the Roman Church) thus divided the populace, and was accompanied by the same bloody atrocities as had been witnessed in the time of Damasus and Ursicinus. Eulalius had taken possession of the Lateran; Boniface retired to S. Paul's. The prefect sending a tribune to summon the latter to his presence, the people rose in indignation and maltreated the messenger. Symmachus immediately caused the commands of the Emperor to be made public, and, in order to prevent the return of Boniface, had the gates of the city closed. But the party of the excluded candidate hastened to Ravenna, represented to the Emperor that Eulalius had been un-canonically elected, Boniface nominated bishop with all due ceremony by the majority; and Honorius finally declared himself willing to lay the schism before a council. The contending parties appeared at his command first in Ravenna; then before a synod at Spoleto; and until the matter was decided, both candidates were forbidden to return to Rome. Boniface obeyed, taking up his abode in the Coemeterium of Felicitas on the Via Salaria;[1] Eulalius, however, who had been living at Antium at the church of S. Hermes, forced his way into the city to baptise, and to celebrate mass at the Lateran on the occasion

[1] We must not, however, assume that the catacombs still served as a place of refuge. The exclusive use of subterranean burial ceased with the fifth century. Tombs were then also constructed on the surface of the ground, and oratories, and even convents, all called Coemeterium, built over the ancient crypts. De Rossi, "Il Cemetero di Massimo nella via Salaria nuova," *Bullettino*, June 1863, Nr. 6. A monastery *in Catacumbas* erected by Sixtus III. is mentioned in the life of the Pope given by the *Lib. Pont.*

of the Easter festival; his opponent, meanwhile, being satisfied to perform the sacred functions in the basilica of S. Agnes outside the gate. In consequence of this act of audacity, Eulalius was renounced by the Emperor and banished from the city to Campania, while Boniface was legally recognised and succeeded to the chair of Peter in 418.[1] After political life had passed away from the Roman people the choice of their bishop, as being their only independent action, became an event of the greatest importance.

Boniface I., 418–422.

Soon after they were called to deal with a matter of weightier moment, a right formerly exercised by the senate and people, namely, the nomination to the Imperial throne. On August 15, 423, the Emperor Honorius, after a long and inglorious reign, rendered memorable solely by the ruin of the Empire, died at Ravenna in his fortieth year. His body was brought to Rome and buried in the Mausoleum of S. Peter. The Western Empire was thus left without any appointed successor, the male line of the great Theodosius having with him become extinct. Placidia, already the widow of Athaulf, had, shortly before her brother's death, betaken herself on account of court intrigues to Byzantium with the son (Valentinian) whom she had borne to her second husband, Constantius. The Emperor Theodosius II., at first undecided as to whether he should unite the Eastern with the Western Empire, or place the crown of the West on the head of a boy, at length yielded to the wishes of his aunt Placidia, and appointed her Augusta and guardian of her son,

Death of Honorius, 423.

[1] Pagi, *Critica* with regard to this year.

promising at the same time to bestow on Valentinian the Imperial title and the hand of his little daughter Eudoxia. He forthwith sent mother and son, accompanied by a fleet, to Ravenna, where a usurper, John, Primicerius of the Notaries, had assumed the purple. This bold adventurer might with ease have made himself master of Italy, and been acknowledged Emperor even of Rome, had not the Byzantine generals, Ardaburius and Asper, who were escorting Placidia and Valentinian, fortunately arrived in time to put a stop to his progress. Taking Ravenna, they caused the usurper to be put to death.

Valentinian III., 425.

Placidia and her son hastened to Rome, where the boy received the Imperial robe from the hands of Helion, the Byzantine plenipotentiary, and was, as Valentinian III., declared Augustus at the age of seven. The young Emperor established his court in strongly-fortified Ravenna, where his mother brought him up among the women and eunuchs of the palace, whilst she herself, too weak to guide the corrupt State, remained the prey of court intrigues. This princess, whose eventful life excites a romantic interest, possessed no talents for government, and although the abilities of two great generals, Aetius and Boniface, stood at her command, through feminine frivolity and a passion for intrigue she deprived herself of the services of both. The result of her own weakness and the cunning of Aetius was the loss of the province of Africa. Boniface, impelled to treason by the ignoble jealousy of his rival, in the heat of his resentment summoned the Vandals from Spain. But simultaneously with their

Galla Placida, Regent.

landing in Africa (429) he saw with dismay the error he had committed, and his heroic soul was torn by the anguish of unavailing remorse. Genseric, in the course of ten years, won Africa for himself, and with this rich province, the granary of Rome, became possessed of the key to Italy.[1] The city was soon called upon to suffer the consequences of these events, but the destinies of the Empire were no longer decided either in the deserted palace of the Caesars or in the ruined Capitol, and Rome was forced silently to bow to the decrees of fate.

Sixtus III. Pope, 432–498.

The history of the city itself is at this time animated solely by the activity of the Bishop, Sixtus III., a Roman who ascended the chair of S. Peter on July 31, 432. Under his predecessor, Celestine I. (422–432), the condemnation of the Byzantine patriarch Nestorius had been pronounced at the Council of Ephesus in 431. The patriarch's offense had consisted in denying to the mother of the Founder of the Christian religion the monstrous title of "Mother of God." Sixtus now celebrated his dogmatic triumph over the Nestorian party in the magnificent restoration of the basilica of Liberius, which he dedicated to the Virgin Mary, the "Mother of

[1] Prudentius could now no longer have written the verses which, inspired by the consciousness of Imperial power, he had penned in 403.

Respice, num Libyci desistat ruris arator
Frumentis onerare rates et ad ostia Tibris
Mittere triticeos in pastum plebis acervos?
—*Contra Symmach.*, ii. v. 936.

God."[1] He adorned the interior of this, probably the first temple to Mary in Rome, with mosaics, many of which still remain. These mosaics, next to those of S. Pudentiana and the somewhat rough decorations in S. Costanza, are the oldest in Rome. The church of S. Sabina on the Aventine having, however, been built by Bishop Peter in the time of Sixtus III., it is probable that the mosaics in this beautiful basilica are contemporary with those in S. Maria Maggiore.

He restores and adorns S. Maria Maggiore.

The style of the mosaics in S. Maria still preserves the traditions of ancient art, and bears no traces of the so-called Byzantine influence perceptible a little later, as, for instance, when the Arch of Triumph in S. Paul's was decorated by Placidia.[2] They are

[1] See Gruter, 1170, Nr. 7, and De Rossi, *Inscr. chr.,* ii; 71, the ancient inscription over the main door of the church:—

Virgo Maria, tibi Xystus nova tecta dicavi
Digna salutifero munera ventre tuo.
Tu genitrix ignara viri; te denique foeta
Visceribus salvis edita nostra salus.
Ecce tui testes uteri tibi praemia portant
Sub pedibusque jacet passio cuique sua,
Ferrum, flamma, ferae, fluvius, saevumque venenum:
Tot tamen has mortes una corona manet.

According to the Archives (see Marini, *Papira diplom.,* n. xci. p. 142), the church was known in the sixth century as Basilica S. Dei Genitricis ad Praesepe. Hence is rectified the statement of Valentini (*La Patriarcale Bas. Liberiana descritta ed. ill.,* Rom, 1839), that it only received the title in 642, when the Holy Manger was brought thither from Jerusalem. Criticism cannot, however, accept the Holy Manger.

[2] I have followed Giovanni Ciampini (*Vetera Monumenta in quibus praecipue Musiva opera,* &c., Roma, 1690) with regard to the chronological order of the Roman mosaics. That we owe those in S. Maria Maggiore to Sixtus III., the inscription on the Arch of Triumph

also the only mosaics in Rome which illustrate the development of Christianity in a series of Biblical histories. These histories are so distributed, that the representations of the Old Testament on the walls of the nave lead to the history of Christianity on the Arch of Triumph. Both of these walls are decorated above the entire length of the architrave with thirty-six square pictures, divided into two rows, one above the other. Beginning with the greeting of Abraham and Melchisedek, they represent the lives and deeds of the patriarchs, of Moses and Joshua, up to the entrance into the Promised Land. The first, in their idyllic character, are the most beautiful; possessing much of the grace of the antique, they appear as predecessors of Raffaelle's celebrated little frescoes in the Loggie. The scenes of war and combat depicting the history of Joshua which follow, seem, on the other hand, to have been the work of artists inspired by the style of the sculptures on the column of Trajan.[1]

The history of Christ adorns the Arch of Triumph erected by Sixtus over the high altar to commemorate the victory of the Orthodox Church. In the middle is the throne; before it lies the mystic Book with the Seven Seals; at the sides stand SS. Peter and Paul and the symbols of the four Evangelists; next, the Annunciation by the Angel to the Virgin, a graceful

informs us: *Xystus Episcopus Plebis Dei.* These mosaics have not suffered unduly by restoration. See De Rossi, *Mosaici Cristiani.*

[1] See the representations in the II. Dissert. of Fr. Blanchini's edition of the *Liber Pontificalis,* vol. 1, p. 123, and in the *Basilica Liberiana descr. ed illustr.,* Rome, 1839. Nine scenes which had perished were replaced by colour paintings, in imitation of mosaics, in the sixteenth century.

seated figure. But nowhere is the Virgin honored with the nimbus. Next follows the presentation of Christ in the Temple, or Mary carrying the Child whose head is surrounded with the aureole. In the second row of mosaics follows the adoration of the Magi, a curious conception. The Child sits alone on the throne, while two kings, slender youths, with crowned Phrygian caps resembling the oval helmets of the Dioscuri, or the berrettas of the Dacian prisoners of war on Trajan's arch, stand upright with their gifts. Behind the throne are four angels, and the star in the heavens;[1] on the other side is Christ teaching in the Temple, with two angels behind him. The third row to the right of the beholder is a scene representing some act in the life of Herod, not easily understood; on the left, the Massacre of the Innocents. Later art has chosen to depict this scene with a certain rough brutality, but the ancient mosaic only shows us a group of anxious women, children in their arms, towards whom three soldiers advance with rapid steps.[2] The series ends at each side of the arch with the customary representations of the towns of Jerusalem and Bethlehem, to which lambs, typical of the believers, look up. Such are the most remarkable of the mosaics of S. Maria Maggiore; a

[1] Some of these figures have been the subject of later alterations. In Kugler's *Kunstgeschichte* it is erroneously stated that these mosaics on the triumphal arch consist "principally of representations of the Apocalypse," see pp. 394, 395.

[2] This beautiful *motif* has also been borrowed and imitated in a fresco in the church of S. Benedetto at Subiaco. This later work appears to belong to the twelfth or thirteenth century, to the time probably when Conxolus and other artists were working at Subiaco.

beautiful monument of the last days of Roman art in the fifth century.

The *Liber Pontificalis* enumerates the lavish adornments with which Sixtus endowed the church of S. Maria, but, according to the catalogue here given, it would appear that gold had become scarce after the Gothic sack, since only one cup of pure gold, 50 lbs. in weight, finds mention. All the remaining consecrated vessels are silver, and among them we are told of an altar covered with plates of silver amounting to 300 lbs. and a stag 30 lbs. in weight, from whose mouth water flowed into the baptismal font. Meanwhile, Valentinian III., at the request of the Bishop, obtained from the exhausted treasury money sufficient to erect in S. Peter's a relief of the Saviour and the twelve Apostles in gold and adorned with jewels, to replace in the basilica of the Lateran a silver tabernacle (*Fastigium*). For the latter had been carried off by the Goths,[1] in spite of their respect for the churches, and since this treasure alone weighed 511 lbs. we may imagine how rich were the spoils which the barbarians must have collected from the other churches of Rome. Honorius, Placidia and Valentinian, together with the bishops of their time, eagerly strove to repair these losses, and the despoiled churches were soon refilled with precious objects in massive gold and silver. There is not one among succeeding bishops who is not extolled by the *Liber Pontificalis* for the different vases, candlesticks, altars, statues, which he has had placed in the

Increasing luxury in the churches.

[1] *Lib. Pont.* in S. Sixto III. *Fastigium argenteum in basilica Constantiniana, quod a barbaris sublatum fuerat.*

various churches. In vain did S. Jerome denounce this luxury. "The marble walls shine," he said, "the roofs sparkle with gold, the altars with precious stones, but the true servants of Christ are without splendour. Let no one reply that the temple in Judea was rich, that the table, lamps, censers, vessels, cups, cauldrons and all other utensils were of gold; now that the Lord has made poverty his temple, we should think of the cross, and esteem riches as worthless." So spoke S. Jerome.[1] The ostentatious priesthood, however, held a different opinion, striving instead to render each church a replica of Solomon's temple, and imitating an oriental splendour in the sacred utensils with such success, that within a period of forty years there was again collected in Rome a rich booty for such barbarians as fortune and audacity might bring to the city.

3. Leo I., Pope, 440—African Fugitives in Rome—Heresies—Death of Placidia, 450—Her Fortunes—Her Daughter Honoria—Attila summoned by Her—Battle of the Catalaunian Fields—Attila Invades North Italy—Valentinian in Rome—Embassy of the Romans to the King of the Huns—Leo before Attila—A Celebrated Legend—Attila's Retreat and Death—Statues of the Capitoline Jupiter and the Peter of the Vatican.

Leo I., 440–461.

On the death of Sixtus III. (August 440) the deacon Leo, son of the Roman Quintianus, was

[1] Hieron, Epist. 52, ad Nepotianum, c. 10. Agincourt, in his *History of Art,* has taken the trouble to compile a catalogue of the various works of art bestowed upon the churches by successive popes and emperors from the fourth to the ninth century. See end of vol. i.

unanimously elected his successor. Never had the city cause to regret her choice. On the contrary, it was to this illustrious man that in after years she owed her preservation from the enemy. Leo, sent by Valentinian to Gaul to effect a reconciliation between the great Aetius and his rival Albinus, was absent at the time of his election. Returning, however, to Rome, after having been consecrated in S. Peter's on September 29, he won the favour of the people by a sermon in which he displayed his powers as an orator; and never did Pope better understand how to employ such gifts. The times were difficult; the Imperial power, wielded by a boy, tottered to its fall; the provinces became one after another the prey of German tribes. In such dire necessity the Roman Emperor could, without scruple of conscience, effect a compromise with the barbarians, but the Roman Bishop, who witnessed the daily progress of disruption, only strove the more zealously to defend the Church against the entrance of heresies from the East, to make the orthodox dogma felt to its full extent, and to win supremacy for the Roman chair. From Carthage, conquered by the Vandals, from the devastated provinces of Numidia, swarms of African fugitives came to seek shelter in Rome. Amongst these fugitives the Pantheistic sect of the Manichaeans was numerously represented. The Pope awarded the unfortunate exiles a refuge, only on condition that they abjured their heresies. Their writings he ordered to be publicly burnt.[1]

[1] Prosper, *Chron. ad Anni.,* 443.

It undoubtedly cost Leo some trouble to maintain the purity of the orthodox faith. The unemployed intelligence of men, withdrawn from all that concerned the State, set itself with energy to work out theological systems. Manichaeans, Priscillians, Pelagians raised their heads in the provinces; and the newly arisen heresy of the Monophysites entangled the Bishop of Rome in a wearisome controversy with the East, from which, however, he issued victorious. Leo I. established the supremacy of the Apostolic chair in Rome, and his efforts found ready supporters in a bigoted woman, the Augusta Placidia, and a feeble-minded Emperor, her son Valentinian. Both came several times to Rome, where they visited the graves of the Apostles, enriched their churches with costly offerings, and where Galla Placidia covered with mosaics the tribune of S. Paul's. She herself died in Rome on November 27, 450. Her body was taken to Ravenna, where, seated on a throne of cypress wood, it was preserved in its wondrous tomb for many centuries.[1]

Death of Placidia, 450.

Her extraordinary career is coincident with the downfall of Imperial Rome, as Cleopatra's had been with that of Republican Rome. It is a remarkable historic phenomenon, that in periods of decadence some female figure generally rises into prominence—some woman exercises a great influence upon her epoch, and in her fate we see reflected the moral standard of her time. The period of Rome's decline

[1] Gibbon, c. 35; Muratori, *Annal. ad. Ann.*, 450. The Mausoleum of Placidia at Ravenna, with its mosaics, in excellent preservation is one of the most remarkable of monuments of Italy.

is marked in the West, as in the East, by Placidia, Pulcheria, Eudocia, and Placidia's daughters, Eudoxia and Honoria, women whose human passions light up and mitigate the darkness of the age. Amidst such histories there are few, if any, of greater importance, perhaps none, which, owing to its changeful and adventurous circumstances and the fascination of its backgrounds, arouses a higher interest than that of Galla Placidia. The daughter of the great Theodosius and the sister of Honorius, when a girl of twenty-one, was taken prisoner by Alaric, carried off to Calabria, and married to the Gothic King, Athaulf, at Narbonne. Later, having buried her son Theodosius at Barcelona, and lost her husband himself by assassination in 415, she was ignominiously thrust out of the palace by the murderer, Singarich, loaded with chains, and compelled to walk twelve miles before his horse. Sent back by the new King Wallia to her brother at Ravenna, the widow of Athaulf was obliged, against her will, to give her hand to the general Constantius. This brave man, a Roman from Illyria, had been celebrated even in the time of Theodosius for his warlike deeds; he had freed Gaul from the tyranny of the usurper, Gerontius; and was the greatest Roman general of the time. His was a highly attractive figure, and one calculated to command respect. Before Placidia resolved to marry Athaulf, Constantius had sought, though in vain, to win the love of the Emperor's beautiful sister. The voice of the people pronounced him the most worthy successor to the throne of Honorius, at whose court he soon became all powerful. Finally Placidia married the general on January 1, 417, and bore him two children, Valentinian and Honoria. Constantius, declared Augustus and co-regent by Honorius, died suddenly September 21, 421,[1] to the great misfortune of the Empire. The Emperor, credited but a short time before by evil report with criminal desires towards his sister, now turned from love to hatred and banished the unhappy woman with her children to Byzantium. We have seen that she soon after returned with an army, and, after many dangers at sea, landed in Italy, set the son of Constantius on the throne of the West, and for twenty-five years ruled the Roman Empire as guardian or regent.

Fate of Honoria.

Immediately after her death the fate of her daughter Honoria became curiously linked with that of the Empire. This maiden, brought up at the court of Ravenna, impelled by sensual passions in the solitude of her cloistered life, had, at the age of seventeen, been induced to yield herself to Eugenius, her own steward. Placidia, discovering that her beautiful daughter was about to become a mother, sent her to the court of Constantinople, where the strict Pulcheria ordered her to be imprisoned. Here the daughter of Placidia languished until 434, when, in the tedium of her loneliness, she conceived the desperate idea of calling upon Attila King of the Huns in Pannonia, the most terrible figure of the times, to be her deliverer. As the reward of her release she offered him her hand and with it, as dowry, her claim on a portion of the Empire. The recollection of the singular for-

[1] See Sievers, *Studien zur Gesch. der röm. Kaiser,* Berlin, 1870, p. 449 f.

tunes of the beautiful Athenais or Eudocia, the wife of Theodosius II., and of the wandering fate of her own mother, who had not disdained marriage with a barbarian king, the pillager of Rome, dispelled her scruples, if any she entertained. She found an opportunity of sending a eunuch to Attila, who conveyed to him her letter and betrothal ring. This took place before the death of Theodosius, and scarcely had the Senator Marcian married Pulcheria and been raised to the Imperial throne in the East, when Attila demanded the fulfilment of the suppositious claims accorded him by this betrothal with Honoria.[1] The court of Constantinople forthwith hastened to send the princess back to Ravenna in order to relieve itself of the object of Attila's demands. No sooner had Honoria arrived in Italy than she was forced into a conventional marriage with an official of the court, who might oppose, by legal right, the claims of the King of the Huns, and immediately after the marriage the daughter of Placidia was again condemned to a lingering imprisonment.

She summons Attila.

Various reasons meanwhile, impelled the King of the Huns, instead of throwing himself on Constantinople, to scatter his Sarmatian and German troops

[1] Jordanes, *De Regnor. success.* See Muratori, *T. I. P.,* i. p. 239, and *De Reb. Get.,* 42. Priceus, a contemporary (*Excerpta de Legat.,* pp. 39, 40), and Marcell. Com. relate the history of Honoria and her connection with Attila. Marcellin.: *Ariobinda et Aspare coss. Honoria Valentiniani Imp. soror ab Eugenio procuratore suo stuprata concepit, palatioque expulsa Theodosio principi de Italia transmissa Attilanem contra occidentalem remp. concitabat.* Honoria was born in 418.

over the West and the provinces of Gaul. We shall not attempt to follow the traces of these frightful devastations. We only see with satisfaction, the same Visigoths who had previously sacked Rome now joining the troops of Aetius, as defenders of Roman civilization, and valiantly fighting the hordes of Attila on the Catalaunian Fields. The dying Roman Empire roused itself to fight with heroic valour one of the greatest battles recorded in European history. Its downfall is lightened by this great deed of arms, which, reflecting lustre also on the memory of the Visigoths, cleanses it from the stain left by the sack of Rome.[1]

Battle of the Catalaunian Fields, A.D. 451.

The defeated King of the Huns gathered together the remnants of his troops and returned to Lower Pannonia. He employed the rest of the winter in the accumulation of fresh forces, with which he intended to descend on Italy by way of the Julian Alps in the spring of 452, and to gain possession at the same time of the hand of his betrothed, her inheritance, and the title to which he laid claim. On his march from Friuli he crushed the unfortunate towns of Venetia, of Insubria and the Emilia, but halted at the junction of the Mincio and the Po. Between him and Rome stood neither fortress nor army, for the Roman general Aetius, who had collected but few troops, could with difficulty defend the passes of the Apennines, and the walled towns which might have hin-

Attila enters Italy.

[1] The childish prejudice against the Goths is found occasionally amid Italians of the present day, who should instead be influenced by the dispassionate judgments of Muratori. See *Annal. ad Ann.,* 482, towards the end, and other passages.

dered the advance of the barbarians did not promise, like the heroic Aquileia, to sustain a three months' siege. The cowardly Valentinian would have been unable to defend himself in Ravenna; he was, however, brought by Aetius to Rome, more defenceless than even Honorius had been. The badly equipped city saw itself exposed to an inhuman enemy, and the despairing populace, incapable even of the thought of arming in defence of their walls, said to themselves with horror, that from Attila, whose hands still dripped with the blood of Aquileia, they dared not hope for the mercy which they had experienced from the magnanimous Alaric.

In their extremity, Emperor and Senate decided upon sending a solemn embassy to implore the King of the Huns to make peace and to withdraw. The foremost men of Rome, the consul Gennadius Avienus the head of the Senate, Trigetius, formerly prefect of Italy, and the Bishop Leo, were chosen to execute the desperate mission. The venerable Leo was associated with the senators in order that their importance might be strengthened by the halo of his spiritual position, the dignity of his person, and the charm of his extraordinary eloquence. The people of Rome undoubtedly had also desired him as their ambassador.[1] Here appears for the first time the Bishop as an active agent in a political matter, and we may well suppose that he, like all other bishops

[1] *Hist. Misc.,* xv. Cassiodorus, *Variar.,* i. Ep. 4, cites among the envoys the names of the father of Cassiodorus and Carpilio, son of Aetius. Jordanes, *De reb. Get.,* c. 42; Prosper, *Chron.*; and *Lib. Pontif.*

in the towns of the West, already possessed a great and officially recognised influence in the Curia of the city.[1]

Seldom has a priest been entrusted with a more grateful commission. His appearance before the terrible barbarian leader, who was approaching to destroy the capital of the world, won for him, more perhaps through the favour of ecclesiastical legend than through his actual services, the gratitude of mankind and a deathless renown. An Attila probably felt no more reverence for the person of a bishop than for that of a senator; nevertheless, Leo was the true representative of human civilisation, the salvation of which already lay in the spiritual power of the Church.

Leo I. before Attila, A.D. 452.

The delegates met the "Scourge of God" at his camp on the Mincio, and on gaining entrance to his tent found him already assailed by doubts, and therefore more easy of access than they had dared to hope. It appeared as if the account of the sudden death which had snatched Alaric away a short time after the conquest of Rome had made a deep impression on the mind of the superstitious Hun. It was said that his friends wished to dissuade him from marching against Rome, by the example of the great Goth.[2] A later legend however, relates that close to

[2] The Curiae had at this period become utterly degenerate. The churches alone formed influential corporations; the bishops not only exercising supervision over the magistrates, but even appointing the *Defensores.* This applied, it is true, to the provinces only, and although they did not exercise the same authority in Rome, yet there also their voices were heard in political affairs. Guizot, *Historie Générale de la Civilization en Europe,* II. Leçon.

[2] Jordanes, *De reb. Get.,* c. 42.

the warning figure of Leo, Attila had seen the supernatural form of a strange and venerable old man, clad in priestly vestments, who, holding a drawn sword, menaced him with death, and gave him to understand he must obey the warnings of the holy Bishop. This celebrated legend, an ingenious fiction, does honour to the genius of the Christian religion, and awakens our sympathy with unfortunate Rome, who, from the protection of heroes and citizens, now found herself reduced to that of a celestial apparition. Neither Raffaelle in one of the Stanze of the Vatican, nor Algardi in a chapel of S. Peter's has been able to express the simple beauty of the legend, representing, as they have done, Attila shrinking back from SS. Peter and Paul, who with drawn swords, hover over him.[1]

The compliance of the King of the Huns is, in the main, as much of a riddle as was the sudden withdrawal of Alaric. We cannot attribute the renunciation of Attila to the spell which the name of Rome still exercised on the imagination of mankind, Alaric having lessened, if not extinguished, the charm. But as the Hunnish hordes rolled like a devastating storm

[1] The Fathers honour both Apostles as patrons of the city; so Paulinus Natal., xiii., *Fragm. de Gothor. exercitus cum ego Rege interitu.* Cassiodorus terms them tutelary deities of Rome, *Var.,* xi. 13. The legend is of late origin. The editors of Leo's works (Lugdun, 1700) maintain that, since it does not appear in the older MSS., it has been interpolated in the MS. of the *Hist. Misc.,* edited by Janus Gruter, Dissert. I., *de vita et reb gest. S. Leonis M.,* p. 165. Baronius believes in the apparition, for the authenticity of which he quotes the *Historia Miscella.* Bower, a disciple of Voltaire, points out, however that he might with equal justice have appealed to the authority of Raffaelle.

over the land, laying waste with brutal fury farms and cities, they destroyed their own means of subsistence; they suffered at the same time from hunger, pestilence and the malaria of Italy, and intelligence reaching them that the Emperor Marcian had sent an army into Pannonia which menaced their retreat, Attila may have esteemed it more prudent to satisfy himself on this occasion with humiliating the city. He forced her to sue for peace, and, with the promise of a yearly tribute he agreed to withdraw July 6, 452.[1] Had he conquered Rome, the fury of his Mongolian hordes would doubtless have reduced the city to a smoking heap of ashes. The world was happily spared the frightful catastrophe, and Rome continued to exist as the sacred tradition of centuries, the centre of civilisation and of political and religious ideas.

Attila withdrew to Pannonia, threatening that he would return to destroy Rome and Italy, if Honoria and with her a proportionate dowry, were not made over to him. He was fortunately prevented from carrying out his threat by death, which overtook him in the arms of a beautiful woman the night after his marriage in the following year (453).

Legend of the Capitoline Jupiter.

The deliverance of Rome gave rise to a later legend. It is related that Leo, having returned from his honourable embassy, in thanksgiving for the fulfilment of his mission and the aid lent him by the prince of the Apostles, had the bronze statue of the Capitoline Jupiter recast in the figure of S. Peter, which we now see seated on a throne in the basilica. In this

[1] See Amédée Thierry's *Attila,* &c.

legend the majestic tutelary divinity of the Roman Empire, the most sacred image of its temples vanishes from sight, and while the statue, which in the general overthrow of the gods met an unnoticed end, is here mentioned for the last time, its fate offers a striking symbol of the transformation which had taken place in Rome.[1] The Capitoline Jupiter had been the supreme deity of the West; in the Hellenised East the marvellous Colossus of Zeus, erected by the great Phidias in Olympia, had been enthroned for centuries as the supreme god. He also existed no longer. In tragic loneliness he had remained in his temple until the end of the fourth century, when he was removed to Constantinople, and it is said, was there destroyed by fire in the reign of Leo the Isaurian.[2]

Rome for a short time celebrated her delivery from Attila by a religious ceremony. The great Bishop, however, in a sermon on one of these anniversaries upbraided the people because, instead of offering thanksgivings at the grave of the Apostle, they flocked to witness the Circensian games. "The religious festival," he said, "on which, as recording the day of our chastisement and release, the whole company of the faithful were wont to gather to praise God, has almost become forgotten, as is testified by the small number of the congregation, and the fact troubles me

[1] Marangoni, *Cose Gentilesche,* c. xx. p. 68; Torrigius, *De Cryptis Vat.,* p. 126, and *Sacri Trofei Romani,* p, 149; Bonanni, *Templi Vaticani Historia,* p. 107; Cancellieri, *De Sacrariis Nov. Basil. Vatican.,* p. 1403 f.; Card. Dom. Bartolini, *Della celebratiss. Statua di Bronzo del Princ. d. Apost., S. Pietro,* Roma, 1850 (see below), vol. ii. book iv. chap. i.

[2] Lasaulx, *Untergang des Hellenismus,* p, 110.

and fills me with fear. I repeat it with shame, and yet I ought not to let it remain unsaid, that more follow the demons than the Apostles, and that more throng to the disgraceful spectacles than to the graves of the Martyrs. What saved this city? Who redeemed her from bondage? Who delivered her from death? The Circensian games or the guardianship of the saints?"[1]

The passion which the Romans still retained for the Circus and the pantomimes justly excites our astonishment. The taste for this form of pleasure had been inherited from their fathers, and while the populace regarded with dull indifference the fate of the declining Empire, the contests between the Greens and Blues awoke the most furious party feeling. A Gaulish bishop of the time of Leo was horrified by this rage for spectacles, and passionately exclaimed, "Who can think of the Circus in the face of captivity? Who can go to execution and laugh? We play with the fear of slavery hanging over us, and laugh while the terror of death is upon us? One might suppose that the whole people of Rome had

[1] *Sermon in Octava Apost. Petri et Pauli,* lxxxi. Muratori, *ad Ann.,* 455, believes the festival to have been instituted after the withdrawal of the Vandals, and although the editors of Leo's works maintain the same opinion, the view of Baronius, namely, that the sermon refers to Attila, seems the more probable. I cannot believe that Leo could apply to the fearful sack of the Vandals terms so mild: *qui corda furentium Barbaror. mitigare dignatus est;* or would have spoken as he does of redemption from bondage. Papencordt, *Gesch. der Vandal. Herrsch. in Afrika* (Berlin, 1837), even holds that the sermon was preached immediately after the departure of the Vandals. Is it possible, however, that the despoiled city could at once turn its mind to the games of the circus, or defray their expenses?

become satiated with the sardonic herb; it laughs even in death."[1]

[1] Salvianus of Marseilles, *De vero Judicio et provid. Dei,* vii. p. 78. The preachers of the time were truly provided with weighty texts of world-wide significance. The phrase describing the sardonic laughter of the Romans after their tremendous defeat is a terrible one: *Sardonicis quodammodo herbis omnem Romanum populum putes saturatum. Moritur et ridet.* (Procopius, *De bello Goth.,* iv. 24, has some remarks on the sardonic herb and laughter.) Salvian is at heart more of a Roman than the African Augustine, and his discourse at times takes a higher flight. This remarkable man, apparently a native of Treves, survived the crash of the Roman dominion in Gaul, and accompanied the decline of the corrupt Empire with his lamentations and invectives as Jeremiah had accompanied the fall of Judaism. Zschimmer, *Salvianus, der Presbyter von Massilia und seine Schriften,* Halle, 1875.

CHAPTER VI.

1. Fall of Aetius—A Romance of Court Life— Murder of Valentinian III. 455— Maximus Emperor—Eudoxia summons Genseric, the Vandal King.

Fall of Aetius, 455.

THE Western Empire was already tottering to its fall, although the death of two Emperors and a second sack of the city—a sack which, like the first, followed hard upon the tragic death of a hero—were yet to intervene.

The fall of the valiant Aetius, which, like that of Stilicho, is hidden in the darkness of court intrigue, was linked with the fortunes of two beautiful women. The conqueror of the Huns, adored by the Romans as their deliverer, hated by the envious, the possessor of boundless wealth, and at the summit of power, cherished the natural ambition of allying himself yet more securely with the Imperial house through the ties of blood. He was the father of two sons, Carpilion and Gaudentius; Valentinian of two daughters, Eudocia and Placidia. By a solemn oath the Emperor had promised to marry one of these princesses to one or other of the youths. The courtiers, amongst them the eunuch Heraclius, however, apparently thwarted the union, and while recollecting perhaps his double dealing with Boniface, they represented Aetius as an overbearing traitor, whispered that he had secret understandings with the Huns, who, since the days of the tyrant John, had been his devoted friends, and asserted that with the help of his barbarian allies he hoped to gain supreme power.

In 454 Valentinian, who frequently visited the Imperial city, came to Rome. Here, one day in the palace, he was attacked by Aetius, who, relying on the greatness of his fame and his services, demanded the fulfilment of the Emperor's sworn promise. The scene had apparently been planned by the enemies of the general in order to bring about his overthrow. Aetius, who had never believed the cowardly Valentinian capable of any manly action, saw the Emperor suddenly draw his sword, and at the same moment felt himself stabbed. Falling on the marble floor, he was thrust through and through by the swords and daggers of a swarm of eunuchs and courtiers. Exulting in their revenge they fell on the prostrate body of Rome's last great general and covered it with wounds, while, probably the effeminate Valentinian lay fainting in the arms of a eunuch, overpowered by the exertion of the blow he had dealt.[1]

Many of the friends of Aetius were entangled in his fall, amongst them the Praetorian Prefect, Boethius, a member of the family of the Anicii, and

[1] For particulars of the fall of Aetius, see Victor Tununensis in Canisius, t. i.; Prosper Tiro, Prosper, *Chron. Pithoean, ibid.*; Procop., *De bello Vand.,* i. c. 4; Idatius' *Chron.* in Sirmond, t. ii.

grandfather of the afterwards celebrated philosopher. The followers of the general were murdered.

This simple account of the fall of Aetius is also the most probable. It is, at all events, more in accordance with the natural course of things that the powerful, meritorious and ambitious general, like others of his kind, fell a sacrifice to envy or suspicion, than that some love romance was the cause of his overthrow. A romance, however, was enacted in the palace, and played an important part in the fortunes of the city.

Valentinian, tiring of the charms of his Empress Eudoxia, the daughter of Theodosius the Younger and the Greek Athenais, had become attracted by the wife of the Senator Petronius Maximus, now the head of the family of the Anicii, a woman who, combining virtue with beauty, was destined to be the last Lucretia of Rome. His overtures not being favourably received, he called the dice-board to his aid. In playing with the Emperor, Maximus lost a sum of gold, for which he gave his ring as pledge. With this token in his hand, a eunuch hastened to the house of the senator, and showing the wife her husband's ring, feigned to have been sent to fetch her in a litter to the palace to greet the Empress. Arrived at the palace the unsuspecting woman was conducted to Valentinian in a distant part of the building.

When Maximus returned to his house he found his wife in tears of shame and despair; but subduing her emotion, the unfortunate woman overwhelmed him with denunciations as having been the vendor of her honour. Informed of the true state of the case,

Maximus devised a scheme of revenge. He decided to wash out the insult in the blood of the miserable Emperor. It is here that Procopius, who is our informant (his dates are confused), asserts that Maximus, regarding Aetius as the chief hindrance to his scheme, cleared the general out of the way, in order to carry out his plan with the greater certainty.[1] He was himself the richest and most prominent man in Rome, had been twice Consul and four times Prefect of the city, also Praetorian Prefect of Italy, and had been honoured with a public statue in the Forum of Trajan. It followed, therefore, that both he and the Anicii family were not devoid of means to execute his projects of revenge.[2]

A striking instance of Valentinian's blunted and despotic character is shown in the fact that, after the murder of Aetius, he took several of the general's former retainers into his own service, and insulted their sense of honour by assuring them that he trusted none of them, and could never believe barbarians, such as they were, capable of any noble emotion. He undoubtedly gave them occasion for revenge, and it is not improbable that Maximus himself may have brought these men into the service of Valentinian in order to avail himself of their swords. As the Emperor stood one day (March 16, 455) watching the military exercises from the Villa *ad duas Lauros,* at the third milestone on the Via Labicana, he was suddenly struck down by assassins, amongst whom

Murder of Valentinian III., March 16, 455.

[1] Procop., *De bello Vand.,* i. 4; Marcell. Com., *Chron.*; Nicephor. Callist., *Hist. Eccl.,* xv. c. 11; Evagrius, *Hist. Eccl.,* ii. c. 7.

[2] Aschbach, *Die Anicier,* &c., p. 39.

were two Goths, Optila and Traustila.[1] No sword was drawn from its sheath in his defence, and thus expired Valentinian, and with him the direct line of Theodosius the Great, another and a heavy blow for Rome.[2]

Maximus Emperor, March 17, 455.

Owing to the wealth which gave him an advantage over Majorianus the rival candidate, Maximus succeeded in getting himself proclaimed Emperor (March 17), and in him the celebrated family of the Anicii ascended the Imperial throne. After having had the remains of his predecessor buried beside S. Peter's (his unfortunate wife had meanwhile died of grief), he strove to induce the widow of Valentinian to forget in his arms the death of her unworthy husband, hoping by this union with one of the Imperial line to conciliate the adherents of the house of Theodosius and the more firmly to secure

[1] Cassiodorus (*Chron.*) and Victor Tununensis represent the Emperor's death as taking place on the Field of Mars; Prosper Tiro, on the contrary, on the spot known as *ad duas Lauros.* See also *Hist. Misc.*, xv., and Marcell. Com., Idatius' *Chron.*: *occiditur in campo, circumstante exercitu.* Clinton gives the chronology, *Fasti Romani.*

[2]

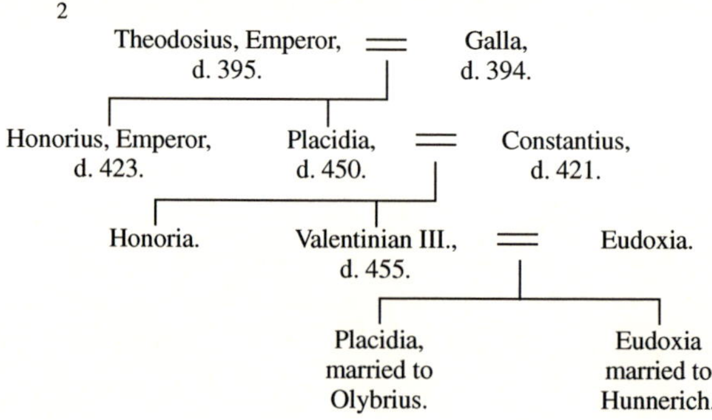

the throne. The proud daughter of Theodosius the Younger (as yet ignorant that Maximus was the disguised murderer of her husband), yielded to menace and force, and after the new Emperor had compelled the widow of his wife's seducer to marry him a few days after the murder, he was vindictive enough to apprise her of what he had done. The unfortunate woman, wounded to the innermost soul, conceived on her side the idea of avenging herself on the usurper of her husband's throne and the betrayer of her own honour.

Eudoxia summons Genseric.

While, as Byzantine historians relate, she racked her brains for some means of revenge, recognising that nothing was to be hoped from Constantinople, since her mother Eudocia was living in banishment at Jerusalem, and her father Theodosius and her aunt Pulcheria were already dead; unreasoning hate suggested the thought of appealing to Genseric, King of the Vandals in Africa; a man as wild, as hideous, and as terrible as Attila. She accordingly sent messengers imploring his speedy departure for Rome.[1] We have strong grounds for doubting the truth of this account, and it is not improbable that the legend may owe its origin solely to the imagination of the Greeks. Inasmuch, however, as it is incapable of proof, we may allow the tale to rest on its own

[1] Our chief authorities are Procop., *De bello Vand.,* i. c. 4; Evagrius, ii c. 7. Niceph., xv. c. 11, repeats and amplifies the statements of Evagrius. Marcell. Comes. Jordanes, *De Regni success.,* p. 127. The truth of this legend was doubted as early as Muratori's time. G. Morosi ("L'invito di Eudossia a Genserico," *Pubbl. del. R. Instituto di studi sup.,* Florence, 1882) has demonstrated its improbability in detail.

merits; and the historian may follow the example of an earlier chronicler, who, after relating the fall of Valentinian and the usurpation of Maximus, simply adds that the usurper of the throne quickly expiated the excesses of his passion, when, in the second month of his reign, the fleet of Genseric arrived at the mouth of the Tiber.[1]

2. THE VANDALS LAND AT PORTUS—MURDER OF MAXIMUS —LEO CONFRONTS GENSERIC—THE VANDALS ENTER ROME, JUNE 455—FOURTEEN DAYS' SACK OF ROME—SACK OF THE PALATINE AND THE TEMPLE OF JUPITER—THE ANCIENT SPOILS OF THE TEMPLE OF JERUSALEM—THEIR FATE—MEDIAEVAL LEGENDS.

Scarcely had the squadron of the foreign King, with its swarms of rapacious Vandals and heathen Berbers, appeared, when the despairing people rose in insurrection. Maximus had effected a marriage between his son Palladius and the daughter of Eudoxia, and had caused Palladius to be proclaimed Caesar, but this seems to have been the sole act of his reign. He instituted no preparations for defence; almost as if numbed in intellect, he discharged his followers, gave permission to all to go where they willed, and hurried out of the palace to save himself by flight, already the foremost object in the minds of all. In the street he was stoned by the servants of the palace, and his mangled body thrown into the Tiber. Thus fell Petronius Maximus after a reign of seventy-seven days.[2]

Murder of Maximus, June 455.

[1] Prosper, *Chron. ad Ann.*, 455.

[2] Τῆς δὲ πόλεως ἐξιέναι μέλλοντα βαλών τις λίθῳ κατὰ τοῦ

Genseric, summoned by the news of the revolution in the palace, had meanwhile landed on the coast, and with his terrific army was approaching by the Via Portuensis. No one opposed him but the same Bishop who had previously withstood the yet more terrible Attila. Surrounded by his clergy, Leo fearlessly interrupted the advance of the enemy, and addressed Genseric with the same eloquence as that with which he had once addressed the King of the Huns. No vision of an indignant Apostle bearing an unsheathed sword met the gaze of the Vandal leader, who nevertheless promised the venerable Bishop to spare the city the horrors of sword and fire, and to limit himself to the pillage of its treasures.

Genseric enters Rome, June 455.

The third day following the murder of Maximus the Vandals entered the defenseless city by the Portuensian gate.[1] The unfortunate Romans, who, five and forty years before, had beheld the rude children of the Pannonian Steppes ransack their palaces, were now forced to look on whilst rapacious Bedouins from the land of Jugurtha, together with German Vandals, pillaged in like manner the

κροτάφου ἀνεῖλε. Καὶ τὸ πλῆθὸς ἐπελθὸν τόν τε νεκρὸν διέσπασε καὶ τὰ μέλη ἐπὶ κόντῳ φέρον ἐπαιωνίζετο—*Jo. Antiocheni Fragam.*, p. 615 (vol. iv. *Historicor. Graecor.*, ed. Carl Müller).

[1] Prosper, *Chron.*: *Post hunc Maximi exitum confestim secuta est multis digna lacrymis Romana captivitas.* Victor Tun.: *Tertia die postquam Maxim. occiditur Gensericus—ingreditur.* Papencordt collects all the accounts of the Vandal capture, but although he holds June 2 to have been the probable day of the catastrophe, does not venture to assert it. Appendix iv. to his *Gesch. der Vandalen.* On the evidence, however, of Prosper and Victor Tun., we may infer June 14 to have been the date of Genseric's entrance into Rome. See Clinton's *Fasti.*

treasures of their city. While the Goths in a three days' sack had hastily carried off as much as they were able to seize, astounded all the while at their own audacity, the Vandals plundered at their leisure with unscrupulous avidity during the fourteen days accorded them by Genseric. The spectacle is appalling. The records of history disclose scarcely any more disgraceful sight than that offered by the utterly degraded city while at the mercy of these African Vandals. No contemporary historian attempted to describe the scene of devastation, nor has the lament of any Roman come down to us.

The Vandal sack.

Every article of value in palace, church, or public building that had been left unheeded by the Goths, or that the Romans had since replaced, now fell into the hands of the plunderers. The sack was carried out according to system. All quarters of the city were pillaged at the same time, and hundreds of waggons laden with booty were driven out of the Portuensian gate, bearing their burthens to the vessels which covered the Tiber. The barbarians fell first of all upon the Palatine, the Imperial headquarters, where the hapless Eudoxia had already been made the prisoner of Genseric, and robbed with such avidity as not to leave a single copper vessel. On the Capitol they sacked the hitherto untouched Temple of Jupiter, collecting not only the statues which yet remained, and which Genseric designed for the adornment of his African palace, but stripping half the roof of its tiles of gilded bronze, and carrying these also away on board their vessels.[1]

[1] Procop., *De bello Vand.*, i. 5.

Robbery of the spoils of Jerusalem.

Still more deplorable was the capture of the ancient spoils of Jerusalem. The traveller of the present day in Rome still gazes with interest on the remains of sculpture on the Arch of Titus, and there beholds the imperfect representations of the sacred vessels of the Temple of Solomon—the Seven-branched Lychnuchus, the Holy Table of Sacrifice, with the two censers, two long trumpets and an ark.[1] He knows that here are represented the sacred spoils, as described by Flavius Josephus, brought by Titus from Jerusalem to Rome. Vespasian, dividing these spoils, caused the Veil of the Temple and the books of Jewish law to be conveyed to the Palace of the Caesars, the golden Candlestick and the costly vessels to be deposited in his Temple of Peace.[2] And although this latter building was destroyed by fire under Commodus, time was found to save the Jewish treasures, which, removed to some spot unknown to us, remained hidden for ages. Among the treasures which Alaric accumulated at Carcasonne were some of the beautiful vessels decorated with chrysoprase from Solomon's Temple, which had fallen into his hands in Rome.[3] Other Jewish relics, however, he

[1] Hadrian Reland, *De Spoliis Hierosolym. in arcu Titiano Romae conspicuis,* points out that the representations on the Arch of Titus are lacking in accuracy, the first and seventh branches of the Lychnuchus being dissimilar, all of them too thick, and finally animals, sea-monsters, and eagles being represented at its base, contrary to the Jewish faith.

[2] Josephus, lib. vii. c. 24.

[3] Procop., *De bello Goth.,* i. c. 12: ἐν τοῖς ἦν καὶ τὰ Σολόμωνος τοῦ Ἑβραίων βασιλέως κειμήλια ἀξιοθέατα ἐς ἄγαν ὄντα. πρασία γὰρ λίθος αὐτῶν τὰ πολλὰ ἐκαλλώπιζεν, ὅπερ ἐξ Ἱεροσολύμων Ῥωμαῖοι τὸ παλαιὸν εἷλον.

must have left unheeded, since, together with the spoils acquired from the churches, some of the sacred vessels of the Temple, brought by Titus from Jerusalem, were shipped by Genseric to Carthage.[1]

The singular errant fate of the ancient treasures of the Temple does not end here. Eighty years later Belisarius discovered them in Carthage, and with the spoils of the Vandals brought them amid solemn rejoicings to Constantinople, where the sight of their sacred vessels stirred the Byzantine Jews with such profound emotion that, sending a deputation to the Emperor, they demanded the restoration of their property. Procopius at least speaks of an enthusiastic Jew in the service of Justinian, who appeared before the Emperor and warned him that he must not retain the mystic vessels in the palace of Byzantium, since nowhere would they find rest save in the place originally prepared for them by Solomon. Their removal from the ancient Temple is said to have been Genseric's motive in conquering the fortress of the Caesars, and again to have impelled the Roman army to capture the palace of the Vandals, where the relics lay concealed. Procopius further relates that, seized by superstitious fears, Justinian commanded the vessels of the Jewish Temple to be conveyed to one of the Christian churches of Jerusalem.[2] Whether this anecdote of a contemporary of Belisarius be wholly or partially true, it proves that, nearly

[1] Theophan., *Chronogr.*, p. 93, and Cedrenus, *Hist. Comp.*, i. 346: ἐν οἷς ἦσαν κειμήλια ὁλόχρυσα καὶ διάλιθα ἐκκλησιαστικὰ καὶ σκεύη Ἑβραικά, ἅπερ ὁ Οὐεσπασιανοῦ Τίτος Ἱεροσολύμων ἀθείλετο.

[2] Procop., *De bello Vand.*, ii. c. 4.

five hundred years after the time of Titus, the recollection of these sacred vessels still survived, and we may suppose that throughout the course of centuries the eyes of the children of Israel had continuously watched over them from one generation to another. Thenceforward all trace of them disappeared. The relics of Solomon's Temple, did they ever reach Jerusalem, may have been lost in the East, a prey to the marauding Arabs. At the same period in the time of Justinian, the Armenian Bishop Zacharias, who compiled a register of the public works in Rome, asserts that five and twenty bronze statues representing Abraham, Sarah, and the Kings of the House of David, which Vespasian had brought with the gates and other monuments of Jerusalem to Rome, were still preserved in the city, and Roman tradition in the Middle Ages boasted that the Lateran basilica still preserved the Sacred Ark of the Covenant, the Tables of the Law, the Golden Candlesticks, the Tabernacle and even the priestly vestments of Aaron.[1]

It is possible that on board the same vessel that

[1] Breviar. Zachar.: *similiter alia aenea XXV., referentia Abrahamum, Saram regesque de stirpe Davidis, quae Vespasianus imperator Romam detulit post deletam Hierosolymam cum ejusdem Urbis portis aliisque monumentis.* We thus see how early the legend arose. The redaction of the *Mirabil. urbis Romae, Graphia aureae urbis Romae,* in Ozanam, *Docum. ined.,* p. 160, further says: *In templo Pacis juxta Lateranum* (sic!) *a Vespasiano imperatore et Tito filio ejus recondita est archa testamenti, virga anû* (probably Aaron), *urna aurea habens manna, vestes et ornamenta Aaron, candelabrum aureum cum VII. lucernis tabernaculi, septem cath. argentee,* &c. The register enumerates other relics in the Lateran basilica, which still boasts the possession of the *arca foederis* and the *virga Aaronis.*

sailed to Carthage, laden with the spoils of Rome, the Lychnuchus of Solomon and the statue of the Capitoline Zeus, symbols of the oldest religions of the East and West, may have rested side by side. Procopius expressly mentions one vessel freighted with statues which alone perished at sea, while all the others reached the harbour of Carthage in safety.

3. WITHDRAWAL OF THE VANDALS—FATE OF THE EMPRESS EUDOXIA AND HER DAUGHTERS—S. PIETRO IN VINCOLI—LEGEND OF S. PETER'S CHAINS—THE MONUMENTS UNHURT BY THE VANDALS—CONSEQUENCES OF THE SACK.

Departure of Genseric.

The fate of Rome strangely resembles that of Jerusalem. Many thousands of the inhabitants, of every age and condition, were carried off by Genseric as slaves to Lybia; among them Eudoxia, and Gaudentius the son of Aetius. The daughter of a Byzantine and the wife of two Roman Emperors expiated the crime of high treason against Rome (if such indeed she had committed) not only by witnessing the sack of the city and the indescribable sufferings of the people, but also by her own imprisonment and that of both her daughters. Of these, Eudocia, forced to give her hand to Hunnerich, the son of Genseric, lived for sixteen years in reluctant wedlock in Carthage, escaped, encountered manifold adventures, finally made her way as a pilgrim to Jerusalem, and there died and was buried near the celebrated grandmother whose name she bore.[1] The other daughter,

[1] Theophan., *Chronogr.*, p. 102. The singular fortunes of the

Placidia, regaining her liberty after the death of the Emperor Marcian, accompanied her mother Eudoxia to Constantinople and rejoined her husband Olybrius who had there sought refuge. Such were the fortunes of these women, the last survivors of the race of the great Theodosius.

S. Pietro in Vincoli, a monument of Eudoxia.

Rome, where the memory of Eudoxia is inseparably associated with that of the Vandal sack, still preserves a memorial of the unfortunate Empress in one of its churches. Shortly before the invasion of Genseric Eudoxia had built a basilica to S. Peter. This church, situated in the neighbourhood of the Baths of Titus on the Carinae, at first bore the name Titulus Eudoxiae, later that of S. Pietro ad Vincula or in Vincoli. Legend relates, with regard to its foundation, that Eudocia, the mother of the Empress, had brought the chain of Peter with her from Jerusalem, that she presented half the relic to Constantinople, sent the other half to her daughter in Rome. The chain which the Apostle had worn before his death had also been preserved in Rome, and as Pope Leo held the two chains in his hands, the ends joined indissolubly together, forming one chain of thirty-eight links. The account of the miracle induced the wife of Valentinian to build the church, where the fabulous relics are still venerated, and where the Pagan festival of Augustus (the 1st August) transformed into that of the Chains of Peter.[1]

beautiful Athenais or Eudocia the Byzantian Empress are related by Nicephorus, xiv. 23. See also the author's *Athenais, Gesch. einer byzantin. Kaiserin.*

[1] For this legend, see Ugonio, p. 58. The *Feriae Augusti,* now known as the *Ferrare Agosto,* are still celebrated on this day.

Nature of the Vandal sack.

The Vandal fleet having set sail, the Romans were at liberty to bewail undisturbed the frightful havoc of their city. As after the withdrawal of Alaric, so now after that of Genseric, no enemy remained within their walls. No political change had taken place, but the city, covered with ruins and corpses, bore witness to the extent of its sufferings. The pillage had been so general that it seemed as if everything of value must have fallen into the hands of the Africans. It is hard to believe that, out of respect to the Apostles, Vandals and Moors could have spared the three principal churches, and only sacked the titular or parochial churches.[1] We have nevertheless evidence that many articles of value, more particularly in S. Peter's, either escaped their notice or were spared by the barbarians.[2] Even had we no other definite account of the character of the sack (and the information which we

[1] Baronius founds this inference on the following passage from the "Vita Leonis" in the *Lib. Pont.: Hic renovavit post cladem Vandalicam omnia ministeria sacrata argentea per omnes titulos de conflatis hydriis sex argenteis; basilicae Constantinianae duabus, bas. B. Petri duabus, bas. B. Pauli duabus, quas Constantinus Aug. obtulit, quae pensabant singulae libras centum. Quae omnia vasa renovavit sacrata.* De Rossi, *Bull. d. Arch. Cristiana,* 1865, p. 8, believes the inscription in Gruter, 183, 9 (*C. I. L.,* vi. 1663), to refer to the sack of Genseric, and holds that by the words *Barbarica Incursione Sublata Restituit* are to be understood the Pagan statues which Castalius Innocentius Audax, prefect of the city, had caused to be restored.

[2] The gold reliefs representing the Saviour and the Apostles had apparently been erected by Valentinian over the Shrine of S. Peter in the time of Sixtus III. (*Lib. Pont.* in Xysto). Pope Adrian, in his celebrated letter to Charles the Great respecting the worship of images, refers to this work of art, saying that it was still held in veneration in his own day (*et a tunc usque hactenus apud nos— venerantur*). Labbé, *Concil.,* viii., 1591.

derive from later writers is very scant), the expression "Vandalism," which has become a proverb, testifies to the grounds of its origin. Although the Visigoths had pillaged Rome, their name had escaped the stigma which popular belief has affixed to that of the Vandals, a proof how indelibly the remembrance of the second sack had been imprinted on the mind of the people. Calm investigation, however, leads us to reject the legend of the destruction of the buildings at the hands of the African invaders. Not a single historian who alludes to the sack instances the ruin of any single building, and Procopius, who is careful to inform us of the havoc caused by fire to the palaces of Sallust during the Gothic sack, merely tells us that the Vandals pillaged the Palatine and Capitol. Byzantine chroniclers, writing at a later period, and transcribing one from the other, are our sole informants concerning the rumoured burning of the city and the destruction of its monuments.[1] We shall presently have occasion to speak of these buildings and the care evinced by Theodoric for their preservation, and shall hear them extolled and described by Cassiodorus. We therefore close our present inquiry, quoting the verdict of a Roman

[1] Evagrius, *Eccl. Hist.*, ii. c. 7: ἀλλὰ τὴν πόλιν πυρπολήσας, πάντα τε λησάμενος. Nicephorus, *Eccl. Hist.*, xv. c. 11: ἀλλὰ τὰ μὲν πολιορκήσας (which is sheer nonsense), τὰ δὲ τῶν τῆς πόλεως πυρπολήσας. The real fact is stated by other writers:—Prosper, *Chron.: per quatuordecim igitur dies secura et libera scrutatione omnibus opibus suis Roma vacuata est.* Isidorus, *Chron.: direptisque opibus Romanorum per quatuordecim dies*; Jordanes, *De reb. Get.*, c. 45: *Romamque ingressus cuncta devastat*; and *De Regni succ.*, p. 127: *urbe rebus omnibus exspoliata.*

author on the subject. "So far as can be discovered," says Muratori, "it is not shown that Genseric destroyed either the buildings or the monuments of Rome."[1]

The damage inflicted was nevertheless incalculable. After the Vandals had made themselves masters of the rich province of Africa, and had appropriated the 'Latifundia' of the Roman patricians and the patrimony of the Church, the majority of the senatorial families were reduced to beggary, and the population, through misery, flight and slavery terribly diminished. We venture to assert that, within five and forty years after the conquest of Alaric, Rome was the poorer by 150,000, or an even greater number, of her citizens. Many ancient families had entirely disappeared, others survived to lead a miserable existence, falling, like the deserted temples, rapidly to decay. Huge palaces stood empty and forsaken; the people stalked like spectres through the streets of the desolate city, too vast to receive any semblance of animation from the reduced ranks of her citizens. Men began to marvel at the great extent of Rome, which, filled with temples, basilicas, colonnades, and pleasure resorts of every kind, had never in her prime possessed a population in proportion to her size. How much more evident were her vastness and desolation when, after the middle of the fifth century, the solemn hush which had already invaded the once animated streets and squares of the city of Trajan began to deepen into the silence of the grave.

[1] Fea, *Sulle rov. di Roma,* p. 270; also the treatise of Bargaeus.

CHAPTER VII.

1. Avitus Emperor, 455—Panegyric of Apollinaris Sidonius and the Statue in his Honour—Deposition of Avitus by Ricimer — Majorianus Emperor, 457—His Edict with Regard to the Monuments—Beginnings of Vandalism amongst the Romans—Fall of Majorian, 461.

THE capture of Rome by Genseric left no political consequences of any importance. It had been nothing more than an African "razzia," a piratical expedition successfully carried out, such as in later centuries Saracens from the same coasts more than once sought to repeat.

The throne of the West, no longer claimed by any family of Imperial birth, again became the prey of ambitious generals, and soon after the death of Maximus it was seized by a noble from Gaul. This still prosperous and powerful province, aided by the interested friendship of the Visigothic King, Theodoric, raised in Toulouse the General Avitus to the highest dignity. At Arles, in the presence of an assenting army and people, he shortly afterwards (July 10, 455) assumed the purple. The Roman Senate, although still jealously guarding its right of election, was forced to sanction this already accomplished act, and to invite Avitus to the city. The Gaul, a man of good education, here received ratification of the election, and his son-in-law, the celebrated Apollinaris Sidonius, on Jan. 1, 456, in presence of the assembled Fathers, read the customary panegyric on the new Emperor, which brought him the honour of a bronze statue in the Forum of Trajan. The fortunate poet himself relates that the "purple-clad Quirites" (*i.e.,* the Senate) unanimously awarded him this distinction, and he flattered himself with the thought that Trajan had beheld the monument erected to his (the poet's) honour among the illustrious authors of Greek and Latin literature.[1] Even with the horrors of the sack still present to their minds, the Romans held fast to the honoured customs of their ancestors, and we have in this passage from Sidonius a proof that the Vandals had neither seized on the Ulpian library nor on the statues, which still continued to decorate their halls.

The Roman Senate meanwhile, could not forget that it had recognized an Emperor who, with the help of provincials and barbarians, had usurped the throne.

[1] *Sistimus portu, geminae potiti*
Fronde coronae:
Quam mihi indulsit populus Quirini
Blattifer, vel quam tribuit senatus:
Quam peritorum dedit ordo consors
Judiciorum:
Cum meis poni statuam perennem
Nerva Trajanus titulis videret
Inter auctores utrinsque fixam
Bibliothecae.
—Apollin. Sidon., Ep. xvi., ad Firmianum, lib. ix. p. 284.

A secret agreement was entered into for the overthrow of Avitus, the chief party to the plot being Count Ricimer, a foreigner who had risen to power in Italy.[1] Ricimer, who was a descendant of the Spanish-Suevic house, his mother having been a daughter of King Wallia, had learnt the arts of war in the school of Aetius, and had served with distinction successively under Valentinian, Maximus and Avitus. Bravery, cunning, and ambition qualified him, as they had previously qualified Stilicho, for a distinguished career in these troubled times, when, under a declining Empire there was nothing to prevent a German soldier from rising to the highest power, or even from seizing the throne of Italy. Ricimer, who was General of the Empire, had acquired renown by a victory which he had recently gained over the Vandals in Corsican waters. With the cooperation of the Senate he rebelled against Avitus. The Senators having pronounced his deposition, the aged and defenseless Emperor fled from Rome and betook himself to Placentia. There he exchanged the purple for the vestments of a bishop, but finding himself still insecure and proscribed by the Senate, he sought to escape to his native land, Auvergne, when death met him by the way (Sept. 456).[2]

The extinction of the Imperial line of Theodosius, and the state of universal anarchy into which the Empire had

[1] *Nam patre Suevus, a genetrice Gethes,* says Sidonius, *Paneg. Anthemii* (carm. ii. v. 361). More bombastic even than Claudian, Sidonius found his Stilicho in Ricimer; he makes the Emperors Avitus, Majorianus, and Anthemius in turn the theme of the traditional panegyrics.

[2] Gregory of Tours, *Hist. Franc.,* ii. c. 11.

fallen, had given a passing vigour to the Senate, the highest lawful authority in the State. Rome, which since Valentinian III. had frequently been the Imperial residence, was again recognised as head of the Empire. All power, it is true, lay in the hand of the German stranger Ricimer, and with this audacious upstart begins the rule of the mercenaries in Italy. Under this rule, after two decades of terrible confusion, the Empire sank. In vain had the national Roman party sought to strengthen itself since the time of Honorius, to deprive the barbarians of influence, and to drive back the advancing tide of Teutonism. The decay of the Roman constitution, and the system of mercenaries, which had become indispensable, frustrated all efforts of the Senate. Insolent barbarians, generals of armies in the service of mere shadows of emperors, now formed an aristocracy of the sword—a foreign military nobility side by side with the remnant of the ancient hereditary nobility of Rome. Nothing but some specially favourable opportunity was required to constitute the boldest of these invaders ruler of Italy. Ricimer, however, was not the man fitted for such high office. Satisfied to govern Rome as tyrant under puppet-emperors, creatures of his own, he but prepared the way for the hero of the German future.

Rise of the power of Ricimer.

The throne of the Caesars remained vacant six months, during which interval Ricimer continued sole ruler. He allowed himself to be nominated Patricius, Feb. 28, 457, while he bestowed the dignity of Magister Militum upon Julius Valerius Majorianus, a former companion-in-arms under

He raises Majorian to the throne, April 1, 467.

Aetius. His favourite was then allowed to ascend the throne, and Majorian was proclaimed Emperor in the camp at Ravenna (April 1, 457). The wishes of the people, the State, and the Senate, even those of the Eastern Emperor Leo I., were satisfied by this election.[1] Rare virtues adorned the character of the new Emperor. The Latins hailed him with rejoicings. His accession to the throne recalled to his astonished contemporaries memories of the best of the Caesars, amid whom he was worthy to have reigned; and in Majorian posterity recognised with admiration the last noble Emperor of Rome. In his rescript to the Senate, we seem to hear the voice of Trajan. The manifesto of an Emperor, who, in the midst of ruin and distress determined to rule according to the laws of the State, filled Rome with satisfaction, and all ensuing edicts issued by Majorian called forth the admiration of mankind for the wisdom and humanity by which they were dictated.

Edict for the protection of Roman monuments.

Among these laws, one concerning Rome particularly claims our attention. The noble-minded ruler, anxious to restore the disordered Empire, to improve the administration of the finances, and to infuse new

[1] Apoll. Sidon. in the *Panegyr. Majoriani* Carmen v. 385, &c.

Postquam ordine vobis
Ordo omnis regnum dederat, plebs, curia, miles
Et collega simul.

With regard to the share taken by the Senate in his election, Majorian himself, in his letter, uses the words: *favete nunc Principi, quem fecistis.* The words: *Erit apud nos cum parente patricioque nostro Ricimere rei militaris pervigil cura,* denote Ricimer's position. Novell. Major. in Cod. Theod., s. Curtius, *Commentarii de Senatu Rom. post Tempora Reipublicae,* &c., v. c. 1, p. 130.

life into the servile Curiae of the cities, took Rome under his special protection. Her desolate aspect, the rapid decay of the monuments, now no longer cared for, still more the wilful destruction of ancient buildings by the rapacity of the Romans themselves, filled him with shame. He therefore promulgated the following edict:—"We, the rulers of the State, with a view to restoring the beauty of our venerable city, desire to put an end to the abuses which have already long excited our indignation. It is well known that in several instances public buildings, in which all the ornament of the city consisted, have been destroyed with the criminal permission of the authorities, on the pretext that the materials were necessary for public works. The splendid structures of ancient buildings have been overthrown, and the Great has been everywhere destroyed in order to erect the Little. From this has arisen the abuse that whoever has built a private house has, through the favour of the judges appointed by the city, presumed to appropriate the necessary materials from public buildings, whereas all such buildings as contribute to the splendour of the city should have been restored and upheld by the loving reverence of the citizens. We accordingly command, by a universal law, that all buildings which were of old erected for the public use or ornament, be they temples or monuments, shall henceforward neither be destroyed nor touched by anyone whomsoever. Any magistrate permitting the infringement of this law shall be punished by a fine of fifty pounds of gold; any servant of the law, or any Numerarius, acting on such order, or not resisting such work of destruction, shall, after undergoing flogging, also suffer the loss of both his hands, because, instead of protecting the monuments of antiquity, he has damaged them. Such places as have been appropriated by their present occupiers by unfair means must remain unharmed. Should any of their contents have been removed, we command that they be given back to the State. We order the restoration of what has been alienated; and we suppress for the future the *licentia competendi.* Should it be found anywhere necessary to construct a new building, or should the restoration of an old be impossible, the illustrious and venerable Senate shall collect all necessary information, and if, after due consideration, they find such building requisite, the matter shall be laid before our sovereign judgment. For what can in no wise be restored shall at least be employed to the adornment of some other public building."[1]

The state of barbarism to which this edict bears witness had set in under Constantine, since whose days the populace had continued to wage destruction to the monuments of antiquity.[2] The impoverished

[1] *Legum Novell Liber.,* at the end of the *Cod. Theod., tit. vi.* 1, *De aedif. publ.* The edict is dated: *VI. Idus Jul. Ravennae,* under the consulate of the Emperors Leo and Majorianus, A.D. 458, and addressed to the Praef. Praet. Aemilianus.

[2] Earlier Emperors had been obliged to issue similar edicts; thus Valens and Valentinian, A.D. 376: *Novum—opus qui volet in urbe moliri, sua pecunia, suis operibus absolvat, non contractis veteribus emolumentis, non effossis nobilium operum substructionib., non redivivis de publico saxis, non marmorum frustis spoliatarum aedium deformatione convulsis.* To the Senate, Cod. Theod., lib. xv. 1, n. 19. Edicts of a like nature were issued by Valentinian, Theodosius, Honorius and Arcadius.

descendants of Trajan regarded with ever increasing indifference the neglected monuments of Imperial greatness, and if nobler minded patriots still cherished the traditions of antiquity, rapacity proved on the whole stronger than reverence, and the officials, many of whom would have had difficulty in tracing their ancestors on the banks of the Ister or the Rhine, remained either indifferent or corruptible. Colonnades, basilicas, and temples, probably also a theatre or circus here or there attracted the desire for the possession of their valuable materials, and it seemed more rational to apply the slabs of marble to private uses than to leave them to the destruction of the elements. No one ventured to touch the more conspicuous buildings, but the smaller and more obscure were plundered with impunity, and many deserted temples, together with the foundation and soil upon which they stood, had already passed over into the possession of private persons. The building of Christian churches since the time of Constantine had given an irresistible impulse to the pillage of ancient monuments. The priests, to whom the edict in great part applied, carried off marble and material of different kinds to build or beautify their churches. The time had come when Rome, preying on her own vitals, became little better than a great lime-pit or public stone-quarry, and as such served the Romans themselves for more than a thousand years.

Whatever wise laws Majorian might issue, he could arrest neither the ruin of the city nor that of the Empire. He sank under the heavy burden—the last support of Rome. The chief object of his ambition had been the chastisement of Genseric and the reconquest of Africa. After quelling an insurrection in Gaul, he concluded a fresh alliance with Theodoric, King of the Visigoths, equipped a fleet and a numerous army, and set forth from Gaul to march against the Vandals at Saragossa in May 460. The loss, however, of a portion of his fleet in the harbour of Carthagena, where, perhaps with the treacherous connivance of Ricimer, it had been surprised, obliged the Emperor to return to Gaul, and he soon after met his fall. Ricimer had discovered that Majorian reigned independently as a Roman, and with ease overthrew the defenceless Emperor. As Majorian was about to return to Rome, he took him prisoner at Tortona, August 2, 461. The noble-minded Emperor yielded to the demands of the tyrant, laid aside the purple, and on the 7th August was beheaded. "A man," says the Greek historian, "just to his subordinates, terrible to the enemy, who excelled in each and every virtue all who had previously ruled over the Romans."[1] Rome's last hopes were buried in the grave of this noble Emperor.

Fall of Majorian, August 7, 461.

[1] Procopius, *De Bello Vandal,* i. 7, informs us that Majorian died of dysentery, a report in all probability spread by Ricimer. We cannot doubt, however, that the Emperor met his death by violent means. *Occisus est ad fluvium Hyram VII. Id. Aug.* (*Incert. Chron.* in Clinton). Τῆς κεφαλῆς ἀπετέμνετο: *Jo. Antiocheni Fragm.,* p. 616. The latest authority regarding this Emperor is Luigi Cantarelli, *L'imperatore Maioriano* (*Archivio della Società Romana di Storia Patria,* vol. vi.).

2. DEATH OF LEO I., 461—HIS FOUNDATIONS IN ROME— THE FIRST CONVENT BESIDE S. PETER'S—BASILICA OF S. STEPHEN ON THE VIA LATINA—ITS DISCOVERY IN 1857 — HILARY POPE — SEVERUS EMPEROR— ANTHEMIUS EMPEROR — HIS ENTRY INTO ROME —OBLATIONS OF HILARY.

Death of Leo I. 461. Foundation of the primacy of Rome.

The year of Majorian's death also witnessed the vacancy of the Papal chair; Leo, who had honourably filled it during a reign of more than twenty-one disastrous years, dying on November 10. A great priest, his memory is justly sacred to the Romans, not only as a legendary deliverer of the city from Attila, but also as the alleviator of its misery in the sack of Genseric. Bold, prudent and resolute, eloquent and learned, Leo was a true bishop, and the first great Pope in the annals of the Roman Church. With unsparing severity he subdued Manicheans, Priscillians, and Pelagians, and in the Synod of Chalcedon (451)—the first Synod over which the Legates of Rome presided—he vanquished the Monophysite heresy of Eutyches. He further subjected the recalcitrant Bishops of Illyria and Gaul to the supremacy of S. Peter's chair,—a supremacy which, by his means, was established as a doctrine, and confirmed by Imperial edict.[1] In his writings,

[1] This supremacy was confirmed in the West as early as 445, by a decree of Valentinian III. (*Leo. Op.,* Ep. xi., ed. Ballerini). A decree was also passed at Chalcedon, which accorded to New Rome the same privileges as belonged to Old Rome, and this canon, disputed by Leo, laid the foundations of the Eastern schism. The clause proclaiming Peter Primate of the Universal Church was carried by Leo.

consisting of numerous sermons and letters, there rests a kind of reflected glory from the times of Jerome, Augustine and Paulinus no longer apparent in the works of his successors. Leo was the first Pope buried in the vestibule of S. Peter; and to him, the founder of the dogmatic supremacy of Apostolic chair, the grateful Church awarded the name of Great.[1]

Rome, however, retains scarcely any memorial of his reign. After the Vandal pillage he strove to restore the injury and robbery done to the churches. He decorated the tribune in the Lateran; also those in S. Peter's and S. Paul's; and founded in the Vatican the first monastery of SS. John and Paul. But if the zealous Bishop seemed to encourage monasticism, he restricted celibacy in the already depopulated city by an edict forbidding any maiden to take the veil before she had reached her fortieth year. He built a basilica in memory of Bishop Cornelius in the Coemeterium of Calixtus on the Via

Ep. x.: *sed hujus muneris sacramentum ita Dominus ad omnium Apostolorum officium pertinere voluit, ut in B. Petro Apostolor. omnium summo, principaliter collocaret; et ab ipso quasi quodam capite, dona sua velit in corpus omne manare: ut exortem se mysterii intelligeret esse divini, qui ausus fuisset a Petri soliditate recedere. Hunc enim in consortium individuae unitatis assumtum, id quod ipse erat, voluit nominari, dicendo Tu es Petrus,* and Ep. xiv. Ed. Perthel, *Papst Leo's I. Leben und Lehren,* Jena, 1843, p. 218; Joseph Langen, *Gesch. der Röm. Kirche van Leo I. bis Nicol. I.,* Bonn, 1885, p. 104, f.

[1] Perthel, whose work is directed against the theory held by W. A. Arendt (*Leo der Grosze und seine Zeit.,* Mainz, 1835), disputes Leo's claim to the title, maintaining that he was only great as compared to the insignificance of his contemporaries. He forgets, meanwhile that no light can shed its rays but in the dark: "nell' etadi grosse," as Dante tells us.

Appia, and his pious friend Demetrias of the Anician family presented him with her beautiful estate on the Via Latina, three miles beyond the gate, as a site for a basilica to S. Stephen. These churches, although mentioned in the books of the pilgrims of later times, disappeared in the Middle Ages, and it was only at the end of the year 1857 that, in some excavations on the Via Latina, workmen came upon the traces of an ancient basilica, which a marble inscription proved to be the long-forgotten basilica of Leo.[1]

Hilary Pope, 461–465. Severus Emperor, 461–465.

The Sardinian Hilary succeeded to the chair of Peter, November 461, at a time when a creature of Ricimer, the Lucanian Libius Severus, filled the Imperial throne. The unimportant reign of this puppet-Emperor lasted from Nov. 19, 461, until the autumn of 465, when the all-powerful minister found him no longer necessary.[2] Supported by an

[1] The inscription, which belongs to some period between the years 844 and 847, was copied from the remains of the choir screen by the present writer: *Canpaa Expensis Mei Feci Temp. Dn. Sergii Ter Beassim. Et Coangelico Junioris Pape Amen.* On the other side: *Stephani Primis Martiri Ego Lupo Gricarius.* The basilica was erected on the remains of an ancient villa, which, apparently originally belonging to Domitian, afterwards passed into the possession of the Sulpicii or Servilii and later into that of the Anicii. Several basilicas on the Campagna rose on the remains of country houses. Vaults in good preservation and belonging to Imperial times were likewise discovered on the Via Latina in the immediate neighbourhood of the church. Demetrias was the friend of Augustine, to whom Pelagius addressed the *Epistola ad Demetriadem,* which has found a place among the letters of Jerome.

[2] According to *Incert. Chron.,* Severus died August 15. Clinton, however, denies this, and seeks to prove that he lived until November. That he was entirely governed by Ricimer is proved by a copper coin of his reign, which, quite without precedent, bears, instead of the

army of German mercenaries and his inexhaustible wealth, feared and hated, Ricimer reigned alone nearly two years, but, although usurping the rights of Imperial power, he did not venture to make an end of the Empire, or exchange the title of Patrician with which the Emperor had invested him, for that of King. On the other hand in these death struggles of the Empire the Senate gave signs of patriotic courage. The corporation of the Roman Fathers still lived on, the only support of the tottering State; it still possessed men of the highest worth, who, like Gennadius Avienus and Caecina Basilius, "in the illustrious company of senators, next to the purple-clad ruler, were worthy to rank as princes." So says Sidonius, but he adds, "if one does not take into consideration the prerogative of the army."[1] The Senate openly opposed an active resistance to Ricimer, which the foreigner could the less overcome, since the Roman government had found a powerful supporter in Leo I. the Emperor of the East. The provinces outside Italy having fallen into the possession of various German tribes, Burgundians, Franks, Visigoths, and Vandals, the dissolution of the Western Empire seemed inevitable, and dishonoured Rome gradually sank into a position of ever increas-

Imperial monogram, that of Ricimer. Jul. Friedländer, *Die Münzen der Ostgothen,* Berlin, 1844, p. 5. The *Zeitschr. für Numism.* of A. v. Sallet, vol. ix., 1882, p. 1, f., contains an explanation and illustration of the *Exagium Solidi* of Ricimer, a bronze tablet with three silver bands, bearing on the obverse the words:—SALVIS DOMINIS NOSTRIS ET PATRICIO RICIMERE.

[1] Apoll. Sidon., i., Ep. 9, p. 22: *seposita praerogativa partis armatae, facile post purpuratum Principem principes erant.*

ing decrepitude, and caused Constantinople to appear as the true head of the Empire. The more noble-minded of the Eastern Emperors felt the duty of uprightly maintaining the unity and indivisibility of the Empire, and whilst they regarded declining Italy simply as a province, they prevented the Germans from making it their own. The National Roman party itself called on the Greek Emperor to protect the legitimate Imperial power.

Upon the death of Severus the throne remained more than a year unoccupied, and Ricimer was obliged, not only to allow the Senate to treat with Leo on the question of a new Emperor, but also to agree to the election of a Greek. He was, however, appeased by the promise of receiving as wife the daughter of the new Augustus. The newly elected Emperor was Anthemius, one of the foremost senators of the East, the husband of Euphemia, daughter of the Emperor Marcian. With solemn pomp, and with a train that resembled an army, Leo sent his protégé to Rome. Three miles from the gate he was received at Brontotas, a spot unknown to us, by the Senate, people, and army, and here, on April 12, 467, he accepted the Imperial dignity[1] and entered the city, which gladly and expectantly awaited his arrival. Ricimer himself shortly after celebrated his marriage with the Imperial princess, at which the poet Sidonius was present in the capacity of an orator from the Gallic provinces. The city overflowed in a sea of rapture (as a court poet

Anthemius Emperor, April 12, 467.

[1] Cassiod., *Chron.* For an account of the procession of Anthemius, see Idatius, *Chron.: cum ingenti multitudine exercitus copiosi.*

of our own days would express it), and marriage odes were declaimed in all the theatres, markets, forums, temples, and gymnasia. All occupations were at a stand, the law courts were closed, and all serious affairs were forgotten in the universal turmoil of festivities.[1] Rome, fallen as she was, still appeared to the Gaul as the capital of the universe; even in the fifth century he terms her the seat of law, the abode of learning, the curia of honour, the summit of the world, the birthplace of freedom, the city in which barbarians and slaves alone are strangers.[2] In the description of the Gallic poet, Rome appears for the last time in the festal robe of her ancient splendour, and, although the life of the people may have been reduced to a smaller scale, we perceive that as yet none of the ancient institutions for public pleasure or benefit had disappeared.[3] Sidonius delivered his

[1] Apoll. Sidon., Ep. 1, 5, p. 12: *vix per omnia theatra, macella, praetoria, fora, templa, gymnasia, talassio fescenninus explicaretur.... Jam quidem virgo tradita est, jam corona sponsus, jam palmata consularis, jam cyclade pronuba, jam toga senator honaratur, jam penulam deponit inglorius,* &c. Towards the end of Carmen ii., *Panegyr. Anth.,* the poet makes Rome appear in the form of a goddess, and travelling to Constantinople (represented as Aurora) implore the latter city to bestow Anthemius upon her as Emperor. The passage is the most original in the whole of the overladen panegyric.

[2] Epist. i. 6.

[3] At this period not only were the Baths of Diocletian in use, but also those of Nero and Alexander:—

Hinc ad balnea non Neroniana,
Nec quae Agrippa dedit, vel ille cujus
Bustum Dalmaticae vident Salonae:
Ad thermas tamen ire sed libebat
Privato bene praebitas pudori.

Sidon., carm. 23, ad Consentium, written A.D. 466; Fea, *Sulle rovine di Roma,* p. 271.

panegyric on Anthemius on January 1. The poet, an insipid flatterer, indifferently played the rôle of Claudian; happier however than his predecessor, his bombastic verses were rewarded with the Prefecture of Rome. Three years later he renounced this office to become Bishop of Clermont.

Amidst the festivities which were celebrated on the accession of Anthemius, astonished historians have especially dwelt on the Pagan festival of the Lupercalia, which was actually celebrated under the eyes of Emperor and Pope by the Christians of Rome, according to ancient custom in the month of February. In like manner twenty years later we shall come upon other memorable relics of Paganism in Rome, and see them invested with the garb of Christianity. The Roman priesthood had in other respects opportunity for doubting the Catholic orthodoxy of the new Emperor; they discovered unsound views in the Greek Anthemius, and among his followers the heretic Philotheus. Discord respecting dogma threatened to break out between the clergy and Emperor, and the Pope demanded the suppression of Byzantine teaching in Rome.

While the treasury was exhausted in the preparations of Anthemius for war against the Vandals, Hilary spent great sums of money in decorating churches. If we may credit the list of offerings, the churches, constantly enriched by emperors and private persons, found themselves in spite of the sack, in possession of inexhaustible sources of wealth. This is quite intelligible; the barbarians robbed the churches, but the estates remained, and since the estates were extensive, the revenues continued undiminished. The Roman Church had already acquired a territory greatly exceeding that possessed by the Patriarch either of Constantinople or of Alexandria, and was by far the richest Church of Christendom. Hilary replaced the treasures robbed by the Vandals from the Lateran, from S. Peter's, S. Paul's, and S. Lorenzo's by the most costly ornaments, and the imagination is excited by the account of the works of art to which decaying Rome gave birth.[1] After the downfall of the gods and of sculptors, art in the fifth century seemed to have found a refuge in the workshops of jewellers, brass-founders, and designers in mosaics. Skill and fancy were exercised in the making of vessels of various forms in massive metal, barbarously overladen with ornament; lamps and candelabra, golden doves and crosses; altars were covered with silver and gold, fonts were adorned with silver stags, arches of gold were placed over the shrine, which, borne on pillars of onyx, enclosed a golden lamb. Whilst Rome became impoverished and sank to decay, the churches abounded with treasures; and the nation, which was unable to equip an army or fleet for war against the Vandals, saw the basilicas accumulate fabulous wealth in gold and precious stones.

[1] *Lib. Pont.*, "Vita Hilarii." With regard to his buildings in the Lateran, see also book iii. chap. v. of the present history.

3. TRIAL OF ARVANDUS—FRUITLESS UNDERTAKINGS AGAINST AFRICA—ARROGANCE OF RICIMER AND HIS RUPTURE WITH ANTHEMIUS—HE BESIEGES ROME—THIRD SACK OF THE CITY, 472—OLYBRIUS EMPEROR—DEATH OF RICIMER—HIS MONUMENT IN ROME—S. AGATHA IN SUBURRA—GLYCERIUS AND JULIUS NEPOS EMPERORS—THE GERMAN MERCENARIES REVOLT—ORESTES CAUSES HIS SON ROMULUS AUGUSTULUS TO BE PROCLAIMED EMPEROR—ODOACER RULER OF ITALY, 476 — EXTINCTION OF THE EMPIRE OF THE WEST.

Trial of Arvandus.

The rule of Anthemius proved devoid alike of success and power. It was, however, distinguished by one remarkable event; the trial of Arvandus, Prefect of Gaul. This overbearing official had oppressed the great province, had been accused by the nobles of the country, and been forced to appear before the Senate in Rome. The illustrious Curia of the Empire constituted the highest judicial tribunal, and the accused was imprisoned on the Capitol itself. The last State trial of Rome in its character of Republic excites our curiosity in the highest degree, the more that Sidonius, the personal and courageous friend of the accused has described the incidents. Arvandus, in the custody of Flavius Asellus Count of the Treasury, was treated with the consideration due to his rank, and permitted to move about freely on the Capitol.[1] In the white robe of a candidate, he pressed the hands of the numerous nobles who came

[1] *Qui adhuc in eo semifumantem praefecturae nuper extortae dignitatem venerabatur,* i., Ep. 7.

to visit him, spoke with contempt of the abuses of the State, sparing neither the Senate nor Emperor, and amused himself in wandering round the square, or inspecting the silk stuffs and ornaments which the jewellers exposed for sale in their shops.[1] At the time appointed for the trial, the four Gallic accusers appeared in the unpretentious garments of suppliants, and with becoming moderation brought forward their charges against the proud aristocrat, who, with defiant scorn, acknowledged a letter which contained proof of his treason against the Emperor, and of his scheme for dividing the province between the Visigoths and Burgundians. This remarkable incident recalled the time of Verres and of Catiline, and restored once more to the Senate the consciousness of judicial majesty. Unanimously it pronounced Arvandus guilty, and the Prefect of Gaul was cashiered, degraded to plebeian rank, and finally condemned to death by the hand of the executioner. Arvandus awaited his doom in a prison on the island of the Tiber dedicated to Aesculapius. Before, however, the end of the thirty days appointed to elapse between a sentence and its execution, his friend Sidonius and other persons of influence contrived to get the sentence changed into one of exile.[2] This trial was one of the most honourable deeds which graced the dying days of the Senate. For Gaul, however, it was but an empty and formal satisfaction, since the governors of the province

[1] *Reus noster aream Capitolinam percurrere albatus:—modo serica, et gemmas, et praetiosa quaeque trapezitarum involucra rimari, et quasi mercaturus inspicere.*

[2] Sidonius still speaks of the island as *insula serpentis Epidaurii.*

continued, not only to drain it with the same rapacity as before, but further betrayed it into the hands of the Visigoths; in fact the immediate successor of Arvandus, Seronatus (a new Catiline), was for these offenses punished by the Senate with death.[1]

The preparations against the Vandals made by the united forces of the East and West, was one of the greatest efforts of the Empire, the existence of which was threatened by the incessant raids of the Africans on the coasts of the Mediterranean, and exhausted alike Byzantium and Rome. In spite of these immense preparations, the campaign in Africa under the conduct of Basiliscus and Marcellinus (468) had ended in misfortune. The prestige of Anthemius suffered a heavy blow by these reverses. Rome, counting on his alliance with Constantinople, had expected from him the restoration of Africa. As the power of the Emperor declined, the presumption of Ricimer increased. The Eastern Emperor had known how to free himself from Aspar, a formidable man, who had held a similar position in the Empire, but Anthemius found himself unable to fling off the yoke of his all-powerful minister and son-in-law. After an open rupture Ricimer removed from Rome to Milan, where he fixed his abode, and Rome was terrified by the report that he had there entered into an alliance with the barbarians on the other side of the Alps. A contract between him and the Emperor, effected through the mediation of Bishop Epiphanius of Ticinum or Pavia only brought about an apparent

[1] Sidonius gives a spirited account of his offenses, Ep. ii. 1, v. 13 and in vii., Ep. 7, relates the circumstances of his death.

reconciliation.[1] Ricimer started with his barbarian army from Milan, pushed on to Rome and besieged the city, setting up his camp near the Bridge of the Anio beyond the Salarian Gate[2] (472).

Ricimer besieges Rome, 472.

While Ricimer thus harassed Rome, Anicius Olybrius, with whom he had long before entered into an agreement, arrived from Constantinople. At the time of the capture of Rome by Genseric this Senator of illustrious family had saved himself by flight to Constantinople, and had there become the husband of Placidia, daughter of Eudoxia. Through his wife he was the only heir to the claims of the family of Theodosius the Great, and therefore the man most fitted to overthrow the Greek Anthemius. In spite, however, of the insignificance of his forces, and of the fact that the city was filled both with adherents of Ricimer and with Arians, the Emperor made a manful resistance. Pestilence broke out, and famine prevailed within the walls. The people began to talk of surrender.[3] Surrender was, however, delayed by the arrival of a foreigner, the Goth Bilimer the Commander of Gaul who, advancing by forced marches to the relief of the garrison threw himself with his troops into Rome. But the Trasteverine portion of the city found itself already in the power of Ricimer, who, from the side of the Vatican and the tomb of Hadrian, which is not yet spoken of as a fortress, strove to enter the city by the bridge and the Aurelian Gate. After a fierce struggle, in which

[1] Ennodius in the *Vita S. Ephiphan. Ticin. Episcopi.* in Sirmond, ii.

[2] *Hist. Misc.,* xv.; Sigonius, *De Occid. Imp.,* xiv. p. 385.

[3] Theophan., *Chronogr.*

Conquers and sacks the city, July 11, 472.

Bilimer fell, Ricimer forced the gate, whereupon his mercenaries, a mixed throng of Germans and others of Arian faith, flung themselves into the city, murdering and robbing all who came in their way (July 11, 472).

We have no definite information with regard to this sack, or of the fate of the monuments in the city. Writers of the time make no mention of any injury by fire, nor of any building having been destroyed.[1] A single inscription, however, informs us that the Prefect of the city, Anicius Acilius Aginatius Faustus, restored a statue of Minerva, whose temple had been burnt.[2] According to an ancient report the only two regions spared were those occupied by Ricimer, *i.e.,* the Vatican, at that time a territory already filled with convents, churches and hospitals, and the Janiculum or Trastevere, a portion of the city which formed a single region. It therefore follows that S. Peter's suffered no pillage, although the entire city was given up without reserve to the German mercenaries.[3]

Olybrius Emperor, 472.

Into this city, laid waste by pestilence, famine, murder and robbery, Flavius Anicius Olybrius now entered to take the diadem which he had so long

[1] With regard to this sack, Fea tells us: *si contentò di darle il sacco* (p. 274); and Bargaeus: *sic tamen, ut praeda contentus aedificiis pepercerit.*

[2] *Simulacrum Minervae abolendo incendio tumultus civilis igni tecto cadente confractum. Annal. d. Inst.,* 1849, p. 342. Anicius Faustus was Prefect of the city previous to the year 483.

[3] *Hist. Misc.,* xv.: *Praeter famis denique, morbique penuriam quibus eo tempore Roma affligebatur, insuper etiam gravissime depraedata est, et excepto duabus regionibus, in quibus Ricimirus cum suis manebat, caetera omnia praedatorum sunt aviditate vastata.*

coveted from the head of the dead Anthemius.[1] Already proclaimed Emperor with the consent of Leo and by the desire of the Vandal King, he took possession of the Palace of the Caesars, and allowed himself to be confirmed by the Senate in his dignities. But the spoiler of Rome, the murderer and tyrant of so many Emperors, was snatched away by pestilence.

Death of Ricimer, Aug. 18, 472.

Ricimer died suddenly on Aug. 18, 472. The memory of this German leader is still preserved in a church which he either built or restored on the slopes of the Quirinal. This is the present diaconate of S. Agatha in Suburra, one of the churches originally granted to the Arian Goths; for Arianism, the faith to which Germans who already swayed the Empire obstinately adhered, enjoyed at this time complete toleration in Rome. Ricimer had adorned the tribune with mosaics, of which only a drawing now remains. It represents Christ between the Apostles sitting on a globe, with a beard and long hair, his right hand raised, in his left a book; near him is S. Peter, who, curiously enough, bears only one key. Ricimer was undoubtedly buried in this church.[2]

Basilica of S. Agatha.

[1] On July 11, 472, according to the *Incert. Chron.* According to *Joh. Antiocheni Fragm.* (vol. iv., *Historicor. Graecor.*, ed. Karl Müller, p. 617), Anthemius, in seeking to escape, was captured and beheaded near S. Chrysogonus by the Burgundian Gundebald.

[2] Baron. and Murat., *ad Ann.* 472. Ciampini, *Vet. Mon.,* i. c. 38, gives a poor illustration of the mosaic, which fell in 1592. It contained the inscription: *Fl. Ricimer V. J. Magister Utriusq. Militiae Patricius Et Exconsul Ord. Pro Voto Adornavit.* For the inscription already mentioned on a bronze tablet: *Salvis DD. NN. Et Patricio Ricimere Eustatius VC. Urb. P. Fecit.,* see Muratori, *Thesaur Nov. Inscr.,* p. 266, and *Annal. ad Ann.* 472.

Death of Olybrius Oct. 23, 472.

Olybrius bestowed the dignity of Generalissimo of the Army on a Burgundian prince, named Gundebald, a nephew of Ricimer; but the Emperor himself dying of pestilence on the 23rd Oct., the throne was again left a shuttlecock in the hands of the barbarians. On the death of Anthemius and Olybrius, the last representative of Roman legitimacy, the dominion of the barbarians was re-established over Rome and Italy; but the question now was, where to find a leader, who should invest the anarchic rule of mercenaries with the principles of solidity and dignity.

Glycerius Emperor, March 5, 473.

Julius Nepos Emperor, June 24, 474.

In the frightful confusion of these last years, the unhappy forms of Emperors appear before us but as passing shadows.[1] Gundebald had bestowed the dignity of Emperor on Glycerius, of whose antecedents we have no information, at Ravenna on March 5, 473. The Burgundian general, however, soon left Italy and returned home to occupy the throne of his father Gundioch, and the barbarian army passed under the leadership of Roman generals.[2] Glycerius meanwhile was overthrown in 474 by Julius Nepos, son of Nepotianus, a Dalmatian by birth, who had been despatched by the widowed Empress Verina with an army from Byzantium to Ravenna. Marching against Rome, he overtook Glycerius at the harbour of the Tiber, forced him to abdicate, to

[1] The period is well described by Amédée Thierry, *Récits de l'histoire Romaine au Ve. siècle,* Paris, 1860.

[2] Hence arose the later rebellion of the mercenaries under Odoacer; see Pallmann, *Gesch. der Völkerwand.,* ii. p. 292. According to the *Fragm. Johis Antiocheni,* Glycerius had been Comes Domesticor.: τὴν τοῦ Κόμητος τῶν δομεστικῶν ἀξίαν ἔχοντα.

become a priest, and to take leave of public life as Bishop of Salona.[1] The repeated transformation of a dethroned emperor into a bishop testifies perhaps to the high esteem which the episcopal dignity enjoyed, although not on account of its spiritual, but of its worldly attributes. In a later age Avitus or Glycerius would have been simply invested with the cowl of a monk. Nepos, having been proclaimed Emperor in Rome on the 24th June, returned to Ravenna, and here entered into negotiations with Eurich, King of the Visigoths, whose friendship he had purchased with the cession of Auvergne. Orestes, whom he himself had shortly before made Patrician and General of the army in Gaul, now advanced against him in rebellion, and Nepos, escaping from Ravenna (Aug. 28, 475) across the sea, took refuge in the same Salona whither he had just banished Glycerius.

Overthrown by Orestes, Aug. 28, 475.

Orestes, a Roman from Pannonia, had formerly been secretary to Attila, but, after the death of the King of the Huns, had served the emperors as leader of barbarian troops.[2] He had commanded the army of mercenaries which had been led by Ricimer, and which was at that time in a state of the wildest ferment. The motley collection of Sarmatians and homeless Germans objected to march to Gaul, whither Nepos wished to remove them, and proposed instead to bestow on their general the crown of Italy. Orestes,

[1] Jordan, *De reb. Get.,* c. 45; *Incert. Chron.*; *Anonym. Valesii,* or the *Excerpta* at the end of Ammian. Marc.

[2] He was born at Pettau in Illyria. His wife was the daughter of the respected Comes Romulus. Amédée Thierry, *Récits,* p. 191.

however, judging it better to invest his youthful son with the Imperial purple, caused Romulus Augustulus to be proclaimed Emperor of the West, Oct. 31, 475. By the irony of fate, this, the last Emperor of Rome, united in his person the names of the first founder and the first Augustus of Rome.[1]

Romulus Augustulus, Emperor, Oct. 31, 475.

Only for a short time did he wear the purple, being soon overthrown by the same rebellious mercenaries to whom he had owned his dignity.[2] Since the time of Alaric and Attila, the dying Empire had taken as allies into its armies, Scyrri, Alans, Goths, and other barbarian tribes. These, with their leaders, now governed the Empire, and weary of servitude they became naturally masters of the country, the military power of which had completely died away. The head of these bands at that time was Odoacer, the son of Edecon, a Scyrrian in the service of Attila, a man of the most adventurous spirit, to whom as a youth, a prophecy had awarded royal power in the future. "Go to Italy," was the command of Severin, a monk in Noricum, "go as thou art, clad in wretched skins; soon thou wilt have power to confer great wealth."[3] After an adventurous and heroic career,

Odoacer leader of the barbarian mercenaries.

[1] The *Anon. Vales.*: *"Augustulus, qui ante regnum Romulus a parentibus vocabatur, a patre Oreste Patricio factus est imperator."* For the coins of the last Emperor with the inscription, *D. N. ROMULUS AUGUSTUS P. F. AUG.*, see Cohen, vol. viii. The Greeks corrupted the name Romulus into Momyllus, and, on account of his youth, that of Augustus was likewise transformed into Augustulus. The name of Romulus had been that of his maternal grandfather. Sievers, *Studien,* p. 523.

[2] Procopius, *De bello Goth.,* i. 1, at the beginning.

[3] The *Anon. Val.* relates this in his life of S. Severinus. *Vade ad Italiam, vade vilissimis nunc pellibus coopertus, sed multis cito plurima*

passed chiefly amid the din of battle (he had distinguished himself under Ricimer in the war against Anthemius), Odoacer had become the foremost leader in the motley company of mercenaries. These homeless warriors, Rugians, Heruli, Scyrri, and Turcilingians, persuaded by him that it would be more to their advantage to become settled masters of this beautiful land of Italy than to wander in the pay of miserable emperors, impatiently demanded from Orestes the third part of the soil of Italy. On his refusal to comply, they rose in indignant rebellion, and ranged themselves under the standard of Odoacer. Originally ambitious to become as powerful in the State as Ricimer had been, Odoacer ended by far surpassing his predecessor. Having been proclaimed King by his motley army, he immediately proceeded to Ticinum or Pavia, where Orestes had stationed himself. The town was stormed and Orestes beheaded soon after at Piacenza, while the last Emperor of Rome, Romulus Augustulus, fell at Ravenna into the hands of the first real King of German descent who reigned in Italy.

Becomes King in Italy, Aug. 23, 476.

Odoacer assumed the title of King, and at once obliged the abject Senate in Rome to satisfy him in the dignity. He refrained, however, from adopting the purple and diadem. His elevation took place in the third year of Zeno the Isaurian, the ninth year of Pope

largiturus. The name, which is, strictly speaking, Odovacar, signifies "guardian of property" (Pallman, ii. 168). He was an ordinary freeman of low birth, and was held to have been a Rugian or Scyrrian. The remarkable *Fragm. Johannis Antiocheni* says: 'Οδόακρος γένος ῶν τῶν...Σκίρων πατρὸς δὲ 'Ιδικῶνος καὶ ἀδελφὸς 'Ονοούλφου.

Simplicius, the second of the consulate of Basiliscus and the first of Armatus, on Aug. 23, 476 A.D.[1] The fortunate barbarian did not, however, entertain the idea of setting himself up as Emperor of the West, or even of making Italy an independent Teutonic kingdom apart from the Imperium. The majesty of a single and indivisible Empire, the centre of which Constantinople now was, still survived as a political principle recognised by the barbarians with respect. Odoacer merely desired to be lawful ruler in Italy, the last province which remained to the Empire in the West, and founded here no national, but only a barbarian, military monarchy, without foundation and without stability.[2] To his soldiers he gave the third part of the soil of Italy, and, to avoid all appearance of usurpation, forced Augustulus to a formal resignation before the Senate, and the Senate to the declaration that the Western Empire was extinct. The last political act of the Senatorial Curia excites a melancholy sympathy: it sent to the Emperor Zeno at Constantinople ambassadors, who, in the name of the Imperial Senate and people declared that Rome no longer required an indepen-

[1] Cassiodor., *Chron.*: *nomenque regis Odoacer adsumpsit, cum tamen nec purpura, nec regalibus uteretur insignibus*; Theoph., *Chronogr.*, pp. 102 and 103; *Incert. Chron.*: *Basilisco II. et Armato coss. Levatus est Odoacer rex X. Kal Sept. Eo etiam anno occisus est Orestes patricius Placentiae V. Kal. Sept. Item eo anno occisus est Paullus frater ejus in Ravenna prid. Non. Sept.*

[2] He was not, however, King of Italy. Pallman justly terms him a King of Mercenaries—a German King, and Felix Dahn speaks of his followers not as a race or people, but as an army of henchmen—"Landsknechtsregimenter" (*Die Könige der Germanen*).

dent Emperor, that a single Emperor was sufficient for both East and West. They had chosen, they said, as protector of Italy, Odoacer, a man experienced alike in the arts of war and peace, and they entreated Zeno to bestow the dignity of Patrician and the government of Italy on the man of their choice. The deplorable condition in which Rome found herself lessens the ignominy of this declaration; Imperial rule had become impossible, and the afflicted people recognised that the dominion of a German patrician, under the supremacy of Imperial power still existing in the East, was preferable to the continual change of powerless puppet emperors.

Negotiations with Zeno.

Zeno, himself a barbarian from Isauria, received at the same time an earnest application for aid from the dethroned Nepos, who desired his restoration as lawful Emperor of the West. Zeno replied to the Senators that, of the two emperors he had sent to Rome, one had been banished and the other put to death; that as the former was still living they must again receive him, and that it rested with Nepos to confer the Patriciate on Odoacer. Zeno, nevertheless, recognised that his client, Nepos, had no longer any hopes of regaining the throne, and that he must accept what was already an accomplished fact. The Emperor of the East received the diadem and crown-jewels of the Western Empire committed to his keeping, and deposited them in his palace. The usurper, who had presumed to snatch for himself the sovereignty of Italy, he endured for just so long a time as he himself was powerless to remove him. In his letters to Odoacer, Zeno merely bestows on him the title of "Patrician of the Romans." Abandoning Nepos, he resigned Rome and Italy to the rule of the German leader, under his Imperial authority.[1] Thus was the country received again as a province into the universal Empire, the division between East and West again removed, and the whole united under one Emperor, who now had his residence in Constantinople. The ancient unity of the Empire, as it had existed in the time of Constantine, was restored, but Rome and the West were given over to the Germans, and the ancient Latin polity of Europe expired.

Fall of Imperial power in the West, 476.

The extinction of the Roman Empire, from which the Germans had already snatched one province after another, only set the seal to the inward decay of the Latin race and the ancient Roman traditions. Even the Christian religion, which had everywhere replaced the old faith in the gods, no longer awoke any life in the people. The Gallic bishop Salvian casts a glance over the moral condition of these effete but now Christianized nations, and pronounces them all sunk in indolence and vice; only in the Goths, Vandals, and Franks, who had established themselves as conquerors in the Roman provinces, does he find purity of manners, vigour, and the energy of youth.

[1] An account of this embassy is given in the Excerpt of the lost history of Malchus in Photius (*Corp. Scriptor. Hist. Byz.*, ed Bonn, i. 235, 236). The Excerpts of Candidus pass it over in three words (*ibid.*, p. 476). Such are the scanty crumbs concerning this memorable event which have fallen to us from the table of Photius. The *Anon. Vales.* is silent. As all readers are aware, the last Roman Emperor, the beautiful boy Romulus Augustulus ended his unhappy life in Castellum Lucullanum, near Naples. Nepos was murdered at Salona, on May 9, 480.

"These," said he, "wax daily, we wane; they advance, we decay; they bloom, we wither—and shall we therefore be surprised if God gives all our provinces to the barbarians, in order that through their virtues these lands may be purified from the crimes of the Romans?" The great name of Roman, ay, even the title which was once the proudest among men, namely "Roman citizen," had already become contemptible.[1]

The Empire, dying of the decrepitude of age, was finally destroyed by the greatest conflict of races recorded in history. Upon its ruins Teutonism established itself, bringing fresh blood and spirit into the Latin race, and reconstituting the Western world through the assertion of individual freedom. The overthrow of the Roman Empire was in reality one of the greatest benefits which mankind ever received. Through it Europe became reinvigorated, and from out the chaos of barbarism a many-sided organism arose. The process of development was, however, slow and attended by terrible struggles. For Rome herself, the extinction of the Imperial power was followed by momentous consequences; now sinking into the position of a provincial town, her buildings fell into ever deeper decay, and her last political and civil life died out. No longer dominated by the Emperor of the West, the Papacy gained ascendency, and

[1] Salvian, *De vero judicio,* v. 32, p. 53: *Itaque nomen civium Romanorum aliquando non solum magno aestimatum, sed magno emptum, nunc ultro repudiatore ac fugitur; nec vile tantum, sed etiam abominabile pene habetur.* Further, lib. vii., and his lamentations at the end of lib. vi.: *vendunt nobis hostes lucis usuram, tota admodum salus nostra commercium est. O infelicitates nostrae, ad quid devenimus!—quid potest esse nobis vel abjectius vel miserius!*

the Church of Rome grew mighty amid decay. It assumed the place of the Empire, and, already a firm and powerful institution when the Empire fell, remained unshaken by the fate of the ancient world. It filled, for the time, the void caused by the disappearance of the Empire, and formed the bridge between antiquity and the modern world. Admitting the Germans who had destroyed the Empire into the civic rights of the Roman Church, it sought in them to prepare the elements of the new life in which it was to take the ruling place, until, after a long and extraordinary process, it became possible to restore the Western Empire under a Germanised Roman form. Amid terrible conflicts, through dark and dreary centuries, was accomplished the metamorphosis which is alike the grandest drama of history and the most noteworthy triumph of the ever-advancing, ever-developing Genius of Man.

BOOK SECOND.

FROM THE BEGINNING OF THE REIGN OF ODOACER TO THE ESTABLISHMENT OF THE EXARCHATE IN RAVENNA, 568.

CHAPTER I.

1. Reign of Odoacer—Simplicius Pope (468–483)—Building of New Churches—S. Stefano Rotondo—S. Bibiana—Odoacer Commands the Election of Felix III.—Theodoric enters Italy with the Ostrogoths—Overthrow of Odoacer's Rule—Theodoric becomes King of Italy, 491.

Rule of Odoacer.

Incapable of forming any new political conception, the ignorant but powerful and benevolent Odoacer took into his keeping the ruins of the Empire, upon which he settled his warlike followers. Supported by these followers, but depending for counsel on Latins, he governed Italy from Ravenna according to traditionary usage. The forms of government remained unaltered; the Emperor it is true was absent, but a shadow of the Senate still survived. The barbarian king allowed Roman affairs to be administered as heretofore through the Prefects. From the year 480 onwards, he probably even appointed the accustomed Consuls for the West, and the Consuls, on their entrance into office, gave the people the customary gifts of money and games in the Circus.[1] The Curia

[1] The West was without a Consul for seven years. In 480 the office is found again, Basilius junior being appointed Consul. He was

of hereditary Senators still enjoyed a traditional respect as Council of the Empire and representative of Rome, as the assembly of the ancient patricians, and boasted amid its ranks Basilius, Symmachus and Boethius, Faustus, Venantius, Severinus, Probinus, and other consular names. We possess no information, however, either as regards the number or the constitution of this corporation.

Rome itself remained tranquil and devoid of history during the thirteen years of the tolerant reign of Odoacer; the sole facts recorded being the erection of churches and the gradual development of the worship of the saints. The mythology of the heathen survived in Christianity in the creation of a new polytheism founded on the deeply rooted instincts of mankind, Latin and Greek races alike finding it impossible entirely to renounce the beliefs of their forefathers. Accustomed to a thousand temples and a thousand local gods, the descendants of Pagans baptised into the family of Christ, required in the place of the temples and deities they had abjured a thousand churches and a thousand saints. Hence a form of religion, in its origin purely spiritual and unconnected with images, became again in the cities

succeeded the following year (481) by Placidus junior. Sigonius, *De Occ. Imp.*, xv., without any foundation, asserts with regard to Odoacer: *Romani Senatus auctoritas, et consulum dignitas ad feroces contundendos spiritus dempta.* We are only acquainted with a single coin of Odoacer, which represents him (curiously enough) with mustachios, without a diadem, and is inscribed FL. ODOVAC. The only other memorial of his rule is the papyrus of the *Mus. Borbon.*, which speaks of him as DN.ODOVACAR. REX. J. Friedländer, *Die Münzen der Vandalen.*, Leipzig, 1849, p. 58.

and provinces a worship of local altars and of national patrons.

Simplicius, successor to Hilary, dedicated a basilica on the Coelian (the present S. Stefano Rotondo) to the proto-martyr Stephen. The building is now supposed to have been originally either the ancient Temple of Faunus, or that erected to the deified Claudius. In either case, then, must S. Stefano have afforded the earliest instance in Rome of the transformation of a Pagan temple into a Christian church. The beautiful circular form of the building lends support to the belief, the few other churches of like form being all of Pagan origin; and the fact that, after the adoption of the nave, the erection of a circular building was of rare occurrence, still further justifies the supposition.[1]

Simplicius, 468–483.

Consecrates S. Stefano Rotondo.

Simplicius also dedicated a church beside S. Lorenzo without the Walls to the proto-martyr, and built a basilica on the Esquiline close to S. Maria Maggiore in honour of S. Andrew. This basilica, which in the ninth century received the curious designation of "Cata Barbara Patricia," was erected on an estate which a Goth, Flavius Valila, a general of the Imperial army, had bequeathed to the church. An ancient aula, intended for secular purposes, built

[1] Italian archaeologists are mostly agreed in holding S. Stefano to have been a temple, and Agincourt (*Storia dell' arte italiana,* ii. 120) upholds the supposition. The *Mirabilia Romae* assert: *S. Stephanus rotundus fuit Templum Fauni.* The brickwork of the church testifies to a period of utter decadence. In the days of Gregory XIII. the walls were disfigured by a series of frescoes by Tempesta and Pomerancio, in which the Muse of Painting was degraded by the representation of scenes of utmost horror and brutality.

by Junius Bassus, Consul in the year 317, already occupied the spot. The aula was a beautiful square hall, richly inlaid with mosaics in variegated marble, representing mythological scenes—Diana engaged in the chase, and other subjects of a like nature. Simplicius, by the addition of an apse, transformed the hall into a Christian church. This apse he covered with mosaics, while, with the singular taste characteristic of the fifth century, he allowed the Pagan decorations to remain untouched. The mosaics survived until the seventeenth century, when this remarkable basilica was destroyed.[1]

The same Pope also consecrated the church of S. Bibiana beside the Licinian Palace. The origin of the palace itself is unknown, but the Vicus where it stood, near the gate of S. Lorenzo on the Esquiline field, bore the name of Ursus Pileatus.[2]

[1] The church stood close to S. Antonio Abbate. Piper, *Mythol. und Symbolik der Christl. Kunst,* i. 49. De Rossi has dealt with it thoroughly in *Bull. di Arch. Crist.,* 1871, p. 5, f. The name *Cata barbara patricia* he explains by the fact that the Patricius Valila being a Goth, was also a barbarian. The word *Cata* is equivalent to *ad* or *juxta.* Thus there were churches in Rome named *Cata Galla patricia* and *Cata Pauli.* The old inscription in the apse began with this couplet:

Haec Tibi Mens Valilae Decrevit Praedia XPE
Cui Testator Opes Detulit Ille Suas.

Valila is undoubtedly the same Goth who made the deed of gift for a church (celebrated as the Cata Cornuziana, of which we shall hear later) in Tivoli.

[2] Pompon. Letus, *De vetustate urbis,* explains the name Ursus Pileatus: *quod ibi fuit imago ursi habentis pileum in capite.* See Donatus, *De urbe Roma,* iii. 310; Niebuhr, in *Röm. Stadtbeschr.,* iii. 2, 332. The so-called Temple of Minerva Medica stood in the neighbourhood. Since the gardens of the Emperor P. Licinius

The death of Pope Simplicius in 483 gave rise to a point of controversy destined in the course of time to develop into a question of the highest importance. The Bishops of Rome had hitherto been nominated by the assembled congregations, or churches of the city, that is to say, by the people of all classes. The nomination accomplished, the returns of the election were laid before the Emperor, and not until after their validity had been examined into by an official, did the Emperor confirm the election of the bishop, his subordinate. Odoacer now claimed this right of ratification. He was Patrician and King, and filled the place of the Western Roman Emperor. He did not, however, belong to the Catholic Church, but instead, like all of German race at this period, was a follower of Arianism, the form of faith which most readily adapted itself to the untutored German intellect. Odoacer sent to Rome as his plenipotentiary, Cecina Basilius, Prefect of the Praetorium, his chief official, with authority to enforce the royal claim on the Senate and people and to inquire into the election. Before the clergy and laity assembled in the mausoleum of the Emperor Honorius in S. Peter's, Cecina Basilius laid a decree, to which Simplicius must already have given his assent. This decree ordained that no Papal election henceforward could take place without the co-operation of the royal plenipotentiary. The conclave yielded to the will of the King, whose justice was recognised alike by

Gallienus lay in the district, the entire complex of the adjacent buildings may have been known as the Palatium Licinianum. Lanciani, *Bull. comm.*, 1874, p. 55.

Arians and Catholics. The Arains still, however, retained undisturbed possession of all their churches both in Rome and elsewhere. A Roman of the renowned family of the Anicii was now elected Pope as Felix III.[1]

Felix III. 483–492.

Forbearance towards the Church, as towards all the State institutions, was for the German conqueror a necessity of self-preservation. His followers did not form a nation in Italy, only a mixed swarm of warlike adventurers, whose rude barbarism placed an impassable chasm between them and Roman civilisation. The rule of Odoacer was consequently nothing more than the rule of a military camp, and although endowed with the highest dignity of the Empire, he remained in Ravenna a foreigner, dreaded and hated, and powerless to bequeath the Italian crown to his descendants. The Byzantine Emperor regarded him as a usurper, and only awaited the first opportunity to set him aside. For this undertaking there was at hand a yet greater tribal leader of German race, and an entire people who had forsaken their devastated homes on the slopes of the Haemus, to descend upon the fertile plains of Italy. These were the warlike Ostrogoths, ruled at that time by Theodoric. The Emperor Zeno, fearing that in his repeated incursions across the frontiers of the Eastern

[1] Pope Symmachus refers to this Synod *in Mausoleo quod est apud b. Petrum ap.*; A. Thiel, *Ep. Rom. Pont. Genuinae,* Braunsberg, 1868, i. 685. It is, moreover, difficult to decide whether Odoacer issued this decision as a decree intended to apply to future occasions, or only to that in question. Dahn, *Könige der Germanen,* iii. Abt. p. 203, holds the latter view, while Staudenmaier, *Gesch. der Bischofswahlen,* p. 63, maintains the former.

Empire the Gothic King might prepare for Byzantium the fate which Italy had suffered at the hands of Odoacer, constituted Theodoric his ally, bestowing on the barbarian the titles of Consul and Patrician. In order to remove him from the East, the Emperor exhorted him to turn the thirst of his people for spoil and adventure towards the West and to snatch the land of Italy from the "tyrant" Odoacer. By virtue of a formal treaty Zeno made over to him and his people the investiture of this province of the Empire. Theodoric accordingly led his entire tribe across the Alps in 488, and appeared in formidable power on the banks of the Isonzo, in the summer of 489. The Goths of Theodoric had been more or less imbued with the influences of the civilisations both of East and West, and although judged by the standard of Latin culture, they may have been deemed barbarians, they were not altogether barbarians, such as the followers of Alaric had been. They formed moreover a nation which presented to the enervated and effeminate Italians the unusual spectacle of heroic manhood. It was in short the conviction of their own superiority as free men to which the Goths owed the subjugation of the ancient world.[1]

Theodoric and the Ostrogoths enter Italy, 488.

The struggle of the two military leaders for the possession of the beautiful and unhappy country was

[1] The probable number of Theodoric's followers remains unknown. Gibbon estimates it at a million. Later investigators, such as Köpke and Dahn, are content with from 200,000 to 250,000, with about 60,000 fighting men. But is it possible that the Ostrogoths can have found accommodation in Pavia side by side with the former inhabitants? (Sartorius, *Regierung der Ostgothen,* p. 15.)

long and fierce. Defeated on the Isonzo and afterwards at Verona, Odoacer threw himself on his last stronghold, Ravenna. The isolated assertion of a chronicler that, after the defeat at Verona he retreated to Rome, there to entrench himself, and that out of revenge for his rejection by the Romans he laid waste the Campagna, is very doubtful. The Roman Senate, whose adhesion had been gained by the Byzantine Emperor, had already arrived at a secret understanding with Theodoric, and, after Odoacer had been driven to bay at Ravenna, had openly declared in favour of the Gothic King. As early as the year 490 Theodoric, therefore, was able to send the Patrician Festus, the head of the Senate, to Zeno to request the royal mantle.[1]

Conquers Ravenna, March 5, 493.

For three years Odoacer made a gallant resistance at Ravenna. At length, reduced to despair, he opened the gates to Theodoric (March 5, 493). A few days later the victor faithlessly broke the treaty he had made with his valiant enemy, stabbing Odoacer with his own hand, and causing all his followers to be slain. Without waiting for the ratification of Anastasius, who, on the death of Zeno (April 9, 491) had succeeded to the Imperial throne, Theodoric had already adopted the title and insignia of King of Italy. Not until 498 did he receive recognition, the Emperor then surrendering all the jewels of the Imperial palace previously sent by Odoacer to Constantinople. Theodoric was by right of his people King of the Goths; by that of conquest, the election of his followers and the allegiance of the conquered

[1] *Anon. Valesii,* 53: *Fausto et Longino Coss., i.e.,* A.D. 490.

also King of Italy; by the surrender of the insignia of Empire, he now received the Imperial ratification of this right—the right, that is to say, to govern Italy as it had been previously governed by the Emperors of the West.[1] But while the Byzantine Emperor had only commissioned Theodoric to rescue the prefecture of Italy from the possession of a usurper, the Goth was himself little better than a usurper in his eyes. The new conqueror, on his side, recognised the legitimate authority of the Emperor, professing subjection to Anastasius, although at the same time regarding himself as nothing less than ruler in a country, the third part of which he had bestowed on his soldiers. He also fixed his residence at Ravenna, thence resolved to govern, according to Roman institutions, Rome, Italy, and perhaps the West. The project was, however, one which threatened danger, owing to the fact that Theodoric professed the Arian faith. The people whom he had led into Italy were a heretic people, and in Rome he found himself opposed by the already powerful bishop, the recognised head of the Church in the West.

[1] *Anon. Vales.*, 64: *Facta pace cum Anastasio imperatore per Festum de praesumptione regni, et omnia ornamenta palatii, quae Odoacher Constantinopolim transmiserat, remittit.* Dahn, *Die Könige der Germanen,* ii. 162, justly lays stress on this surrender of the insignia of the Western Empire, by which the views held by Belisarius, Justinian and Procopius regarding Theodoric's usurpation are deprived of all legal ground.

2. Dispute in Rome concerning the Pagan Festival of the Lupercalia—Its Abolition—Schism on the Election of Symmachus, or Laurentius—Synod of Symmachus in 499.

The Goths established themselves permanently in Italy, which now, for the first time, suffered an entire barbarian race to found a colony upon her soil, and henceforward had no choice but to admit an infusion of German principles into her Latin nationality. The succession of wars and devastations had completed the ruin of her native population. In Tuscany and the Emilia everything had been laid waste.[1] The unfortunate Latins assembled in the decaying towns, where the laws of Rome, the municipal forms and the scanty remnants of the ancient civilisation still lingered, and the Latin bishop, through the organism of the Church, alone upheld the rapidly decaying tradition of national unity. Rome, although reduced to the lowest ebb, had at least been spared the horrors of war. Neutral in the midst of the great struggle which decided the fate of Italy and resigned the country into the power of the German, the Roman people were occupied with the affairs of the Church, in which they found compensation for the political life which had passed away. Precisely at this time the city was stirred by a curious contest concerning the last publicly tolerated remnant of the heathen faith—the festival of the Lupercalia.

[1] *Quid Tuscia, quid Aemilia, caeteracque provinciae, in quibus hominum prope nullus existit,* says Pope Gelasius in his *Apologia adversus Andromach.* Baronius, *Anal. A.* 496. The words, however, must not be taken altogether literally.

Abolition of the festival of the Lupercalia.

The sanctuary of the Lupercal or the wolf-averting Pan, the oldest of all the Roman sanctuaries, was a dark cave at the foot of the Palatine. The Arcadian Evander, according to the legend, had dedicated it to Faunus, and the mythic she-wolf had here suckled Romulus and Remus. Here stood the ancient bronze group of the nursing wolf, perhaps the same statue which we now see in the Palace of the Conservatori.[1] The festival of the Lupercal, which centred round this sanctuary, was celebrated every year on February 15, and was followed on the 18th by the Februatio, or purifying of the city from the influence of demons. The Luperci (youths, members of the sacred college) uncovered themselves unabashed before the eyes of the people, and clad only with an apron of the skins of the goats slain in the sacrifice, ran from the Lupercal through the streets, swinging straps of leather, with which they hit the women strokes on the right hand, thereby to bestow the blessing of fruitfulness.[2] In such a procession had the celebrated Mark Antony once been seen in Rome. All other ancient festivals (many of which were indecent in the extreme) had yielded to the influence of Christianity. The Lupercal, however, still survived, and, as we have seen, was celebrated on the accession of Anthemius; so great being the reverence of the Romans for this, the most ancient of their national customs, that even as Christians they could not renounce it. And although the altered sense of decorum had already excluded people of rank from taking part in it, and had rele-

[1] Andreas Fulvius (*Antiq. R.,* ii. c. 51) holds this opinion.

[2] Preller, *Röm. Myth.,* i^3. 388, f.

gated the carnival-like festival to slaves and the lower classes, to the horror of the bishop it was still celebrated every year.

The Christians asserted that the attempt of the bishops to suppress it had provoked pestilence and famine. They even averred that the sack of the city at the hands of the barbarians, and the fall of the Empire, were due to the neglect of the worship of the God Februus. These views, which found support in the Senate, called forth a memorable work on the part of Pope Gelasius, a Roman who had succeeded Felix III. in March 492. This theological and critical treatise was addressed to Andromachus, head of the Senate and defender of the festival. Although nearly five hundred years had passed since Paul preached the gospel in Rome, the ancient worship of the gods was not yet extinct, and a remnant of former social and political beliefs still struggled against the new order which the Middle Ages had ushered in. So obstinately did the traditions of the ancient Fathers still linger among the aristocracy, so deeply rooted was Paganism among the members of the Senate, that consuls could still have been found who, in remembrance of their ancestors, observed the omens of the sacred hens, the auguries, and other ancient ceremonies which the religion of their forefathers had associated with their office.[1] Gelasius strove to make the Romans understand

Gelasius Pope, 492–496.

[1] Salvian., *De vero judicio,* vi. 19, p. 62: *quid enim? numquid non consulibus, et pulli adhuc gentilium sacrilegiorum more pascuntur, et volantis pennae auguria quaeruntur, ac paene omnia fiunt, quae etiam quondam pagani veteres, frivola atque irridenda duxerunt?*

that "they could not at the same time eat at the table of the Lord and at that of demons, nor drink from the chalice of God and that of the devil. Not the Lupercalia," he averred, "were to blame for the misery of Rome, but the vices of her inhabitants. To heathen magic and the continuance of godless customs were to be ascribed the fall of the Roman Empire, and the fact that the Roman name had almost become extinct."[1] It is probable that the zeal of the Pope succeeded in inducing the Senate to abolish the Lupercalia. The Church, however, accommodating herself from motives of a somewhat dangerous policy to the traditions of Paganism, transformed the old festival of purification in the Lupercalia into the feast of the Purification of Mary, when the procession bearing lighted tapers (Candelora) vividly recalled the earlier Pagan ceremony. The 2nd February was the day appointed for the Christian festival, and the same date has ever since witnessed its annual celebration.[2] The instance here described

[1] *Gelasius Papa adv. Andromachum Senatorem, ceterosque Romanos, qui Lupercalia secundum morem pristinum colenda constituebant, apologeticus Liber*; see Baron., *ad An.* 496; A. Thiel., *Ep. Rom. Pont Genuinae,* i. 598–607. This work belongs to the series of Apologies of Augustine, Orosius, and Salvian, and follows the same train of thought: *Numquid Lupercalia deerant, cum Urbem Alaricus evertit? Et nuper, cum Anthemii et Ricimeris civili furore subversa est, ubi sunt Lupercalia, cur istis non profuerunt. Postremo, quod ad me pertinet, nullus baptizatus, nullus Christianus hoc celebret, sed soli Pagani, quorum ritus est, exequantur. Me pronunciare convenit, Christianis ista perniciosa et funesta indubitanter existere.* He now proceeds to give the causes of the fall of the Empire: *ideo haec ipsa Imperia defecerunt: ideo etiam nomen Romanum, non remotis etiam Lupercalibus, usque ad extrema quaequae pervenit.*

[2] With reference to the transformation of some Pagan festivals into

serves to show us the form which Christianity had assumed in Rome towards the end of the fifth century.

Anastasius II., 496–498.

A few years later a more dangerous strife arose. Gelasius died in 496, and his successor, Anastasius II., a Roman, also dying shortly after his election (498),[1] the greater part of the clergy chose the Sardinian Symmachus as Pope (Nov. 22). The Senator Festus, however, had just now returned from Constantinople, whither he had gone to negotiate with the Emperor not only with reference to the recognition of Theodoric, but also with regard to the Henotikon, an edict of 482. This edict, by which Zeno hoped to silence the disputes concerning the Incarnation and nature of Christ, had been accepted by the East, but was refused recognition by the orthodox Bishops of Rome. Festus, who sided with the Emperor, with the aid of Byzantine gold bribed a part of the Roman clergy, and succeeded in obtaining the election of the deacon Lawrence to the episcopal office. Lawrence, in return for his promotion to the Apostolic chair, promised to sign the Henotikon. Both candidates were ordained the same day, Symmachus by the more numerous party in S. Peter's, Lawrence by a smaller body of adherents in the

Schism.

Christian ones, see Marangoni, *Cose Gent.,* c. 26, p. 99, and also Baron., *ad Ann.* 44: *gentilicii ritus in ecclesiam aliquando translati.*

[1] *Anastasius, natione Romanus, de reg. V. caput Tauri* (*Lib. Pont.*). Pope Alexander I. is likewise spoken of as belonging to the region Caput Tauri. This region (Esquiliae) is reckoned V. according to the civil division. The name Caput Tauri (variant, Tauma) is explained by the skull of an ox on the arch of the Porta S. Lorenzo, and is used to designate a spot near S. Bibiana.

Basilica of S. Maria, and thus clergy, people and Senate were again divided into two hostile camps. The faction of Lawrence was headed by the Consuls Festus and Probinus, leaders of the Senate, that of his opponent by the Senator Faustus.

The schism took the form of the fiercest civil war, and streets and churches became the scenes of constant strife. At length Theodoric, as royal umpire, called the heads of both factions to Ravenna. The Arian King in the fulness of his power pronounced with perfect justice the decision, that he who had been elected first and by the greater number, should be recognised as Pope. Symmachus therefore, ascended the Apostolic throne, and, after tranquillity had for a short time been restored to the city, held his first Roman Synod in S. Peter's (March 1, 499). This Council occupied itself principally with regulations for the Papal elections, which it sought to place beyond the influence of intriguing factions. The Council of Symmachus had a special importance for Rome as a city, in that the signatures appended to the Acts of the Synod afford us a list of the titular churches in existence at the time.[1]

Symmachus Pope, 498–514.

[1] *Synodus Romana I., Ann. 499, de tollendo ambitu in comitiis pontificiis,* tom. v. of Labbé, with the emendations of Baluzius, p. 446; also A. Thiel, *l. c.,* i. 651. The signatures of the presbyters are also given by Panvinius, *Epitome Pontif. Roman.,* p. 19, and Mabillon, *Mus. Ital.,* t. ii., in the Commentary to the *Ordo Roman.,* p. xiii : he enumerates thirty titles.

3. THE TITULAR BASILICAS OF ROME ABOUT THE YEAR 499.

These were as follows:—

1. Titulus Praxidae. The basilica on the Clivus Suburanus of the Esquiline, dedicated to the sister of Pudentiana.

2. Vestinae. This church (the present S. Vitale), which stands in the valley of the Quirinal, had been already consecrated by Innocent I. (between 401 and 417), in accordance with the will of the Roman lady Vestina, to S. Vitalis and his sons, Gervasius and Protasius.

3. S. Caeciliae. The beautiful church in Trastevere founded by Bishop Urban in the third century in the dwelling of the saint.

4. Pammachii. The basilica of SS. Giovanni and Paolo on the Clivus Scauri behind the Colosseum, built over an ancient Vivarium. It first appears in the Council of Symmachus with the name of Pammachius. Pammachius was apparently the Roman Senator to whom, on the death of his wife Paulina, S. Jerome addressed his letter of consolation.[1] Bestowing his wealth on the poor, Pammachius embraced monasticism and founded this church, which, in the time of Gregory the Great, was called after SS. John and Paul, two Roman brothers, and martyrs under Julian the Apostate.

5. S. Clementis. The celebrated ancient church between the Colosseum and the Lateran.

[1] S. Hieron., *Ep. ad Pammachium.*

6. Julii. The present S. Maria in Trastevere which, although owing its foundation to Bishop Julius I. (337–354), bore the name Calisti. According to a later legend, a spring of oil which appeared in the time of Augustus within the Taberna Meritoria, and which announced the birth of Christ, was the origin of the building of this basilica.[1]

7. Chrysogoni. This basilica also stands in the Trastevere and is dedicated to a Roman martyr of the time of Diocletian. The builder is unknown, and the church is mentioned for the first time in the Council of Symmachus.

8. Pudentis. The Basilica Pudentiana on the Esquiline, the oldest titular church in Rome, also called S. Pastor. It was originally named Pudentis, or "Ecclesia Pudentiana," *i.e.,* of Pudens, the Christian Senator who founded it in his own house.[2]

9. S. Sabinae. The largest and most beautiful church on the Aventine was erected either by Celestine I. or Sixtus III. in the first half of the fifth century and dedicated to Sabina, a Roman lady who suffered martyrdom under Hadrian. It was

[1] The legend is given in the *Mirabilia*: *Transtiberim ubi nunc est S. Maria fuit Templum Ravennatium, ubi terra manavit oleum tempore Octaviani, et fuit ibi domus meritoria, ubi morabantur milites, qui gratis serviebant in senatum.*

[2] This is shown by the ancient inscription belonging to the year 384, LEO PARDUS LECTOR DE PUDENTIANA, which, with the almost contemporary mosaic in the tribune, is the oldest historic monument in the church. On a document in the hand of Christ, represented in the mosaic, we read the words: DOMINUS CONSERVATOR ECCLESIAE PUDENTIANAE. De Rossi, *I monumenti del secolo IV. spettanti alla chiesa di S. Pudenziana,—Bullettino Arch.,* 1867, n. 4, and *Musaici Cristiani.*

founded, as we are informed by the mosaic inscription over the principal door,[1] by the Presbyter Peter of Illyria, and its splendid columns must undoubtedly have belonged to one of the temples on the Aventine, perhaps to the celebrated Temple of Diana.[2]

10. Equitii. The church of S. Martinus in Montibus on the Carinae near the Baths of Trajan, built by Pope Sylvester in the house of the Presbyter Equitius. Named at first after its founder Titulus Sylvestri, it bore the appendix "ad Orphea," derived perhaps from some ancient statue which may have stood on the spot. Later restored by Symmachus, it was dedicated to S. Sylvester and S. Martin of Tours, but as the restoration was not effected till the year 500, the church appears under its earlier title in the Council of Symmachus in 499. Some remains of the ancient church of Sylvester are traceable even in the present building.[3]

[1] *Culmen Apostolicum cum Caelestinus haberet*
Primus et in toto fulgeret episcopus orbe,
Haec quae miraris fundavit Presbyter urbis,
Illirica de gente Petrus, vir nomine tanto
Dignus, ab exortu Christi nutritus in aula,
Pauperibus locuples, sibi pauper, qui bona vitae
Praesentis fugiens meruit sperare futuram.

[2] Celestine filled the papal chair from 422 to 432. It is probable that the Emperor Honorius gave him permission to take columns from the ancient temples to use in the construction of his church, the laws for the protection of the buildings having been set aside since the Visigothic invasion. Martinelli believes the church of S. Sabina to have been the ancient Temple of Diana; Ampère that of Juno in remembrance of the fact that Juno was a Sabine deity. Ingenious derivations of this kind, however, were not in vogue in the fifth century (*Histoire Romaine à Rome,* ii. 532).

[3] *Ristretto di tutto quello che appartiene all' antichità e venerazione*

11. S. Damasi. The basilica known to us as that of S. Lorenzo by the Theatre of Pompey.

12. S. Matthaei. This church, which derived from an ancient palace the additional name "in Merulana," and which stood between S. Maria Maggiore and the Lateran, has disappeared.[1]

13. Aemilianae, as this church was called even in the time of Leo III. It can no longer be identified.

14. S. Eusebii. S. Eusebio stands near the so-called Trophies of Marius on the Esquiline. Its patron, a Roman priest, suffered martyrdom under Constantius for the Athanasian faith.

15. Tigridae, or Tigridis. The present S. Sixtus, on the Via Appia within the city, occupying the supposed site of the ancient Temple of Mars. The origin of the title is unknown. The church is, however, dedicated to the memory of Bishop Sixtus II., beheaded in the reign of Decius or Valerian, and under whom S. Lawrence held the office of archdeacon.[2]

16. Crescentianae. Neither basilica nor titular can any longer be defined with any degree of certainty. The *Liber Pontificalis,* however, mentions under the life of Anastasius I. (399–401) a Basilica

della chiesa de' SS. Silvestro e Martino (Roma, 1639), and Pougard, *Monumenti esistenti in S. Martino* (Roma, 1806).

[1] According to Niebuhr in Bunsen's *Stadtbeschr.,* iii. 2 Abt. p. 304, the ancient parish church of S. Matteo in Merulana was built about the year 600. It is not, however, mentioned by the *Lib. Pont.* in the life of Gregory I. It was rebuilt by Paschalis II. in 1110. Adinolfi, *Roma—di Mezzo,* i. 295.

[2] Severanus, *Memorie sacre delle 7 chiese di Roma,* p. 473. In Ugonio, p. 167, the church is called S. Sisto in Piscina; this author seeks to prove that the church occupies the site of the Temple of Mars.

Crescentiana in the second region, in the Via Mamurtini, a street which may have occupied the site of the present Salita di Marforio.[1]

17. S. Nicomedis. A church dedicated to S. Nicomedes is mentioned on the Via Nomentana; but as, amongst the basilicas enumerated in the *Acts of the Synod,* none outside the city gates find mention, the title must have been accorded elsewhere. The church, however, soon fell to ruin when the title was transferred by Gregory the Great to the Basilica S. Crucis in Hierusalem.[2]

18. S. Cyriaci. The ruined church *S. Cyriaci in Thermis Diocletiani,* the title of which was transferred by Sixtus IV. to SS. Quiricus and Julitta, a building which stands beside the present Arch of the Pantani. The ancient basilica dedicated to Cyriac, a Roman who suffered death under Diocletian, probably stood within the precincts of the baths. Although in use about 466, in the time of Sidonius Apollinaris, these baths were so spacious that a church may well have been constructed in one of the smaller chambers. A convent for women was also established within the building.[3]

19. S. Susannae. This church bears the designation

[1] *Lib. Pont.* in Anast.: *Hic fecit basilicam, quae dicitur Crescentiana in regione II. via Marmurtini* (variant: Mamertina).

[2] Nicomedes was a Roman presbyter who was beaten to death with clubs, and his body cast into the river from the Pons Sublicius. *Emerologio Sacro di Roma Cristiana,* by Piazza, ii. 161, on the 15th September.

[3] Ugonio, p. 197. Nardini, *Roma Ant.,* ii. 91, beheld the remains of the church of Ciriacus in the vineyard belonging to the Carthusians near the granary of Urban VIII. See also Martinelli, p. 354. Ciriacus, a deacon of the Roman Church, was sentenced to serve as

ad duas domos, by which is understood the house of Gabinus, father of the saint, and that of her uncle, the Bishop Caius. It stood on the Quirinal between the Baths of Diocletian and the Gardens of Sallust, and still remains, although in altered form. It is mentioned by Ambrosius as early as the year 370. Susanna, a Roman national saint, was, according to legend, a member of the family of Diocletian. The brutal Maximian desired to wed the young princess, but, by force of her personal charms, she converted his various envoys to Christianity. Attempts which, by the Emperor's orders, were made upon her chastity were averted by an angel; and the golden statue of Zeus, to which she was commanded to sacrifice, was destroyed by the mere breath of her lips. Susanna was beheaded by order of Diocletian; but Serena, the Emperor's wife, in secret a Christian, caused the remains of the saint to be enclosed within a silver coffin and buried in the Catacombs of Calixtus. Whether to the church of S. Susanna was united the neighbouring Titulas Caii, or whether each church remained separate and distinct, is a matter of uncertainty.[1]

20. S. Romani. Not a trace of this church remains. A basilica dedicated to the Roman martyr

hodman in the Baths of Diocletian. For the remarkable legend concerning him, see the Bollandists, 8th of August.

[1] Ugonio, 190, &c. Piazza, *La Gerarchia Cardinalizia* (*Titoli distrutti ovvero soppressi*), is of opinion that the two churches were distinct from the time of Gelasius I. All such statements are, however, very inexact, and Panvinius, whose authority is adopted by the greater number of later ecclesiastical writers, is not distinguished for accuracy.

is, however, mentioned outside the Porta Salaria in the Ager Veranus, near S. Lorenzo.[1]

21. Vitantii, or Byzantis. We are equally ignorant with regard to this title.[2]

22. S. Anastasiae. The ancient basilica of S. Anastasia, called Sub Palatio on account of its position under the Palatine. Its founder is unknown. Anastasia, a national saint of the Romans, is asserted by legend to have been the daughter of Chrysogonus, and to have followed her father to Aquileia. Under Diocletian, she was first exiled to the island of Palmaria and afterwards burnt in Rome.[3]

23. Sanctorum Apostolorum. Whether the present Church of the Apostles in the Baths of Constantine, in the region Via Lata, built by Pope Pelagius about 560, bore this title, or whether the titular church which existed in the time of Symmachus stood on some other site, is uncertain. The assertion, however, that Constantine had already built a church to the Apostles, is entirely unfounded.

24. Fasciolae. An ancient basilica on the Via

[1] Martinelli, &c., 387. Piazza does not bestow a single syllable on this church. Prudentius celebrated the *Passio Romani Martyris* under Galerius in *Peristephanon,* x.

[2] Severanus, p. 443, gives an inscription from the church of S. Sebastian: *Temporibus Innocentii Episcopi Proclinus et Ursus Presbyt. Tituli Bizantis S. Martyri ex voto fecerunt,* and Panvinius believes that the title belonged to S. Sabina. Bosio, *Roma Subt.,* iii. c. 12, holds it instead to have belonged to S. Susanna. The name in some manuscripts is written Vizantis, Vitantii, S. Susannae. See A Thiel, *l. c.*

[3] The history of this church has been written by Crescimbeni: *Istoria della Basil. di S. Anastasia,* Roma, 1722; Filippo Capello: *Brevi notizie dell' antico e moderno stato della Chiesa Collegiata di S. Anastasia,* 1722.

Appia, opposite S. Sisto. It is now dedicated to the canonised eunuchs Nereus and Achilleus, the alleged pupils of S. Peter, whose names recall the extinct mythology of Paganism. The title Fasciola cannot now be explained.[1]

25. S. Priscae. This now ancient church on the Aventine is erroneously supposed to have been the house of Aquila and his wife Priscilla. Here, according to tradition, Peter dwelt, and here baptised his converts from the fountain of Faunus. Aquila and Priscilla, the faithful friends of the Apostle, and the earliest members of the Christian community in Rome of whom we have any knowledge, were banished from the city by the edict of Claudius against the Jews, and appear to have died in Asia. At what time the church of S. Prisca arose on the Aventine we cannot now discover. It is probably, however, contemporary with S. Pudenziana;[2] consequently one of the oldest churches in Rome.

26. S. Marcelli. Tradition asserts that Bishop

[1] Probably derived from the name of a Roman matron. It is first mentioned in an inscription of the year 377, which runs as follows: CINNAMIUS. OPAS. LECTOR. TITULI. FASCIOLE. AMICUS. PAUPERUM. QUI. VIXIT. ANN'. XLVI. MENS'. VII. D. VIII. DEPOSIT'. IN. PACE. KAL. MART. GRATIANO. IIII. ET. MEROBAUDE. CONSS. (De Rossi, *Inscriptiones Christ.* , i. n. 262.)

[2] The Coemeterium of Priscilla, who was in all probability the mother of the Senator Pudens, stands on the Via Salaria. There were buried Pudens, Praxedis and Pudenziana; also a certain Prisca, believed by De Rossi to be the same as the saint whose church stands on the Aventine. This fact, and more inscriptions, lead him to the conclusion that a connection subsisted between the family of Pudens in the Vicus Patricius and that of Prisca on the Aventine, also that Prisca may have been the freedwoman of Pudens. *Bullett. Arch.,* 1867, n. 3.

Marcellus consecrated a house in the Via Lata belonging to Lucina, a Roman lady, as a basilica, and that here the Bishop himself suffered martyrdom, being torn to pieces by wild beasts. To Marcellus is ascribed the establishment of twenty-five titular churches.

27. Lucinae. The celebrated church of S. Lorenzo in Lucina, beside the Sundial of Augustus.[1]

28. S. Marci. The church of the Evangelist Mark in the Via Lata, under the Capitol and in the neighbourhood of the Circus Flaminius, probably built by Pope Marcus about 336. The spot on which it stood was called "Ad Pallacinas," from the ancient baths known by this name.[2]

4. LOCAL CHARACTER OF THE SAINTS TO WHOM THESE CHURCHES WERE DEDICATED—THEIR LOCAL DISTRIBUTION—THEIR TITLES IN THE TIME OF GREGORY THE GREAT, ABOUT 594 A.D.—THEIR NATURE—THE CARDINALS—THE "SEVEN CHURCHES" OF ROME.

Saints worshipped at this period.

For the history of the Roman religion it is instructive to bestow a glance on the different saints

[1] The *Acts of the Synod* of Symmachus give the signatures, Presbyter Lucinae and Presbyter Luarentii; different forms, apparently, of the same title.

[2] *Juxta Pallacinas,* according to the improved reading of the *Liber. Pont.* in the life of Marcus. Platina erroneously reads Palatinas, and Vignoli holds that it is to be explained from the Circus Flaminius which in times of barbarism was known simply as Palatium. Nevertheless, Sex. Roscius was murdered *ad balneas Pallacinas* (Cicero, *Pro Roscio,* vii. 18). The inscription of the sixth century, ANTIUS LECTOR DE PALLACINE, shows the name to be correct. De Rossi, *Inscript. Chr.,* i. 62. The Pallacinae, Baths, Porticoes, with which was also connected a monastery dedicated to S. Lawrence, must be thought of as situated opposite the present Palazzo Mattei.

to whom these ancient parish churches were dedicated. We observe that the principle of local relations was firmly adhered to; with the exception of the Apostles, all the holy men and women thus distinguished had been either Romans by birth, in the service of the Roman Church, or through martyrdom deserving of honour at its hands. No Greek saint has as yet obtained recognition. We find a parish already dedicated to each Apostle, but alone among the evangelists Matthew and Mark have received the distinction, and of Roman bishops none but Clement is thus early honoured by the dedication of an altar. After Clement came apparently Sylvester and Marcellus, while the basilicas of Julius, Calixtus, and Caius bear simply the names of their founders. Among priests and deacons many are distinguished: first and chiefly Lawrence, then Chrysogonus, Eusebius, and Nicomedes. Of senators Pudens and Pammachius, the first Roman monk of noble birth. Greater was the multitude of martyrs to whom churches were dedicated; more numerous still the crowd of holy women. Foremost among the latter the names of Agnes, Praxida, Pudentiana, Sabina, Cecilia, Susanna, Anastasia, and Prisca shine conspicuous, while the pious matrons Lucina and Vestina gave their names, if not to any altar, at least to two churches. The multitude of feminine saints finds explanation in the share which the matrons of Rome had borne in the extension of the Church, and in the fact that, according to the statement of Ammianus, they had also been its most liberal benefactors.

As regards local distribution, we find the greater number of these parish churches on the widespread Esquiline, the district inhabited by the lower classes—namely four, Praxida, Pudentiana, Matthaeus, and Eusebius; on the side of the Viminal, which adjoins the Quirinal, three, Cyriacus, Susanna, and Vitale; the Carinae boasted two, Equitius and S. Pietro ad Vincula, with which we are already acquainted; the Coelian two, Clemens and Pammachius. In the Via Lata, were those of Marcellus and Marcus; under the Palatine, that of Anastasia; on the Field of Mars, the two churches dedicated to Lawrence; on the Via Appia, the titulars Tigridae and Fasciolae; on the Aventine, two parish churches, Sabina and Prisca; in Trastevere, three parish churches, S. Maria, which still bore the title Juli, Chrysogonus, and Cecilia.

A later ecclesiastical writer who, in his work, has restored these twenty-eight titular churches from the list given in the records of the Synod of Symmachus and the *Liber Pontifcalis,*[1] has omitted the titulars Romani and Byzantis, substituting in their place those of Caius and Eudoxia Augusta or S. Pietro ad Vincula, in spite of the fact that neither of these churches is quoted as a titular in either the acts of Symmachus or those of Gregory the Great.[2] In the Synod, however, convened by Gregory in 594, the presbyters of

[1] Panvinius, in his work on the seven principal churches in Rome. Mabillon, through an error in counting, has, wrongly, thirty titular churches.

[2] I find these churches quoted as titulars for the first time in the life of Leo III (795–816) in the *Lib. Pont.,* where, however, it is not shown that, as some ecclesiastical writers assert, they had been raised to this rank by Leo I.

the following churches are recorded as having taken part:—1. Sylvester; 2. Vitalis; 3. John and Paul; 4. Lawrence; 5. Susanna; 6. Marcellus; 7. Julius and Callistus; 8. Marcus; 9. Sixtus; 10. Balbina; 11. Nereus and Achilleus; 12. Damasus; 13. Prisca; 14. Caecilia; 15. Chrysogonus; 16. Praxedis; 17. Apostolorum; 18. Sabina; 19. Eusebius; 20. Pudens; 21. Marcellinus and Petrus; 22. Quiriacus; 23. Quatuor Coronatorum.[1] Thus, in the time of Gregory the Great, we see that five of the titular churches of Symmachus are omitted, *i.e.*, Aemiliana, Crescentiana, Nicomedes, Matthaeus, and Caius.[2] On the other hand, the basilicas of S. Balbina on the Aventine, and on the Coelian that of SS. Marcellinus and Petrus, and that of the Quatuor Coronati are distinctly spoken of definitely as new titulars.[3]

Idea of the titular churches.

The titular churches were such as had been built to the honour of saints or martyrs, and which bore either the names of their patrons or those of their founders.

[1] Labbé, *Concil.*, tom. vi. 917. Gregory's Ep. ix. 22, gives a document, signed by the presbyters, of nine titular churches here mentioned.

[2] Panvinius is mistaken in asserting that the Aemiliana had disappeared before the time of Gregory: this titular being still mentioned in the *Lib. Pont.*, "Vita Leonis," iii. n. 403, in the passage speaking of the churches which stood between S. Balbina and S. Cyriacus. Piazza, *La Gerarch. Card.*, p. 531, also overlooks this passage.

[3] Panvinius maintains that Gregory I. had founded five new titular churches in place of those that had disappeared:—S. Balbina, S. Marcellinus and Petrus, S. Crux in Hier., S. Stephanus on the Coelian, and SS. Quat. Coronatorum. Neither in the *Acts of the Synods,* nor in the *Lib. Pont.,* can I discover any information respecting the elevation of S. Stephanus or S. Crux into titulars at this period. Great confusion, however, prevails with regard to the question.

They were destined for the baptism of, and for penitential retreats for, converts from Paganism to Christianity; also for the worship of the martyrs; and Bishop Marcellus in 304 seems first to have fixed their number at twenty-five.[1] They corresponded to the dioceses or parishes, and were really the parish churches of Rome. Distinct from the later eighteen diaconates or institutions for the maintenance of widows, orphans and the poor, and from the many small houses of prayer (oratoria, oracula), in them alone could the sacraments be administered. Restricted in the beginning to one presbyter or priest, the number of clergy was increased to two, three or more, when the first or most important was designated "Cardinalis," or Presbyter-cardinal.[2]

[1] *Lib. Pont.,* "Vita Marcelli": *et XXV. Titulos in urbe Roma constituit, quasi Dioccesis, propter baptismum et poenitentiam multorum, qui convertebantur ex paganis, et propter sepulturas martyrum.*

[2] According to Panvinius (*De Presbyt. Cardinal. orig. et* 28, *ipsor titulis, et* 21 *novis*), the title of cardinal arose before the time of Sylvester; according to Macer's *Hierolexicon,* in that of Stephen I. (257). *Cardinalis* from *incardinare,* i.e., *addicere alicui Ecclesiae.* Lexicons of Ducange and Macer; Piazza, *La Ger. Cardin.,* p. 351; Cardella, *Memorie Storiche de' Cardinali,* Roma, 1793; and the 61 Dissert. of Muratori. The title was also later borne by the seven bishops appointed to the Lateran, the fourteen regionary deacons, the four *Diaconi Palatini,* and the Abbots of S. Paul and S. Lorenzo. Sixtus V. was the first to fix the number of cardinals at seventy (Const. 50, Bullar. 2). Of these fifty-one were presbyters, since, in addition to the original twenty-eight titulars, he confirmed thirteen new, himself creating ten new ones. Sixtus also fixed the number of deacons at fourteen, and confirmed the reduction of the Lateran cardinal-bishops from seven to six. The remaining cardinals (since there were seventy-one) is explained by the fact that the title "in Damaso" was always associated with the dignity of cardinal-vice-chancellor. At present there are only forty-eight titles of the

The Cardinals.

According to the opinion of ecclesiastical writers the number of Cardinal-presbyters in the Roman Church, fixed in 336, in the time of Julius I., at twenty-eight, was not exceeded for a long time.[1] The number corresponded to the four patriarchal churches, S. Peter, S. Paul, S. Lorenzo without the Walls, and S. Maria Maggiore, in each of which principal churches seven Cardinals read mass each one day in the week; while subsequently to the episcopal church of Rome, that of S. John in Lateran, seven bishops from the neighbourhood of the city (Suburbicarii), namely, the Bishops of Ostia, Portus, Silva-Candida, and Sancta Rufina, the Sabina, Praeneste, Tusculum and Albanum, were assigned as Cardinal-bishops.[2] Under Honorius II., from the year 1125, the titulars fell into neglect, and twenty-one churches were created new titulars. Still it would seem that, from early times, in addition

presbyter-cardinals and fifteen of the deacons, to whom are added the Commendator of S. Lor. in Dam. and the six bishoprics, thus giving the seventy members of the *Sacrum Collegium.*

[1] In Joh. Diacon., *De eccl. Lateran.* (Mabill., *Mus. Ital.,* ii. 566, &c.), a writer of the middle of the thirteenth century, we find: *septem episcopi cum XXVIII. Cardinal. totzidem in ecclesiis intra muros urb. Romae praesidentibus* (p. 567).

[2] With regard to these seven cardinal-bishoprics, see Ughelli (*Italia Sacra,* t. i). Ostia was united to Velletri about the year 1150; Portus with Silva-Candida and S. Rufina about 1120. Silva-Candida, an ancient bishopric, formerly *ad Silvam Nigram,* was situated on the Via Aurelia, eight miles distant from the city. The martyrdom of two sisters, Rufina and Secunda, about the year 260, gave occasion to the foundation of a church in the time of Pope Julius; a farm in the locality still preserves the name of S. Rufina. The Saracens destroyed these creations of the Church. Nibby, *Anal.,* iii. 41; Tomasetti, *Della Campagna Romana, Archiv. Stor.,* Rom., 1880, iii. 306, f.

to the great titulars, small churches of the same character existed for the tombs of the saints, and this circumstance may explain the confusion which prevails in the accounts concerning the old cardinal-titles.[1]

Distinct from these parish churches, five basilicas, three within, two outside the city, already attracted a peculiar reverence, namely, the churches of S. John in Lateran, S. Peter, S. Paul, S. Lawrence without the Walls and S. Maria Maggiore. These churches were not assigned to any cardinal, belonged to no definite parish; their priest was the Pope as Bishop of Rome, and their congregation the whole body of believers. Associated with these, as early as the fourth century, another basilica is mentioned as enjoying universal honour, that of S. Sebastian, on the Appian Way, standing as it did above celebrated Catacombs. Later the Basilica of the Holy Cross in Jerusalem was also added to the list. Such are the so-called "Seven Churches of Rome," visited and venerated through the whole of the Middle Ages by the pilgrims of the West.[2]

[1] Mabill., *Mus. Ital.,* ii. p. xvi.

[2] See the works of Panvinius and Severanus, which treat of them in detail.

CHAPTER II.

1. Theodoric's Attitude towards the Romans—His Arrival in Rome, 500—His Speech to the People —The Abbot Fulgentius—The Rescripts in Cassiodorus—Condition of the Public Buildings— Theodoric's Care for their Preservation— Cloacae—Aqueducts—The Theatre of Pompey— The Palace of the Pincii—Palace of the Caesars —Forum of Trajan—The Capitol.

Theoderic maintains the traditionary forms of government.

Theodoric, a foreigner like Odoacer, had already acquired the respect if not the affection of the Romans; his justice, and yet more his acquiescence, in all existing forms of government had endeared him to the people. Long usage, moreover, had accustomed Italy to German rule and taught Italians to regard it as an inevitable necessity.

The Gothic King did not meddle with any of the existing institutions of the Roman Republic, but rather sought to flatter the people by awarding them a pompous recognition. The political and civil character of Roman administration remained unaltered; the conditions both of public and private life as entirely Roman as in the times of Theodosius or Honorius. Theodoric himself adopted the gentile name of Flavius. The Senate he treated with peculiar distinction, although the illustrious Fathers no longer retained any share in the administration of the State, and were now only regarded as the centre of such dignities as entitled their occupants to a seat in the Curia. The Petronii, Probi, Fausti, and Paulini, all members of the great family of the Anicii, were those who still held the highest offices in the State. In political affairs Senators were sent as ambassadors to the Court of Constantinople, while in the city itself they exercised a share in the criminal jurisdiction, retained all matters connected with the public well-being under their protection, and, lastly, possessed an influential voice in the papal elections and in ecclesiastical affairs. The collected letters of Cassiodorus contain seventeen Rescripts of Theodoric to the Patres Conscripti, in which the King, in the official style of the Empire, expresses his high esteem for the Senate and his intention to uphold and increase its dignity.[1] The Council of the Fathers appears in these Rescripts as the most dignified ruin of the city, and the reverence of the barbarian King was shown no less in his anxiety to preserve the

[1] See the first rescript to the Senate in which he notifies the appointment of Cassiodorus to the Patriciate,—*Var.,* lib. i. ep. 4 and 13: *quicquid enim humani generis floris est, habere curiam decet: et sicut arx decus est urbium, ita illa ornamentum est ordinum caeterorum,* and iii. ep. 6. In the *Paneg.* of Ennodius we find: *coronam curiae innumero flore velasti.* Theodoric writes to the Senate: *Domitori orbis, praesuli et reparatori libertatis, Senatui urbis Romae Flavius Theodoricus rex.* So in the *Praeceptum—contra illos sacerdotes, qui substantiam Ecclesiae—vendere aut donare praesumunt.* A. Thiel, *Ep. R. P.,* i. 695.

ancient institution than in his care for the Theatre of Pompey or the Circus Maximus. In appointing men of merit from among his retainers, or from the provinces, to the Patriciate, Consulate, or to other high offices, Theodoric politely recommended these candidates to the Senate, begging it to receive them as colleagues. From the titles of his officials— Magister Officiorum (Chancellor), Count of the Household troops, Prefect of the City, Quaestor, Count of the Patrimony (the private domain), Magister Scrinii (Director of the Chancery of State), Comes Sacrarum Largitionum (Minister of the Treasury and Commerce)—and still more from the two books of Formulas of nomination left us by Cassiodorus, we perceive how firmly Theodoric held to all the appointments of Constantine and his successors, and even sought to revive them in the public esteem. Roman legislation suffered no change.[1] The safety of his position as a foreigner in Italy required that the military dominion of the Gothic intruders should be concealed under the titles of the Republic, and that for the Romans Roman laws should be preserved. The position, however, of a German nation isolated amid Italians, and governed

[1] The well-known edict of Theodoric (issued in Rome in the year 500) contains only 144 short paragraphs, all taken from the Imperial codes, and referring more particularly to landed proprietors, slaves, and women. The only innovation was the appointment of the Gothic Count endowed with judicial power (Cassiodor., viii. 3). With regard to the offices of State under Theodoric, see Manso, *Gesch. des Ost-Gothischen Reichs,* Breslau, 1824, p. 92, &c., and Appendix, p. 342; and F. Dahn, *Die Könige der Germanen,* Abtheil. iii. and iv., which treats of the *Edictum Theodorici* and *Athalarici regis.*

by Roman institutions, brought with it its inevitable downfall; the instability of the political constitution and the lifelessness of political forms, which, resting on artificial support, endured like the ruins of antiquity, made the civil reorganisation of Italy impossible, and served only to further the rising power of the Church, which waxed powerful as the State decayed.

Comes to Rome, 500.

Theodoric came to Rome in the year 500.[1] The foreign King who now ruled over Italy showed himself for the first time to the Romans in the capital, not only in the hope of gaining the good will of the people, but also in that of quieting party strife, which still raged over the papal election. His entry was celebrated with the honours due to an Emperor, and by Roman flatterers he was saluted as another Trajan. Outside the city, either at the bridge of the Anio or at the foot of Monte Mario, he was received by the Senate and people, and by the Pope at the head of the clergy. The Arian King, from motives of policy, forthwith proceeded to the basilica of S. Peter, knelt in prayer, "with great reverence and like a Catholic," at the grave of the Apostle, and then advanced in triumphal pomp across Hadrian's bridge into the city. Following the precedent set by Theodoric, his German successors, bearing in later times the Imperial title, on their solemn entry into Rome, always proceeded direct to S. Peter's, and it is interesting to

[1] *Hoc anno dn. rex Theodoricus Romam cunctor. votis expetitus advenit et senatum suum mira affabilitate tractans Romanae plebis donavit annonas, atque admirandis moeniis deputata per singulos annos maxima pecuniae quantitate subvenit.* Cassiodorus' *Chronicle,* ed. by Th. Mommsen, vol. iii. of the *Abhandlungen der Sächs. Gesellsch. der Wissensch.*

observe that this ritual of Imperial reception, which survived throughout the entire Middle Ages, was established three hundred years before the days of Charles the Great.

The Gothic King made his dwelling in the now deserted Imperial palace on the Palatine, and gladdened the hearts of the Romans by appearing in the Curia, where the sight of their sovereign had long been an unfamiliar spectacle. Here the noble Boethius delivered the customary panegyric. The King then proceeded to the "Senatus," the building erected by Domitian beside the Arch of Severus and near the Janus Geminus, and delivered a public address. The spot where he stood, called "ad Palmam" or "Palma Aurea," must have been a platform belonging to the "Senatus."[1] Theodoric, a rude unlettered warrior, had never even learned to write, and his address in the corrupt Latin, acquired in the camp rather than amongst rhetoricians, must naturally have been brief. It may, perhaps, have been spoken through the mouth of a secretary.[2]

[1] *Anon. Valesii: venit ad Senatum et ad Palmam populo alloquutus.* Fulgentius or his biographer ("Vita B. Fulgentii," c. 13, t. ix., *Max. Bibl. Veter. Patr.,* Lugduni, 1677): *in loco qui Palma aurea dicitur, memorato Theodorico rege concionem faciente.* In Cassiodorus., *Var.,* iv. 30, it is expressly called *Curiae porticus, quae juxta domum Palmatam posita.* We must not, however, confuse this building with the *porticus palmaria* in S. Peter's. *Lib. Pont.,* "Vita Honorii": *in Porticu b. Petri Apos., quae adpellatur Palmata* (al. *Palmaria*). In the life of Sixtus III., on the other hand, *Domum Palmati intra urbem.* Preller, p. 143, quotes a passage from *Acta SS. Mai.,* t. vii. p. 12: *juxta arcum triumphi ad Palmam.* The *arcus triumphi* can be none other than the Arch of Severus.

[2] Theodoric had spent ten years in Byzantium, where Latin still

He explained to the Romans that he would conscientiously uphold all existing institutions of the Emperors, and in testimony of his sincerity had his promises engraved on tables of bronze.

Amid the applauding crowd of degenerate Romans who, at the foot of the plundered Capitol, beside the mutilated statues of their ancestors and the Rostra, listened to the official speech of a barbarian King, and where togas mingled with the cowls of monks and priests, was an African Abbot, Fulgentius, a fugitive who, escaping from Vandal persecution, had come from Sicily to Rome. Our informant, his old biographer, tells us, that Senate and people being alike moved to transports of rejoicing by the presence of the King, even the pious Fulgentius was unable to resist the prevailing enthusiasm. "When he" (these are the words of the biographer) "regarded the noble bearing and distinguished splendour of the Roman Curia, ranged according to order of precedence, and heard the shouting applause of a free people, the splendour and pomp of this world became suddenly revealed to him. The poor fugitive, shocked at himself, turned his glance from the magnificence of Rome towards Heaven, and astonished the surrounding crowd with the sudden ejaculation: 'How beautiful must be the heavenly Jerusalem when

remained the official language. The Gothic tongue survived in the Gothic race, but has left no monument of its existence behind in Italy, partly from the fact that but few Goths were able to write, and also because Latin was the language of the Church, the State and the Law. Edicts of Gothic kings to subjects of their own race were drawn up in Latin.

earthly Rome shines in such splendour.'"[1] The naïve outburst of admiration on the part of an African abbot testifies to the overpowering impression which the venerable city, already falling into ruin, but still essentially the Rome of antiquity, yet possessed over the minds of men.

The invaluable collection of the rescripts of Theodoric, —which we owe to the pen of Cassiodorus,— however, gives fuller information of the condition of Rome at this period, as well as of the active care of the Gothic King for the preservation of a city over which he was more worthy to rule than many Emperors had been before him. These edicts, in the turgid language of the minister, are a mixture of official pomposity and pedantic loquacity; while the admiration of the monuments of antiquity, and the effort to conceal the barbarian descent of the ruler under learned dissertations upon the origin and aim of individual buildings, and finally, the repeated allusions to antiquity, betray but too plainly that the period of barbarism had set in. To the passionate enthusiasm of the historian for his ancestral city is united the bitter grief of the Roman, who, watching the splendours of Antiquity hopelessly falling to decay, bids them a last farewell. Watching as he did the age of barbarism irresistibly draw near,[2]

Cassiodorus his minister.

[1] *Vita B. Fulgentii,* and Baron., *ad. Ann.* 500, *quam speciosa potest esse Hierusalem coelestis, si sic fulget Roma terrestris.*

[2] The term "barbarian" was generally used at this period without any sense of disparagement. Among the rescripts of Theodoric are some addressed simply to Romans and "barbarians" (*i.e.,* non-Romans). It is frequently used in documents of the sixth century, and after the fall of the Goths we frequently find the expression *barbaricum tempus*

Cassiodorus, by the exercise of his abilities succeeded in delaying its approach so long as he remained Theodoric's councillor. These two men, the Roman and the German, the last Senator and the first Gothic King of Italy, the representative of ancient civilisation and the intelligent northern barbarian, present in their coalition an interesting sight, and one which not only serves to illumine the first of many centuries of union between Italy and Germany, but also to typify the whole of Germanic-Roman civilisation.[1]

Condition of the monuments in the time of Theoderic.

After having impartially examined the accounts of the various sacks which the city had endured at the hands of German invaders, we are no longer surprised to find those celebrated buildings, upon which the eyes of Honorius had rested in 403, still existing in 500. The multitude of marble and bronze statues which still adorn the public squares may, however, awake our surprise. For Cassiodorus speaks of a numerous population of statues and an immense multitude of horses,—meaning equestrian statues.[2] Neither the horror of the Christians for the Pagan

Great number of statues.

naïvely employed as signifying war in opposition to peace (*pax*). Marini, *Papiri Dipl. Annot.,* 7, p. 285, and Ducange's Glossary. In the same way, in the language of civil law, the words *Sors barbarica* signify the third part of the landed property which fell to the Goths. We find the term "*campus barbaricus*" still surviving in the eighth century.

[1] As Theodoric stood towards the Latin world of his time, so Peter the Great stood towards the German world of a later age. Since, however, the character of the rude Czar cannot be compared with that of the noble Goth, the parallel only holds good so far as culture, generally speaking, is concerned.

[2] Cassiodor., *Var.,* viii. 13: *nam quid populus copiosissimus statuarum, greges etiam abundantissimi equorurm sunt cautela servandi.* He describes their beauty and form with enthusiasm. *Var.,* lib. vii. 15.

gods, the robbery of Constantine, nor the successive sacks of Visigoths, Vandals, or the mercenaries of Ricimer had been able wholly to exhaust the boundless wealth of Rome. Were the multitude of statues no longer so great as, according to the exaggerated estimate of Cassiodorus, almost to equal that of the inhabitants, yet the number still remaining was almost incalculable.[1] A separate official, distinguished with the title *Comitiva Romana,* or that of a Roman Count, subordinate to the Prefect of the city, was appointed for their protection, Theodoric or his ministers finding that in their degenerate age the buildings could no longer be entrusted to a public in whom the sense of beauty seemed extinct, but required the custody of watchmen. These "Vigiles" were obliged to parade the streets by night, to seize or prevent robbers from removing or injuring the statues, no longer valued for the sake of art, but for that of the material alone. Some relief was found in the thought that bronze statues betrayed by their clang the pickaxe of the destroyer. "The statues are not entirely dumb, since, through their bell-like sound, they warn the watchman as soon as they are struck by the blow of the thief."[2]

[1] *Quas amplexa posteritas pene parem populum urbi dedit, quam natura procreavit. Ibidem.*

[2] *Var.,* vii. 13: *statuae nec in toto mutae sunt: quando a furibus percussae custodes videntur tinnitibus admonere.* Perhaps this is the source of the legend in the *Mirabilia,* which relates that the statues of the various provinces which stood on the Capitol, were provided with bells (*tintinnabulum*), and that the statues gave notice as soon as a revolution broke out in the province they represented. The *Comes Romanus* was known in Imperial times as the *Curator statuarum.* Panciroli, *Notitia, &c.,* c. 16–122.

Theodoric protects the statues against the barbarism of the Romans.

Theodoric had taken the defenceless population of metal and marble under his special protection, a protection which he extended to all provinces of the Empire. This is shown by an edict issued with regard to a bronze statue which had been stolen in Como. The reward of 100 pieces of gold was offered for its recovery and the discovery of the robber.[1] But the barbarism of the Romans had already become so great that the edicts of the Gothic King could no longer restrain the universal cupidity, and Theodoric repeatedly laments the disgrace which the Romans brought on their ancestors by their mutilation of works of art. The rapacious people, however, continued their practices, and, when unable to carry the statues bodily away, struck off the limbs of such as were of bronze, and tore the metal clamps from the blocks of marble and travertine in theatres and baths. The later descendants of these plunderers looked with astonishment, towards the end of the Middle Ages, at the holes in the walls of the ruins, and, in the audacity of ignorance, set them down to the score of the very Goths who had sought to preserve the splendour of the city.

He preserves Rome.

A hundred passages in the rescripts of the Gothic King testify to his sincere respect for Rome, "the city which is indifferent to none, since she is foreign to none; the fruitful mother of eloquence, the spacious temple of every virtue, comprising within herself all the cherished marvels of the universe, so that it may in truth be said, Rome is herself one great marvel."[2] To preserve the splendour of antiquity, and to add

[1] *Var.*, ii. 35, 36.

[2] *Variar.*, iv. 6: *Universa Roma—miraculum. Var.*, vii. 15.

new buildings worthy of the old, Theodoric held to be his duty, although never at any time did he think of making his residence in Rome. He appointed a City Architect, under the Praefectus Urbi, and entrusted to this official the care of the monuments, charging him with regard to new buildings, to study the style of the old, and in nowise to deviate from ancient examples.[1] According to the precedent of earlier Emperors, he reserved a certain proportion of the yearly revenues for restorations. For the repair of the city walls he not only set apart the revenues received from the Lucrine harbour, but further imposed a yearly contribution of 25,000 bricks from the brick-works of the State, and showed himself, moreover, resolute in requiring that the money was really devoted to the purpose assigned. To procure the necessary lime, a special official was employed; and although the destruction of temples or statues was prohibited by severe penalties, permission was given to take such blocks as lay strewn on the ground or were otherwise utterly useless.[2]

The walls.

[1] *Var.,* vii. 15. Under the Emperors this official was known as *Curator operum publicorum.* Pancir., *Notit.,* c. 14, 15, p. 122. In Imperial times there was also a *Tribunus rerum nitentium,* or of cleanliness, an official much needed in the Rome of present times, notwithstanding the fact that an officer of *nettezza publica* (*rerum nitentium*) still continues to be appointed. Theodoric only repeated the edicts of earlier Emperors, Valentinian and Valens having in 364 issued the following edict to the Prefect Symmachus: *Intra urbem Romam aeternam nullus judicum novum opus informet, quotiens serenitatis nostrae arbitria cessabunt, ea tamen instaurandi, quae jam deformibus ruinis intercidisse dicuntur, universis licentiam damus.* Cod. Theod., xiv. 1, n. 11.; similarly, n. 19.

[2] *Ut ornent aliquid saxa jacentia post ruinas. Var.,* ii.7. For the

Cloacae.

The same care was extended to the Cloacae, those marvellous canals of the city, "through which, as if enclosed within vaulted mountains, flowed copious streams," and "through which alone," exclaimed Theodoric's minister, "can be understood, O mighty Rome, the nature of thy greatness. For what city could ever attain thy height, when even thy subterranean depths can find no equal."[1]

Aqueducts.

The colossal Aqueducts demanded no less careful attention. Although age and neglect had mantled these gigantic structures with underwood, the ancient conduits still continued flowing over the desolate Campagna to supply the baths and fountains of the city. Cassiodorus describes them in magniloquent language.

"No less worthy of our admiration than the architecture is the unrivalled excellence of the water. And since these stone canals have borne the force of the rivers which have flowed through them for centuries, even as through some mountain of artificial construction, we might esteem the aqueducts the

restoration of the city walls, see i. 21, 25, ii. 34, vii. 17. Cassiod., *Chron.*; *Anon. Val.,* 67. Ennodius, in his barbaric panegyric on Theodoric, says with regard to these restorations: *date veniam Lupercalis genii sacra rudimenta, plus est occasum repellere, quam dedisse principia.* Marangoni, *Memorie sacra e profane dell' anfiteatro Romano,* p. 44, accuses Martinelli and Blondus, *Romae instatur.,* i. c. 3, of gross ignorance, because they refer to an edict of Theodoric, issued for Catania, to Rome, and assert that he had sanctioned the use of the stones of the Colosseum for the restoration of the walls. The Colosseum at this period stood intact.

[1] *Variar.,* iii. 30. The expression: *videas structis navibus per aquas rapidas non minima sollicitudine navigari, ne praecipitato torrenti marina possint naufragia sustinere,* is somewhat strong.

natural bed of the river. The mountain which has been undermined crumbles away, the bed of the river wears in the course of time, but the works of antiquity remain, if care be but bestowed upon them. See the beauty conferred upon the city by the copiousness of her streams, and besides, of what avail were the magnificence of the baths apart from the excellence of the water? The Aqua Virgo flows clear and joyous, meriting its name by its unsullied purity. For while other aqueducts are polluted with soil after violent rains, the Aqua Virgo seems, in its undefiled depths, ever to reflect bright and unclouded skies. Further, who can sufficiently explain how the Claudia is so borne by a colossal aqueduct to the brow of the Aventine, that, falling from the height, it waters the highest summit of the city, even as though it were a valley?"[1] Cassiodorus finally comes to the daring conclusion that the Roman Claudia surpasses the Nile of Egypt in magnificence. Under the rule of Theodoric the Aqueducts were relegated to the care of a special official, who bore the title of *Comes Formarum urbis,* or Count of the Aqueducts of the city, under whom stood a numerous body of overseers.

Meanwhile many buildings began of themselves to show signs of decay, sinking under the pressure of their own weight, as for example the theatre of Pompey, the celebrated building which, on account of its size, had been called simply "Theatre" or "Theatrum Romanum." Under Honorius both in-

The Theatre of Pompey.

[1] *Var.,* vii. 6. With regard to the *Comes Formarum,* see the *Notitia,* c. 7, p. 121.

terior and exterior had been restored.[1] Theodoric, however, finding it again in ruinous condition, entrusted the necessary restoration to the most distinguished of the Senators, the patrician Symmachus, who had won no small favour in the King's eyes by the erection of some splendid new buildings in the suburbs. It is on this occasion that Cassiodorus exclaims, "How is it, O age, that thou dost not destroy, when thou hast shaken that which is so mighty."[2] "It appears," he says, "as if the mountains would more easily fall from each other than this colossus, which was built so entirely of stone that it seemed a natural rock." He extols the vaulted galleries, which, fitting with invisible joints, resembled the grottos of a mountain; speaks, in the name of Theodoric, of the origin of the theatre, and of all manner of dramatic matters, like an archaeologist of to-day; and, after having in his antiquarian enthusiasm declared that Pompey better merited the title "Great" from having built this theatre than from any other of his actions, he charges Symmachus to strengthen the structure by buttresses and other necessary repairs, and directs him to apply to the royal "cubiculum" for the required funds.

Cassiodorus gives us but scanty information as regards the condition of the other buildings of the city, and but few of these are mentioned by name in the

[1] Anon. of Einsiedeln, n. 50, and *C. I. L.,* vi. 1191. Dedicatory inscription to the same Emperor by the Prefect of the City, Aur. Anic. Symmachus (between the years 418, and 420), in the portico of the theatre, n. 1193.

[2] *Var.,* iv. 51: *quid non solvas, o senectus, quae tam robusta quassati?*

Rescripts. Amongst such, however, is the Pincian Palace, which must have been in an utterly ruinous condition, since Theodoric, in defiance of his own command, ordered blocks of marble and columns to be removed from the Pincio to Ravenna, where his own royal palace was in process of construction.[1] In later years, however, we shall see the Pincian Palace once more inhabited, this time by Belisarius. The Palace of the Caesars, sacked by the Vandals, served Theodoric as a dwelling during his sojourn in Rome, but this colossal building, where Emperors had once squandered the wealth of the world, which by turns they had enslaved or wisely ruled, had now long stood empty and deserted, and was already falling into ruin on account of its own vastness. For the restoration of the palace and that of the walls, Theodoric allotted from the wine tax the yearly sum of 200 pounds of gold.

Splendid beyond all other monuments of Rome as they gradually sank to ruin, stood the grandest memorial of antiquity, the Forum of Trajan. "The Forum of Trajan," cries Cassiodorus, in his enthusiasm, "is a miracle, however long one may consider it. He who ascends the lofty Capitol sees a work exalted above human genius."[2] This memorable passage seems to prove that, in spite of the Vandal sack, this

The Forum of Trajan.

[1] *Marmora quae de domo Pinciniana constat esse deposita. Var.*, iii. 10. It nevertheless appears that this palace had been an Imperial Palatium. It is also called *Palatium Pincianum* in the *Lib. Pont.*, "Vita Silverii."

[2] *Trajani Forum vel sub assiduitate videre miraculum est. Capitolia celsa conscendere, hoc est humana ingenia superata vidisse. Var.*, vii. 6.

Forum, as well as the Capitol, still retained its splendour; since, had either building been in ruin, Cassiodorus could not have spoken of one or other in such terms. He says not a word, however, of the desolate aspect of the Temple of the Capitoline Jupiter, which, robbed by the Vandals of its roof stood, with bare rafters, empty, despoiled, and open to the light of day.

2. THE AMPHITHEATRE OF TITUS—SPECTACLES AND PASSION FOR SPECTACLES AMONG THE ROMANS— ANIMAL-HUNTS — THE CIRCUS, ITS GAMES AND FACTIONS.

The Amphitheatre of Titus.

Cassiodorus dwells at length on the Amphitheatre of Titus and on the Circus Maximus. These world-renowned buildings, dedicated to the favourite amusements of the Romans, under Gothic rule were still thronged by vast crowds on any occasion when wrestling matches, the chase of wild animals, or chariot races were to take place. The dramatic art of the Romans, which never even in its prime had at all approached the nobility of the Greek stage, had sunk in the general decay to obscurity and buffoonery. The actors deferred to the brutal tastes of the populace, and with the actors were numbered the very drivers of the chariots.[1] In the Odeum of Domitian, which contained more than ten thousand seats, perhaps also in the theatres of Balbus, of Marcellus and of Pompeius, singers, organ-players, or dancers gratified the senses

[1] This is evident from *Var.,* iii. 51.

of the Romans. Recited comedies or mimes encouraged sensuality by indecency of language; while the pantomimes, with their choruses and dumb gesticulations, surpassed all else in the unbridled representation of obscenity. The lament of Salvian over the deterioration of such spectacles in the other cities of the Empire is not exaggerated. "In the theatres," says the bishop, "such shameful things are represented that modesty renders it impossible even to mention, much less to explain them. At one and the same time the soul is polluted by the desire of sensual pleasure, the eye by the sight, and the ear by language. Words fail to express the limitations of unchastity, the indecent motions and gesticulations."[1] We may understand scenes to be meant such as were presented in the infamous game called "Majuma." In Rome it cost the bishops a long and weary struggle to suppress the ridiculous festival of the Lupercal; but the influence which the clergy undoubtedly exercised on the customs of the public did not avail to abolish the frightful exhibitions against which, as against the works of the devil, the Fathers of the Church had already been preaching for three hundred years. Nor did the decrees of the Byzantine Emperors—an edict

Grossness of the Roman theatre.

[1] Salvian, *De vero jud.*, vi. p, 62, speaks like a theologian of Geneva: *spectacula, et pompae—opera diaboli.* Procopius, *Anecdot.*, c. 9, enlightens us as to the character of the plays represented in the sixth century in the description of the scene in which the Empress Theodora appeared in public on the Byzantine stage. Salvian enumerates the various scandalous spectacles: *longum est nunc dicere de omnibus, amphitheatris scilicet, odeis, lusoriis, pompis, athletis, petaminariis, pantomimis, &c. Petaminarii,* from πετάμενοι, *qui more avium sese ejaculantur in auras,* tumblers. Ducange's Glossary.

of Anastasius I. issued in 494 forbade obscene comedies—produce any result. Even Theodoric could do no more than lament that the mimes had sunk to absurdity, that the refined ideas of pleasure of the ancient Romans had degenerated in their corrupt descendants into the lowest vice, and that what had formerly been decorous enjoyments had become perverted into scenes of sensuality and licence.[1] The Roman populace would not relinquish these spectacles: its last passion was pleasure,—it would die laughing. Amongst the "Formulae" in Cassiodorus there is one concerning the Tribunus Voluptatum, an official who acted as Director of public amusements in Rome, and whose function it was to exercise a judicial and moral supervision over all actors.[2]

Lamenting the corruption of the public amusements the King found himself forced to support them, since the Romans would have given up the last remnant of their national independence rather than renounce their games. On the occasion of any

[1] *Var.*, iii. (*ad fin.*): *ut aetas subsequens miscens lubrica priscorum inventa taxit ad vitia: et quod honestae causa delectationis repertum est, ad voluptationes corporeas praecipitatis mentibus impulerunt.*

[2] *Var.*, vii. 10: *Teneat scenicos si non verus, vel umbratilis ordo judicii. Temperentur et haec legum qualitate negocia, quasi honestas imperet inhonestis.* The following inscription, referring to a Tribunus Volupt., belongs to as late a date as the year 523.

Fl. Maximo VC.
Concessum Locum Petro
Rome Ex. Trib. Volupt.
Et Conjugi Ejus Johan
Papa Hormisda et Tra(nsmundo)
Praepst. Basc. B. P.

(In the Crypt of the Vatican; see Dionysius, t. xxv.)

festival, on the entrance into office of a Consul, or other high official, these games which were still public were invariably celebrated; and the few historians of the time have taken occasion to point out, as an important event, that Theodoric, during his sojourn in the city, gave the people spectacles in the Amphitheatre and Circus. These two theatres alone are mentioned as in use, while profound silence already prevails concerning the Circus Flaminius and that of Maxentius.

The fights with animals continue.

The Amphitheatre of Titus stood practically unchanged. It had apparently, however, suffered to some extent from a great earthquake, which in 422 injured many buildings in Rome,[1] since, as an inscription informs us, restorations seem to have been effected under Valentinian III.[2] Further restorations were made between 467 and 472.[3] It appears to have been again damaged by a second earthquake in the beginning of the sixth century, in consequence of which it was again restored by the City Prefect Decius Marius Venantius Basilius in the reign of Theodoric (508).[4]

The poverty of the State treasury and of the Senate,

[1] Paul Diac., *De gestis Long.,* iv. 47: *tam terribili terrae motu Roma concussa est ut plurimae aedes ejus et aedificia corruerint* (year 422).

[2] *Corp. I. Lat.,* vi. 1763.

[3] Inscription according to which the amphitheatre was restored by a certain Messius Phoeb...*C. I. L.,* vi. p. 860, n. 100; and *Bull. della Comm. Arch. Com.,* 1880, viii. 229.

[4] *C. I. L.,* vi. 1716, a. See also *Bull. d. Comm. Arch., l. c.,* p. 223, f. For the history of the Colosseum at this period, Parker, *The Flavian Amphitheatre,* 1876.

also the code of Christian morality no more allowed the imposing but hideous spectacles of ancient times. We may assume that gladiatorial combats had ceased in the arena from the time of Honorius, since Cassiodorus, in the memorable letter where he speaks at length and in detail of the representations in the Amphitheatre, is silent with regard to them.[1] Gladiatorial exhibitions had also been abolished in Byzantium, an edict of the Emperor Anastasius putting an end to them in 494. The Romans, accustomed to the sight of blood, however, could not forego the pleasing spectacle of watching men, who, for a miserable pittance, yielded themselves up to be mangled before the eyes of the public and to die with Roman dignity. These were the Venatores, or hunters of beasts, who, alternately with the wrestlers, enlivened the arena. Now and then, through a great outlay, these exhibitions recalled those of past times, as, for instance, when Eutharic, son-in-law of Theodoric, in 519, upon his solemn entrance into Rome, celebrated his election to the Consulship by liberal largesses in gold and sports in the Amphitheatre. Africa on this occasion, as in old times, contributed wild animals, the strange forms of which, as Cassiodorus in his chronicle tells us, astonished the spectators. The chronicler describes the arts of the huntsmen, as they had been practised from antiquity; how the Arenarius, armed with a wooden lance, springs from the advancing lion or bear; how, on knees and

[1] *Variar.*, v. 42. Rescript concerning the petition of a huntsman. The varieties of these sports were, Cassiodorus tells us, as numerous as the torments of Virgil's Hell.

stomach, he creeps to meet it, or glides towards it in a wooden rolling machine, or holds himself entrenched like a hedgehog, in a case of thin and yielding rods. As a Christian, he accompanies this description by a humane lament over the fate of these men. Such a lament in the mouth of a minister even in the time of Hadrian or of the Antonines would have seemed ridiculous or indeed have been impossible. "If these anointed champions of the ring," says Cassiodorus, "or these organ players or singers have claims on the liberality of the Consuls, the Venator, who gives his life for the applause of the spectators, who sheds his blood to give them pleasure, who exerts his fatal skill to delight the people who do not desire his escape, has surely much greater claims. Abominable spectacle! Unholy strife! to combat with wild beasts which he cannot hope to subdue by force." And at the end: "Woe to the lamentable infatuation of the world! had it any insight into what is right, those riches which are now devoted to destroying life would be spent on doing good to mankind." A noble expression of regret, and one which every benevolent minister in a state resting on military force must still re-echo.[1]

Survival of the races in the Circus Maximus.

With less indignation Theodoric opposed the ancient Circensian games, which also gave occasion to scenes of bloodshed, owing to the bitterness of

[1] *Heu mundi error dolendus! si esset ullus aequitatis intuitus, tantae divitiae pro vita mortalium deberent dari, quantae in mortes hominum videntur effundi.* Salvian utters a like lamentation: *nihil ferme vel criminum, vel flagitiorum est quod in spectaculis non sit: ubi summum delitiarum genus, mori homines, aut—lacerari, expleri ferarum alvos humanis carnibus, comedi homines, cum circumstantium letitia, conspicientium voluptate. De vero jud.,* vi. 142 (Venice, 1696).

party feeling. The Roman Circus had been the work of centuries; Trajan had completed the building after the Neronian fire, and Constantine added its latest ornament in the great Egyptian Obelisk, which overshadowed by forty palms the neighbouring obelisk of Augustus. Both obelisks still remain in Rome, but, once close together on the Spina of the Circus, they have been widely separated by fate, one now standing in front of the Lateran, the other in the Piazza del Popolo. Our sympathy is aroused by hearing the wonders of Roman greatness extolled for the last time in their unimpaired splendour, as Cassiodorus on this occasion, and with many allegorical explanations, extols them.[1] The diminished population of Rome no longer filled the immense, elliptical, many-storied building, 150,000 or 200,000 seats far exceeding the needs of the citizens of the time. When Trajan had celebrated the games, and the Circus was not sufficiently large to meet the requirements of the city, no Roman could have believed that a time would come when the Circus would be too large for the entire population; yea, when a fourth of the accommodation would more than suffice for all the inhabitants of Rome. Probably in the year 500, many of the marble seats were already worn and broken; many portions of the portico already injured; the shops and arches outside already deserted; and of the statues placed there by Severus, many apparently had been carried away by the Vandals, while others stood broken in their niches. The Circus was old and weather-beaten; and the whole giant structure, worn by

[1] *Var.*, iii. 51.

centuries of use, must in colour and aspect have assumed a time-worn character like that of the neighbouring Imperial palace, from which it was only separated by a street. It was still, however, in constant use; the twelve-fold door of entrance, the Spina with its two obelisks, the seven-pointed column or Meta, the Euripus or canal which surrounded the arena, even the Mappa, at the signal of which the "desultores" or "Equi desultatorii" (the equestrian performers) rushed forward to announce the beginning of the races; in short, all essentials of both Circus and games are mentioned by Cassiodorus. The solemn pomp with which the procession, bearing the images of the gods and the animals for the sacrifice, once moved from the Capitol to the Circus was observed no longer, and the people were forced to content themselves with a greatly diminished splendour. But the Consuls still continued to celebrate the games on their entrance into office, and one we even find immortalising them in verse.[1]

It would seem that at times distinguished charioteers from the Hippodrome at Constantinople appeared in the Roman Circus, or fled to Rome for

[1] Turcius Rufius Apronianus Asterius, Consul, A.D. 494, in his celebrated MS. of Virgil (Laurentian Library at Florence), dedicates an epigram to the subject (Tiraboschi, iii. 1, c. 2, and Mabillon, *De Re Dipl.*, p. 354):

> *Tempore, quo penaces Circo subjunximus, atque*
> *Scenam Euripo extulimus subitam,*
> *Ut ludos currusque simul, variumque ferarum*
> *Certamen junctim Roma teneret ovans:*

a proof that races, armed dances, mimes, and hunts were at the same time celebrated in the theatre.

shelter in the heat of party strife. In the Rescript of Cassiodorus which treats of the Circensian games, he mentions with regard to the charioteer Thomas, that a monthly salary was assigned to him, "since he," as the minister with a certain respect expresses it, "is the first in his art and has renounced his native country in favour of the Western Empire."[1] As in Byzantium, so also in Rome, the Circus gave rise to the most furious contests, the rival factions of the Prasina or Green and the Veneta or the Grey-Blue now dividing the populace. Originally four colours had been employed in the Circus, and these colours Cassiodorus explains to have denoted the Four Seasons, the Prasina signifying the greenness of spring; the Veneta the cloudy winter; rosy red the flaming summer; and white the ripe harvest. Since low-minded Emperors had degraded themselves to appear as drivers of chariots and had sided with either the green or the blue faction, this division of the Circus became fixed,[2] and the people having ceased to take part in public life, derived a certain compensation from this rivalry of factions, in the tumult of which their political opinions found some degree of expression. If in Rome struggles so furious did not arise as were frequent in Byzantium (where, in 501, more than 3000 men were slain on the occasion of a combat between the Greens and Blues), still Rome also witnessed many a bloody scene.

Circus factions.

[1] *Var.,* iii. 51: *nostri sedes fovere delegit imperii*; *fovere* sounds almost like *honour.*

[2] On the origin and history of the factions of the circus, see L. Friedländer, *Darstellungen aus der Sittengeschichte Roms,* ii.

"It is surprising," says Cassiodorus, "how, more than in any other game, the mind is carried away by unreasonable passion. A Green conquers, immediately half of the people lament; a Blue excels in running and the greater part of the city complains; do they win nothing, their insults increase; while if they lose nothing they feel themselves deeply aggrieved, and the unimportant strife occupies them as much as if the safety of their country depended on it."

In 509 a dispute arose in the Circus, when two Senators, Importunus and Theodoricus, partisans of the Blues, were assailed by the Greens, and a man was slain in the tumult. In Byzantium, the people of the Prasina (such is the significant expression of the Rescripts) would in the heat of their passion have set fire to the city, but in Rome they calmly turned to seek help from the authorities, and Theodoric ordered both patricians to be arraigned before the ordinary tribunal. The King passed a law, punishing severely any offence committed by a Senator upon a free man, and any offence offered to a Senator by a man of inferior rank, and finally sought to protect the chariot drivers of the weaker party.[1] At the same time he admonished the Senators, who, in aristocratic arrogance, could not bear the cries of derision of the populace, to remember the place in which they were—"since in the Circus they must not look for Catos."[2]

[1] *Var.,* i. 27, 30, 31, 32, 33.

[2] The famous saying: *Ad Circum nesciunt convenire Catones. Var.,* i. 27. The freedom of masquerade was permitted at the circus; *locus est, qui defendit excessum.*

He protests from the bottom of his heart that he despises amusements which banish all serious thought, excite to the most foolish quarrels, and reduce that, which in the time of their ancestors had been an honourable institution, to mere buffoonery among the degenerate population of a later age. He further admits that he only supports the Circensian games because he is unable to resist the childish importunity of the people, and because prudence also sometimes counsels folly.[1]

Thus did the magnanimous Goth seek to preserve the monuments of Rome and the customs of the people, and such were the ideas which animated his reign; a reign far in advance of the time, worthy of the most humane centuries, and which honours alike the King who supported the minister, and the minister who, through his culture, directed and influenced the King.

3. Theodoric's care for the Roman People—Roma Felix—Tolerance towards the Catholic Church —The Jews in Rome—Their Oldest Synagogue— Outbreak of the Populace against the Jews.

Roma Felix.

With no less solicitude did Theodoric, as far as his limited means allowed, care for the welfare of the people. We must guard ourselves, however, against describing by too exalted praise his reign as an absolutely golden age; it was golden only in comparison to the misery of the immediate past. The exhaustion was great, and the wounds were many.

[1] *Expedit interdum desipere, ut populi possimus desiderata gaudia continere. Var.,* iii. 51.

The accustomed distributions of oil and meat were renewed, and the officials annually measured out to the hungry city mob the wholly insignificant sum of 120,000 modii of corn, yielded by granaries filled with the harvests of Calabria and Apulia.[1] The poor in the hospitals of S. Peter, as expressly noticed by Procopius, received also a special annual distribution of 3000 medimni of corn.[2] The Prefecture of the Annona, for the provision of the public necessities, was again raised to an honourable office. At least the minister of Theodoric flattered the official by the recollection of his great forerunner Pompey, and by pointing out to him the distinction he enjoyed in driving in the carriage of the City Prefect before the eyes of the people, and in occupying a place beside the Prefect at the Circus. But the formulae of appointment are not altogether to be trusted, and Boethius says, "In former days, when anyone had care of the welfare of the people, he was highly respected, but what is more despicable than the present Prefecture of the Annona?" Shortly before, he had also remarked, "the Prefecture of the city was once a great power, now it is only an empty name and a heavy burthen of the Senatorial census."[3]

[1] *Anon. Val.,* 67. Gibbon, reckoning the measure of 120,000 modii as equal to 4000 bushels, infers that a great reduction had taken place in the population. As sixty modii were reckoned per head, Theodoric's distributions could not have sufficed for more than 2000 men. Lud. Friedländer, *Sittengeschichte Rom's,* i. 22.

[2] Procop., *Histor. Arcana,* 26: τοῖς τε προσαιτηταῖς οἳ παρὰ τὸν Πέτρου τοῦ ἀποστόλου νεὼν δίαιταν εἶχον.

[3] The formulae of the *Praef. Annon. Var.,* vi. 18. Passage in Boethius, *De Consolat.,* iii. prosa 4.

Care was taken to see that the Magazines on the Aventine and the Pig-market (Forum suarium) in the region Via Lata were well supplied, a special tribune having from of old been appointed for the purpose. The bread was good and of full weight, the price so cheap that in the time of Theodoric sixty modii of wheat were bought for one solidus, and thirty amphorae of wine for the same sum.[1] "The public wealth grew," says Ennodius, in his panegyric on the King, "through the gains of private individuals, and since the court is without covetousness, the sources of prosperity flow in every direction." If this eulogy be somewhat exaggerated, since no sudden transformation could have taken place in the character of Roman officials, nor Goths all at once have renounced their avarice, it is nevertheless true that Rome returned, after her terrible sufferings, to a condition of peace and security. The Senators enjoyed again, as in the days of Augustus and Titus, their now dilapidated villas on the Gulf of Baiae, in the Sabine Mountains, or in Lucania on the Adriatic,[2]

Eulogy on Theodoric.

[1] *Anon. Val.* A solidus was the $^{1}/_{72}$ part of a pound of gold. The *Liber Junioris Phil.,* in Angelo Mai, t. iii., Class. Auctor. e Vatican. Cod. Nr. 30, celebrated in the fourth century the wines of Bruttium, Picenum, Sabina, Tibur, and Tuscany; the ham and lard of Lucania: *Lucania regio optima, et omnibus bonis habundans lardum multum aliis provinciis mittit.*

[2] The villas of the nobility of the time may have presented as ruinous an aspect as many of the country houses of the Roman nobility of present days. Cassiodorus describes some districts in his native province: the Market of Leucothea in Lucania (*Var.,* viii. 33), Baiae (ix. 6), Mons Lactarius (xi. 10), and Squillace (xii. 15). He tells us how the people of Lucania, Apulia, Bruttium, and Calabria flocked to hear mass at the Fountain of Leucothea, as they throng to Nola at

and the diminished population, no longer dreading barbarian pillage, well nourished and amused with games, protected by Roman laws and in the enjoyment of a certain degree of national independence saw no irony in their ancient city adopting, for the last time, the title Felix.[1]

If this condition of peaceful welfare (and there is no old author, whether Latin or Greek, whether friendly or hostile, who does not extol the rule of Theodoric) was disturbed in the city, such disturbance did not occur through any fault of the enlightened government, but through that of ecclesiastical fanaticism. Theodoric, an Arian in faith, had throughout his reign treated the Roman Church with perfect respect, so that not even his bitterest enemy could accuse him of ever having forced a Catholic to change his faith, or of having persecuted a bishop. On his entrance into Rome he "prayed like a Catholic" at the grave of the Apostle, and among the offerings

the present day; and we read how the priests already understood the art of deceiving the crowd by wonders worked by the miraculous water. The blood of S. Januarius was as yet undiscovered.

[1] *Felix Roma*: *Var.,* vi. 18; Fabretti, *Inscr.,* c. vii. p. 521; *Regn. D. N. Theodorico Felix Roma.* Herr Henzen has allowed me to share the materials collected by him for his *Corpus Inscr. Latin.,* with reference to the stamps of Theodoric. Of these there are twelve in all, six of which bear the words *Felix Roma,* five *Bono Romae* (see his work, Nr. 149–160). Stamps of the time of Athalaric are rare. Nr. 161 is distinguished by its inscription of *Roma Fida.* Stamps with *Regn. Dn. Athalaric.... Felix Roma* have been discovered in the Columbaria within the Porta Maggiore. Gori in Buonarotti, 1872, p 133. There are also autonomous Roman copper coins belonging to the Gothic time; the obverse bears with the helmeted head of Rome, the inscription INVICTA ROMA, the reverse the she-wolf or an eagle. J. Friedländer, *Die Münzen der Ostgothen,* p. 56, f., and Plate iii.

which the rulers of the time brought to S. Peter's, two silver candlesticks of seventy pounds weight were given by the Arian King. The discovery of some tiles in the church of S. Martina in the Forum, and even on the roof of the buildings adjacent to S. Peter's, with the stamp, *"Regnante Theodorico Domino Nostro, Felix Roma,"* has given rise to the opinion that the King had provided for the roofing of these churches. Such a supposition, however, is erroneous. The church of S. Martina was not built at this time,[1] and we therefore incline to the belief that the tiles had been brought from elsewhere and at a later date, or were a product of the public manufactory. Theodoric's tolerance was in advance of his century, and his Chancellor Cassiodorus almost exhibits the traits of a minister of the later period of philosophic humanism. Even the contempt for the Jews, which the Romans, whether Pagan or Christian, had inherited, was kept in check, and the edicts of the King show perfect toleration, mingled with compassionate disdain, towards the religion of Moses.[2]

Tolerance towards the Jews.

The Jews, who had come to Italy as slaves of war

[1] See the representations of the stamps in Bonanni, *Templi Vatican. Hist.,* p. 54. Similar tiles were found in the Temple of Faustina, on the Via Labicana, on the roof of S. Peter's, on that of S. Stefano degli Ungari, in the ruins of the Secretarium of the Senate, in S. Gregorio, in an ancient aqueduct beside the Colleg. German., in S. Giov. e Paolo, on the roofs of S. Paul, S. Costanza, S. Martina, S. Giorgio in Velabro; on the roof of the chapel of John VII. in S. Peter's; on the Palatine, where Theodoric seems to have instituted restorations.

[2] To the Jews in Genoa he writes: *religionem imperare non possumus, quia nemo cogitur—ut credat invitus. Var.,* ii. 27. *Var.,* v. 37: *concedimus—sed quid, Judaee, supplicans temporalem quietem quaeris, si aeternam requiem invenire non possis?*

in the time of Pompey, possessed synagogues in Genoa, Naples, Milan, Ravenna, and, yet earlier than in any of these cities, in Rome, where, in the reign of Tiberius, their numbers had risen to more than 50,000. Their talent and ceaseless activity had brought wealth to many members of the community, although the majority remained sunk in the direst poverty. The hatred of the Romans towards this remarkable people, whose tenacious vitality outlived the downfall of every nation and Empire, is to be seen in both poets and prose writers since the time of Augustus. Their attitude of hostile reserve towards all other religions was incomprehensible to the Roman with his cosmopolitan instincts, and on account of this exclusiveness they are denounced by Tacitus as a race hateful to the gods.[1] The Romans, nevertheless, gazed with astonishment on the deeply religious character of the Hebrews, while not a few fell under the moral spell of Judaism: a religion which made many proselytes among the Roman nobility, more especially among its women. The wanton Poppaea, wife of Nero, had been received into the synagogue, and had desired to be buried as a Jewess. No sooner had Christianity made its appearance, however, than its disciples, as a Jewish sect, were abhorred by the followers of Paganism. Rutilius has given expression to the hatred of the Latins towards the Semitic race in his farewell poem, in words where he laments that Pompey had subjugated and Titus destroyed Jerusalem, for since

[1] *Genus hominum ut invisum deis.* Tacit., *Hist.,* v. 3. The *odium humani generis* was also a reproach against the Christians, who were at first, very naturally, identified in the popular mind with the Jews.

then the plague of Judaism had spread and the subjugated nation had conquered its conquerors.[1] Thus early does Judaism appear as a serious social question.

The Synagogue in Rome.

The oldest synagogue in Rome lay in what, since the days of Augustus, had been the densely populated Jews' quarter in Trastevere, where, even in the time of Martial and Statius, Jewish pedlars went about the streets crying their wares, even as they cry their *Stracci ferraci* now. The short distance which lay between the harbour and the Trastevere had led both Jews and Syrians to establish their quarters in this part of the city.[2] Here their descendants continued to dwell throughout the entire Middle Ages, and Trasteverines of the present day have pointed out to the writer of this history the site of the first synagogue in the Vicolo delle Palme. It is possible that during Imperial times Jews may have also dwelt in

[1] He finds himself domiciled in Faleria—

Namque loci quaerulus curam Judaeus agebat.
Humanis animal dissociale cibis...
Quae genitale caput propudiosa metit...
Atque utinam numquam Judaea subacta fuisset
Pompeii bellis, imperioque Titi.
Latius exciscae pestis contagia serpunt,
Victoresque suos natio victa premit.

—*Itiner.,* v. 383, &c.

Basnage, *Histoire des Juifs* (la Haye, 1716), has dedicated the 8th chap. of lib. vii. to the history of the Jews in Rome from the time of Pompey to that of Nero. His information is, however, frequently erroneous. More exhaustive is the treatment this remarkable subject receives at the hands of Bosio and Aringhi, *Roma Subterranea,* t. i. lib. ii. c. 22 (c. 23). Still more recently it has been dealt with by Emil Schürer, with the aid of the inscriptions in Jewish burial places. *Die Gemeindeverfass. der Juden in Rom in der Kaiserzeit,* Leipzig, 1879; also A. Hausrath, *Neutestamentliche Zeitgesch.,* iii. 71 ff.

[2] Renan, *Saint Paul* (Paris, 1869), p. 101, f.

the Vatican quarter; since as late as the thirteenth century the Bridge of Hadrian, the Pons Aelius, is called in the *Mirabilia* Pons Judaeorum, a name which it may have received from the fact that in the Middle Ages the stalls with which it was lined were occupied by Jews, who here exposed their goods for sale to the passers by.[1]

In their synagogue, which owed its origin to the Libertini, or Jewish slaves set free after the time of Pompey, the children of Israel had sought to represent a likeness of the Temple destroyed by Titus. Here they assembled on Sabbaths and festivals by the light of a seven-branched Menora, while the true Lychnuchus and the sacred vessels of Jerusalem, their desecrated property, were preserved in the Temple of Peace. Their House of Prayer was almost three hundred years older than S. Peter's or the Lateran, and the Pagan Romans, as early as the days of Horace and his friend Fuscus Aristius

[1] Basnage maintains that another Jewish quarter was the island in the Tiber. A third was the Vale of Egeria, where the Jews continued to dwell for a length of time. In the days of the Empire they had their own cemetery on the Via Appia, discovered afterwards in the Vigna Randanini and Cimarra. Here, however, the inscriptions, being mainly Greek, lead to the supposition that these catacombs were appropriated to the use of Alexandrian Jews. On the grave-stones the seven-branched candlestick is frequently represented. The catacombs, even the tombs (also marble sarcophagi) and the very paintings display symbolism similar to that in the Christian cemeteries, and these were derived from the earlier examples in Judea and Egypt. Garucci, *Cimitero degli antichi Ebrei,* Rome 1862. The authors of *Roma subterr.* have in addition pointed out the ancient Jewish cemetery outside the Portuensian Gate. Here also the inscriptions are for the most part Greek. A Jewish burial-place has also been discovered at Portus.

or of Juvenal, had witnessed as intrusive guests the same Mosaic mysteries which, at the Feast of the Passover, call forth the contemptuous smiles of the Romans of to-day. The ancient House of the Jews in the Trastevere was doubtless more splendid than the present synagogue in the Ghetto; a temple resting on columns, the interior furnished with costly hangings and golden sculpture of pomegranates and flowers. But the Roman populace had several times desecrated the Synagogue, and at last under Theodosius had burnt it, and Goths and Vandals had robbed it of all its ornament. Under the mild rule of Theodoric, however, the Jews enjoyed complete toleration until 521, when a fresh outburst of fanaticism on the part of the Christians condemned them to further ill-treatment. One day the populace burnt the synagogue, and from the complaint of the Jews to Aligern, Theodoric's envoy in Rome, it appeared that Christians in the service of rich Jews had slain their masters, and that in consequence of the murderers having been convicted, the people revenged themselves on the synagogue. Theodoric, on receiving the news of this outrage, addressed a Rescript to the Senate, charging it to punish the offenders with the utmost severity.[1]

[1] *Var.*, iv. 43. From the expression employed: *ad eversiones pervenerint fabricarum, ubi totum pulchre volumus esse compositum,* we assume that the building was by no means insignificant. It is undoubted that a synagogue had stood in the Trastevere from very ancient times. Bosio maintains that this synagogue was transformed into S. Salvatore in Curte (*Roma subterranea,* ii. c. 22); but Martinelli, with more probability, derives the name of the church from an ancient Curia, where law was administered in the Trastevere.

4. FRESH SCHISM IN THE CHURCH—SYNODUS PALMARIS—PARTY STRUGGLES IN ROME—SYMMACHUS DECORATES S. PETER'S—BUILDS THE ROUND CHAPEL OF S. ANDREAS, THE BASILICA OF S. MARTINUS, THE CHURCH OF S. PANCRATIUS—HORMISDAS POPE, 514— JOHN I. POPE—RUPTURE OF THEODORIC WITH THE CATHOLIC CHURCH.

Schism between Symmachus and Lawrence.

Scenes much more disgraceful than this isolated outbreak on the part of the populace, or the disputes between the Greens and Blues, had long filled Rome with confusion. We have already spoken of the schism in connection with the election of Pope Symmachus. After Theodoric had confirmed this election, and after, by his six-months' sojourn in the city, he had succeeded in restoring quiet between the factions, the quarrel broke out afresh with greater violence than before.[1] By investing the Antipope Lawrence with the bishopric of Nucera, which had been granted to him, Symmachus had removed his rival from the scene; but the heads of Lawrence's faction who sided with Byzantium, priests as well as Senators and amongst them Festus and Probinus, had brought the exile back to Rome. They addressed a detailed accusation against the Pope to Theodoric, and the King sent to Rome Bishop Peter of Altinum to inquire into and judge the matter. Theodoric himself, anxious to avoid imperilling his own position by interference in ecclesiastical affairs, summoned a Council in Rome

[1] See the difficult chronology in Jaffé. According to this, the first meeting of the Synod took place between May and July 501.

and had left it to the assembled clergy to restore peace.[1] This Synod of 115 bishops, called Palmaris from the Portico of S. Peter's where it was assembled in 501, was afterwards held in the Basilica Julii (S. Maria in Trastevere), but on account of a sudden tumult was removed to the Sessorian Church of Santa Croce in Gerusalemme. On the way Lawrence's adherents attacked the clergy with arms in their hands; many followers of Symmachus were slain, and Symmachus himself was in danger of being stoned. The Council, again assembled in S. Peter's, had time to acquit the accused Symmachus, and after the solemn condemnation of Lawrence had been pronounced, his rival, amid the din of arms, was reinstated in the chair of Peter. He immediately summoned another Synod (Nov. 6, 502), when the assembled bishops and Roman clergy annulled the decree of Odoacer, which had ordained that the Papal election could only be ratified in the presence of the Royal plenipotentiary. The election henceforward was to be removed beyond the influence of the secular authorities.[2] But peace did not return. On the contrary, for three or four years Rome was sprinkled day and night with the blood of the slain. The Senators, at enmity with each other, fought fiercely in the streets, and apparently it is only through oversight that writers

[1] That this Council, the fourth Synod convened in the affairs of Symmachus, was summoned by Theodoric himself, with the approval of the Pope, is shown by Pagi, p. 131, xiii., from the *Acts of the Synod.* The bishops wrote to the King: *ideoque nos toto affectu et obsequio jussioni vestrae parere voluimus.* Thiel, *l. c.,* Ep. 5, p. 657.

[2] J. Langen, *Gesch. d. R. K. von Leo I. bis Nicol I.,* 1885, p. 232.

have omitted to mention that the factions of the Greens and Blues in the Circus were drawn into the struggle. The friends of Symmachus were massacred, many presbyters were slain with clubs in front of the churches, even nuns were maltreated in their convents, while to these horrors was added that of pillage.[1] Quiet was not restored to the city until 514 under the Consulate of Aurelius Cassiodorus. The celebrated minister writes in his chronicle—"When I was Consul, to the glory of your (Theodoric's) age, after clergy and people had been assembled, the longed-for union was restored to the Roman Church."

During the intervals of the strife, and in spite of his differences with the Emperor Anastasius, in whose party we assuredly recognise the defeated faction of Lawrence, Symmachus found leisure to beautify the city. The dangers which he had happily overcome increased the zeal of this perhaps not wholly blameless priest, and he hastened to show his gratitude to the saints by adorning their churches or building other churches in their honour.

Symmachus adds to S. Peter's.

His care was more especially directed to the Basilica of S. Peter, where he covered the atrium with plates of marble and decorated the cantharus or fountain with an aedicula of porphyry columns and the walls of the Quadriporticus with mosaics.[2] He also

[1] *Lib. Pont.,* Vita Symmachi; Theod. *Lector, Hist. Eccl.,* ii. 17; *Hist. Misc.,* xv., and the memorable fragment of the Vita Symmachi in Muratori, *Script.,* iii. p. 2, where the reign of disorder is estimated to have lasted four years. Theoph., *Chronogr.,* p. 123: ἔνθεν λοιπὸν ἀταξίαι πολλαὶ καὶ φόνοι καὶ ἁρπαγαὶ γεγόνασιν ἐπὶ τρία ἔτη. A fifth Synod was held under Symmachus in 502. Thiel, i. 682, f.

[2] *Lib. Pont.,* Vita Symm., n. 79, and Duchesne's note on it, p.

supplied the public piazza in front of the basilica with a fountain for the use of the people—the modest predecessor of the two splendid fountains which now beautify with the rainbow and rush of their waters the grandest piazza in the world. He further widened the staircase of the entrance hall of the basilica by the addition of wings. And since he also built episcopia, that is to say, dwellings for the bishops, to the right and left of this staircase, he may be regarded as the founder of the later Vatican palace.[1] He further erected several oratories or chapels in S. Peter's; and built a church to S. Andrew near the basilica. The brother of Peter, named by the Greeks Protokletos, which signifies the "first called," had enjoyed universal veneration even before the time when, under the Pontificate of Simplicius, a basilica had been erected in his peculiar honour. Symmachus built him a second church with vestibule, staircase and cantharus, and of circular form. This church was at that time second in size only to S. Peter's, before Stephen II. and Paul I., in the eighth century, transformed the Imperial mausoleum of Honorius into a circular chapel in honour of Petronilla. The chapel of S. Andrew stood near the Obelisk, and being round gave rise to the erroneous belief that it

First beginnings of the Vatican palace.

Chapel of S. Andrew.

266. Petrus Mallius, c. 7, n. 127, informs us that Symmachus adorned the cantharus with the bronze pine cone, *quae fuit coopertorium cum sinino aeneo et deaurato super statuam Cybelis matris deor. inforamine Pantheon.* This ancient pine cone, which emitted a jet of water, at present stands in the Cortile della Pigna of the Vatican. For the description of the fountain, see also the *Mirabilia Romae,* p. 27 (ed. Parthey).

[1] *Item episcopia in eodem loco dextra levaque fecit. Lib. Pont.*

had been originally a building of Nero, namely, his Vestiarium, or the house where his treasures and robes were kept. It later received from an image of the Virgin the name of S. Maria Febrifuga, and finally, in the sixteenth century, served as sacristy to S. Peter's.[1]

As early as the beginning of the sixth century the Vatican basilica was consequently surrounded by many neighbouring buildings, chapels, mausoleums, and one or two monasteries; although we only recognise with certainty that of SS. John and Paul. Symmachus also built hospitals beside S. Peter's, S. Paul's and S. Lorenzo without the Walls, and founded a Xenodochium at Portus; a fact which shows that the concourse of pilgrims by sea must already have been considerable.

We pass over the restorations effected in S. Paul's under this Pope, but may add that to him is due the rebuilding of the Basilica of S. Martino (the ancient Titulus Equitii) beside the baths of Trajan, also the foundation of S. Pancrazio on the Via Aurelia.[2] The latter church still remains, although in altered form, over the Catacombs of the Roman Martyr Callepodius.

Symmachus died July 19, 514, and Hormisdas, a native of Frusino in Campania, was elected Pope. Hormisdas Pope, 514–523.

[1] *Cancellieri de secretariis novae Basil. Vatican.,* Roma, 1876, cap. ii. p. 1153, &c.

[2] According to legend, Sylvester had erected the titular church Equitii, and Symmachus seems to have built an entirely new church to S. Martin of Tours beside it. The two churches united then formed the *Basilica sanctor. Silvestri et Martini. Lib. Pont.*

During his nine years' reign the Church on the whole enjoyed peace.

John I., 523–526.

Under his successor, John I., a Tuscan, however, the previously existing relations between Theodoric and the Catholic Church became troubled. In 523 the Emperor Justin issued an edict of persecution against the Arians throughout the entire Empire, commanding that the Arian churches should be restored to the adherents of the Catholic faith. These violent measures were adopted with the intention of undermining, by means of religious divisions, the power of the barbarian King; and perhaps Justinian, the imperious nephew and declared successor of Justin, already counted on the expulsion of the Goths from Italy and the restoration of Imperial authority in the West. Latin nationality, excited by Greek influences and the Roman clergy, asserted itself more strongly than ever against the Northern foreigners, who, without renouncing their Arian heresy, had made themselves masters of Italy. A Byzantine party existed within the Senate and amongst the Roman clergy, and Theodoric began to suspect ingratitude and treason in the city on which he had bestowed innumerable benefits. His indignation against the edict of Justin was heightened by the consciousness of the perfect toleration which he had observed towards the Catholic faith; and he now vowed to revenge the persecution of the Arians in the East by the suppression of the Catholic ritual in Italy. As a warning, or as deserved punishment of some unknown fanatical step on the part of the Romans, he caused an oratory in

Persecution of the Arians in Byzantium.

Verona to be thrown to the ground, and at the same time prohibited all Italians from bearing arms.[1] The unhappy King now learnt by experience that not even the wisest or most humane of princes, if he be an alien in race, in customs and religion, can ever win the hearts of the people. After a reign of almost three and thirty years, during which he had loaded decaying Italy with the blessings of peace, finding himself a stranger amidst strangers and enemies, he was forced in self-defence to adopt a tyrannical course of conduct.

5. TRIAL AND EXECUTION OF THE SENATORS BOETHIUS AND SYMMACHUS—POPE JOHN UNDERTAKES AN EMBASSY TO CONSTANTINOPLE AND DIES IN RAVENNA—THEODORIC COMMANDS THE ELECTION OF FELIX IV.—DEATH OF THE KING IN 526—LEGENDS CONNECTED WITH IT.

Fall of Boethius and Symmachus.

The tragic overthrow of Rome's two most distinguished Senators, Boethius and Symmachus, followed, the shades of his victims remaining to darken for ever the fame of the noble Gothic King. We might attempt to prove, as many historians have done already, that motives of State required the execution of these two men,[2] did not Boethius, with the world-famous *Consolations of Philosophy* in his hand, seem to us a too powerful accuser, and the manner of his

[1] *Item ut nullus Romanus arma usque ad cultellum uteretur vetuit.* Anon. Vales., 83.

[2] Giannone, *Storia Civile del Regno di Napoli.,* vol. i. iii. § 6; Manso, *Gesch. d. Ostgoth. Reichs.,* p. 164.

death too barbarous, even judged by the standard of that barbarous age.[1]

Both men (Boethius was sentenced in 524, Symmachus in the following year) fell sacrifices to Theodoric's but too well-founded suspicion of the Senate. Blameless before the tribunal of the King they were not, but what may appear as crime before the judgment bar, is frequently esteemed virtue in the eyes of the people. It would scarcely increase the fame of the Senator, certainly not that of the philosopher, Boethius, could his treason be ascribed to love of his native Rome. Anicius Manlius Torquatus Severinus Boethius united in himself the names of the most illustrious families of Rome, and, in the twilight of his age, talents so varied as sufficed to shed over his native city an after-glow of philosophy. The muse of antiquity appeared to the Roman in his imprisonment for the last time in a dignified half-Greek form, after (already wearied with the vain searchings of the Christian theologians into the essence of, or likeness between, the Father and Son and the confusion of the dual natures) she had already taken leave of earth.[2] Boethius certainly had not studied in Athens, the last seat of the Neo-Platonic philosophy in Greece, although his researches into the teachings of Plato and Aristotle have connected his intellect,

[1] *Qui accepta chorda in fronte diutissime tortus, ita ut oculi ejus creparent, sic sub tormenta ad ultimum cum fuste occiditur.* Anon. Val.

[2] Her attire, however, says the unfortunate Platonist, already betrayed negligence and was somewhat begrimed with smoke: *caligo quaedam neglectae vetustatis obduxerat. De cons. phil.,* prosa 1.

as posterity has done his name, with the learning of antiquity, which was irretrievably fading away.[1] The honours which he had borne in the State (he himself had been Consul in 510), and the success with which twelve years later his two youthful sons, Symmachus and Boethius, had together conducted the Consulship, may well have filled his noble spirit with sadness for the present, and with lively recollections of the past greatness of Rome. He causes his consolatory goddess to hold up the mirror of memory, that he may gaze therein upon the picture of his Consular honours. He sees his sons, accompanied by the solemn procession of Senators and people, conducted from the Anician Palace to the Curia, where they take their place upon the Curule chairs. According to custom, he pronounces the panegyric upon the King, constantly interrupted by the acclamations of the people; finally, he rejoices in retrospect over the greatest day of all, when, finding himself in the Circus between his two sons, both Consuls, he divides the triumphal gifts amongst the people.[2] The Roman Senator may perhaps have deemed the return of past greatness still possible. Boethius, however, was a man of study, not of action. Five or eight hundred years after the fall of the Roman Empire the dream of its restoration on the

[1] According to Corsini, *Fasti Attici,* iv. 201, Boethius studied eighteen years in Athens, where he was the pupil of Proclus, in the year of whose death (485) he returned to Rome. This, however, is a mistake. The passage in Cassiodorus, *Var.,* i. 45: *longe positus Athenas introisti,* proves the contrary. Gibbon, v. c. 34, gives the erroneous reading *positas*; all good manuscripts have *positus.*

[2] *De consol.,* ii. prosa 3.

ruins of the ancient city might appear as madness, but in 524, only fifty years after its extinction, the delusion may well be pardoned. We observe with surprise, however, that the vain dream, which ruled the city like a spell throughout the entire Middle Ages, was already cherished in the time of Boethius. The Roman of ancient nobility and of classic education must in his heart have despised the Goths, even while admiring the wisdom and power of the King. Boethius himself contemptuously makes use of the term "barbarian" when enumerating to Philosophy his deeds in the service of his country, and recalls the names of those Romans whom he had rescued from the violence of the "dogs of the palace" and the unpunished greed of "the barbarians."[1] His proud idealism outweighed his gratitude for the great benefits of Theodoric, who in the learning of Boethius respected Rome's greatest ornament; and scorn for his base accusers induced the philosopher to give way to utterances the most imprudent.

When the King suspected that the same Senate that he had distinguished with honours, maintained treasonable a treacherous understanding with the Byzantine court, he appeared almost to desire that his suspicions might prove founded, so that he might have the right to punish the offenders. Base tale-bearers were found on the spot,—Opilio, Gaudentius, and Basilius. The King heard that a plot existed in the Senate, and insisted on believing the entire Curia guilty of high treason, because the Consul Albinus had been accused of having written certain

[1] *De consol.*, i. prosa 4.

letters to the Emperor Justin. Boethius, the head of the Senate, hastened fearlessly to Verona, and while he defended Albinus before the King, and maintained the innocence of the Senators, he was himself accused of having written letters expressing "hope" for the freedom of Rome.[1] His bold words, "the accuser Cyprianus lies; if Albinus did that of which he is accused, the same did I and the whole Senate with him," fell heavily on the ears of the irritated King. Accused of high treason, and, moreover, disliked for his orthodoxy by the Arian sovereign, Boethius was imprisoned in Pavia; where his only regret was for the loss of his sumptuous library, its panels inlaid with ebony and various coloured glass. In his imprisonment he wrote the *Apology,* which unfortunately has perished, and his *Consolations of Philosophy.* His trial was stormy and devoid of every observance of legal form, the accused being allowed no defence, but doomed by the King and the timid Senate to a speedy death. From the responsibility of this arbitrary proceeding it is impossible to exonerate Theodoric.[2] The noblest of the Senators, the aged Consul Q. Aurelius Sym-

[1] *Quibus libertatem arguor sperasse Romanam. Ibid.,* i. prosa 4. The Roman, nevertheless, betrays himself, when he says: *nam quae sperari reliqua libertas potest? atque utinam posset ulla!* Gibbon places the words of Canius in his mouth: *si ego scissem, tu nescisses*; this, however, is erroneous, since Boethius only says, that he would have answered as Julius Canius had done, had he cherished any hope.

[2] The two most powerful voices on this point are *Anon. Val.,* p. 87: *inaudito Boethio, protulit in eum sententiam*; and Procop., *De bello Goth.,* i. 1, towards the end: ἀδίκημα—ὅτι δὴ οὐ διερευνησάμενος, ὥσπερ εἰώθει, τὴν περὶ τοῖν ἀνδροῖν γνῶσιν ἤνεγκε.

machus, bitterly lamenting the death of his son-in-law, soon shared his fate, suffering death at the hands of the executioner in the Palace at Ravenna. All ancient writers are agreed in pronouncing accusations and depositions of witnesses against Boethius both alike false, and Theodoric guilty of an unjust and arbitrary act. The records of the trial are no longer forthcoming, not a single document throwing light upon the case being found among the Rescripts of Cassiodorus, the unfortunate minister, who could not, or dared not, save his fellow-citizens, and who was obliged to reject the plans of the National party, because he too clearly recognised the inevitable ruin of political power. The attitude of the Senate with regard to Theodoric is clearly seen in the books of Boethius, and the nature of things does not serve to contradict the assumption that secret dealings with the court of Byzantium had actually been in progress.

With these two illustrious men, philosophy, the last appearance of which recalls the times of Cicero and Seneca, for ever took leave of Christian Rome. Its departure is imperishably united with the site of one of the noble Anicii who was condemned by the incongruities of the time to die for the phantom of a Senate which displayed, for the last time in Roman history, the illusion of Roman virtue.

Pope John sent to Byzantium.

The Roman Bishop was to suffer the weight of the royal anger. John, summoned from Rome to Ravenna, was obliged to set forth for Constantinople attended by a few priests and four Senators, Theodore, Importunatus and the two Agapiti, to demand from the Emperor the reinstatement of the oppressed

Arians in the East. In despair, the chief bishop of the West undertook the difficult embassy. The people and the Emperor Justin, however, received the first Pope who ever set foot in the Greek capital, before its walls, not as ambassador of the Gothic King, but with ostentatious honours, as the head of Catholic Christendom, and led him in triumph to S. Sophia's, where he celebrated the Easter festival in 525. He obtained some seeming concessions from Justin, but cannot have executed the more important points of the embassy; else were the subsequent anger of the King entirely inexplicable. On the return of the embassy to Ravenna, Theodoric, enraged, threw not only the Senators but the Pope also into prison, where John I. died (May 18, 526). The grateful Church later honoured his memory by conferring on him the crown of martyrdom.[1]

Felix IV., 526–530.

Theodoric now firmly resolved no longer to concede any of the privileges he had hitherto granted to the Catholic Church, but to exercise the royal authority in the papal elections. He therefore nominated to the Senate, clergy and people, as candidate for the vacant chair, Fimbrius, son of Castorius of Benevento, whom the trembling Romans elected and consecrated as Felix IV. This act of regal authority, concerning which the *Liber Pontificalis* maintains a deliberate silence, was destined to lead to important results; the successors of Theodoric claiming in consequence the right of confirming each successive papal election.[2]

[1] *Lib. Pont.,* "Vita Joh. I."; *Anon. Val.*; *Histor. Misc.*

[2] The rescript of Athalaric to the Senate (*Var.,* viii. 15) stands in

Death of Theoderic, Aug. 30, 526.

The *Liber Pontificalis* maintains that his death was a divine judgment, following on that of Pope John, and another author asserts that it took place on the same day as a written decree of the "Jew" Symmachus—a jurist of the King— ordering the Catholic churches to be made over to the Arians, was to be carried into execution.[1] Procopius relates the childish legend, that the King, sitting one day at table, imagined that he saw, within the wide-open jaws of a huge fish, the head of the murdered Symmachus, and that, terrified by the sight, he was seized by a sudden fever, and died a few days after, tortured by remorse.[2] Assuredly remorse and painful thoughts must have added to the death agony of the great prince. Jordanes only veils them in silence, in giving us the picture of the calm and peaceful death of the noble Goth. "After," he says, "the King had reached old age, and recognised that his end was approaching, he called the Gothic Counts and the heads of his people before him, and nominated, as his successor, the boy Athalaric, who was barely ten years old (son of his daughter Amalasuntha and the dead Eutharic), enjoining his followers, even as by his dying testament, that they

black and white: *oportebat enim arbitrio boni principis obediri, qui quamvis in aliena religione, talem visus est pontificem delegisse.* Muratori also terms this election *un comandamento*. Henceforward (apparently if the election were contested and negotiated before the royal court), the popes, like all bishops, had to pay down a sum of money; in the case of the popes 3000, of other patriarchs 2000, and in that of the bishops of the smaller cities 500 solidi. *Var.,* ix. 15.

[1] *Anon. Val.,* towards the end.

[2] Procop., *De bello Goth.,* i. 1.

should cherish the King, should love the Senate and people of Rome, and should always seek to preserve conciliatory and friendly relations towards the Greek Emperor."[1] Theodoric died in August 30, 526. Fanatical theologians, on the other hand, inform us that the soul of Theodoric, naked and fettered, was borne through the air by the angry spirits of Pope John and the Patrician Symmachus, and thrown into the crater of Lipari. An anchorite on the island testified to having seen it with his own eyes; a malicious legend which Pope Gregory was not ashamed to repeat in his dialogues.[2]

In the heroic form of Theodoric appears the first attempt of the Germans to erect, on the ruins of the Empire, the new world of civilisation which resulted from the alliance of the Northern barbarians with Roman culture and nationality. Theodoric, the predecessor of Charles the Great, was the first to bring his wandering people to a stand. His powerful rule extended from Italy to the Ister, from Illyria to Gaul, and he cherished the bold intention, like an Emperor, of uniting German and Latin

[1] *De reb Get.,* towards the end.

[2] S. Gregor, *Dial.,* c. 30. Even in the eighth century, S. Wilibald speaks of Volcano, a fire-vomiting island belonging to the group of the Lipari, as the Hell of Theodoric (*ibi est infernus Theodorici*). *Vita seu Hodoeporicon S. Wilibaldi,* in Titus Tobler, *Descriptiones Terrae Sanctae,* p. 42. The legend that Theodoric had fallen a prey to the spirits of evil reappears in the poem of Etzel's Court, where Dietrich, the son of an evil spirit, who builds him the fortress at Bern (Verona) is finally borne by a demon horse into the wilderness, and there has to defend himself incessantly against two serpents. He is also represented as a wild huntsman on the porch of S. Zeno at Verona. See Fr. v. d. Hagen, *Briefe in die Heimat,* 1818, Band ii. p. 60.

races in one feudal system. But the plan was not yet ripe. A union of the West, such as this, required the co-operation of the Church, and the Church had not yet been able to incorporate the Arian German races into her organism. It further required the emancipation of the West from the Imperial authority of Byzantium. The memory of the Gothic King, the noblest foreigner who ever ruled Italy, still lingers in several cities restored or beautified by him.[1] Ravenna still preserves his great mausoleum with its huge monolithic cupola, over which, it was said, stood the porphyry urn containing the ashes of the dead.[2] In Pavia and Verona Lombards still show the castles of Theodoric; even in Southern Terracina the ruins of a fortress bear his name, and an ancient inscription records that Theodoric restored the Appian Way and drained the Pontine Marshes. Thus did a Gothic ruler, in the time of the decadence, achieve an honour which Caesar had not been able to win.[3] In Rome, however, where the Senate honoured

[1] *Sub cujus felici imperio plurimae renovantur urbes, munitissima castella conduntur, consurgunt admiranda palatia, magnisque ejus operib. antiqua miracula superantur.* Cassiod., *Chron. ad A.* 500. Dahn (iii.) gives a detailed list of all Theodoric's buildings and restorations in Italian cities.

[2] The porphyry urn is said to have been overthrown by a cannon ball in 1509, and inserted in 1563 in the wall of Theodoric's palace. See Peringskiöld's note, p. 594, on Cochlaeus' *Vita Theodorici.* After, however, having seen the urn at the Palace in Ravenna, I hold the above statement to be entirely fabulous.

[3] The Patrician Decius caused the Decemnovian Swamp to be drained at his own expense, together with the profits derived from the land reclaimed. *Var.,* ii. 32, 33. But the service rendered by Pius VI.

his memory with a gilt statue, and where several other monuments were erected to him, no memorial remains; only the tomb of Hadrian, which he made the model of his own mausoleum at Ravenna, was for several centuries known as "the house or prison of Theodoric," perhaps because that under the Gothic King this building was transformed into a fortress or state prison.[1] The memory of Theodoric is, however, inseparably connected with the city, and such Romans as forget the outrages committed by their own forefathers on the monuments of antiquity during the rude times of the Middle Ages, may associate with the name of the Goths the recollection that, to the benefactor of Italy in a seven and thirty years' reign is owing the preservation of these monuments. Italian historians have shown themselves without prejudice in extolling the virtues of the great Gothic hero.[2]

in the construction of the *Linea Pia* was even greater than that rendered by Theodoric. The inscriptions were found in two copies in 1743, on the Via Appia, near Terracina; see Gruter, p. 152, and the more correct version of Friedländer, *Die Münzen der Vandalen,* p. 62. The tracts in question are *Decennovii Viae Appiae id est a trib.* (sc. *tribus tabernis*) *usq. Terracinam,* &c., according to Cluver's reckoning nearly thirty miles. Bergier, *Histoire des grands chemins,* ii. c. 26, p. 214. Contatore, *De Histor. Terracinensi,* Roma, 1706, gives a brief history of the draining of the Pontine Marshes especially.

[1] Statues were erected to Theodoric in several Italian cities. The Roman Senate honoured his memory by the erection of a gilt statue, as Isidor., *Chron. Gothor.,* tells us: *per hunc dignitas urbis Romae non parva est restituta: muros enim ejus iste redintegravit: ob quam causam a senatu inauratam statuam meruit.* Later Rusticiana, widow of Boethius, caused the statues of the king to be overthrown.

[2] Giannone, in his *History of Naples,* is still warmer in his laudations than either the Bishop of Pavia or Cassiodorus. His observations

CHAPTER III.

1. Regency of Amalasuntha—Her Genius—Encouragement of Learning—Her Conciliatory Government—Growing Importance of the Bishop of Rome—Felix IV. Builds the Church of SS. Cosma and Damiano—Its Mosaics—Origin of the Worship of these Saints.

Athalaric King under the regency of Amalasuntha.

The comparatively prosperous condition of the Romans lasted for some years after the death of Theodoric, so long, in fact, as his daughter Amalasuntha, widow of Eutharic (who had died in 522), retained the guardianship of her son Athalaric. For the Gothic nation, however, this regency was an misfortune, and one of the chief causes of its downfall, proving, as it did, that the Gothic dominion in Italy had depended entirely on the individual energy of the King who had been its founder. Procopius, as well as Cassiodorus, has awarded to Amalasuntha the praise of unusual strength of character, states-

(l. iii. § 3) are instructive. "The institution of the magistrates who exist in our kingdom in the present day, namely, the appointment of governors and judges in every town, is due, not to the Romans, but to the Goths." Baronius also extols the Gothic King, in that he calls him *saevus barbarus, dirus tyrannus, et impius Arianus.* Agincourt, i. c. 8, deals well with Theodoric's encouragement of Art.

man-like prudence, and high literary attainments.[1] If Theodoric had been an object of ridicule in the eyes of the Romans because he was unable to do more than sign the first four letters of his name, following with the stylus the tracings already prepared for him, the abilities of a woman who spoke Greek with the Greeks, Latin with the Latins, and who held lively conversations with the learned on the philosophy and poetry of antiquity, excited their astonishment, and they were obliged to concede to the Goths the merit of upholding civilisation.

The Rescripts of Cassiodorus prove that Amalasuntha strove by every means in her power to promote the welfare of the Romans. During her regency, perhaps even more zealously than in the days of her father, learning was cherished and cultivated. Professors of the liberal arts, of grammar, "the teacher of language which is the ornament of mankind," of eloquence and of law were encouraged by liberal salaries to settle in Rome.[2] The city maintained her reputation as the seat of learning, so that Cassiodorus was able to say, "other districts furnish wine, balsams, and aromatic herbs, but Rome dispenses the gift of eloquence, to which it is inexpressibly sweet to listen."[3] Some scanty remains of the ancient University founded by the Antonines

[1] Procop., *De bell. Goth.*, i. 2; Cassiod., *Var.*, xi. 1: *jungitur his rebus quasi diadema eximium, impretiabilis notitia literarum.* Her history proves, however, that her statesmanlike abilities were of no very high order.

[2] *Var.*, ix. 21.

[3] *Var.*, x. 7.

survived into Gothic times, and youths in the pursuit of learning still resorted thither.[1] The Goths, in the proud consciousness of their warlike vigour, deliberately left the Romans in undisturbed enjoyment of the arts of peace. No military service was exacted from them. The cities were garrisoned solely by Gothic troops. None but Goths bore arms. But among these barbarian settlers many had already begun to acquire, together with a love of study, the customs of the Romans and a taste for peaceful occupations, while, on the other hand, many Romans, whether from a desire to flatter the foreign rulers, or from a fashionable love of change, assumed a show of Gothic manners and dress, and even attempted to stammer the heroic language of Ulfilas.[2]

[1] Bishop Ennodius recommends his nephew Parthenius, who had gone to Rome for this purpose, to the notice of Pope Symmachus: *sancta sunt studia literarum, in quib. ante incrementa peritiae vitia dediscuntur;* also another, who *profutura ad testimonium ingenuitatis studia Romana requirit.* A. Thiel, *Ep. R. Pont. Genuinae,* i., Ep. 22, 23 of Symmachus.

[2] Theodoric said: *Romanus miser imitatur Gothum, et utilis Gothus imitatur Romanum. Anon. Val.,* 61. Cesare Balbo, in the fervour of modern patriotism, distorts this perfectly clear passage as follows: *un Romano povero s'assomiglia ad un Goto, e un Goto ricco a un Romano. Storia d'Italia,* i. c. 11, p. 89. Peringskiöld (note, p. 576, to Coehlaeus), without any justification, emends "*utilis*" into "*vilis,*" an interpretation which, moreover, Eyssenhardt in his edition of the Excerpta, at the end of Ammian. Marcellin., has accepted. Sartorius, like Balbo, translates *utilis* as well-off. *Pueri stirpis Romanae nostra lingua loquuntur, eximie indicantes exhibere se nobis futuram fidem, quorum jam videntur affectasse sermonem.* So writes Athalaric to the Patricius Cyprian. *Var.,* viii. 20. Honorius had already issued a law forbidding the Romans to adopt the dress of the Goths. *Usum tzangarum atque bracharum intra urbem venerabilem nemini liceat usurpare—majores crines, indumenta pellium—praecipimus inhiberi.* Cod.

The first act of Amalasuntha's regency was to conciliate the Roman Senate and people so deeply wronged by her father. Letters from the pen of Cassiodorus, who continued to serve the grandson of Theodoric as minister, announced in respectful terms to the Romans the change on the throne; and through his ambassadors the young King tendered to the Senate and people his solemn oath faithfully to preserve the rights and laws of Rome. Further, to prove by deeds the desire for reconciliation, Amalasuntha reinstated the children of Boethius and Symmachus in their hereditary possessions. Lamenting the last cruel act of her father's reign, she sought to efface it from her memory, and during the whole of her regency never punished a Roman either in life or property. As in the days of Theodoric, honours continued to be heaped upon the Assembly of the Fathers. Their numbers also were increased by the introduction of Gothic heroes; and the descendants of the Scipios could scarce feel themselves offended when it was said "that it was fitting the family of Romulus should receive as colleagues the followers of Mars."[1] With these sons of Mars it was hoped to strengthen the Gothic party in the Senate.

The honours of the Senatorial Curia were but pompous titles; not so the rights which, in order to re-establish the former relations, the Gothic government conceded to the Pope. The power of this

Theodos, t. v. lib. xiv. tit. 10, 237; quoted by Am. Thierry, *Récits de l'histoire Romaine au V. siècle,* p. 5.

[1] *Convenit gentem Romuleam Martios viros habere collegas. Var.,* viii. 10.

bishop (he was also already recognised by the East as head of the Christian Church) waxed continually greater. The fact that the Gothic rulers continued to reside in Ravenna was advantageous to his position; still more advantageous the circumstance that they, as Arians, remained outside the Roman Church. Thus it came to pass that the Pope, as head of Catholic Christendom, felt himself raised above the heretical kings, and thus, standing between them and the orthodox Emperor (whom they recognised as their Imperial overlord), he gradually became a man of importance and finally acquired a greater degree of influence in the internal affairs of the city.[1] Among the Rescripts enumerated by Cassiodorus is an edict of Athalaric appointing the Roman bishop arbitrator in disputes between the laity and clergy. Anyone having a dispute with a member of the clergy in Rome was directed henceforth to appeal first to the judgment of the Pope, and only in case the Pope rejected his complaint, was he to carry the action before the secular jurisdiction. Anyone refusing to submit to the decision of the Pope was sentenced to be fined in ten pounds of gold.[2] Felix IV.

[1] Athalaric's letter to Justin, notifying his accession to the throne, indicates the recognition of the Imperial supremacy. *Var.,* viii. 1. The silver coins of the Gothic Kings, bearing on the obverse the head of the Emperor, on the reverse the monogram of the King, surrounded by a wreath or the words INVICTA ROMA, supply us with a further indication. J. Friedländer, *Die Münzen der Ostgothen,* Berlin, 1844.

[2] *Var.,* viii. 24. Muratori refers this law to the year 528. G. Sartorius (*Versuch über die Regier. der Ostgothen in Italien,* p. 145) considers that this privilegium, the importance of which he depreciates,

appears to have been the Pope who succeeded in obtaining this decree so favourable to the influence of the Roman Curia. The episcopal power of arbitration between laity and clergy had been exercised from of old, but the privilege may be regarded as simply exempting the clergy from all secular jurisdiction. Such was the decree which laid the foundation of the political power of the Papacy. It was evident that the regal government felt itself insecure after the death of Theodoric, and that it hastened to conciliate the Roman Church.[1]

Felix IV. builds the church of SS. Cosma and Damiano.

The chronicle of the city cannot pass over the short reign of Felix IV. (526–530) without mention of a remarkable church, the first built on the confines of the Roman Forum and on the Via Sacra. This is the church of SS. Cosma and Damian, Arabian physicians and twin brothers, who suffered martyrdom under Diocletian, and to whom Felix built a basilica on the Sacred Way, not far from the Forum Pacis, near the Temple dedicated to the City of Rome.[2] For the reason that an ancient rotunda serves as a vestibule to the single-naved basilica, which has also developed out of an ancient building, an attempt has been made to identify this rotunda

only applied to the clergy in the city of Rome. S. Marc, however (*Abrégé chronologique de l'histoire d'Italie,* p. 62), says: *c'est sur cette condescendance des princes pour un etat infiniment respectable en lui-même, que dans la suite les Ecclésiastiques ont prétendu qu'ils etoient de Droit divin exemts de la jurisdiction séculaire.*

[1] During the reign of Theodoric, however, the clergy remained subject to the secular Forum.

[2] *Lib. Pont.,* "Felix IV.": *hic fecit basilicam SS. Cosmae et Damiani in urbe Roma, in loco, qui appellatur Via sacra juxta templum urbis Romae* (according to one MS, *vel Romuli*).

either with the Temple of the City of Rome, or with that of Romulus, or, thirdly, with the Temple of the Twin Brothers Romulus and Remus, and in support of one or other opinion a passage from Prudentius has been quoted, a passage, however, which clearly refers to Hadrian's twofold Temple of Venus and Rome.[1] Recent investigation confirms the supposition that this so-called "Templum Romuli" was a temple dedicated to Caesar Romulus by his father Maxentius, whose large basilica stood in the neighborhood.[2] The church of Felix IV. originally arose out of three ancient buildings, of which one, and undoubtedly the last, the present sacristy, was called in the sixth century Templum Urbis Romae, apparently from the fact that to its walls was affixed the marble plan of the city, placed there in the time of Septimius Severus.[3] There seems to have been

[1] Prudent. in Sym., i. 219. The history of the church by Bernardinus Mezzardi: *Disquisitio Historica de s. martyr. Cosma et Dam.,* &c., Roma, 1747, although uncritical, is worth reading. The *Mirabilia* say: *S. Cosmatis ecclesia, quae fuit templum Asyli.* This was also the locality of the legend of the fall of Simon Magus: and as late as the twelfth century men pointed out *silicem, ubi cecidit Simon Magus juxta Templum Romuli.* Mabill., *Mus. Ital.,* ii. 144.

[2] De Rossi, *Bullettino,* 1867, n. 5. Canini had already connected the spot with Romulus, son of Maxentius, and his opinion is supported not only by the evidence of a coin which bears the representation of a circular temple dedicated to Romulus by Maxentius, but also by an inscription with the name of Constantine, which was found on this building. We know that the Senate consecrated all the buildings of Maxentius to the victorious Constantine.

[3] De Rossi, *Piante iconografiche di Roma,* p. 54, f. The celebrated marble plan of the city was discovered here in the sixteenth century, in fragments, attached as an outer facing to a wall. A further portion of the plan, found in prosecuting some excavations near SS. Cosma

found on the spot a document belonging to the city prefecture, which contained a register of the census and a plan of the city.[1] In any case, this is one of the first instances in Rome where an ancient building in perfect preservation was adapted to the uses of a church.[2] Standing on the Via Sacra, beside the ruins of the Forum, in the immediate neighbourhood of Vespasian's celebrated Temple of Peace, and surrounded by the magnificent remains of antiquity, its site is one of the most noteworthy in the city. The porphyry columns at the entrance of the church, the other shafts of the columns of the portico close by, and the antique bronze doors also deserve our attention as interesting relics of the past.[3]

Its mosaics.

The building of Felix IV. was striking from the fact that it deviated entirely from the character of a basilica, the architect constructing it from the existing Pagan buildings which lay to hand. The circular temple he transformed into an entrance hall, placing before it a pillared portico: pierced this rotunda by opening a passage into the ancient hall-like building (Templum Urbis Romae), which was richly inlaid

and Damiano in Sept. 1867, seems to decide the site of the Templum Pacis. Jordan., *Forma urbis Romae,* Berlin, 1874.

[1] Lanciani, *Bull, di arch. com.,* x. p. 29, f.

[2] In the list of Roman churches which have arisen out of temples, given by Marangoni, *Cose Gent.,* c. 52, Cosma and Damian stands second, S. Stefano being reckoned by him the first. The church adjoins the ruins of an ancient building, and behind the *Orator. della Via Crucis* is a wall of peperino, which probably belonged to an outbuilding of the Temple of Peace.

[3] In the year 1879 the circular building was disclosed to view, and the bronze doors were replaced on their original site. The excavations have now changed the aspect of the whole neighbourhood.

with marble. Here he designed the apse, and also made a passage into a third building, or, more strictly speaking, to the further part of the aula.[1] He adorned the arch of triumph and niches with mosaics, which, on account of their character and antiquity, may rank amongst the most remarkable in Rome. Representations in a style not yet free from the antique spirit cover the arch, visions from the Apocalypse, a source from which were borrowed numerous subjects for mosaic art. Christ as the Lamb rests upon a splendid throne, before Him lies the Book with the Seven Seals; at the sides stand the Seven Candlesticks, slender candelabra of somewhat debased design, although the two winged seraphs beside them are strikingly graceful figures. Two Evangelists with their attributes stand at each extremity of the arch; further below, the four and twenty Elders offering their crowns to the Saviour.[2]

The large picture in the tribune is especially worthy of attention. Upon a gold background figures of superhuman size are represented in a vigorous and effective style, the draperies in particular being treated with great success. The colossal central figure, depicting the Saviour, with bearded head and long locks surrounded by a nimbus, powerful and majestic, is one of the best representations of Christ in Rome. The draperies of yellow gold fall in massive simple folds. In the left hand He holds

[1] Lanciani, *l. c.*

[2] Of the elders, two defaced forms in the corner of the arch alone remain, and in the series of evangelists the two outer figures have disappeared. See the illustration in Ciampini, *Vet. Mon.,* ii. 7.

a roll of parchment; the right is raised in the act of blessing. Originally a hand with a wreath over His Head signified the First Person of the Trinity, who in the early centuries of Christianity was represented by this symbol and not as yet in the likeness of an old man.[1] Right and left stand Cosma and Damiano, led by Peter and Paul (larger and more imposing figures) to the Saviour. Both saints, and especially those on the right, have powerful, stern, and magician-like faces; their great, gloomy eyes are animated with reverent awe at the thought of approaching Christ, and lighted with such a glow of religious fervour as seems to herald the coming triumph of the Church over the world. Their attitude, as they advance in rude bashfulness, is very lifelike. These are two indomitable champions of Christ. Their robust forms, expressing an energetic barbarism, convey the idea of men of a wild, epic existence, such as belonged to the heroic, warlike times of Odoacer, Dietrich of Bern and the Byzantine Belisarius. The mosaic in its vigorous and effective treatment is alone of its kind in Rome. The grace of the antique has passed away, while the characteristics of Byzantine art, visible in Justinian's celebrated mosaics in Ravenna, are not yet apparent in these of earlier date. The picture is independently Roman, an original work of the sixth century, and with it mosaic art in Rome sinks to decay for long ages to come.

Near these saints we still see Pope Felix (the figure entirely restored) and the saintly warrior

[1] The hand with the wreath of laurel has vanished.

Theodore. Felix is clad in yellow gold drapery over a blue under-garment, wears the stole, and presents a model of his church to the Saviour. This building is represented with a vestibule, but without a tower.[1] Among these figures Christ alone wears the nimbus, a proof that at the beginning of the sixth century the custom had not yet arisen of bestowing the halo on the saints.[2]

Two palms incline their slender branches towards the heads of these figures. Over one hovers to the right of Christ the fabulous bird, the phoenix, a star above its head. The star, an emblem of immortality, and one of the loveliest symbols of art, had been derived from Pagan antiquity, the phoenix with the star having been engraved on Imperial coins from the time of Hadrian onwards.[3] Below

[1] The figure of the Pope (Felix IV.) belongs to the time of Alexander VII., by whom the mosaic was restored, a resemblance to the original figure being however retained. The ancient figure fell to pieces during the reign of Gregory XIII., and was replaced by that of Gregory the Great, until finally Cardinal Francesco Barberini restored Felix IV. to his original place. The church owes its present form to Urban VIII. Ugonio, p. 178.

[2] Marangoni, *Delle cose Gentil.,* c. xxxv., shows that the glory (borrowed from the representations of Apollo and the deified Emperors) had been bestowed on the martyrs in the Catacombs before the time of Constantine.

[3] On coins of the elder and younger Faustina is found the type of AETERNITAS, holding the globe, on which is the phoenix with the star (Vaillant, ii. 175, iii. 132). A beautiful coin of Constantine represents Crispus handing the globe with the phoenix to his father, who is seated. A coin of Constantine the Younger displays the Emperor with the globe and phoenix in his right hand, the Labarum with the monogram of Christ in the left (Vaillant, iii. 247). The phoenix with the star is found on Egyptian monuments, as a symbol, it is believed, of the period of Sirius—1461 years. The legend concerning the phoenix

this remarkable picture are represented the flowing waters of the Jordan; still lower, in the last division of all, twelve lambs, symbolising the apostles, approach the Saviour from the towns of Jerusalem and Bethlehem. Christ, depicted a second time in the form of a lamb, is placed in the midst on a richly covered chair, His head crowned with the nimbus. An inscription in large characters, and arabesques in gold mosaics, form a pleasing frame to the whole of the decorations of the tribune.[1]

Thus, within this church on the Via Sacra, we find two Arabians from the far East distinguished by an honour which hitherto had only fallen to the share of Roman martyrs. The worship of the saints was, as we have seen, local in its origin. With the Roman martyrs were afterwards associated other martyrs from the provinces; the principle of universality, to which the Church of Rome laid claim, showing itself in the admission of some of the Eastern saints within the bounds of her worship. The enmity, however, that existed later between

is first related by Herodotus. Pliny adds that the fabulous bird dies in the aromatic bed which it had made, that from its ashes arises a worm, from which in turn issues a young bird that buries its father. Thus arose the legend of the burning of the phoenix. Piper, *Mythol. und Symbolik der christl. Kunst,* i. 446.

[1] The inscription runs:—

Aula Dei claris radiat speciosa metallis,
In qua plus fidei lux pretiosa micat.
Martyribus Medicis populo spes certa salutis
Venit, et ex sacro crevit honore locus.
Obtulit hoc domino Felix antistite dignum
Munus ut aetheria vivat in arce poli.

See the illustration of the mosaic in De Rossi's *Musaici cristiani.*

Rome and the East, and the complete separation which afterwards took place, set a limit to the worship of Greek saints. The true motive of Felix in thus distinguishing Cosma and Damiano, who, as the "Anargyri," already enjoyed universal veneration throughout the whole Byzantine Empire, may have been of a political nature. It was perhaps an act of diplomatic homage towards the orthodox Emperor, with whom the Roman Church stood at that time in friendly relations. Or it may have been that the Pope, on account of the Goths, wished to flatter the Greeks. Or, again, perhaps pestilence approaching from the East actually threatened Italy, and Felix may have deemed it prudent to propitiate the twin brothers, whose mere prayers had once cured the Emperor Carinus of a fatal malady, and who were already in great repute as workers of miracles. The mosaic inscription expressly honours both martyrs as physicians who "assured to the people the means of recovery." The site of the church beside the Forum had been expressly chosen as having been that occupied in olden days by the dwelling of the celebrated Galen, and as the spot where physicians had formerly been accustomed to hold their meetings. In the reign of Justinian these two miracle-workers were honoured at Cyrus on the Euphrates (their burial-place) as new Aesculapii. Churches had also been built to them in Pamphylia and in Constantinople. The East, the birth-place of the plague, was rich in sainted physicians, and Cyrus, John and Pantaleon, Hermolaus and Sampson, Diomedes, Photius and others, after having cured the living and restored the dead to life, were placed, like Empedocles, in heaven.

2. BONIFACE II. POPE, 530—SCHISM BETWEEN BONIFACE AND DIOSCORUS—JOHN II.— DECREE OF THE SENATE AGAINST THE SIMONISTIC PRACTICES OF THE PAPACY—EDUCATION AND DEATH OF ATHALARIC—THEODATUS CO-REGENT— FATE OF QUEEN AMALASUNTHA—JUSTINIAN'S AIMS AND VIEWS—EXPIRATION OF THE WESTERN CONSULSHIP IN 535.

Felix IV. had ventured to appoint as his successor the Archdeacon Boniface, and had gained the consent of a part of the clergy to the appointment. The Senate refused, however, to sanction an action so outrageous, and issued a decree which threatened the punishment of exile against anyone who attempted to appoint a successor to the Papacy during the lifetime of a Pope.[1] The death of Felix (Sept. 530) was followed by a schism; his followers actually electing and ordaining Boniface in the Lateran basilica, on Sept. 22, while at the same time the more numerous body of their opponents consecrated the Greek Dioscorus (a highly respected man) in the Lateran Aula, known as the Basilica Julii.[2] The former candidate belonged to the Gothic, the latter

[1] *Praeceptum Papae Felicis* and *Contestatio Senatus,* important documents discovered at Novara by Amelli in 1883, printed by Duchesne in *Mélanges de l'Ecole de Rome,* iii. (1883) 239, f., and in his edition of the *Lib. Pont.* (1883), p. 282. See also P. Ewald, *Acten z. Schisma d. J. 530,—Neues Archiv.,* 1885, p. 412, f.

[2] *Lib. Pont.*: *Qui Dioscorus ordinatur in basilica Constantiniana, Bonifacius vero in basilica Julii* (a place in the Lateran Palace).

to the Byzantine faction. Dioscorus dying (fortunately for the Roman Church) immediately after (Oct. 14, 530), the brief schism came to an end, and the presbyters of the opposite party, now professing subjection to Boniface, condemned Dioscorus as an intruder.[1]

Boniface II., 530–532.

The ambitious Boniface, the first Pope of German race, was the son of Sigibold, whose name was not wholly new to Rome. As early as 437 a Sigisboldus had borne the consular dignity along with Aetius, and the present Pope belonged to the ancient and powerful German house which had entered the service of fallen Rome. He had been trained from his earliest youth in ecclesiastical discipline, had risen to the office of Archdeacon, and had become the confidant of Felix IV. The Gothic court had probably favoured, the Senate opposed his election; nevertheless he does not seem to have responded to the aims of Amalasuntha's government.[2] The disputes on the occasion of the papal election, and the wish of the Arian Queen to renounce all influence upon it, caused Boniface to renew the attempts of his predecessor. In his first Synod in Rome, he himself appointed his successor, the deacon Vigilius, and deposited the Deed of Election, signed and sworn to by the thoughtless clergy, in the Shrine

[1] *Libellus quem dederunt praesbiteri LX. post mortem Dioscori Bonifacio Papae.* See Duchesne, *l, c.*

[2] The German origin of Boniface allows us to suppose that he owed his elevation to the influence of the court. Nevertheless, neither in his case nor in that of his successor are we aware that the election was compulsory. Silverius was the first who ascended the papal chair by command of Theodatus.

of the Prince of the Apostles. Neither Amalasuntha nor yet the Senate could, however, sanction this despotic act, which, had it been allowed to become law, would have altered the entire nature of the ecclesiastical hierarchy; and in a second Synod Boniface was obliged solemnly to withdraw the decree.

John II., 532–535.

Boniface dying in 532, the Roman Mercurius, son of Projectus of the Coelian Hill, was elected as John II.[1] It had long since become customary for the aspirants to the powerful Roman bishopric to seek the dignity during the lifetime of the Pope by means of simony or purchase, bribing the most influential senators and court officials by gifts of money. In order to raise the requisite sums these candidates for the Papacy frequently had recourse to selling the property of their churches, and even the vessels of the altar. In consequence of this abuse, the Senate, under Felix IV., had already issued a decree forbidding this illegal means of acquiring the papal office, and this decree (so far as we are aware, the last ever passed by the Senate) received confirmation from Athalaric upon the election of John II.; when the

Edict against simony.

[1] One of the earliest inscriptions that makes mention of a Pope mentions this John, and tells us that he was raised to the pontificate from the titular church of S. Clemens: SALBO. PAPA. N. JOHANNE. COGNOMENTO. MERCURIO. EX. SCE. ECCL. ROM. PRESBYTERIS ORDINATO EX. TIT. SCI. CLEMENTIS. AD. GLORIAM PONTIFICALEM. PROMOTO. BEATO. PETRO. AP. PATRONO. SUO A. VINCULIS. EIUS SEVERUS. PB. OFRT.

ET. IT. PC. LAMPADI. ET. ORESTIS. V.V. CC. URBI †. CLUS CEDRINUS EST. (Marble tablet belonging to the year 532 on the wall of S. Pietro ad Vincula.)

King commanded Salvantius, the City Prefect, to have the law engraven on a marble tablet and placed before the Atrium of S. Peter.[1] This memorable decree shows the active part the Senate legally possessed in the papal election, and further, that at this period it gave laws to the Church in matters of discipline. In virtue of its wealth and constitutional power, the Senate still possessed a considerable degree of importance. It was treated with respect by the Gothic Kings; and, as it directed the papal elections, and as even the decrees of the synods were subject to its decisions, the Bishops of Rome strove also to maintain friendly relations with the august Fathers. The Senate, the highest secular authority, asserted its right, as representative of the laity or of the people of Rome, to have a voice in ecclesiastical affairs.[2] In such acts the once glorious corporation of Rome, the former ruler of the world displayed a last semblance of political life before it entirely vanished from history.

The Roman people itself no longer showed any signs of life. Far from the eyes of its ruler, nourished as hitherto, though more sparingly, by the provinces, it was occasionally startled from its lethargy by the dread of approaching famine, and tumults perhaps arose, or suspicions of rebellious tendencies were awakened. This appears to have

[1] *Var.,* ix. 16, and Athalaric's letter to Pope John, ix. 15.

[2] The *Synodus Palmaris* recognised the right of the Senate to pass an opinion on its decrees. In 507 the Senate resolved that no bishop could provide for the cession of ecclesiastical property. H. Usener *Das Verh. des röm Senats zur Kirche in der Ost-Gothenzeit* (*Commentat, Mommsen.* 1877, p. 759, f.).

been the case in the reign of Athalaric, when Pope John himself complained that Romans were kept too long in imprisonment on mere suspicion.[1] Rome was, however, soon to be roused out of her condition of quiet, though inglorious, prosperity under the Gothic rule, and plunged into the most terrible distress. An awful calamity, followed by long centuries of barbarism, in the darkness of which her history is well-nigh lost, lay before the unfortunate city. Before entering, however, on this period of her annals, we must briefly follow the fortunes of the house of Theodoric, with which the fate of Rome was interwoven.

The Goths rise against Amalasuntha.

The family of the great King suffered the penalty of the contradiction in which the national spirit of the Goths stood towards Roman culture in spite of the reconciliation which Amalasuntha in vain had attempted to effect between these opposing elements. Educating her son in the liberal arts of the Romans, she excited the contempt of the rough Gothic warriors, who, not unreasonably, detested Roman civilisation as the enemy of the manliness, as also of the dominion of their race. Scarce anywhere do we find an educational problem of greater moment than that which arose with regard to this German boy. The Gothic Counts snatched him, as they said, from the dishonouring discipline of the pedagogues, and left him to the teachings of nature. They would have no grammarian for King, but a brave soldier, such as his forefathers of the stock of Amal had been. His mother was an enthusiastic lover of

[1] *Var.*, ix. 17.

Roman culture and ideas, and already estranged from her own unlettered people. Owing to this estrangement, the party opposed to the firm rule of Theodoric and his Romanising schemes attained a greater degree of power. The Gothic nobility despised the regency of a woman. Such regencies had been frequent in Roman and Byzantine history during the last century, but were at variance with German custom. The Goths, therefore, longed to overthrow Amalasuntha, and the threatened princess was forced secretly to secure herself a safe retreat at the court of Byzantium. The murder, by her orders, of three of the most dangerous of the opposing Goths, restored her courage; and, renouncing the treacherous thought of escaping to the East, she continued to wield the sceptre in the palace of Ravenna. Meanwhile, she recognised the inevitable downfall of the Gothic kingdom in Italy, where the non-catholic and northern warrior race could, with difficulty, take root. Worn out by his early excesses, her son languished beneath her eyes. She therefore, as Procopius informs us, resumed negotiations with the Emperor Justinian with regard to the abdication of Italy; a step against which every Gothic heart rebelled. Athalaric dying in 534, at Ravenna, in his eighteenth year, and the throne of Theodoric being thus left without an heir, the Gothic kingdom was thrown into utter confusion, and the noble Cassiodorus was unwillingly forced to recognise that the Roman Empire, resting as it did on the support of the Amali, must perish in the coming overthrow. The learned Roman, who had

Death of Athalaric, 534.

remained the faithful minister of Amalasuntha and Athalaric, had not disdained to write the history of the Gothic nation in order to justify the Amal race and to exalt it in the eyes of the Latins.[1]

Upon the death of her son, Amalasuntha, whose position was desperate, elected her cousin co-regent, and, while bestowing on him the kingly title, herself retained regal power. Theodatus, son of Theodoric's sister Amalafrida, was a determined opponent of Amalasuntha. She hoped, however, to convert an enemy into a friend, to secure her own throne and life, and to tranquillise the mutinous Goths.

Theodatus co-regent.

In Theodatus the influence of Italy, to which so many Goths had already succumbed, was exemplified in the most striking manner. Weak and unwarlike, he was nevertheless a thorough scholar in ancient literature, and was versed in the study of Plato. Living on his ample estates in Tuscany, he had exchanged the court for the villa, and, but for the torments of an insatiable avarice, might have led an enviable existence in his olive-shaded retreat. All Etruria, however, had cause to execrate his

[1] *Iste reges Gothorum longa oblivione celatos, latibulo vetustatis eduxit. Iste Amalos cum generis sui claritate restituit, evidenter ostendens in decimam septimam progeniem stirpem nos habere regalem.* Thus speaks the unfortunate Athalaric of Cassiodorus. *Variar.*, ix. 25; and *Originem Gothicam historiam fecit esse Romanam.* The twelve books of Gothic history by Cassiodorus have unfortunately perished, as also the Gothic history of Ablavius. The history of the Goths by Jordanes, an extract from Cassiodorus, has alone been preserved. Jordanes, a writer of Gothic race, was the contemporary of Cassiodorus, and a resolute supporter of Roman Imperial power.

greed, and already Amalasuntha had been forced to compel her cousin to surrender the spoils of others; an act which he never forgave. Theodatus now came to Ravenna, and took the crown which he was to wear with such disgrace.[1] Scarcely did he find himself its possessor when he executed his vengeance on the princess to whom he owed it. Backed by her enemies, he banished her to an island in the lake of Bolsena, and here forced her to write a letter to her friend, the Emperor Justinian, in which she declared herself satisfied with her position, while Theodatus himself sent two Roman Senators, Liberius and Opilio, to Byzantium to appease the Emperor. Before these messengers returned, however, the daughter of Theodoric was already dead. Relations of the three Gothic chiefs who had been executed by her orders, thirsting for revenge, not without the knowledge of Theodatus, forced their way one day into her prison and strangled her. The greater number of the Goths acquiesced in the not wholly undeserved fate of the unfortunate woman, who had stooped to conceive the thought of betraying her own nation and the kingdom of her noble father.[2] The murder took place in 535, at the time when Belisarius, having overthrown the kingdom of the Vandals in Africa, was free to turn his genius to the conquest of Italy. The Byzantine

Murder of Amalasuntha, 535.

[1] See the letters of Amalasuntha and Theodatus which announce the latter's accession to the throne. *Var.*, x. 1–2. Horst Kohl, *Zehn Jahre ostgothischer Geschichte, vom Tode Theodorich's bis zur Erhebung des Vitigis,* Leipzig, 1877.

[2] Procopius gives an account of all these occurrences in the beginning of his history of the Gothic war.

Empire had developed increased strength, and Justinian had formed the ambitious resolution of once more uniting East and West; of annihilating the German intruders, destroying the dominion of Vandals and Goths, and subjecting the western province to the authority of a Greek governor. Fortune had favoured the accomplishment of this design in providing him with a great general; and the ease with which Belisarius triumphed over the African Vandals seemed to promise a like success with the Goths in Italy, where the Latin nation and the Catholic Church awaited the Greeks as their deliverers from the yoke of the barbarian.

On receiving the intelligence of Amalasuntha's murder, Justinian feigned indignation, but in silence congratulated himself on the favourable combination of events which had prepared a way for him in Italy. While his ambassador Peter treated with Theodatus for the surrender of the once Vandal Lilybaeum in Sicily, and some other concessions, the Emperor made over the command in Dalmatia to the General Mandus, with orders to attack the Goths, at the same time giving the fleet to Belisarius for the conquest of Sicily. The island fell into the power of the Greeks at the end of 535, in which year, memorable in Roman history, Belisarius alone held the Consulship. From this time onward, until the complete extinction of the Consulship of private persons in 541, no Western Consul was registered in the Fasti. Decius Theodorus Paulinus the Younger, son of Venantius, of the family of the Decii, enjoyed the distinction of closing the long line of Romans

Extinction of the Western Consulship.

who filled the illustrious office. From the time of Constantine onwards it had been the custom to appoint each year one Consul for old, the other for new, Rome. So long as the Gothic Kings ruled Italy they themselves appointed the Consul of the West, the Emperor apparently ratifying the appointment. After 534, however, only one Consul was appointed in the East until 541, when, after the Consulship of Flavius Basilius the Younger, the Emperor Justinian allowed the office to become extinct; because, as Procopius informs us, he would no longer agree to the customary distributions of money. On the inauguration of a Consul more than 2000 pounds of gold had usually been expended on the poor and on entertainments, of which sum the greater part was paid by the Emperor himself out of the treasury. Thus expired this celebrated institution, which, through a long course of centuries, had served to give its name to the government and the measure to time. Only once more, in 566, was the title of Consul again resumed by the Emperor Justin, after which the accession of an Emperor and the beginning of the Consulship were made to coincide.[1]

Complete extinction of the consulship, 541.

[1] Murator., *ad Ann.* 534, 541, 566; Baronius and Pagi, *ad Ann.* 541; and the *Dissertatio Hypatica* of the last, Lugd., 1682, p. 301; Procop., *Hist. Arcan.*, c. 26; Onuph. Panvin., *Commentar., in libr. iii. fastor.*, p. 310. From the year 541 until 566, five and twenty years are designated as *post consul. Basilii.* With regard to chronology, from the year 584 onwards the Roman Church used the Indictions; the system of reckoning from the Incarnatio Domini not coming into use until 968. Jaffé's Introduction to the *Regesta Pontif.*

3. NEGOTIATIONS OF THEODATUS WITH BYZANTIUM— LETTER OF THE SENATE TO JUSTINIAN—EXCITEMENT IN ROME—THE ROMANS REFUSE TO RECEIVE GOTHIC TROOPS—POPE AGAPITUS UNDERTAKES AN EMBASSY TO BYZANTIUM—HIS DEATH—NEGOTIATIONS FOR PEACE BROKEN OFF.

Negotiations between Theodatus and the Emperor.

Scarcely had Theodatus received the news of the fall of Sicily than, his courage completely forsaking him, he agreed to the conditions offered by Peter in the name of the Emperor; namely, to surrender Sicily, to pay a yearly tribute of 300 pounds of gold, and, as often as was required, to furnish an auxiliary force of 3000 Gothic troops. Neither Senators nor patricians were henceforth to be appointed by the King of Italy without permission of the Emperor, and both life and property of priest and senator were to be held sacred from royal jurisdiction. At the games at the Circus the acclamations of the people were to be first for Justinian, then for the King, and, should a monument anywhere be erected to the latter, it was ordained that a statue to Justinian should be placed on the right beside it. The Byzantine, having concluded the treaty, hurried away, but on reaching Albanum was overtaken by messengers from Theodatus and brought back to the King. "If the Emperor refused the peace," Theodatus asked with anxiety, "what would then follow?"[1] "Excellent sir," replied the

Weakness and indecision of Theodatus.

[1] Procop., *De bell. Got.,* i. 6: ἐν 'Αλβανοῖς. Since Albanum alone can be meant here, it follows that Theodatus must have been in Rome at the time, and not, as Muratori holds, in Ravenna. Of the ancient Alba Longa only some scanty ruins remained in the days of Pliny.

messenger, "then you would have to make war;" and he represented that, though it would scarcely beseem a student of Plato to shed the blood of his people, it well befitted the Emperor to make good his rights over Italy. Theodatus consented to yield to a much more humiliating treaty, pledging himself to renounce the kingdom of the Goths and the Romans to Justinian for a yearly pension of only 1200 pounds of gold. Fear depriving him of judgment, he demanded from Peter the sworn assurance that he would only lay the second contract before the Emperor in case he rejected the first.

The Senate intercedes with the Emperor.

Peter was accompanied to Constantinople by the Presbyter Rusticus in the capacity of envoy, and the Senate also roused itself to despatch a letter to the Emperor, praying for peace. The letter, composed by Cassiodorus himself, is in the highest degree valuable as one of the Senate's last assertions of life. The assembled Fathers cause Eternal Rome to appear before the Emperor in person and say,—"If our entreaties do not suffice, give ear to our native city, which expresses itself in these imploring words. If I were ever dear to thee, then oh! most pious of princes, love my defenders.

When the town of Albano arose on the site of the Villa of Pompey and of the Emperors, the Albanum Caesaris, is uncertain. In the *Lib. Pont.* (life of Sylvester, n. 46) it is said, however, of Constantine: *fecit—basilicam in civitatem Albanense sancti Johannas Baptistae.* The architect Franconi has discovered this church, and written a treatise upon it: *La catacomba e la basilica constantiniana in Albano,* Rome, 1877. According to De Rossi (*Bull.,* 1869, p. 76, f., 1873, p. 102, f.) the town of Albano took its rise in the camp of the second legion (Parthica), stationed by Septimius Severus in the Imperial villa. Concerning the earliest bishops of Albano, see Ughelli, *It. Sacra,* i. 248.

They who rule me must live in unison with thee that they may not be guilty of any offense against me which is contrary to thy wishes. Thou, who hast always contributed to my happiness, canst not be the cause of my cruel fall. See, under the protection of thy peace, I have doubled the number of my children; I shine in the splendour of my citizens. If thou shouldst permit such a misfortune to overtake me, how wilt thou deserve the name of pious? What further canst thou do to me, since my Catholic religion, which is also thine, is so flourishing? My Senate continues to increase in honours and possessions, thou shouldst not therefore destroy through discord that which it is thy duty to protect, even by arms. I have had many kings, but none who were so advanced in knowledge; many sages, but none who have been more learned and pious.[1] I love the Amal, whom I have nourished at my breast; he is brave, civilised by intercourse with me, endeared to the Romans by his wisdom, and honourable in the bravery of the barbarian. Unite thy wishes, thy judgment with his, that, through the increase of my fortune, thy own glory may increase. No—do not come to seek me so as not to find me. And since I nevertheless belong to thee in love, do not allow anyone to tear my limbs asunder. If Libya deserved to regain her freedom, it were cruel that I should lose what I have openly possessed. Illustrious Conqueror! control the impulses of thy anger! the universal voice of entreaty is more powerful than the indignation aroused

[1] *Habui multos Reges, sed neminem hujusmodi litteratum,* a curious tribute to a barbarian from the lips of Rome! *Variar.,* xi. 13.

in thy heart by the ingratitude of others. Thus speaks and entreats Rome through the mouth of her senators. And if this do not suffice, then may thy spirit give heed to the holy supplications of the blessed apostles Peter and Paul. For what could thy princely mind refuse to the merits of those who so often, as protectors of Rome, have shielded her against the enemy?"

From some passages in this letter (written under compulsion of Theodatus) it would seem that the Senate, which upon the death of Athalaric had taken the oath prescribed by the Constitution, had suffered the indignity of threats from the King. The statement of a contemporary author that Theodatus had threatened to kill the Roman senators, together with their wives and children, unless they would use their influence to restrain the Emperor from the conquest of Italy, is not without foundation.[1] The letters of Cassiodorus clearly prove that, on the accession of Theodatus, Senate and people were stirred to the highest pitch of excitement. As we read these documents we see the impassable chasm which separated Romans from Goths. The secret negotiations of Justinian with the Romans are inaccessible to us, but Rome seems to have been seized with a feverish dread of some coming catastrophe. It was believed that the King would destroy the Senate, since he had now summoned it to appear before him in Ravenna.[2]

[1] Liberatus Diaconus of Carthage in the *Breviar.*, c. 21.

[2] I take this from *Var.*, x. 13: *quod praesentiam vestram expetivimus, non vexationis injuriam—tractavimus. Certe munus est, videre principem* &c.

People ran together in the streets telling each other that Theodatus would destroy the city, or have the citizens murdered, and that already a Gothic army was marching upon Rome. Theodatus had certainly ordered a garrison of Gothic troops to be stationed in the city, to overpower it in case of insurrection, and to defend it against a sudden attack of the Greeks by sea. The Rescripts of Theodatus to the Senate and people show, however, that the Romans raised a strong protest through their representative bishops, and we may therefore infer that the city had previously received from Theodoric a ratification of the constitutional privilege exempting it from subjection to any garrison. This ancient right the city obstinately guarded even to late mediaeval times, when Emperors of German race lay encamped with their armies on the field of Nero. As the people now rose in uproar, and refused entrance to the Gothic garrison, Theodatus exerted himself to tranquillise the city, and by letters bade the Romans "disperse the shades of fear, and put down the foolish insurrection." "To your enemies, not to your defenders," he said, "must you show resistance; you must invite the auxiliaries in, not exclude them. Are the faces of the Goths strange that you shrink from them?[1] Wherefore do you fear those who, until now, have been called kinsfolk? who have left their families to hasten to you, only concerned for your safety. And what shall become of the good name of the ruler, if

[1] Since the passage refers to the Goths, I thus translate *gentis. Numquid vos nova gentis facies ulla deterruit? Cur expavistis, quos parentes hactenus nominastis? Var.,* x. 14.

we (far be it from us) should permit your ruin? Do not imagine that which we certainly do not intend."

At the same time Theodatus addressed a conciliatory letter to the Senate. He had already, to some degree, tranquillised that august body by requiring only a few Senators to come to Ravenna, and explaining that these were to serve rather as counsellors than as hostages.[1] He further added in his letter that the Goths had no other intention than to defend Rome, a city which was without equal in the world. This defense should inflict, he promised, no additional burden on the citizens. And lastly, he agreed that the garrison should take up its quarters outside the gates.[2]

These dissensions between the Goths and the Romans occurred while the King was negotiating with Justinian and when Belisarius was already on his way from Sicily. The occupation of the city by the Gothic troops must therefore have taken place at a later date, and, as we shall see, under the command of Vitiges.

Agapitus I. 535–536.

The Pope was also forced to go as ambassador to Byzantium to sue for peace.[3] This was Agapitus I., a Roman, who, having by Theodatus' desire been

[1] *Var.*, x. 1 3: *Sed ne ipsa remedia in aliqua parte viderentur austera, cum res poposcerit aliquos ad nos praecipimus evocari: ut nec Roma suis civibus enudetur, et nostra consilia viris prudentibus adjuventur.*

[2] This memorable passage, *Var.*, x. 18: *quos tamen locis aptis praecipimus immorari: ut foris sit armata defensio, intus vobis tranquilla civilitas; and further: defensio vos obsidet, ne manus inimica circumdet.*

[3] *Lib Pont.*, "Vita Agapiti"; *Var.*, xii. 20, also gives evidence of this embassy. Only the chronology affords ground for perplexity.

elected as successor to John, had ascended the apostolic chair June 535. Reluctantly he submitted to the command, and declared himself without the means necessary for the expenses of the journey. He therefore pledged the valuable vessels of S. Peter's to the officials of the royal treasury.[1] Arrived in Constantinople, he began, as the *Liber Pontificalis* naïvely tells us, to dispute with Justinian over religious questions, and, later, appears to have executed his commission as an enemy to the Goths. Death, which overtook him in Byzantium, April 22, 535, alone preserved him from the fate of John I.

Justinian meanwhile received the envoys, Peter and Rusticus, and after having rejected the articles of the first treaty, accepted the second, which deprived the unworthy Goth of Italy and the crown. The Emperor sent Peter and Athanasius with the ratification of the treaty to Theodatus;[2] but, on appearing before the King in Ravenna, they found themselves, to their surprise, received with scorn. The news of some slight advantage to his arms in Dalmatia had suddenly changed the temper of this characterless prince; he threw the envoys into prison and ventured on war.

[1] *Var.,* xii. 20. The *Arcarii* Thomas and Peter were instructed by Cassiodorus to restore the forfeited property to S. Peter, and this occasion is taken to praise the generosity of the King. The Arian monarch never thought of providing his envoy, the Pope, with money for his journey. The excited letters written by Theodatus and his wife Gudelinde to Justinian and Theodora repay the trouble of reading.

[2] Procopius gives Theodatus's letter as well as Justinian's.

4. BELISARIUS COMES TO ITALY—FALL OF NAPLES— THE GOTHS ELECT VITIGES KING—END OF THEODATUS—THE GOTHS WITHDRAW TO RAVENNA— BELISARIUS ENTERS ROME, DEC. 9, 536.

Belisarius begins operations.

Belisarius arrived in Italy in the summer of 536. The treachery of Ebrimut, son-in-law of Theodatus, had opened all unhoped-for means of entrance into the powerful Rhegium, and the conqueror of the Vandals received with joy messengers from the people and towns of Southern Italy, who came to wish success to his undertaking, and to aid it with supplies.[1] His army advanced along the coast, the fleet accompanying its progress northwards. Belisarius suddenly found his march interrupted by the heroic resistance of Naples. The ancient and favourite city of Virgil was at the time small in circumference but strongly defended, as was also the neighbouring Cumae. The presence in her midst of many Greek and Jewish inhabitants had kindled in Naples a keen spirit for trading enterprises.[2] The Jews, though hostile to the Emperor Justinian, who had persecuted the companions of their faith, were friendly to the tolerant Goth, and defended the walls no less bravely than did

[1] The rapid success of Belisarius in Italy is explained by the insignificance of the Gothic population in the south and west, the barbarians not having settled in any numbers further south than Samnium and Picenum. This is shown by Dahn, *iii. Abtheilung*.

[2] Πόλιν τε μικὰν οἰκοῦμεν, said the Neapolitan Stephen to Belisarius. Procopius, although minimising the horrors which succeeded the fall of Naples, has left us an interesting account of its siege and capture.

the Gothic garrison. On the twentieth day of the siege, however, Belisarius succeeded in entering the town through an aqueduct, when he punished it by a sack and a cruel massacre of the inhabitants. Leaving garrisons both in Naples and in the fortress of Cumae, which latter place he intended to serve as a basis of operations during his campaign in Southern Italy, he proceeded through Campania to Latium to wrest Rome itself from the Goths.

Here, or in the immediate neighbourhood, Theodatus was stationed. Gothic troops were not quartered in the city, but in its neighbourhood, apparently in the harbour of the Tiber, at both the bridges of the Anio, and on the Appian Way.[1] These forces were but few in number, the greater part of the troops being absent in Gaul, engaged in a war with the Franks; others were in Venetia. Forced to recognise the incapacity of their King, and to foresee that, sooner or later, he would propose a humiliating peace with Belisarius, they revolted, left their camp, and withdrew along the Appian Way. This world-renowned "Queen of long roads" had already exisited for more than nine hundred years, and promised to bid defiance to Time, the constant flow of traffic, which ceased not day nor night, having as yet been powerless to shake the stability of the basalt pavement.[2] Its splendour called forth the admira-

[1] Γότθοις δὲ ὅσοις ἀμφί τε Ῥώμην καὶ τὰ ἐκείνη χωρία. Procopius, i, 11.

[2] *qua limite noto*
Appia longarum teritur regina viarum.
—Statius, *Silv.,* ii. 2, v. 11.

tion of the historian Procopius, when in 536, he traversed and described it.[1] Issuing from the Porta Capena, the Via Appia followed a long straight line over the Alban hills between the Volscian mountains and the sea, across the Pontine and Decemnovian marshes, until, beyond Terracina, having reached the fertile province of Campania, it came to an end in Capua.[2] On each side of the way stood countless ancient tombs already in ruin, gloomy guides to the wayfarer, bearing on their marble inscriptions the names of those Romans who had been celebrated in the history of past ages.[3]

Along this road the Goths now advanced as far as Regeta, a spot lying in the Pontine marshes between the Forum Appii and Terracina, where, finding good pasturage for their horses, they established their camp. The district was watered by the Decemnovius—such, at least, is the name which Procopius gives to the river, and by which it was known for nineteen miles of its course, until at Terracina it emptied itself into the sea. It was the same stream

[1] *De bello Goth.,* i. 14.

[2] Procopius clearly tells us that the Via Appia reached to Capua; the road, nevertheless, extended to Brindisi. See Nibby's exhaustive treatise, *Delle vie degli antichi,* which embodies the greater part of the 4th vol. of Nardini's work.

[3] The *Itinerar. Antonini* gives the following stations on the Via Appia: *Ariciam. M.P. XVI., Tres Tabernas M.P. XVII., Appi Forum M.P. XVIII., Terracinam M.P. XVIII., Fundos M.P. XVI., Formiam M.P. XIII., Minturnas M.P. IX., Capuam M.P. XXVI.* In Theodoric's time the system of posts instituted by the Emperors on the main roads still survived, as we see by *Variar.,* i. 29 and v. 5. Cruelty to horses, a vice which still disgraces modern Italy, was forbidden by law.

on which, running on the right of the Via Appia, travellers in Imperial times were accustomed to embark at Forum Appii, and to proceed for some distance in boats; the road at this point, on account of the marshiness of the soil, having become impassable for carriages, until the Decemnovian swamp was drained under Theodoric.[1] Here the Gothic cavalry pronounced the deposition of Theodatus. In the wild solitude of the Pontine marshes, within sight of the Cape of Circe, which rises like an island from the sea, these warriors, once more wanderers without a home, raised Vitiges on the shield, and saluted him in the ancient fashion of their race as King of the Goths and Romans. In Vitiges they honoured a man of the sword, who had already, under Theodoric, won distinction in the war against the Gepidae, and one who had never exchanged the sword for the stylus of the pedant.

The Goths proclaim Vitiges King.

The new King hastened back to Rome with his forces, Theodatus flying before him to Ravenna by the Flaminian Way. A Goth named Optaris, the personal enemy of Theodatus, overtaking him in his flight, threw him down and strangled him.[2]

Death of Theodatus.

Immediately on his return to Rome, Vitiges issued a proclamation to the whole Gothic people, announcing his elevation, and saying that not by the shouts of courtiers but by the braying of trumpets he had

[1] Concerning Regeta and the Canal, see chapter xii. of Westphal's *Die römische Campagna.* Speaking of Terracina, Procopius mentions the Cape of Circe and its insular form.

[2] Ἐς ἔδαφύς τε ὕπτιον ἀνακλίνας ὥσπερ ἱερεῖόν τι ἔθυσεν. Procopius, ii. 11.

been greeted as King.[1] His election had been the revolutionary act of the army, the right of succession of the Amal had thereby been set aside, and the last Kings of the Goths were again, as in the days of old in Pannonia, freely elected military leaders; Roman civilisation, to which the Amals had done homage, they for ever renounced. Vitiges explained to the Gothic warriors, whom he assembled in the city, that the existing state of things obliged him to leave Rome and hasten forthwith to Ravenna. There he would first end the war with the Franks, gather the dispersed troops, and speedily return to offer war to the Greek Belisarius. Meanwhile, they must not be dismayed by the prospect of the city falling into the hands of the Byzantines, since, with the help of a Gothic garrison, the Romans would either offer a brave resistance; or, on the other hand, did they revolt, from secret they would be changed into open enemies. Vitiges also assembled the Senate and the higher clergy. Reminding them of all the privileges which Rome had enjoyed under Theodoric, he enjoined them to remain faithful to the Gothic rule, and received their oath of allegiance. Leaving 4000 Goths under Leuderis, and taking several Senators with him as hostages, he withdrew to Ravenna.

Vitiges withdraws to Ravenna.

Here, in the chambers of the royal palace, sunk in the deepest grief for the overthrow of her house, lived Matasuntha, the daughter of Amalasuntha and sister of Athalric. Vitiges forced the princess to marry him, hoping that, once possessed of the hand of

[1] *Universis Gothis Vitiges Rex. Var.,* x. 31.

the heiress to the rights of the Amal, he might win the recognition of the entire Gothic nation, and find Justinian disposed to listen to the overtures of peace which he made forthwith.[1] Neither did he lose time in adjusting the relations in which he stood towards the King of the Franks. In his difficulties he found himself, however, reduced to surrender the provinces of Southern Gaul, but, obtaining in return promises of peace and help, he was enabled to recall the Gothic troops from Provence for his more immediate needs.

Whilst Vitiges prepared for war in Ravenna, Belisarius advanced along the Latin Way to Rome,[2] and scarcely had the Romans knowledge of his march when they resolved to send messengers of peace to meet him, and to convey to him the keys of the city. The family of the Anicii, so cruelly wronged by Theodoric, were especially eager in urging the admission of the Greek general. The Pope was also in favour of the measure, foreseeing the restoration of the orthodox faith through the Greeks. The present occupant of the papal chair, Silverius, son of Hormisdas, a former Pope, on the death of Agapitus, had been thrust upon the Romans by

Silverius Pope, 536–537.

[1] *Var.,* lib. x. 32, 33, 34. Vitiges had coins struck in her honour. These coins bear on the obverse the bust of Justinian, on the reverse the monogram of Matasuntha.

[2] The Via Latina separated from the Appia outside the Porta Capena, and in its southward course passed Anagni, Ferentino, Frosinone, and crossing the Liris, after being joined by the Via Labicana and Praenestina, continued to Capua. The ancient road has been destroyed for a distance of nine miles outside the gate; thence onwards it reappears here and there.

Theodatus.[1] Belisarius joyfully received the envoy Fidelius and the members of the Senate and clergy, and continued his march rapidly through the valley of the Trerus or Sacco. Leuderis, perceiving the impossibility of defending a great and hostile city with 4000 men, allowed his garrison, without inflicting injuries on the Romans, to retire to Ravenna; he himself, from a sense of honour, remaining behind. The Goths withdrew through the Flaminian Gate, while the Greeks, hailed by the inhabitants with joy as deliverers, entered by the Asinarian.[2] Among the Romans some rejoiced at the thought of the suppression of the Arian heresy by Byzantine interventon; others flattered themselves with the restoration of the Empire; all wished for a change of government. None could foresee the frightful events in the immediate future, nor perceive that they had hastened to exchange a moderate degree of freedom and a mild rule under the Gothic sceptre for a miserable bondage under the yoke of Byzantium.

Belisarius enters Rome Dec. 9, 536.

Sixty years had passed since the Roman Empire had fallen under the dominion of the Germans, when Belisarius made his entry into the city, Dec. 9, 536.[3]

[1] *Hic levatus est a tyranno Theodato sine deliberatione decreti. Lib. Pont.*

[2] The beautiful remains of the Porta Asinaria still exist close to the gate of S. Giovanni. A bye-way to the right led thence to the Via Latina.

[3] Marcell. Comes tells us that the city was taken by the barbarians during the Consulship of Basiliscus and Armatus (476); it was, according to him, retaken 536; and according to Evagrius on Dec. 9. Cardinal Noris, *Dissert. Histor. de Synod. Quinta,* p. 54 (Patavii, 1673).

CHAPTER IV.

1. Belisarius prepares for the Defence of Rome—Vitiges advances with the Gothic Army against the City—First Assault—Preparations for the Siege—Gothic Intrenchments—Counter Fortifications of Belisarius—Vitiges destroys the Aqueducts—Floating Mills on the Tiber—Despair of the Romans—The Goths demand a Surrender—Preparations for Storming the City.

Although Belisarius sent the keys of Rome and the prisoner Leuderis to Constantinople in token of victory, he nevertheless fully recognised the difficulties of his position in the huge city, the immediate siege of which he foresaw. In spite of Theodoric's restorations, Aurelian's walls in many places proved damaged and ruinous. Belisarius repaired them, strengthening them with trenches, and provided the corners with projecting towers, the skilful building of which awoke the astonishment of the Romans, while the prospect of the siege for which he was making such careful preparations aroused their terror. For he filled the public granaries with grain from Sicily and corn which he had extorted from the colonists on the Campagna. He was not deceived in his expectations.

During the winter Vitiges had collected the entire Gothic army in Ravenna and provided it with weapons and horses; he now set forth for Rome, compelled to haste by the news of the fall of almost all the towns of Tuscany and Samnium. Information which reached him on the way, of the dislike with which the Greeks were already regarded in the city, still further inflamed his desire for war. Without delaying to conquer Perugia, Spoleto or Narni, he marched hastily through the Sabine territory and southwards by the Via Casperia and Salara. It was now the beginning of March 537. Innumerable hosts (estimated by Procopius, with perhaps some exaggeration, at 150,000 men), the strength of the whole Gothic nation, infantry and cavalry,—the very horses clad in mail,—pressed along the Salarian Way against Rome. The Tiber here flows in a gentle bend round some hills of volcanic tufa, receiving the stream of the Anio on its left bank.

Vitiges besieges Rome, 537.

The Goths, finding themselves within sight of Rome, rushed forward to the Anio, which still separated them from the rebellious city. The waters of this lovely stream, swollen by the rains of spring, were difficult to ford, and the bridge was moreover protected by a strong tower.[1] But in the darkness

[1] Gibbon, allowing himself to be misled by Procopius, describes the passage of the Goths as taking place at the Milvian Bridge. This is not the only passage (i. c. 17) where the Greek writer confuses the Tiber with the Anio. Since Vitiges, however, had passed Narni by and come through the Sabina, it is evident that he must have approached the left bank of the Tiber and advanced over the Salarian Bridge.

the garrison had disappeared, and the Goths, bursting open the gates, crossed the bridge. Before reaching the Porta Salaria, however, they encountered the troops of Belisarius, the general having come with a thousand horse to watch the enemy, or to hinder their passage. Procopius has borrowed the colours of the *Iliad* to describe this first furious struggle before the walls of Rome. He shows us Belisarius mounted on a horse with a white forehead; how, foremost in the fight, he mows down one after another of the foe, while a hailstorm of lances and arrows showers upon him, all the shots of the Goths being directed towards him and his horse, conspicuous from afar.[1] But his own sword protected him, the shields of his followers covered him, while the bodies of the fallen Goths as well as Greeks formed a high wall round the general.

After a fierce struggle the Greeks, overpowered by superior numbers, fled backwards up the hill, separated outside the Pincian Gate by a deep gorge from Monte Pincio.[2] The Gothic cavalry, in attempting to enter, were arrested by the dauntless heroism of Valentinus, equerry to Photius, a son of Belisarius's wife, until the fugitives had retired under the walls of the city. The victorious Goths pursued their opponents to the gate. But the watchmen on the walls, fearing that the enemy might gain an

[1] Procop., *De bell. Goth,* i. 18. The horse, he tells us, was named Phalion by the Greeks; by the Goths, however, Balan.

[2] So I understand: ἔς τινα γεώλοφον. It is the hilly ground on which stand the present Villa Borghese and Villa Poniatowski, stretching down to the Acqua Acetosa.

entrance at the same time with the Greeks, and in the belief that their general had already fallen, kept the gates closed, while the despairing fugitives remained crowded together between the trenches and the walls. Here Belisarius encouraged his followers to a last desperate effort. The Goths were forced to retreat to their camp by the river, and the Byzantine general and his exhausted troops succeeded in making good their retreat within the city. The Romans had watched with surprise a fight worthy of their great forefathers; they themselves looking idly on. Thousands lay stretched below the walls adjoining the Porta Pinciana. Amongst the combatants even the enemy had honoured with admiration the bravery of a Goth,—the stalwart Visand, a standard-bearer,—who,[1] foremost in the struggle round the person of Belisarius, had fallen pierced with thirteen wounds. Found, however, the third day after, still breathing, by his countrymen, he was carried into the Gothic camp, and saluted by his countrymen with the title of hero.

Vitiges surrounds the city.

Vitiges, deceived in the hope of taking the city by a first assault, decided on a regular siege. This siege, which is one of the most memorable in history, resembles in its circumstances an heroic epic. The native force of the noblest German race was here pitted against the Roman giants, the walls of Aurelian, and against the genius of the Greek who defended them. The skill of the Goths, accustomed to fight in the open field, was of little avail in laying siege to

[1] Βανδαλάριος. In the Middle Ages the Romans still used the word Banderario.

a city, and Vitiges, overlooking this fact, staked his entire kingdom against the walls of Rome, with the result that a brave warlike race here found their overthrow. The great circumference of the walls did not permit of their being surrounded; Vitiges confined himself to enclosing the weaker part, namely, from the Flaminian to the Praenestine Gate. This being the case, the statement of Procopius that the Gothic army numbered 150,000 fighting men is rendered very doubtful. Within the tract thus enclosed the historian speaks of five principal gates, but apparently omits two from his reckoning. For, while within this territory we find the Flaminia, Pinciana, Salaria, Nomentana, Tiburtina, Clausa, and Praenestina, the Clausa, and, as it appears, the Pinciana also, remained unnoticed.[1] The Goths pitched six entrenched camps before these gates, all on the left side the river; a seventh they erected on the right bank of the Tiber on the Neronian Field, or the plain which stretches under Monte Mario from the Vatican Hill as far as the Milvian Bridge. They thus not only protected the bridge itself, but at the same time threatened the Bridge of Hadrian and its entrance to the city through the inner gate of Aurelian. This gate, already named S. Peter's, stood outside the bridge of Hadrian, and outside the wall, which, from the

[1] The three first gates are undoubted; the Nomentana was destroyed by Pius IV., who built the Porta Pia in its stead. The position of the Tiburtina and Praenestina in relation to the present Porta S. Lorenzo and Porta Maggiore is disputed, topographers holding very diverse views upon the subject.

Porta Flaminia on the inner side of the river, surrounded the field of Mars. Beyond this the Goths directed their attention to the Trasteverine Gate, by which we understand the gate of S. Pancrazio on the Janiculum.[1]

Within the city Belisarius was ceaselessly occupied in placing the gates in a proper state of defence. He barricaded the Porta Flaminia, which lay close to one of the enemy's camps, and entrusted its guardianship to the faithful Constantine; the gate of Praeneste he gave to the charge of Bessas, and established his own quarters between the Pincian and Salarian, both of which entrances lay in the weakest part of the walls, and which were moreover destined to serve as postern gates. Each of the other gates he placed under the custody of a captain, commanding these officers never, under any circumstances, to leave their posts. The Goths, who from time to time pressed forward against the gates, always found the watchmen on their guard, and silent in answer to their shouts that the Romans had been traitors and blockheads in choosing the yoke of the Byzantines in preference to that of the Goths, and adding, not without truth, that Italy had

[1]Procop., *De bello Goth.,* i. c. 19, distinguishes τήν τε Αὐρηλίαν (ἣ νῦν Πέτρου, &c.) καὶ τὴν ὑπὲρ τὸν ποταμὸν Τίβεριν, from which it is apparent that the Aurelia stood on this side. He had already (c. 18) spoken of the Trasteverine Gate, ἣ ὑπὲρ ποταμὸν Τίβεριν Παγκρατίου ἀνδρὸς ἁγίου ἐπώνυμος οὖσα. Even before the time of Procopius popular usage had discarded the ancient name of the gate in favour of that of the new basilica which had arisen beside it. The *Cosmographia* of the so-called Aethicus, which belongs to the last days of the Empire, already speaks of *divi Apostoli Petri portam,* and says, *intra Ostiensem portam, quae est divi Pauli apostoli* (pp. 40, 41).

never gained aught from Byzantium but tragedians buffoons, and sea pirates.[1]

Destroys the aqueducts.

The besiegers, in surrounding the city, cut off all its water supplies, and Belisarius, mindful of Naples, which he and his army had been enabled to enter by means of an aqueduct, had the openings of these Roman aqueducts within the city carefully built up. Thus these colossal structures, the wonder of so many generations, became suddenly doomed to partial destruction, and, for the first time in a long course of centuries, ceased to supply the city. The last remaining baths were consequently rendered useless and fell to ruin, while the aqueducts themselves provided the Romans with building material for several centuries to come.[2]

The inaction of their mills was a loss severely felt by the populace. These mills lay, and still lie, in the Trastevere, on the slope of the Janiculum, opposite the bridge now called Ponte Sisto, where the aqueduct of Trajan descended and drove them with the force of a river.[3] The inaction of these mills gave

[1] Τραγῳδοὺς καὶ μίμους καὶ ναύτας λωποδύτας, an admirable reproof in the mouth of the simple Gothic captain Vacis. See Procop., i. c. 18.

[2] The aqueducts were only cut by the Goths, and it is, therefore, utterly ridiculous to ascribe their wilful destruction to this people. The ancient conduits were gradually destroyed under the hands of the proprietors of the *Fondi suburbani,* in the Middle Ages, as also in more recent times. The architects of Sixtus V. finally ruthlessly sacrificed the remains of the aqueducts to the building of the Acqua Felice. See R. Lanciani, *Commentarii di Frontino,* 1880, p. 361.

[3] Prudentius, *contra Symmach.,* ii. v. 950, asked: *aut quae Janiculae mola muta quiescit?* The time was now come: the mills stood still. ἔνθα δὴ οἱ τῆς πόλεως μύλωνες ἐκ παλαιοῦ πάντες πεποίηνται, says Procop., *De bell. Goth.,* i. 19.

rise to a discovery which remains to the Romans of the present day, a legacy, perhaps, from Belisarius. The general had two boats fastened with ropes to the bridge, and mills placed over the boats, the wheels of these mills being thus driven by the river itself.[1] The Goths attempted to destroy these erections, sending trunks of trees down the stream, but a chain soon intercepted all such obstacles.

Meanwhile the besiegers continued to lay waste the Campagna, and to cut off the supplies from the city. The Romans saw with increasing anxiety the beginning of distress; the mob openly cried out against the insufficient forces, and reproached Belisarius as foolhardy, in wishing to defend a badly protected town with 5000 men against so numerous an enemy. The Senate also murmured secretly. Informed by deserters of the popular discontent, Vitiges sought to turn it to advantage. He sent a messenger to Rome, and this messenger, in the presence of Senators and generals, reproached Belisarius for bringing the Romans, who, under Theodoric, had enjoyed freedom and amusement, to ruin through the horrors of a hopeless defence. The Goth demanded the surrender of the city, and offered to grant in

[1] The writer counted five floating mills on the Tiber between the Ponte Sisto and the Cestian Island Bridge. Fabretti, *De aquis et aquaed. diss.*, iii. p. 170, has subjected Belisarius and his mills to a searching criticism, and establishes the grounds of their destructiveness. The writer can testify that in the spring of 1856, during an unusually high level of the river, a mill was hurled against the Cestian Bridge, and the breastworks seriously injured. Since the works for the regulation of the Tiber have been in progress all these mills have been removed.

return an unmolested retreat to the Greeks and an amnesty to the Romans. The Gothic speaker further asked the Romans, "in what manner they had been so wronged as to have been driven to betray not only the Goths their lawful rulers but also themselves. He explained that they had never received anything but benefits at Gothic hands, and even now the army of Vitiges stood before their walls to deliver them from slavery." Belisarius dismissed the herald, declaring that he would defend Rome to the last man.

Vitiges now hastened the preparation for a decisive assault. Wooden towers, sufficiently high to overlook the walls, were set on strong wheels; projecting battering rams of iron were hung by chains to be thrust against the walls, each manned by fifty men, and long scaling ladders were constructed to be attached to the battlements. To these preparations (at the rude simplicity of which modern science may smile) Belisarius opposed measures all his own. He set upon the walls skilfully contrived catapults or balistrae, and great stone-slings called "wild asses" (*onagri*), constructed to throw a bolt with such force as to pin a mail-clad man fast to a tree. The gates were themselves defended with so-called "wolves," or drawbridges, fashioned out of heavy beams, and furnished with iron pins which were calculated to fall on the assailants with overwhelming force.

2. GENERAL ASSAULT—ATTACK ON THE PRAENESTINE GATE—THE MURUS RUPTUS—HADRIAN'S TOMB— DESTRUCTION OF HIS STATUES BY THE GREEKS— FAILURE OF THE ASSAULT AT ALL POINTS.

General attack.

On the nineteenth morning of the siege, Vitiges undertook an assault. The Goths wished, in a general attack, to climb the walls, and so to make an end of the war; and from their seven camps they advanced in thick masses in full confidence of victory. The sight of the colossal towers, which, drawn by strong oxen, moved slowly against the walls, struck the Romans with dismay, but only excited the derision of Belisarius. With his own hand he let fly a bolt from the Salarian tower, shot the leader of the attacking column, hurled with a second cast another to the ground, and commanded the men who had care of the artillery to direct the next charge against the oxen. The Goths soon saw the vanity of their hopes, the machines remained standing on the field, but they themselves rushed with fury against the walls of the city.

Struggle round the gate of S. Lorenzo.

While they simultaneously attacked each of the beleaguered gates, the struggle raged more violently in two places, where the Goths hoped to effect an entrance; at the Porta Praenestina and at Hadrian's tomb. The walls were especially weak, where, in the neighbourhood of the Porta S. Lorenzo, at that time called the Praenestine Gate, they were adjoined by an ancient Vivarium for wild beasts; the Vivarium only serving to conceal their weakness without adding to their strength.[1] Vitiges here led the assault in person. Belisarius, informed of the danger, hastened from the Salarian Gate to avert it. The Goths had already forced a way into the Vivarium, but, in a furious sortie, were first thrust together into a narrow corner, and then driven in disordered flight back to their distant encampment, while their machines went up in flames.

At the Salarian Gate the assault was repulsed by a like vigorous sally; the Flaminian was not attacked on account of its position; and the "Murus ruptus," between the Flaminian and the Pincian Gates, was defended by the Apostle Peter in person, the saint striking the Goths with sudden blindness.[2] This curious legend, dating from the time when S. Peter was already declared Protector and Patron of Rome, and when his corpse had taken the place of

Round that of the Salaria.

[1] Nardini, ii. p. 17, places the Vivarium close to the Castrensian Amphitheatre sideways from the Porta Maggiore. Niebuhr (*Röm Stadtbeschr.,* i. 657), on the other hand, holds with Piale that the Praenestina was the gate now known as the Porta San Lorenzo. He cites the authority of Flaminio Vacca, who speaks of a Via Praenestina as leading from the Porta S. Lorenzo, and this writer indeed designates the Porta di S. Lorenzo as the Praenestina. For he says (*Memorie,* Nr. 15) that many Gothic cinerary urns were discovered at the Porta San Lorenzo, and that he had read that the Goths had here suffered a defeat. The opinion of the Romans of Vacca's time, based as it was on tradition, seems worthy of attention. The Anon. of Einsiedeln is the first to speak of the Porta Maggiore as the Praenestina.

[2] 'Επεὶ ἐν χώρῳ κρημνώδει κειμένη, says Procop., i. c. 23, speaking of the Porta Flaminia, and either referring to the narrow space between the hills and the river, or confusing the Flaminian with the Pincian Gate. The Flaminian Gate still retains the site assigned it by Aurelian. C. L. Visconti, "Delle scoperte avvenute per la demoliz. delle torri della P. Flaminia," *Bull della Comm. Archaeol. Communale di Roma,* v. p. 206, f,

the ancient Palladium, is related by Procopius with astonishment. The "Murus ruptus" was a part of the wall which supports the Monte Pincio, a mighty structure of buttresses. Nevertheless, it was even in ancient times cracked in the middle, but though in a tottering condition, had remained erect. From time immemorial, Procopius says, the Romans had called it the "Murus ruptus," and we may add that it is now known as the "Muro Torto." When Belisarius, at the beginning of the siege, wished to repair this dangerous place, the Romans dissuaded him with the assurance that repairs were wholly unnecessary, the Apostle having promised to protect the spot in person; and, on the day of the assault, the "Murus ruptus" was spared by the Goths, a fact which gave Procopius occasion to wonder why the enemy, who so often undertook to scale the walls with force by day, and with artifice by night, entirely overlooked this inviting spot.[1]

On the side of the Trastevere the Goths made a fruitless attempt to win the gate of San Pancrazio or the Janiculum,[2] but were more successful in the

[1] Roman legend relates that the wall bowed in reverence as S. Peter was led by on his way to execution. Procop., i. 23. The historian adds that it has never been restored on account of this belief. The present Muro Torto is undoubtedly the Murus Ruptus of history. Padre Eschinardi (*Dell' agro Romana,* p. 286) justly explains its tottering position as due to an earthquake. Pius IX. well restored the walls below the Pincio, but the Muro Torto has hitherto remained untouched.

[2] Procopius already names the Porta Janicul. Pancratiana, adding the words ὑπὲρ ποταμὸν Τίβεριν. In the ninth century the Anon. of Einsiedeln terms it simply Aurelia from the ancient road of this name. There was a Via Aurelia Vetus, as also Nova, but the relation of one to the other remains obscure.

attack which they made on Hadrian's mausoleum. Procopius has described the latter extraordinary episode of the Gothic siege, and to him, on this occasion, we owe the earliest, though unfortunately an incomplete, description of the renowned mausoleum. Earlier authors in their negligence have scarce made mention of the tomb, and the words of Procopius himself neither clearly describe its aspect nor its condition at the time. "The tomb of the Roman Emperor Hadrian," he says, "lies without the Aurelian Gate, a stone's throw distant from the walls. It is a splendid and highly remarkable work, built of blocks of Parian marble, which are fastened to each other, without being otherwise internally joined. Its four sides are alike, the width of each amounting to a stone's throw; the height, however, exceeds that of the city walls. Above stand admirable statues of men and horses made of the same marble." Here the account of Procopius ends, and we are left to imagine the tomb only as a high square building adorned with marble figures; but whether it diminished in successive stories, or whether these stories (if stories there were) were surrounded by rows of columns, or, lastly, whether the whole were a pointed cone, crowned with a bronze pine-cone, he does not say.[1]

Hadrian's mausoleum.

[1] Bunsen gives the diameter of the tower as 329 palms, the circumference as 1033; while the base must have been 15 palms in height. Next in importance to the account of Procopius ranks the certainly somewhat fantastic description of Petrus Mallius about 1160 (*Hist. Bas. S. Petri,* c. 7, n. 131, in the Bollandists, *Acta SS. Junii,* t. vii. 50). The restorations of Labacco, Piranesi, Hirt and Canina give only pretty pictures. A slight history of the fortress in Fea, *Sulle Rov. di*

The size and strength of the mausoleum and its nearness to the city—the bridge of Hadrian leading directly to it from the city walls—long before the time of Belisarius, had suggested to the Romans the idea of converting it into a bridge-fortress and adding it to the fortificatons of the city. "The ancients," the Greek historian remarks, "made this tomb (which looks like an advanced fortress of the city) a part of the fortifications, to which they joined it by two walls."[1] Among the ancients he cannot have reckoned Theodoric, although the Gothic King must have either restored or already made use of the tomb as a state prison, since, in the tenth century, it was called by the people the prison of Theodoric, a name which it only exchanged for that of the tower of Crescentius.[2] More probably Honorius may have joined it to the walls if this junction had not been already made by Aurelian. To understand clearly their connection with the mausoleum we must realize that on the left bank of the Tiber Aurelian's Wall started from the Flaminian

Roma; Donatus, *Roma Vetus ac Recens,* iv. c. 7; and Visconti, *Città e Famigl. Ant. Sec.,* ii. 220. The last-named may answer for his unfounded statements that the sack of the mausoleum and the destruction of Hadrian's funeral urn were due to Alaric.

[1] This important passage in Procopius (i. 22) runs: τοῦτον δὴ τὸν τάφον οἱ παλαιοὶ ἄνθρωποι (ἐδόκει γὰρ τῇ πόλει ἐπιτείχισμα εἶναι) τειχίσμασι δύο ἐς αὐτὸν ἀπὸ τοῦ περιβόλου διήκουσι μέρος εἶναι τοῦ τείχους πεποίηνται.

[2] Fea, p. 385, assumes without any grounds that Theodoric had annexed the mausoleum to the fortifications. Theodoricus of Niem, *De Schismate,* iii. c. 10, p. 63, tells us that in the time of Otto the Great the fortress bore the name of *carcer Theodorici.* The Annalista Saxo *ad. Ann.* 998 speaks of it as *Domus Theodorici.*

Gate, that it was broken at Hadrian's Bridge by the Aurelian Gate, was then continued not only as far as the Janiculan Bridge, but on to the Island Bridge, and ended at the point where Aurelian's Wall enclosing the Janiculum touched the river on the opposite side. Separated by the Tiber from the tomb, the city wall could not otherwise be united to it but by means of the bridge itself; and two walls built from the tomb to the bridge brought both into connection with the city wall on the left side of the river, and with the Aurelian Gate. Thus was this important entrance to the town protected by a bridge fortress, the garrison of which remained in uninterrupted communication with that of the gate.[1] Since, however, the way to S. Peter's was barred by these walls from the bridge to the tomb, a gate had to be made, and this is the second Porta Aurelia, or Porta Sancti Petri in Hadrianeum, as it was called in the eighth and ninth centuries.[2]

[1] Panvin., *Respub. Rom. C.,* p. 113, erroneously places walls in the Borgo, to which he makes the connecting walls lead. Alveri also assumes (*Roma in ogni stato,* ii. 114) that the Porta Aurelia adjoined the Portico of S. Peter's. Nardini, i. 90, admits the connection, but Procopius is very obscure with regard to all these matters. Becker, &c., i. 166; Nibby, *Mura di Roma,* c. vii.; Jordan., *Topogr.,* i. 1, 377, f., ii. 166, ff.; Georg Gött, *De Porta Aurelia Commentatio,* Munich, 1877.

[2] The Anon. of Einsiedeln always mentions this gate and the Hadrianeum or mausoleum with its fortifications as quite distinct: *porta sancti Petri in Hadrianeo*. He reckons therein six towers, 164 *propugnacula* or breastworks, fourteen great and nineteen small loopholes. Procopius in his haste does not mention the gate, forgets even to speak of the bridge, and scarcely bestows a thought upon the river. Neither does he mention the Triumphal Bridge, this structure having already been removed.

Belisarius had entrusted the guard of the mausoleum to his most valued lieutenant, Constantine, ordering him also to cover the neighbouring walls of the city, which, since the river in itself afforded protection, probably remained undefended save by small outposts on the left of the Aurelian Gate. Meanwhile the Goths attempted to cross the Tiber in boats, and Constantine, leaving the more numerous forces in the Aurelian Gate and at the mausoleum as garrison, was obliged to appear in person on the menaced spot. The Goths advanced against the mausoleum. Were they able to take this fortress, they might hope to make themselves masters of the bridge and gate. They brought no machines, nothing but scaling ladders which they covered with their broad shields. A portico or covered colonnade led to the Vatican basilica from the neighbourhood of the tomb, and in this colonnade the approaching party defended themselves against the projectiles of the Greeks stationed in the mausoleum.[1] They approached through the narrow streets which surrounded the ruined circus of Hadrian so cautiously that the besieged in the fortress were unable to use the catapults against them.[2] Then, dashing forward, they shot a cloud of arrows on the battlements of the tomb, and leaned their

Attack on the Mausoleum.

[1] Procop., i. 22. We shall again have occasion to mention this building in the life of Adrian I. From it, in the Middle Ages, the entire Borgo received the name of Porticus or Portica S. Petri.

[2] This circus in the Prata Neronis is held to be a building of the Emperor Hadrian, and must have been identical with the *theatrum Neronis.* Its ruins are represented with stags and other animals in the plan of the city belonging to the thirteenth century; they lasted until the fifteenth century. De Rossi, *Piante Icnogr.,* p. 85.

scaling ladders against it. Pressing forward on all sides they had nearly surrounded and scaled the mausoleum, when despair suggested to the Greeks to make use of the many statues with which it was decorated as projectiles, and forthwith they hurled these statues down upon the Goths. The broken masterpieces, statues of emperors, gods, and heroes, fell like hail in heavy fragments. The attacking Goths were crushed by the bodies of gods which, perhaps, had once adorned the temples of Athens as works of Polycletus or Praxiteles, or had been chiselled in the workshops of Rome four hundred years before.[1] With this wild scene round the grave of an emperor, a scene which recalls the mythic battles of the giants, ended the struggle by the Aurelian Gate. As Constantine hastened from the walls, where he had prevented the enemy from crossing the river, he found the Goths already in retreat from the tomb, at the foot of which lay stretched corpses and statues, alike broken and blood-bespattered.

The Greeks use the statues as projectiles.

His unsuccessful attack cost Vitiges the flower of his army. Procopius, reckoning from the accounts of the Gothic captains, estimates his losses at 30,000,

[1] The mausoleum of Hadrian was thus for ever robbed of its beauty. When, in the time of Alexander VI and Urban VIII., the building was completely transformed into a fortress, the celebrated Sleeping Faun, broken into various fragments, and the colossal portrait bust of Hadrian were found in the line of the trenches. Tacitus relates that Sabinus, brother of Vespasian, defended himself on the Clivus Capitolinus by a barricade of statues against the followers of Vitellius: *Sabinus—revulsas undique statuas, decora Majorum, in ipso aditu vice muri objecisset* (*Histor.,* iii. 71). This, the first instance of this species of Vandalism, was committed by the ancient Romans themselves.

and the historian adds that the number of wounded was yet greater, the projectiles having penetrated thickly packed masses, and the sorties of the Greeks caused fearful havoc amongst the disordered fugitives. As night came on the city resounded with hymns of victory and songs of praise in honour of Belisarius; the Gothic camp, with wild lamentations for the fallen heroes.

3. Continuation of the Siege—Prophecies regarding the Issue of the War—Pagan Reminiscences—The Temple of Janus—The Tria Fata—Two Latin Songs of the Time—Precautions taken by Belisarius for the Defence of the City.

The failure of the attack changed the whole aspect of affairs, and, while paralysing the Goths, it encouraged the Romans, and secured the victory to Belisarius. The Goths remained in their camp, not venturing to approach the walls from fear of sudden onslaughts. Nor did they dare, as heretofore, to scour the Campagna, harassed as they were night and day by the attacks of the light Numidian cavalry. The Roman Campagna forms the most splendid riding ground in the world. Far stretching plains, over which the rider can gallop with loosened rein, spread on every side, here and there interrupted by a narrow brook, or now and then broken by a hill, over which the horseman may hasten with scarcely checked speed. The Numidian bowmen exercised themselves in these classic wastes as on their familiar plains at the foot of the Atlas. Huns from the Ister and Sarmatians from the Tanais here found their grass-grown steppes again; and few periods have witnessed bolder contests of horsemanship than those waged around Rome during this memorable siege.

Since the Goths had not been able to surround the entire city, and as Vitiges had not shown sufficient discernment to take possession of either Albanum or Portus, the connection of the city with the country remained open on the side of Naples and towards the sea. The Romans ceased to deride the foolhardiness of Belisarius; they placed unbounded confidence in his genius, and executed the insignificant services assigned to them zealously and conscientiously. Prophecies encouraged their hopes; for, in spite of their apostles and martyrs, they had not renounced their belief in Pagan omens, and Procopius has preserved some anecdotes which testify to their superstition. Some shepherd lads had been wrestling on the Campagna, two of them personating Belisarius and Vitiges. The boy Vitiges, having been defeated, was punished by the party of Belisarius by being hanged to the branch of a tree, when a wolf chased away the players, and poor Vitiges, left in his painful position, was soon after found dead. The shepherds explained the tragic issue of the game as an omen of Belisarius's triumph, and left the boys unpunished. The incident took place in the mountains of Samnium, but in Naples a yet clearer sign was discovered. A mosaic representing the great Theodoric had been placed in the Neapolitan Forum; within the lifetime

Survival of Pagan superstitions.

of the Gothic King the head of the figure crumbled away, and soon after Theodoric died; eight years later, the middle portion of the figure, and Athalaric died; shortly afterwards the thighs fell to pieces, and Amalasuntha died; and finally, during the siege of Rome, the feet of the picture fell, an occurrence which the Romans interpreted as a sign that Belisarius would issue victorious from the struggle. A witty Jew had uttered to King Theodatus a similar prophecy; he had seen, shut up hungry in their stalls, three times ten swine, which he took to represent Goths, Greeks, and Romans. The Goths were one and all found dead; of the Greeks scarcely any were missing; half of the Romans were dead, the others living, but without bristles.

Meanwhile patricians had also talked in the city of an ancient oracle in the Sibylline books, which had foretold that in the month Quinctilis, that is, in July, Rome would have nothing more to fear from the Goths.[1] Recollections of ancient superstitions were revived by the siege. One day the intelligence startled the Pope that followers of Paganism still existed, and that an attempt had been made to open the doors of the temple of Janus by night, and, though the effort had failed, the lock had been loosened. We know that in ancient times it had been the custom to open the doors of the temple at

[1] According to Procopius (i. 24), the prophecy read: ῆν τι υἱοιμεν ζε καὶ ἱβενύω. καὶ κατένησι γρ΄σοενιπιήυ ἔτι σο πιαπίετα. The historian is, however, of opinion that the oracles found confirmation and explanation only in the successful issue. I have in vain sought for information with regard to this passage in the fragments of the Sibylline Oracles of Opsopaeus, where it is quoted on p. 423.

the beginning of a war. The custom, however, had been abandoned with the introduction of Christianity, since when, as Procopius tells us, the Romans, the most zealous of Christians, had never again opened the doors of Janus in the storm of war. The ancient temple, however, still stood at the foot of the Capitol, on the confines of the Forum and in front of the Senate house. It was, says Procopius, a small temple of bronze, square, and only of such height as permitted space for the statue of the god. This god was also of bronze, five ells in height, and of perfect human form, except that he bore two faces, of which one was turned to the rising, the other to the setting sun. A door stood opposite each face. *The Temple of Janus.*

The mention of the temple and of the statue of Janus proves beyond doubt that neither Goths nor Vandals had touched the ancient sanctuary. From the same memorable passage we further learn that, even at the beginning of the sixth century, a spot within the Forum and close to the ancient Curia was called the Tria Fata. Procopius informs us that "the Temple of Janus lies in the Forum in the front of the Senate house, a short way past the Tria Fata; for so the Romans call the Parcae."[1] The name Tria Fata, which must have been derived from three antique statues of the Sibyls standing in the neighbourhood of the Rostra,[2] as early as the fifth century, was that *Tria Fata.*

[1] Procop., i. 25: ἔχει δὲ τὸν νεὼν ἐν τῇ ἀγορᾷ πρὸ τοῦ βουλευτηρίου ὀλίγον ὑπερβάντι τὰ τρία φᾶτα. οὕτω γὰρ Ῥωμαῖοι τὰς μοίρας νενομίκασι καλεῖν.

[2] Thus at least Carl Sachse, *Gesch. und Beschr. der alten Stadt Rom.*, Hann., 1824, i. 700, Nr, 775, explains it according to a passage in Pliny, 34 5. Bunsen, iii, 2, 120, follows the same opinion. Nibby

by which the Parcae were usually distinguished.[1] We shall later find that in the eighth century it was generally used to designate a district in the ancient Forum, and that down to the twelfth century the bronze Temple of Janus still existed as the so-called Templum Fatale.

The last dying movement of Paganism in Rome exercises a sort of spell on the imagination, and we cannot here deny ourselves the pleasure of quoting a Latin song, one of the last utterances of the ancient faith. It is impossible to translate the verses.

Two ancient songs.

O admirabile Veneris idolum
Cujus materiae nihil est frivolum;
Archos te protegat, qui stellas et polum
Fecit, et maria condidit et solum;
Furis ingenio non sentias dolum.
Clotho te diligat, quae bajulat colum.

Saluto puerum, non per hypotesim,
Sed serio pectore deprecor Lachesim.

(on Nardini, ii. 216, who gives a most inappropriate explanation) rightly holds the site of the Temple of Janus to have been immediately beside the Secretarium Senatus. The Janus Geminus was originally the Porta Janualis in the ancient city walls. Its form is given us by a coin of Nero, which bears the inscription: *S.C. Pace Terra Marique Parta Janum Clausit.* The ancient custom reappears in altered form in Roman Christianity; in the opening and closing of the sacred doors of certain basilicas during the Jubilee.

[1] The proof of this assertion is to be found in a Roman mythographer of the fifth century. (Tom. iii., Classicor. Auctor. of Cardinal Mai, *Mythographus,* i. p. 40.) After having given the explanation, *"de tribus furiis vel Eumenidibus,"* he proceeds:—

110. *de tribus fatis.*

Tria fata etiam Plutoni destinant. Haec quoque destinant. Haec quoque Parcae dictae per antiphrasin, quod nulli parcant. Clotho colum bajulat, Lachesis trahit, Atropos occat. Clotho graece, latine dicitur evocatio; Lachesis, sors; Atropos, sine ordine.

Sororum Atropos ne curet haeresim (?)
Neptunum comitem habeas (perpetim?)
Cum vectus fueris per fluvium Athesim.
Quo fugis, amabo, cum te dilexerim?
Miser, quid faciam, cum te non viderim?

Dura materies ex matris ossibus
Creavit homines jactis lapidibus:
Ex quibus unus est iste puerulus,
Qui lacrimabiles non curat gemitus.
Cum tristis fuero, gaudebit aemulus.
Ut cerva fugio, cum fugit hinnulus.

In answer to this enigmatical song, in which Venus and Love mysteriously appear in the company of the three Parcae or Tria Fata, may have been written another song in honour of SS. Peter and Paul:—

O Roma nobilis, orbis et domina,
Cunctarum urbium excellentissima,
Roseo martyrum sanguine rubea,
Albis et virginum liliis candida:
Salutem dicimus tibi per omnia
Te benedicimus, salve per saecula.

Petre, tu praepotens caelorum claviger,
Vota precantium exaudi jugiter!
Cum bis sex tribuum sederis arbiter,
Factus placabilis judica leniter,
Teque precantibus nunc temporaliter
Ferto suffragia misericorditer!

O Paule, suscipe nostra peccamina!
Cujus philosophos vicit industria.
Factus oeconomus in domo regia
Divini muneris appone fercula;
Ut, quae repleverit te sapentia,
Ipsa nos repleat tua per dogmata.[1]

[1] Niebuhr found both songs in the Vatican and published them in *Rhein. Mus.*, iii. pp. 7 and 8. (See also Daniel, *Thesaur. hymnologicus,*

Glorious defence made by Belisarius.

Belisarius meanwhile required some more powerful support in Rome than that of prophecies. He sent letters to the Emperor Justinian, informing him of the attack so successfully repulsed, and, explaining the difficulty of his position, he earnestly begged for fresh troops. His forces, after the withdrawal of the garrisons which had been obliged to leave in Campania and Sicily, only numbered 5000 men, and of these the siege had already carried away a part. No mention is made of any Roman civic militia; rather would it appear that Rome, which had formerly conquered the world, had already become incapable of providing armed citizens. Procopius only informs us that Belisarius had taken artisans out of work, or day-labourers, into his army, and divided the duty of watching amongst them for which he gave them pay.[1] In divisions, or Symmoriae, they had to supply the ranks of the night watches. Great caution, however, was required

iv. 96.) He attributes them to the last days of the Empire. The above quoted gloss *de tribus fatis* is curiously connected with the first song, where we find a repetition of the same Phrase: *Clotho colum bajulat.* In it we recognise the time of the mythographer, namely, the fifth century. The secular song seems to refer to a statue of Venus, and the line *furis ingenio non sentias dolum* evidently express dread of the robbers of statues. It is possible that some Roman here laments the loss, and takes leave, of a favourite statue. The last stanza is very obscure. Pagans still existed in numbers in the days of Theodoric (*Edictum Theodorici Regis CVIII.* in the Op. Cassiod.), and we can scarcely doubt may have been found even in Rome; although the opening of the doors of the Temple of Janus may probably have been the work of young people, to whose minds the terrible struggle recalled superstitions of the past.

[1] Procop., i. 24: στρατιώτας τε καὶ ἰδιώτας ξυνέμιξε.

to guard against treachery. Belisarius changed the stations on the walls twice a month, and twice in the same time had new keys forged for the gates. The captains were obliged to make the rounds at night, to call the watches by name, and point out the missing to the generals in the morning. Music played at night time to arouse the sleepy, and the Moorish soldiers who stood before the gates at their posts in the trenches had their shaggy watch-dogs by them to aid their own sharp hearing.[1]

4. Exile of Pope Silverius—Famine in Rome— Humanity of the Goths—Vitiges occupies the Roman Harbours—Portus and Ostia—Arrival of Reinforcements in Rome—The Goths repulse a Sortie—Increasing Distress in the City—The Gothic and Hunnish Entrenchments.

Belisarius undoubtedly had reason to suspect the fidelity of the Senate, and can scarcely be accused of harshness in having sentenced some of the

[1] Songs with allusions to the past must assuredly have been in vogue among the sentinels. When, in 924, the people of Modena defended their walls against the Hungarians, the citizens sang the following :—

O tu, qui servas armis ista moenia,
Noli dormire, moneo, sed vigila.
Dum Hector vigil extitit in Troja
Non eam cepit fraudulenta Graecia, &c.

Muratori, Dissert. 40, and Ozanam, *Docum. inédits,* &c., pp. 68 and 69. The goodness of the Latin seems to refer the song to an earlier date, the verses both in rhythm and metre being on a level with those published by Niebuhr.

patricians to banishment. His treatment of Pope Silverius, however, cannot be ascribed to a treacherous correspondence with the Goths, since it was this very Pope who had persuaded the people to open their gates to Belisarius. The painful incident is dismissed by Procopius in a few words: "because it was suspected that Silverius, the chief priest of the city, had plotted treason with the Goths, he sent him forthwith to Hellas, and afterwards appointed another bishop named Vigilius." The fall of Silverius was, however, the result of intrigues with the Empress Theodora, who, with the advent of a new Pope, hoped for the revocation of the decisions of the Council of Chalcedon and the restoration of the condemned patriarch Anthimus in Constantinople. To both of these measures Silverius had steadfastly refused his assent. Taking advantage of difficulties in Rome, Theodora carried on negotiations with the deacon Vigilius, an ambitious Roman and a favourite of her own, who had filled the office of Apocrisiarius, or Representative of the Church, in Constantinople. She wrote letters commanding Belisarius to find some plausible pretext for removing Silverius, and having Vigilius elected to the chair of Peter—Vigilius promising, in return for the Papacy, the restoration of Anthimus and the condemnation of the Council of Chalcedon.

The great Belisarius basely yielded to the orders of two infamous women, the all-powerful Theodora and the crafty Antonina, his own wife; women whom a similarity in lowly birth and licentious life had made confidantes, although each feared and hated the other. Belisarius, who had not the courage to incur their ill-will, forced himself to become the executor of their designs. Antonina and Vigilius procured false witnesses, who were made to swear that Silverius had written to Vitiges: "Come to the Porta Asinaria, near the Lateran, and I will give the city and the Patrician into your hands." The terrified Pope, who had fled for refuge to the church of S. Sabina on the Aventine, was summoned thence by Belisarius to attend him at the Palace of the Pincio, the headquarters of the general during the siege. The unfortunate Silverius, relying on the sworn assurance of safety which he had received, left his asylum. Arrived at the palace, the clergy who attended him were detained in an anteroom, while Silverius was led by Vigilius to an inner chamber where Antonina reclined on a couch, Belisarius at her feet.[1] On the entrance of Silverius, Antonina, an accomplished actress, cried in feigned indignation, "Tell us, Pope Silverius, what have we and the Romans done that you wish to give us up into the hands of the Goths?" While she heaped reproaches upon him, John, subdeacon of the first Region, entered, took the pallium from the neck of the Pope and led him into a sleeping room, there removed the episcopal robes, and put him into the habit of a monk; while another deacon went to the attendant priests, who anxiously waited outside, and briefly informed them that the Pope was deposed and

Silverius deposed by Belisarius, March 537.

[1] The *Lib. Pont.*, "Vita Silverii," says naïvely: *Quo ingresso Silverius cum Vigilio soli in Musileo, Antonina, patricia jacebat in lecto, et Vilisarius, patricius sedebat ad pedes ejus.*

had become a monk. The priests fled in consternation, and the Senate and clergy, under terror of the Greek authorities, elected Vigilius Pope, after his predecessor had already been sent to Patara in Lycia. The arbitrary deposition of Silverius had taken place in March 537, and on the 29th of the same month apparently Vigilius was ordained.[1] This act of despotic interference on the part of the imperial general in ecclesiastical affairs must have shown the Romans that the rule of the Goths was easy to bear, but that the yoke of the Byzantines would press heavily on them. Vigilius, a Roman of noble birth, son of John the former Consul, was the same cardinal-deacon who had been chosen by his patron, Boniface II., to succeed him on the papal chair. The uncanonical act, it is true, had been revoked, but henceforward Vigilius ceaselessly strove to reach the Papacy. As Nuncio at Constantinople he had made many influential friends at the Byzantine court, and had now usurped the papal throne in the violent manner we have just described.[2]

Vigilius, 537–555.

Terrible famine meanwhile raged in Italy, and began its devastations in the city. Belisarius found himself obliged to remove all the inhabitants but such as were available for the defence of the walls. The wretched people were driven forth in great numbers. Some dispersed over the Campagna, others took

[1] Liberatus Diacon., *Breviar.,* c. 22, gives a circumstantial account of the story of Silverius, and ascribes his death in Palmaria (other authorities say Ponza) to the influence of Vigilius. With regard to the chronology, see Jaffé, *Regesta Pontif.,* Rome, 2nd ed.

[2] L. Duchesne, "Vigile et Pelage," *Rev. des quest. historiques.* Oct. 1884.

ship at the harbour of the Tiber, meaning to seek hospitality at Naples, the Goths allowing them to pursue their way unhindered. The humanity of the Northern barbarians during the entire siege compelled the respect even of the enemy, by whom it is recorded that they touched neither the basilicas of S. Peter nor S. Paul, although both churches lay within their territory. Other sanctuaries, however, within the city suffered destruction, the usual accompaniment of war. The Gothic soldiers were accused by Vigilius of having injured the catacombs and numerous cemeteries, and of having broken the marble inscriptions of Damasus.[1] Vigilius himself seems to have acted during the siege as a benefactor of the people.[2]

The anger of Vitiges, however, induced him to commit one bloody and revengeful deed. Sending messengers to Ravenna, he commanded the execution of those Senators whom he had previously sent as hostages from Rome. Finally, the more closely to

[1] Inscription of Vigilius, Gruter, 1171, 4:—

Cum peritura Getae posuissent castra sub urbe,
Moverunt sanctis bella nefanda prius,
Istaque sacrilego verterunt corde sepulcra
Martyribus quondam rite sacrata piis...

[2] The sub-deacon Arator, celebrated as a poet, at this time in the besieged city, begins his *Ep. ad Vigilium* thus:—

Moenibus undosis bellorum incendia cernens,
Pars ego tunc populi tela paventis eram
Publica libertas, Vigili, sanctissime papa,
Advenis incluso solvere vincla gregi.
De gladiis rapiuntur oves, pastore ministro,
Inque humeris ferimur, te revocante, piis.
—*Patrologia,* ed. Migne, vol. 68, p. 73.

Vitiges occupies Portus.

surround Rome and entirely to cut off the supplies, he garrisoned Portus. The Tiber here empties itself by two arms into the sea, forming the sacred island. The harbour of Ostia, on the left shore, had been choked with sand even in ancient times, and on this account the Emperor Claudius had caused a harbour and canal to be excavated on the right bank, and had thrown a mole into the sea. Thus arose the celebrated *Portus Romanus* or *Urbis Romae.* Trajan enlarged these magnificent works by an inner harbour of hexagonal form, which he surrounded with splendid buildings. At the same time he dug a new canal, the *Fossa Trajana,* still to be recognised in the right arm of the Tiber from Fiumicino. Portus henceforward became a place of great importance, and, in the earliest days of Christianity, a bishopric.[1] In the later Pagan times, and even down to the middle of the fifth century, the Romans were accustomed to go in solemn procession, headed by the Prefect of the City or Consul, to the island between Portus and Ostia, to sacrifice to Castor and Pollux, and to enjoy themselves in the fresh green meadows. Neither the heats of summer nor the snows of winter seemed to harm the flowers on this happy island, and, from the fact that in spring it was covered with roses, and filled with the fragrance of

[1] I have followed the authority of Nibby, who has written a learned treatise on the Roman harbour, *Della Via Portuense e dell' antica cittá di Porto* (Roma, 1827). Compare his *Viaggio di Ostia* and the researches of Fea and Rasi concerning the harbours of Ostia and Fiumicino. The celebrated Hippolytus, Bishop of Portus, here suffered martyrdom about the year 229.

aromatic shrubs, it had been named by the Romans the garden of Venus.[1] Theodoric later provided for the maintenance of the port, entrusting the important harbour to a Comes. Even in the time of Procopius, Portus still remained an important town surrounded by massive fortifications; while ancient Ostia, on the left shore, had already lost both inhabitants and walls; and, although both arms of the river remained navigable, Portus commanded the entire traffic. An excellent road led from the Portuensian gate to the harbour, and the river was thronged by vessels, which, bearing the corn of Sicily and the goods of the East, were towed by oxen up to the city.[2]

After Vitiges, who met with no resistance, had occupied Portus with 1000 men, he cut the Romans off from all communication by sea, and the transports were thus obliged to follow the difficult and insecure route by Antium.

The moral impression of this loss was lessened twenty days later by the entrance of 1600 Hunnish

[1] The so-called Aethicus (ed. Gronov, p. 41) writes of this island as follows: *Insula vero, quam facit intra urbis portum et Ostiam civitatem, tantae viriditatis amoenitatisque est, ut neque aestivis mensibus, neque hyemalibus pasturae admirabiles herbas dehabeat. Ita autem vernali tempore rosa, vel caeteris flosibus adimpletur, ut prae nimietate sui odoris et floris insula ipsa Libanus almae Veneris nuncupetur.* The *Ludi Castorum Ostiae,* which were celebrated on January 27, are recorded as late as the year 449. See "I Monumenti cristiani di Porto," by De Rossi, *Bull.,* 1866, n. 3.

[2] This important description of Portus and Ostia is given by Procopius, i. c. 26. Compare his account with that of Cassiodorus, *Var.,* vii. 9. The Tor' Bovaccina, a mediaeval tower standing on the bank of the river, now marks the confines of ancient Ostia. See also Cluver, *Ital. Antica,* iii. 870.

and Sclavonian horsemen. This reinforcement enabled Belisarius to harass the enemy in a series of petty encounters outside the gates, in which the skill of the Sarmatian archers carried the day against the Gothic cavalry armed only with lances. Slight successes inflamed the courage of the besieged; they desired a general attack on the enemy's entrenchments, and Belisarius yielded to their wishes. The greater number of the troops were ordered to make a sally from the Pincian and Salarian Gates; a smaller number were to proceed from the Porta Aurelia to the Neronian Field to cover the Milvian Bridge; and a third division was directed to make a sortie from the gate of S. Pancratius.

The attack of the Greeks repulsed.

The Goths, however, prepared by deserters for the assault, received the Greeks in well-closed lines of battle; the infantry were placed in the middle, the cavalry formed the wings. After a struggle of several hours their bravery won a complete victory; the Greeks neither being able to win the Milvian Bridge, by which they would have cut off the camp on the further side, nor to conquer the entrenchments on the same side. Everywhere driven back, they owed their rescue only to the vigorous action of the slingers stationed on the battlements.

Disheartened by the failure of their attack, the besieged henceforward confined themselves to petty skirmishes, while the Goths sought to increase the famine in the city by enclosing the walls yet more narrowly. They occupied the spot between the Via Latina and the Via Appia, about 50 stadia from the town, where two aqueducts crossing each other formed a favourable site for the construction of a small fort.[1] Having walled up the arches of the aqueduct, they erected on it an encampment for 7000 men, and thus cut off all intercourse with the Neapolitan territory. The distress in the city, in consequence, increased to an extreme degree. The vegetation on the walls was found insufficient for the horses, and the corn reaped by the cavalry at night (the summer solstice was already passed) only appeased the hunger of the wealthy for the moment. Every kind of animal was already used for food; loathsome sausages, made by the soldiers from the flesh of fallen mules, were bought by senators for their weight in gold. The heat of summer united to the horrors of famine the usual fever, and the stench of unburied corpses rendered pestilential the shadeless streets of Rome.

Famine in the city.

No longer able to endure these miseries, the people rose in despair, and through deputies implored Belisarius to make a last desperate attempt. The prudent general, however, tranquillised the clamour by his immovable calm, and consoled the populace with the prospect of relief in the approach of the fleet laden with supplies. He sent Procopius and even Antonina to Naples to freight as many vessels as possible with corn. At last the forces from Byzantium arrived in Southern Italy. Euthalius came to Terra-

[1] Procopius does not mention the names of the aqueducts. According to Fabretti's plan (*De Aquis et Aquaed.,* Tab. 1.), the junction of the Claudia and Marcia may have been at this spot. De Rossi, *Bull.,* 1866, p. 35, and 1870, p. 106, places there the spot in the Patrimonium Appiae, which in the eighth century was still known as the *campus barbaricus.* I, on the other hand, hold that spot to have been Totila's encampment in front of S. Paul's, of which we shall have to speak later.

cina with the pay of the soldiers, and, protected by an escort of a hundred horse, happily reached the city. To ensure the safe transport of the corn, Belisarius occupied the town of Albanum and the fortress of Tibur, which, in some unaccountable way, had escaped the attention of the besiegers. In order to disturb the enemy in their intrenchments on the Via Appia, he advanced the Hunnish cavalry from their quarters in the city to others in the neighbourhood of S. Paul's, a colonnade which extended from the Porta Ostiensis, along the Tiber to the basilica, providing a convenient stronghold.[1] From here, as from Tibur and Albanum, the enemy's camp on the Via Appia was menaced by incessant incursions on the part of the Huns, while the light cavalry of Belisarius checked the forages of the Goths on the Campagna. The marshiness and low situation of the district, however, engendering fever, neither Goths nor Greeks were able to retain their quarters. The encampment of the Huns was removed and the Gothic garrison at the fortress on the aqueducts obliged to withdraw. In consequence of the destruction of the aqueducts a vast track of land outside the city was evidently reduced to a swamp, and centuries after marshy spots still remained in the neighbourhood.

[1] S. Paul's was as yet unprotected, the adjacent fortress not being erected until the ninth century. Procopius, ii. 4: ἐνταῦθα ὀχύρωμα μὲν οὐδαμῆ ἐστί, στοὰ δέ τις ἄχρι ἐς τὸν νεὼν διήκουσα ἐκ τῆς πόλεως, ἄλλαι τε πολλαὶ οἰκοδομίαι ἀπ' αὐτῶν οὖσαι οὐκ εὐέφοδον ποιοῦσι τὸν χῶρον.

5. DISTRESS OF THE GOTHS—THEIR EMBASSY TO BELISARIUS—NEGOTIATIONS—ARRIVAL OF TROOPS AND PROVISIONS IN ROME—TRUCE—ITS RUPTURE—DISCOURAGEMENT OF THE GOTHS—THEIR WITHDRAWAL FROM ROME, MARCH 538.

Privations endured by the Goths.

The Goths, scattered during the summer over the fever-stricken Campagna, had their numbers thinned by malaria day by day, and their ranks further reduced by famine in the midst of a desert, which, scorched by the sun's rays, seemed little else than an illimitable plain of graves. The approach of Byzantine troops spread utter hopelessness. For 3000 Isaurians, under Paulus and Conon, had landed in Naples; 1800 Thracian horse, under the savage General John, had arrived at Hydruntum; and a third troop of cavalry, commanded by Zeno, approached by the Latin Way. Report said that John was already marching along the coast from Naples with a long train of provision waggons drawn by Calabrian oxen, that the supplies had neared Ostia, and that the fleet with the Isaurians already hovered off the mouth of the Tiber. Despairing, therefore, of the issue of the siege, the Goths now thought of raising it. Vitiges sent a Roman and two of his own captains to the city to treat with Belisarius as to the conditions of peace with the Empire. Procopius has minutely described these memorable negotiations, investing them with the decorum of parliamentary forms. The speech of the Goths, a proof of their claims to the possession of Italy of great historic value, was, according to him, as follows:—

Speech delivered by the Gothic envoys in the presence of the Senate.

"You have done us wrong, men of Rome, in taking up arms against friends and companions in war, an act for which you have no justification.[1] Of the truth of our accusations you cannot fail to be convinced. The Goths did not acquire Italy by force from the Romans, since Odoacer had already set aside the Emperor, possessed himself of the kingdom, and changed it into a tyranny. Zeno, at that time Emperor in the East, wishing to avenge his co-regent, to punish the tyrant, and to liberate the country, accepted the aid of Theodoric. Not being himself able to overcome the power of Odoacer he persuaded our King, who was prepared to fight against Byzantium, to renounce his enmity, and, bearing in mind the honours of the Patriciate and Consulate which he had received, to undertake the task of punishing Odoacer on account of the wrong done to Augustulus, and with his Goths to rule the land according to legal usage. While we thus accepted the kingdom of Italy, we, no less than its earlier rulers, have preserved the laws and forms of government with such fidelity that neither Theodoric nor his followers in the Gothic rule have left behind a single law written or unwritten.[2] Faith and worship have been so strictly secured to the Romans that no

[1] The "Romans" here, as always with Procopius, are the Byzantines who speak of themselves as Romans on the strength of the Roman Empire.

[2] The edict of Theodoric is, as already remarked, only a wretched reconstruction of the legal institutions of the Empire, for which Savigny takes it. This edict was renewed and supplemented by the Edictum Athalarici. See Gretschel, *Edictum Athalarici regis.*, Leipzig, 1828.

Italian has willingly or unwillingly changed his religion, nor has a Goth ever been punished for forsaking his faith. The sanctuaries of the Romans have been respected by us; no one who has sought shelter in these sanctuaries ever having been harmed. All the chief magisterial offices have remained in the hands of the Romans; never have they fallen into those of the Goths. Let any one who dares stand up and accuse us of uttering falsehoods. Further, although the Goths have allowed the Romans yearly to receive the dignity of Consul from the Emperor of the East, yet, in spite of this, you, who were not capable of wresting your Italy from the barbarian Odoacer (who for ten long years had ill-treated it), have shown towards its rightful possessors an unjustifiable enmity. Arise then! leave our dominions, and take quietly with you what is yours by possession or spoil."

Belisarius replied, as was to have been expected, that the Emperor, Zeno, had made over to Theodoric not the kingdom of Italy but the war with Odoacer. To the former masters belonged the estranged possessions which must be restored. The Gothic envoys herewith offered the Emperor the possession of Sicily; but Belisarius rejected the offer with scorn, making the Goths instead a present of the larger island of Britain. He would hear neither of Campania nor of Naples, nor listen to any proposal of a yearly tribute, but required the unconditional surrender of the kingdom of Italy. A truce was at length agreed upon for as long a time as was necessary for an embassy to treat with the Emperor for terms of peace.

Truce.

During the progress of these deliberations the city was excited to feverish joy by the news that John had arrived with the transport in Ostia, and that the Isaurian fleet had reached Portus. Troops as well as transports entered Rome as soon as the supplies, packed on the boats of the Tiber, and unhindered by the Goths at Portus, had been brought up the stream. The Goths in their negotiations had not foreseen this occurrence, and were now obliged to permit what, without making impossible the conclusion of the treaty, they could no longer prevent. A truce was, however, agreed to for three months, guaranteed by hostages on each side, and Gothic ambassadors, under Greek escorts, set forth for Byzantium. These events took place in the time of the winter solstice.

Exhausted, and cut off from supplies by sea still more effectually by the presence of the fleet, the Goths could no longer hold the fortresses round Rome. Scarcely had they abandoned Portus than the Isaurians from Ostia entered; scarcely the important Centumcellae (now Civita Vecchia) than Belisarius transferred a garrison thither. The like happened with regard to Albano. Belisarius paid no attention to the complaints that the truce had been broken. On the contrary, he sent John with a strong detachment to Alba in the district of Picenum, commanding him to ride through the country, taking the wives and children of the Goths prisoners, and plundering their treasures as soon as the enemy could no longer resist the temptation of breaking the truce. This enterprise was intended either to threaten

Broken by Belisarius.

the retreating lines of the Goths, or to compel their withdrawal from Rome.

The inclination towards a renewal of hostilities was great, and Vitiges, reduced to despair, may be forgiven a breach of contract. A serious occurrence in the city had also revived the hopes of the Goths. Belisarius had caused the most distinguished of his subordinate generals to be executed in the palace, because this officer, offended by the harsh judgment of his commander in a private matter, had ventured to attack him with uplifted sword. The death of the brave Constantine filled the soldiers who had served under him with indignation, and aroused their hatred against Belisarius; and report, magnifying the event, excited in the Gothic camp hopes of a treasonable alliance. A band of resolute men attempted to enter the city through the Aqua Virgo, the channel of which led under the palace of Belisarius at the foot of the Pincio. The light of their lamps shining through a crevice failed to betray them to the watchmen, but after long subterranean wanderings they found the opening walled up, and were obliged hastily to return. Vitiges now resumed open hostilities, and attempted one morning to storm the Porta Pinciana. The clang of arms aroused the city; the defenders hastened to their posts, and after a short struggle the Goths were defeated. An attempt to enter by the Aurelian Gate, which Vitiges had hoped to carry by bribery, proved fruitless, and was abandoned.

Unsuccessful attempts of the Goths.

Tidings more and more gloomy depressed the spirit of the King. The general John, a "bloodhound," as historians call him, had quickly executed his commission in Picenum. He had fought with and slain Ulitheus, the uncle of Vitiges, had occupied Rimini, and now showed himself before the walls of Ravenna, where the vindictive Matasuntha (who ill brooked the marriage to which she had been compelled by Vitiges) gave the Greeks hope that she would surrender both Ravenna and herself into their hands. On receiving this intelligence the Gothic King yielded to the murmurs of the army, which, now in its turn besieged, threatened utterly to fall to pieces from hunger, pestilence, and the sword of the enemy. It was now spring. The three months' truce was at an end, and nothing had yet been heard of the messengers from Constantinople. A general movement on the plain showed the Romans that something important was taking place. One night they saw the enemy's camp in flames and on the following morning the Goths retreating by the Flaminian Way. Half of the army had already passed the Milvian Bridge when the Pincian Gate opened and infantry and cavalry fell upon the retreating host. The stragglers threw themselves, after a desperate struggle, upon the bridge to gain the opposite bank, which they only reached after heavy loss. The Goths, disheartened and foreseeing the overthrow of their heroic nation, the flower of which lay buried beneath the walls of Rome, resumed their ranks and proceeded along the Flaminian Way. Thus dearly did they pay for the incompetence of Theodatus, which, instead of transferring the war to Neapolitan territory, had brought Belisarius to Rome; as well as for the

Retreat of the Goths, March 538.

mistake of Vitiges, who, concentrating the strength of his army on the unhealthy Campagna, had neglected to undertake other warlike operations either in the South or North, and had utterly overlooked the necessity of providing a fleet. This oversight on the part of Vitiges, this want of a fleet, was the crowning error that decided the fate of the Gothic kingdom in Italy.[1]

The memorable siege had lasted a year and nine days, during which time the Goths had fought in all sixty-nine engagements. Their retreat took place in the beginning of March 538.[2]

[1] Theodoric had undoubtedly constructed a fleet for the defence of the coasts (*Var.,* v. 16, 17), but, since no mention is made of it during the Gothic war, the vessels can scarcely have been available for fighting purposes. Totila was the first to establish a regular navy.

[2] The chronology of Procopius during the first and second year of the war is inexact. Since his reckoning must be taken as dating from the spring or April of 535, it follows that Vitiges withdrew in the spring of 538, therefore at the end of the third year of the war. Cardinal Noris (*Dissert. hist. de Syn.,* v. p, 54) accuses Procopius of having confused in one the second and third years of the war. I, on the other hand, find that after the third year his reckoning is perfectly correct.

CHAPTER V.

1. Belisarius in Ravenna—His Crafty Dealings with the Goths—Totila, King, 541—His Rapid Successes—His Expedition to the South—He Conquers Naples—Writes to the Romans—Departs for Rome—Conquers Tibur—Second Gothic Siege of Rome in the Summer of 545—Belisarius Returns to Italy—The Harbour of Portus—The Gothic Camp.

Belisarius withdraws to Ravenna.

The history of the city does not permit us either to follow the Goths along the Flaminian Way, or to describe the obstinate struggles in Tuscany, the Emilia and Venetia, where the genius of Belisarius vanquished alike the desperation of the enemy and the disobedience of the Imperial leaders. Two and twenty months after the retreat of the Goths from Rome, towards the end of the year 539, the great general entered Ravenna.[1] By making a show of accepting the crown of Italy, offered him by the conquered nation, he deluded the Italians, with the intention of reserving it for the Emperor. Then, sailing for Constantinople he took with him the

[1] Muratori successfully defends the end of the year 539 as the date of this event, against Pagi, *Annal. ad An.* 540 and the 32 Dissert.

treasures of the palace of Theodoric, and the Gothic King who had fallen a prisoner into the hands of John.[1] The account of how Vitiges, having fled from Ravenna to Rome, and there, clinging to the altar of the Basilica Julii in Trastevere, had only surrendered himself to the enemy under the sworn assurance that his life would be spared, seems to be a fable.[2]

But the kingdom of the great Theodoric was not yet annihilated. If the sudden overthrow of the Vandals in Africa arouses our surprise, the splendid recovery of the Goths after so great a fall has just claims on our astonishment. This brave people had laid down their arms in consternation before a hero, their conqueror, sincerely hoping that he would forthwith reign as King over them and Italy. Deluded by this expectation, they arose, and although, out of 200,000 fighting men, barely 2000 remained, they re-established the honour of their nation and their kingdom in a series of almost unexampled struggles; struggles which covered with undying glory their final overthrow.

Ildibad, King of the Goths.

Belisarius had not yet put to sea when the Goths who remained in Pavia offered the crown to Uraias, a nephew of Vitiges. Uraias, however, placed it

[1] Belisarius was guilty of a manifest act of treason, and the indignation awakened by his conduct kindled the Gothic national spirit into flame. Such too is the opinion of Dahn, *Procopius of Cäsaria, ein Beitrag zur Historiographie der Volkerwanderung und das sinken den Römertums,* Berlin, 1865, p. 408.

[2] *Lib. Pont.,* "Vita Vigili.i" Mabillon (*Iter. Ital.,* iii. p. 77) in the year 1685 saw in the Landi Museum in Rome a votive shield of Belisarius in bronze: *Vitigem regem supplicem exhibens.*

instead on the head of the brave Ildibad, whom he had hastily summoned from Verona. The new Gothic King sent envoys to Ravenna to explain to Belisarius that he would himself come to lay the purple at his feet, would he fulfil his given promise, and accept the crown of Italy. A less prudent man would scarcely have resisted the temptation of setting himself up as King of Italy. The genius and power of Belisarius would probably have enabled him to fill with distinction the throne of Ravenna for a few years, but would have been insufficient to retain it. For, since the Gothic Kings, backed by the strength of a whole nation, or at least by that of a numerous military caste, had failed to establish their kingdom on a secure footing, for how could Belisarius, who would have had to fight against the hostility alike of Goths, Italians, and Byzantines, hope to succeed? Instead, however, of setting up as a rebel against the Emperor, the laurel-crowned hero left affairs in Italy to the care of Bessas and John, and quietly set sail for Constantinople to take the command in the Persian War. Scarcely had he departed than circumstances turned to the disadvantage of the Greeks, and in a short time Justinian was startled by the appearance of a new Gothic hero, who recalled the dreaded figure of Hannibal.

Belisarius sails for Byzantium.

Totila, the young nephew of Ildibad, was in command of a Gothic division in Treviso when the tidings of the murder of his uncle at the hands of a Gepidan avenger reached him. In dismay the youth gave everything up for lost, and offered the town of Treviso to Constantianus, then commanding in

Ravenna. He had received the Greek envoys with a view to negotiation when messengers from the camp of his own people at Pavia appeared before him, summoning him to the throne. Sorely perplexed, the young soldier accepted the crown, and the Goths heard at the same time (towards the end of the year 541) of the death of the usurper Erarich and the election of Totila.[1] A spirit of enthusiasm took possession of the warlike people, and everything was changed in a moment as by the wand of a magician.

Totila, King of the Goths, 541.

His triumphs.

A year spent in the reduction of several towns on both sides the Po sufficed to make Totila dreaded, and already in the spring of 542 (with which, according to Procopius, who reckons from spring to spring, began the eighth year of the Gothic war) he was able to advance on Tuscany. He crossed the Tiber, but reserving for another occasion his revenge for his countrymen slain before the walls of Rome, with shrewd foresight he hastened to Samnium and Campania, there to secure the conquest of the more important towns. The terror of his name went before him. It was on this expedition that the young hero visited the holy monk Benedict in the monastery of Monte Casino, and listened to the reproaches and prophecies of the saint. "Thou dost much wickedness, hast done much evil, withhold thyself now from unrighteousness. Thou shalt go over the sea, shalt

[1] Totila bore the surname Baduela. He is thus designated also on the coins: D.N. BADUILA REX., and thus spoken of in the *Histor. Misc.* and Jordanes. In the *Lib. Pont.,* however, the name is written Badua or Badiulla.

enter Rome: nine years thou shalt reign, in the tenth thou shalt die."[1]

He took Benevento in the first attack, threw down the walls of the town and hastened on; set up his camp and sounded his trumpets before Naples, and, while occupied in besieging the city, sent at the same time troops of light cavalry to Lucania, Apulia, and Calabria. All these fair provinces of Southern Italy readily surrendered themselves and the accumulated wealth of the Imperial taxes into the hands of the Goths, whose young King spared the farmer, whilst from Ravenna to Hydruntum the Greek officials greedily sucked the life-blood of both cities and farms. The Italians already recognised their folly in exchanging the just rule of the Goth for the insatiable despotism of the Byzantine. The finances of Italy were at this time administered in Ravenna by Alexandros (an unscrupulous vampire), whom the Greeks wittily named Psalidion (signifying scissors) on account of the dexterity with which he clipped the gold pieces; and the generals in the principal towns—the avaricious Bessas commanded in Rome—were scarcely behind him in their extortions. Procopius significantly remarks that all the distributions of corn allotted by Theodoric to the citizens of Rome had ceased; and that their withdrawal through Alexandros had been sanctioned by Justinian.[2] The

[1] *Multa mala facis, multa fecisti, jam ab iniquitate compescere. Equidem mare transiturus es, Romam ingressurus, novem annis regnabis, decimo morieris. Hist. Misc.*, xvi. p. 458, and the *Annal. Benedict* of Mabillon, *ad A.* 541, t. i. 97.

[2] Procop., *Hist. Arcana,* c. 26.

Byzantine soldiers, however, being defrauded of their pay, deserted in great numbers and went over to the Goths, from whom they received ample food and wages.

Conquers Naples.

Naples, reduced by famine to the direst extremity, opened its gates in the spring of 543, when, even more than his prowess in war, the magnamity of Totila called forth the admiration of mankind.[1] Like a father or a physician he cared for the needs of the Neapolitans. To the starving, food was carefully administered in order that the dangers of over-indulgence might be avoided; property was protected; so, too, was the honour of women. The Greek general Conon and his troops who, according to the terms of the capitulation, should have left by sea, were detained by contrary winds, and Totila, generously providing them with carriages, horses, and provisions, allowed them under a Gothic escort to depart for Rome. Then, as was his custom with all conquered towns, he razed the walls of Naples to the ground, as if, mindful of Rome, before the might of whose walls the Gothic nation had been shattered, he had sworn destruction to the fortifications of other cities. When inflicting this destruction he explained to the Goths that he adopted this measure in order that no enemy might establish himself within the walls, and to free the town for ever from the danger and sufferings of a siege.

[1] The chronology is here a cause of some perplexity. The author who continues the *Chron. Marcell. Com.* seems to accept the year 544 as the date of the fall of Naples. Muratori, on the other hand, seeks to prove that the calamity took place in 543, and in the same year Pagi makes Totila depart for Rome.

From Naples he sent letters to the Roman Senate, which he had already laid under obligations by his courtesy in having sent back the patrician women who had been imprisoned at Cumae.

Writes to the Romans.

"Those who offend their nearest," so wrote the Gothic King," be it from ignorance, or through forgetfulness, have a right to the forbearance of the offended, since the cause of their error for the most part excuses them. When, however, anyone consciously offends, no excuse remains, since the offender must bear not alone the blame of the action but also that of the intention. Examine yourselves and see whether there is any justification for your conduct towards the Goths. Can you allege either ignorance of the benefits of Theodoric or Amalasuntha, or the forgetfulness which time brings. Neither is possible. For not in trifling things nor in times long gone by, but even now and in important matters you have experienced the favour of the Goths. You are acquainted by hearsay or experience with the manner in which the Greeks treat their subjects, at the same time that personal knowledge must have taught you the way in which the Goths have dealt with the Italians. Nevertheless, it appears that you have received the Greeks with the greater hospitality. With the character of the guests you have thus honoured you must be already acquainted, if you call to mind the practices of Alexandros. I do not speak of the soldiers, nor of their leaders, under whose benevolence and magnanimity you have prospered, while they themselves have been brought to this pass. Do not imagine that I, out of youthful ambition, thus reproach them, nor that I speak boastfully as a barbarian King. For I do not assert that the subjugation of these men is the result of our valour; on the contrary, I am convinced that they have been overtaken by punishment for the outrages committed on you. And were it not the most foolish thing in the world that when God thus punishes them for your sake you should willingly continue to endure their ill-usage instead of escaping from the evil? Give yourselves, therefore, one reason to justify the injury you have done the Goths, and to us a reason to forgive you. And this one reason you shall have, if, not pushing us to the last extremity of war and taking your stand upon a futile remnant of hope, you choose the better part for yourselves, and repair the wrongs of which you have been guilty towards us."[1]

Totila forwarded his letter to the Senate by means of some prisoners, and John having forbidden the Senate to return a reply, the King sent yet other letters of a conciliatory nature, which, published in transcripts and placards in the most populous parts of the city, were read with mixed feelings by the Romans. The Greek authorities, suspecting the Arian priests of secret negotiations with the Goths, banished them one and all from the city. They later also banished the patrician Cethegus, a man who enjoyed the doubtful distinction of being Prince of the Senate, to Centumcellae.

After having reduced the whole of Campania to subjection, Totila left for Rome at the end of the

[1] Procop., iii. 9.

winter (543–544). The news that the Emperor Justinian had recalled Belisarius from the Persian war, and had for the second time entrusted him with the command in Italy, caused the Goth no dismay, he having already secured an excellent basis for his operations, both in South and North, and being moreover aware of the insignificance of the forces at the command of the great general.

Belisarius arrived, and, while he was occupied in recruiting troops on the Adriatic coast, the Gothic King appeared in the neighbourhood of Rome. The strong town of Tibur he gained by treachery. The Isaurian garrison within being at variance with the native guards, the latter opened the gates at night to the enemy. The Goths dealt relentlessly with the town, massacred the inhabitants, even the bishop and clergy; and Procopius laments the death of the Tivolese Catellus, a man who had enjoyed a high repute amongst the Italians.[1] Many of the inhabitants of Tivoli were Goths, and among the ancient documents belonging to the bishopric one of the most ancient is a deed of gift, bearing the date 17th April 471, by which the Gothic Count Valila made over to Tivoli the church (which he had founded) of S. Maria in Cornuta.[2] Totila left a garrison behind in the town, and, making himself

Takes Tibur.

[1] Procop., iii. 10. Catellus is an ancient name in Tivoli.

[2] This document (the *Carta Cornuziana*) has been frequently printed the last time in the *Regesto della Chiesa di Tivoli,* by L. Bruzza (*Studi e Docum. di Storia e Diritto,* vol. i., Rome, 1880). The Goth subscribed himself *Valila qui theodovius vir clar. et inlus. et comes et magist. utr. militie.*

master of the upper course of the Tiber, cut off Rome from all intercourse with Tuscany.

Such were the preparations for the siege of Rome; a project which Totila deferred, however, in order to undertake the conquest of several towns in Etruria, Picenum, and the Emilia; enterprises in which the year 544 and a part of the following were spent. Not until the summer of 545 did he encamp before Rome.[1]

Here Bessas lay with 3000 men. Belisarius had sent to his support two able generals, the Persian Artasires and the Thracian Barbation, strongly charging them not to attempt any attack on the enemy. But scarcely did the Goths show themselves before the walls than these generals attempted a sortie. They were defeated, and, escaping with but a few of their followers back to the city, made no further attack.

Totila lays siege to Rome, 546.

The second Gothic siege of Rome differs materially from the first, reminding us rather of the siege under the Visigoth Alaric. While Vitiges placed his army in seven strong camps, and incessantly stormed the walls, defended by one of the greatest generals of all time, Totila pursued the siege with such deliberation that at the same time he directed from his camp other warlike operations in the Emilia, contenting

[1] Undismayed by Cardinal Noris (*Diss. hist. de Syn.,* v. p. 54), I here follow the chronology of Muratori, Pagi, and Procopius. Procopius places the siege of Rome in the eleventh year of the war (therefore in 545–546). Gibbon in May 546; he fails, however, to make good his statement with regard to the month. Baronius, following the continuator of Marcellinus, Marius Aventic. and Theophan., fixes it in 547, an assumption disputed by Muratori.

himself for the present, with regard to Rome, in simply intercepting the supplies. Towards the interior he controlled the river, and a fleet which he had placed in the Neapolitan waters made the chances of succour by sea very doubtful. He had, moreover, little to fear from Rome. The incapacity and carelessness of the commanders proved so great, that he might have taken the city by storm, had he chosen to direct his forces against it. But he was deterred alike by the recollection of the fate of Vitiges and the insignificant numbers of his troops.

Belisarius meanwhile remained inactive at Ravenna. He had earnestly implored the Emperor to send him reinforcements, and, while these were being slowly collected, the unfortunate hero cursed the fate which compelled him to watch from a distance the loss of his glory, together with the very theatre on which it had been won. He blamed his own thoughtlessness in having remained at Ravenna instead of throwing himself upon Rome with the scanty troops which he possessed. Procopius, who seems to agree in the reproach, comforts himself, however, with the philosophical reflection, that "Fate, when pursuing its own dark decrees, frequently reverses the best resolutions of men." Belisarius now hastened to Epidamnum to receive the troops of John and Isaac, and immediately sent Valentinus and Phocas to the mouth of the Tiber to strengthen the garrison at Portus. The Roman harbour still remained in the power of the Greeks, and the fact that Totila had as yet made no attempt to deprive them of this important fortress rendered the siege still more tedious. The Greek generals, however, on arriving at Portus (then commanded by Innocentius), found the Goths masters of the lower portion of the river, Totila having established his camp between the city and the harbour at a spot eight miles from the city, called the Campus Meruli or Field of the Blackbird.[1] The site on the road to Portus had been chosen with discretion. Here all supplies coming by sea could be intercepted, and, as the Goths commanded the Appian, Latin, and Flaminian Ways, the river remained the sole entrance by which the Greeks could attempt the relief of the city.

Valentinus and Phocas, informing Bessas of their arrival, demanded that on a fixed day he should make an attack on one side of the Gothic camp at the same time that they with the troops from Portus attacked it on the other. Bessas, however, would not agree to the proposal, and the attack, conducted only on one side, ended in defeat and rout.

[1] This is known from the passage in S. Gregor., *Dial.,* iii. c. 5, where he says of Totila: *ad locum, qui ab octavo hujus urbis milliario Merulis dicitur: ubi tunc ipse cum exercitu sedebat.* The spot is still known as the Campo di Merlo. Gregory informs us that Totila, having heard that Bishop Cerbonius of Populonium had concealed Greek soldiers, caused the prelate to be brought before him, and at some public spectacle (apparently after the capture of Rome) cast him to a bear, which, however, refused to touch him. The *Liber Pont.,* "Vita Adeodati," names a *Basilica S. Petri juxta camp. Meruli,* the remains of which were discovered in 1860. Angelo Pellegrini, *Cenni Storici intorno ad una basil. di S. Pietro in campo di Merlo,* Rome, 1860.

2. VIGILIUS IS SUMMONED TO BYZANTIUM—THE GOTHS SEIZE THE SICILIAN CORN VESSELS—DISTRESS IN ROME—THE DEACON PELAGIUS GOES AS AMBASSADOR TO THE GOTHIC CAMP—THE ROMANS IN DESPAIR APPEAL TO BESSAS—TERRIBLE CONDITION OF THE CITY—ARRIVAL OF BELISARIUS AT PORTUS—UNSUCCESSFUL ATTEMPT TO RELIEVE ROME—ENTRY OF TOTILA, DEC. 17, 546—ASPECT OF THE DESERTED CITY—SACK—RUSTICIANA—TOTILA'S CLEMENCY.

Vigilius was at this time absent from the city. Having by his intrigues, and with the connivance of Belisarius, procured the banishment of his predecessor to the island of Palmaria (where the unfortunate Silverius had either been murdered or starved to death), the infamous Vigilius had been recognised as Pope not only by the Church but also by Justinian.[1] A misunderstanding had, however, arisen between him and the Empress Theodora, caused by his hesitation to annul the sentence of Agapitus against Anthimus and the sect of the Akephali; and, finally the condemnation (ordered by Justinian) of some doctrines of Origen had given rise to the Dispute of the Three Chapters.[2] Vigilius was summoned to Constantinople and there arrived in 545 or 546, having been brought by force from the church of S. Cecilia on board the vessel, and

[1] Procop., *Hist. Arcana,* c. 1, and Liberat. Diacon., *Breviar.,* c. 22.

[2] In which Theodore of Mopsuestia, the books of Theodoret of Cyrus against the twelve chapters of S. Cyrillus, and a letter of Ibas of Edessa were to be condemned.

followed by the hatred and denunciations of the Romans.[1]

Tarrying some time in Sicily on his way, he was still there when Totila laid siege to Rome. From the patrimony which the Church possessed on the island he now sent corn to the harbour of the Tiber for the relief of the city. The Goths, however, obtaining knowledge of the supplies, proceeded to the mouth of the river, and lay concealed awaiting their arrival. As the ships with the corn drew near, the Greeks, who had observed the Goths from the fortress, waved their cloaks and signalled to the sailors to turn. They mistook the signal, however, for one telling them to approach, and the whole Sicilian fleet fell into the hands of the Goths. In the fleet were several Romans, amongst them Valentinus, whom the Pope in Sicily had appointed Bishop of Silva Candida, and had sent as his vicar to Rome. Brought before Totila and questioned, the Goths accused him of falsehood, and the unfortunate man was punished by the loss of both hands. The capture was made by the besiegers, according to the reckoning of Procopius, at the end of the eleventh year of the war, or the spring of 546.

The vessels laden with supplies are captured by Totilla.

[1] *Lib, Pont.*, "Vita Vigilii": *videntes Romani, quod movisset navis, in qua sedebat Vigilius, tunc populus coepit post eum jactare lapides, fustes et cacabos, et dicere: fames tua tecum, mortalitas tua tecum: male fecisti cum Romanis, male invenias ubicunque vadis.* A characteristic scene which was repeated, as a copy repeats the original, 900 years later in the time of Eugenius IV. Doubts, however, are cast upon it by Baronius, Pagi and Muratori, but not by Platina. Compare also the *Vita Vigilii ex Amalrico Augerio* (Muratori, *Script.*, iii. 2, p. 51).

Within the city famine and distress had reached their utmost limit. In their despair the Romans turned to the deacon Pelagius, a man held in great respect, who a short time before had acted as Nuncio of Vigilius at Byzantium, and on his return had divided his great wealth among the populace. During the absence of the Pope, Pelagius had filled his place, and now willingly undertook the embassy to the camp of Totila. He implored the King to grant a truce; upon the expiration of which, did no relief arrive from Byzantium, the city promised to surrender. Pelagius, starting on his momentous errand, may perhaps have called to mind the mission of Pope Leo, who had once traversed the same road to Portus to claim the mercy of the Vandal King. The Goth received the honoured messenger with every mark of respect, cutting short, however, beforehand all lengthy speech with the explanation that he would agree to every demand save three. He would listen to no intercession in behalf of the Sicilians, nor to any plea for the preservation of the city walls, nor yet to any in regard to the surrender of the deserted slaves. For the isle of Sicily had first of all treacherously admitted the Greeks; the walls of Rome had hindered an open battle and had forced the Goths to the necessity of laying siege to the city and the Romans to the hardships that a siege entailed. Lastly, he would not break his faith with the slaves who had deserted to him. Pelagius turned away, with a sigh, and retraced his steps.

Pelagius goes as envoy to Totila.

The Romans assembled with mournful cries; their deputies repairing to the deserted Palatine, represented

Terrible famine in Rome.

to the Greek commander in words to which hunger lent a terrible eloquence, "The Romans implore you to treat with them, not as friends of a like race, not as citizens under the same laws, but as conquered enemies and as slaves of war. Give your prisoners bread! we do not say sustenance; no, only the necessary crumbs, that our lives may be spared to your service as befits slaves. Does this seem too much to you? Then allow us to withdraw that you may be spared the trouble of burying your slaves, and if this request is too great, well! grant us in mercy to die all together." Bessas answered that he had not food for them; to let them go, would be dangerous; to put them to death godless. Belisarius approached with relief. And he dismissed the fainting speakers to the famished people, who awaited their return in dumb despair.

No hand was raised to slay the wretches. Bessas and Conon, swayed by the lowest greed, prolonged the siege in order to coin money out of the starvation of the people. They shamelessly trafficked with the corn in the granaries; the Greek soldiers even exchanging for money the share which should have fallen to their lot. Rich Romans willingly paid seven gold pieces for a medimnus, or small bushel, of corn, and such as were unable to buy corn held themselves fortunate could they procure a small measure of bean meal for 1 3/4 gold pieces. Fifty gold denarii were eagerly given for a cow, if such were to be had. In the city there was nothing but usury, which sold, and famine, which bought and devoured. When the last gold piece had been exchanged, nobles were seen carrying piece after piece of valuable household furniture to market to exchange for corn; whilst the poor gathered, to fill their stomachs, the very weeds from the walls or ruins of porticos where once emperors had liberally fed their indolent forefathers. At length the corn was exhausted, even to the little supply reserved by Bessas for himself, and rich and poor seized with equal avidity on grass and nettles, which they cooked and devoured. Men might have been seen like hollow-eyed ghosts reeling in the deserted squares, and falling down dead in the act of gnawing nettles. Even Nature at last denied the bitter and common grass; and many ended their sufferings by voluntary death. Amongst the frightful events to which the time gave birth, Procopius recounts but one; no less awful, however, than the scene in the Famine Tower of Ugolino. This was the case of a father of five children! Surrounded by his little ones who, crying for bread, clung to his garments, he heaved no sigh but calmly bade them follow him, and as he came to the bridge of the Tiber, hiding his face in his mantle, like a true Roman he plunged headlong into the river, his children turned as if to stone and his stupefied fellow-citizens looking dumbly on.

At length the commander gave the inhabitants permission to leave the city for a sum of money still to be extorted, and Rome was emptied of its citizens. But the miserable fugitives who went forth in search of food perished, for the most part, from exhaustion by the way; also, according to the statement of the Greeks, by the sword of the enemy. From this accusation of barbarity, however, we may with reason exculpate the Goths. "To such a pass", cries Procopius, "has fate brought the Senate and people of Rome!"

Arrival of Belisarius.

The arrival of Belisarius in the harbour of the Tiber suddenly changed the aspect of affairs. Sailing from Hydruntum he had taken with him the forces of Isaac, and commanded John to march through Calabria and win the Appian Way. He himself proposed to wait in Portus and see whether with his scanty troops he could relieve Rome. It was, indeed, high time for such relief. On reaching the port of the Tiber he found that the Goths had set an obstacle between him and Rome which it was necessary, but difficult, to overcome. Ninety stadia below the city Totila had barred the river by a heavy bridge formed of the trunks of trees, and at each side had erected a strong wooden tower. No vessel could force this bulwark, and none could approach without first bursting an iron chain.

Belisarius, did he wish to bring troops and come into the city, must perforce destroy this bridge. He waited for some time for the arrival of John, but the Goths had barred the way to this bold general at Capua. He ordered Bessas to join him from the city in making a united attack on the Gothic camp, but Bessas did not stir, and the garrison lay armed and idle on the walls. Belisarius now resolved to trust his genius. He would try every method to bring the corn vessels to the city. His scheme was bold and magnificent. Two hundred "Dromons" or cargo vessels were laden with supplies, each made like a floating fortress, its edges surrounded with planks in which loopholes had been cut. While these were disposed in rows on the river, the procession was to be led by a gigantic floating fire-engine. It consisted of a wooden tower, which, resting on two rafts joined together, overtopped the bridge-towers of the enemy, and bore above a movable boat laden with combustibles.

On the day of the undertaking Belisarius entrusted Isaac with the care of the fortress of Portus and the safety of his wife, giving the general strict orders on no account to leave the harbour, even should he hear that he (Belisarius) had fallen or was in the direst need. At the same time he stationed troops in intrenchments at each mouth of the river, and commanded the infantry to accompany the transport vessels along the Portuensian bank.

He makes a vain attempt to relieve Rome.

Belisarius himself entered the first dromon and gave the sign for the procession to move. The rowers struggled with mighty efforts in twenty boats against the current of the Tiber, and from the shore the fire-engine was slowly dragged along. The Gothic guards at the iron chain were overpowered, the chain itself broke, and with redoubled force the rowers attacked the bridge. The fire-ship was applied to one of the towers on the Portuensian side, and set it in flames. Two hundred Goths with Osdas, their captain, perished. A furious struggle now arose round the bridge itself, which, attacked by the dromons on the river and by the infantry on the banks, was defended by the Goths who had hastened from their camp. The fate of Rome depended on a few moments, and would perhaps have been hastily decided had Bessas made a sortie from the city.

As the struggle round the bridge wavered to and fro, a messenger brought the news to Portus that the chain was broken and the bridge won. Isaac, impelled by the desire of sharing the glory of the victory, forgot the commands of Belisarius, crossed to Ostia, there collected a troop of horse, and charged against the enemy's camp on the other side. In the first attack he overpowered the Goths, took their tents, and prepared for a sack. But the Goths quickly turned, thrust out the invaders, and took prisoner the foolhardy general. Unfortunately, the news of Isaac's imprisonment reached Belisarius during the struggle on the bridge. In his alarm he failed to grasp the true state of the case, but, believing that Portus itself, his chests, his wife, and all the means of war were in the hands of the enemy, he immediately sounded a retreat, and vessels and troops withdrew in haste to Portus to reconquer the harbour. Arriving there, he was astonished to find no enemy, but his own faithful guards on the battlements of the fortress. His grief at his own infatuation was so intense that it resulted in a violent attack of fever, and for a time his life hung in the balance.

Thus was the plan of relief frustrated, and Belisarius prevented from adding to the glory of his first defence of Rome by a second. Profound stillness followed. Belisarius lay ill in Portus; quiet reigned in the Gothic camp; the defenceless city seemed a beleaguered tomb. The walls of Aurelian, enclosing the immense desert from which the population had vanished, alone seemed to guard Rome. Scarcely a sentry was to be seen on the battlements; scarcely a patrol made the rounds; those who wished to sleep, slept: no officer disturbed them. In the streets, perhaps, lingered a few famished figures; in the palace Bessas heaping up gold; Totila undecided behind his trenches gazing on the stately city, from which the bloody shades of his people seemed even now to warn him back.

Isaurian sentries at the Asinarian Gate finally betrayed Rome. Letting themselves down several times by night from the walls with ropes, they came to the Gothic camp to propose to the King that he should seize the city. The information of some of his own soldiers overcame the distrust of Totila. One night four sturdy Goths were drawn up on the battlements. Springing into the city they opened the Asinarian Gate, and the Gothic army entered undisturbed on the Dec. 17, 546.[1]

Totila enters Rome Dec. 17, 546.

Day not having yet dawned, Totila did not advance,

[1] Continuat. Marcell. Com., *ad A.* 547: *Totila dolo Isaurorum ingreditur Romam die XVI. Kal. Januarii.* The *Lib. Pont.* says, on the contrary, in the life of Vigilius, that the Goths entered by the gate of S. Paul: *die autem tertia decima introivit in civitatem Romanam indict. XIV. per portam S. Pauli*; whereby the second taking of Rome by Totila must be understood. Procopius is, however, a more trustworthy authority. Muratori and Pagi successfully dispute the grounds on which Cardinal Noris places the date of the capture in the year 547. Note also Clinton's reasons for fixing the date on Dec. 17, 546. The assertions of chroniclers are very confused; according to the *Fragm. Cuspiniani,* it was not until 548 that the walls were destroyed by Totila.

but remained with his troops on the Lateran field. But a tumult had already arisen in the city, and the magnanimous King caused the trumpets to be sounded the rest of the night, so that the Romans might find time to escape by the gates or seek refuge in the churches.[1] The Greek garrison, with their leaders Bessas and Conon, disappeared on the first alarm. Every Senator who remained in possession of a horse followed their example. Amongst these fugitives were Decius and perhaps also Basilius, the last Consul of the Empire, while the Anicians Maximus and Olybrius, Orestes, and other patricians sought safety in S. Peter's.[2] Such as retained strength to drag themselves to the churches, did so. As the Goths marched through the streets by the clear light of day, the silence was that of an uninhabited desert. Procopius says that in the whole city only five hundred people remained; that these with difficulty had fled to the temples, and that all the rest had already disappeared or had perished from hunger.[3] The statement scarcely appears credible, and the number 500 might perhaps be multiplied by 10; but the statements of a contemporary, even though exaggerated, show how incalculable must have been the ruin and depopulation.

[1] This trait of humanity is related by the *Lib. Pont.* in the life of Vigilius: *tota enim nocte fecit buccina clangi, usque dum cunctus populus fugeret, aut per ecclesias se celaret, ne gladio Romani vitam finirent.*

[2] The *Lib. Pont.* mentions three fugitive ex-Consuls, Cethegus, Albinus, and Basilius. Flavius Basilius, junior, was the last Consul in the year 541. The following years are designated: *post consulatum Basilii.*

[3] Procop., iii. 20.

As the Goths at length passed through the streets of the conquered city, around which its people lay in their newly-made graves, they had full opportunity to work their revenge at will; but Rome was so empty that even their hatred could find no food, and sunk in misery so profound as to have become an object fit to excite the pity of the most inhuman barbarian. The vengeance of the Goths was satisfied with the execution of twenty-six Greek soldiers, and of sixty Romans taken from the populace, and Totila hastened to offer his first thanksgiving in Rome at the grave of the Apostle. As the great conqueror ascended the steps of the basilica he was met by the deacon Pelagius, the Gospels in his hand, with the appeal, "Lord, spare thine own." In reply, Totila asked, "Comest thou then as a suppliant, O Pelagius?" And the priest answered, "God has made me thy servant, therefore spare, O my lord, thy servants." The young hero comforted the humiliated priest with the assurance that the Goths would spare the lives of the Romans, but he gave his followers the desired leave to pillage the unhappy city.

Rome is sacked.

Rome experienced a bloodless sack, the deserted houses unresistingly surrendering their possessions. The city was no longer rich as in the days of Alaric, Genseric, or even in those of Ricimer. The hoary palaces of the ancient families stood already in great part empty and ownerless, and but few still retained their works of art or valuable libraries. There was, however, some spoil in the houses of the patricians, and the palace of the Caesars surrendered to the Gothic King the piles of gold which Bessas had there accumulated. Such of the unfortunate patricians as still remained in their palaces were spared; all had claim to the deepest pity, reduced as they were to starvation, and forced to go from house to house in the torn garments of slaves, begging even from their enemies a morsel of bread in the name of God. In such piteous guise an illustrious woman was pointed out to the Goths, a woman beyond all others deserving of sympathy. Rusticiana, the daughter of Symmachus and widow of Boethius, during the siege had given all her possessions towards the alleviation of the common distress, and was now reduced to linger the short span that yet remained of her eventful life in beggary,—an object worthy of tears. The Goths, pointing her out one to the other, and saying bitterly that, in revenge for the death of her father and husband, she had caused the statues of Theodoric to be overthrown, desired the death of the noble widow. Totila, however, respected the misfortunes of the daughter and wife of such illustrious men, and neither to her nor to any woman in Rome did he permit any harm to be done. The clemency of the Gothic King allowed no distinctions, and commanded even the admiration and love of the enemy, by whom it is recorded that Totila lived with the Romans as a father with his children.[1]

Totila's clemency towards the Romans.

[1] *Ingressus autem Rex habitavit cum Romanis, quasi pater cum filiis.* See *Lib. Pont,* life of Vigilius, and the panegyric of Procopius, iii. 20, at the end: μέγα τε κλέος ἐπὶ σωφροσύνῃ ἐκ τούτου τοῦ ἔργου Τωτίλας ἔσχε.

3. Totila's Address to the Goths—He Assembles the Senate—Threatens to Destroy Rome—Letter of Belisarius—Senseless Legend of the Destruction of the City by Totila—Benedict's Prophecies respecting Rome—Totila Surrenders the City—Its Utter Desolation.

Totila addresses the Goths,

The following day Totila assembled the Goths. Addressing them, and comparing their present numbers with their past greatness, he encouraged them, pointing out that the proud army of 200,000, which under Vitiges had been overcome by only 7000 Greeks and reduced to a band of naked and inexperienced soldiers, had nevertheless in turn vanquished 20,000 of the enemy, and reconquered the lost kingdom. He showed that there was a mysterious power which chastised the misdeeds of kings and nations, and admonished his followers to avert the Divine vengeance by their justice towards the vanquished.

and the Senate.

Next he proceeded in kingly wrath to deal with the remnant of the Senate, and this was perhaps the last occasion on which the Patrician Fathers assembled in the Senate House or on the Palatine. The humiliated Senators, in silence, listened to the censures of the Gothic hero, who reproached them with ingratitude for the benefits which Theodoric and Athalaric had conferred upon them, accused them of perjury, treason, and lastly of folly, and explained that henceforth he would treat them as slaves. They answered not a word. Pelagius, however, pleaded for the "unfortunate offenders" until the King at length promised to substitute grace for justice.[1]

Totila felt no hatred against the Romans, but levelled his vengeance entirely against the stones of the city, against those venerable walls which had wrought the overthrow of his nation. Happening at this time to hear that the Goths in Lucania had suffered some slight reverse, the King burst into a transport of rage; he swore to lay Rome level with the ground; he would leave the greater part of his army behind, and hasten to Lucania to punish the wild bloodhound John. Forthwith he gave orders to pull down the walls; and his orders being carried out in several places, the third part of these colossal structures was actually overthrown.[2] The enraged King threatened also to destroy by fire some of Rome's most splendid monuments; "I will turn the whole city," he said, "into pasture for cattle."[3]

Destroys the walls.

Threats such as these were probably uttered by the angry King, but it is scarcely possible that a man so magnanimous could actually have conceived the idea of bringing infamy on his heroic name by so unparalleled an outrage.[4] Report, however, asserted that the Goths were about to destroy the city, and

[1] Ὑπὲρ ἀνδρῶν ἐπταικυτων τε καὶ δεδυστυχηκότων παραιτούμενος, says Procopius himself, iii. 21.

[2] Procopius, iii. 22. It cannot be doubted that the walls between the Praenestine and Pincian Gates were thrown down. This, which is at present the weakest portion of the fortifications, gives evidence of very hurried restorations erected in the Middle Ages.

[3] In the course of time the Forum Romanum actually became the Campo Vaccino.

[4] The judicious Muratori, *Annal. ad A.* 546, says : *laonde gli passò cosi barbara voglia, se pure mai l'ebbe.*

Belisarius, shut up in forced inactivity within the neighbouring port, saw in the fevered dreams of his pain and despair the enemy already in Rome, the city of his glory, ruling, robbing, and burning. He sent a dissuasive letter to the Gothic King. This document, which bears the stamp of a noble mind, deserved to have been engraved in bronze by the grateful Romans and preserved in their city, to deter not so much barbarians as their own barons and popes, who in the Middle Ages waged wanton destruction on the monuments.

Belisarius's letters to Totila.

Belisarius wrote to his noble enemy in the following terms:—

"It is the act of men experienced in intellectual and civil life to decorate towns with beautiful works; the action of the ignorant to destroy these ornaments, leaving their memory branded with disgrace. Beyond all cities upon earth, Rome is the greatest and most wonderful. For neither has she been built by the energy of a single man, nor has she attained to such greatness and beauty in a short time. On the contrary, a long succession of emperors, many associations of illustrious men, countless years and wealth, and also artists from every quarter have been required to bring together all the treasures she contains. Whilst the city, as thou now seest her, has been gradually built, she remains a monument of the virtues of the world to all posterity, and a trespass against her greatness would justly be regarded as an outrage against all time. For such an outrage would rob our ancestors of the monuments of their virtues, and posterity of the sight of their works. Since, then, things are so, admit that one of two things must necessarily happen. In this war thou must either be defeated by the Emperor, or thou must subdue him, if that be possible. Art thou victor? destroying Rome, thou wilt lose not the city of another but thine own. Preserving her, on the other hand, thou wilt enrich thyself with the most splendid possession of the earth. If, however, the worse lot is thy part, then will the preservation of Rome be a plea for pardon in the eyes of the conqueror; the destruction neither a claim for forbearance, nor any advantage to thee. The judgment of the world, which in any case awaits thee, is in proportion to thy deeds. For on their actions depends the reputation of kings."[1] Totila replied to his great opponent, but unfortunately his answer has not been preserved by history.

The monuments of Rome were spared; but many houses were destroyed by fire during the sack, and such was more especially the lot of the Trasteverine quarter, where, however, happily but few of the greater buildings were situated.[2] Perhaps Totila himself may have had some houses set on fire in this quarter as if really intending to carry his threat into execution; and this fire, the glare of which would have been seen on the horizon from Portus, may, in the eyes of Belisarius, have lent an appearance of probability to the report of the impious project. His

[1] Procop., iii. 22,

[2] The continuator of Marc. Com., *ad A.* 547, says: *ac evertit muros, domos aliquantas igni comburens, ac omnes Romanorum res in praedam accepit.* Procop., iii. 22: ἐπεὶ ἐμπρήσας αὐτῆς πολλὰ ἔτυχεν, ἄλλως τε καὶ ὑπὲρ Τίβεριν ποταμόν, and iii. 33: ἐτύγχανε δὲ Τωτίλας πολλὰς μὲν ἐμπρησάμενος τῆς πόλεως οἰκοδομίας.

Idle reports concerning the destruction of Rome.

letter to the Gothic King, the misunderstood, or purposely distorted, passages in Procopius and Jordanes gave rise, however, to the opinion that Totila had really destroyed Rome. Historians of the Middle Ages, and even of later times, have solemnly maintained the assertion, and, while exonerating Alaric, Genseric, and Ricimer from such an outrage, they accuse Totila of the ruin of Rome. Leonardo Aretino, in the character of Virgil, fabricates an awful description of the burning of Rome at the instigation of Totila. "He first," says Leonardo, "tore down the walls, then set fire to the Capitol, the Forum, the Subura, and the Via Sacra; the Quirinal smoked; the Aventine vomited flames of fire; the crash of falling houses filled the air." Other Italian rhetoricians repeated like fables, and, not satisfied with describing the Goths as a horde of ruthless destroyers, who, descending on the Colosseum, disfigured it from top to bottom with holes, asserted that they had designs on the obelisks of Rome, since, having in their own country monuments of the kind from 20 to 30 feet in height, they were filled with envy of the more beautiful obelisks of Rome, and had levelled one and all to the ground, with the solitary exception of that of S. Peter. These senseless fables found acceptance as late as the eighteenth century.[1]

[1] Leonardo Aretino (who died 1444) wrote a history of the Gothic war, in which he very adroitly repeats the substance of Procopius: *de bello Italico adv. Gothos,* libr. iv., appended to the Basle edition of Zosimus. The above marvellous passage is in lib. iii. 333. Both the authors who write of the Roman obelisks,—Mercati, *Degli obelischi di Roma* (1589), and Bandini, *De Obelisco Caes. Aug.* (1750), who slavishly

In other respects the remarkable prophecy of S. Benedict concerning Rome, as related by the great Pope Gregory only forty-seven years later in his *Dialogues,* was fulfilled. When Totila entered Rome fear was universally manifested that the Goths, out of revenge for the fate of their brothers under Vitiges, would entirely destroy the venerable city; and the belief proves that Rome had never ceased to be the object of universal love. The Bishop of Canusium in Apulia came one day to S. Benedict at Monte Casino, and imparted to him these fears. The man of God comforted him with the assurance, "Rome will not be destroyed by the barbarian, but by storms and lightning; scourged by whirlwind and earthquake, the city will putrefy in itself."[1]

Benedict's prophecy concerning the destruction of Rome.

After Totila had thrown a third part of the walls to the ground he voluntarily abandoned Rome to withdraw to Lucania. He left no garrison behind,

follows the former author,—magnify the legends of the ruin inflicted by Totila, more especially on the obelisks. Of the nature of their criticism the following specimen may suffice: Jordanes, *De regn. succ.* (Murat., *Script.,* i. p. 242), says: *omniumque urbium munimenta* (walls) *destruens*; of which Mercati makes *monumenta* (monuments)! Even more blameworthy is Bandini, writing as he did at the time when Winckelmann, a descendant of the Goths, was occupied in instructing the Romans on the art of antiquity and the history of their monuments.

[1] S. Gregor., *Dialog.,* ii. c. 15: *Roma a gentibus non exterminabitur, sed tempestatibus, coruscis, turbinibus, ac terrae motu fatigata marcescet in semetipsa.* "This prophecy," says the Pope, "has been literally fulfilled," and while exonerating the barbarians from the reproach, he gives a satisfactory explanation of the ruin of the city, to which we have something to add in the later Middle Ages. The Romans were again reminded of the same prophecy in the thirteenth century; it stands as a marginal note in the earliest plan of the mediaeval city, that belonging to the time of Innocent III., Cod. Vat., 1960.

but stationed a portion of his troops 120 stadia distant from the city at a spot named Algidus, to prevent Belisarius removing from Portus.[1] He might with good reason consider Rome worthless from a political and strategic point of view, but it appears surprising that he did not throw himself with his whole strength on Portus, and there make an end of the war. He took all the Senators as prisoners with him, and commanded that one and all the inhabitants should leave Rome and disperse over the Campagna.[2] Imagination revolts against the idea of a spectacle so strange and unparalleled, and hesitates to look at the Capital of the World, which we have hitherto been accustomed to think of as populated by nations, as even for a moment under a curse, silent and uninhabited. But the words of Procopius are clear and expressive, and are confirmed by the testimony of another author, who says that Totila had led the Romans prisoners into the Campagna, and that, after her desertion, Rome remained for more than forty days uninhabited that only animals were to be seen, and that not a human soul remained.[3]

Departure of Totila.

Rome entirely depopulated.

[1] Algidus is recognised in the present Castello dell' Aglio, the ruins of which stand on the summit of a height near Rocca Priora. The Algidus of Procopius, however, must have been elsewhere situated, since it is impossible that a camp on the Alban Mount could have directed operations against Portus. Nibby has therefore suggested that we may read Alsium, the present Palo. See his *Analisi della Carta,* &c., i. 129.

[2] Jordanes, *De regnor. succ.* (Murat., i. 242), says with energy: *cunctos Senatores nudatos, demolita Roma(!) Campaniae terra transmutat.*

[3] The continuator of Marcell. Com.: *post quam devastationem XL. aut amplius dies Roma fuit ita desolata, ut nemo ubi hominum, nisi bestiae morarentur.* Procop., iii. 22: ἐν Ῥώμῃ ἄνθρωπον οὐδένα ἐάσας, ἀλλ' ἔρημον αὐτὴν τὸ παράπαν ἀπολιπών.

CHAPTER VI.

1. Belisarius enters Rome—Restores the Walls—Second Defence of the City, 547—Totila Withdraws to Tibur—John removes the Roman Senators in Capua—Rapid March of Totila to Southern Italy—Belisarius leaves Rome—Memorials of Belisarius in the City.

Scarcely had Totila retired towards Apulia than Belisarius made an attempt to enter the unoccupied city. Marching from Portus with only 1000 men, the cavalry, which, on the news of his approach, had hastened from Alsium, forced him to an encounter and a speedy retreat. He resolved to await a more favourable opportunity, left only an insignificant force in the harbour fortress, skilfully deluded the Goths and advanced with all his remaining troops through the Ostian Gate. It was now the spring of 547. No sooner did the great general stand again on the scene of his glory than genius and fortune alike seemed to return to him with redoubled strength.

Belisarius enters Rome, 547.

His first care was to restore the walls, and, having neither a sufficient number of workmen, nor time, nor material entirely to rebuild the parts destroyed, he was forced to do the best that circumstances allowed. The walls were built at random from the ruins that lay around, and many noble fragments of marble or travertine belonging to neighbouring monuments were used without hesitation.[1] No mortar nor other cement united the stones; stakes, however supported them on the outside, and the trenches, which had been previously dug, having been cleared and deepened, served as their best defence. After five and twenty days of hurried work, Belisarius could make the round of the restored walls, and convince himself that they bore at least the outward aspect of solidity. The Romans dispersed over the Campagna gathered again in the city, restoring to it a semblance of animation.[2]

Totila no sooner heard that the enemy had returned to Rome than, as restless, as errant, and as quick as Hannibal, he hastened back by forced marches from Apulia. His expedition, as it was unsuccessful, may appear purposeless, and for the first time the Gothic King may seem deserving of blame, since, without having driven Belisarius from Portus, he surrendered Rome. He had doubtless imagined that, did Belisarius enter, the city would prove utterly untenable, the walls for the most part

[1] Innumerable fragments of white marble, evidences of hasty restorations, are still to be seen in the walls between the Porta San Giovanni and the Porta Maggiore. I do not venture to ascribe these restorations directly to Belisarius, although the material adopted might well belong to this period.

[2] From a longing to dwell in Rome: τῆς τε ἐν Ῥώμῃ οἰκήσεως ἐπιθυμίᾳ, says Procopius, iii. 24, and this is a very ancient longing or malady of mankind.

having been pulled down. He found the Greeks in fact still at work on the gates; he himself had previously removed or destroyed the gates, and Belisarius's carpenters not being yet ready with substitutes, the Greek soldiers instead barred the entrances with their shields and lances. The Goths passed the night in their camp by the Tiber. In the morning: they rushed with fury against the walls, which the lightest thrust of one of Vitiges's battering rams would have overthrown. After a struggle, however, which lasted throughout the day, they found themselves at nightfall driven back to their camp on the Tiber, and recognised with dismay that they had suffered a repulse from the defenceless city. On the following morning they returned to another attack. They found the walls occupied by archers, and, erected before the gates, a number of wooden machines supported on four stakes fastened at right angles, which could be twisted and turned at will.[1] The genius of Belisarius seemed to have been created to defend Rome, and here alone to have been invincible. The Goths, on the other hand, little experienced in the art of beleaguering cities, ever returned, as if impelled by fate, to have their power shattered against these hoary walls. Night again ended the second attack, and a third which Totila undertook after an interval of several days had an

Defeat of Totila.

[1] Gibbon erroneously explains these τρίβολοι as iron spikes; Muratori, with more justice, as *chevaux de frise.* Ducange holds *tribulus* equivalent to *trabuchetum,* a species of mortar, an explanation that does not apply to this case. Although he does not quote our passage he is acquainted with the machine from Vegetius, 3, c. 24.

equally unsuccessful issue, his royal banner being saved with difficulty from the hands of the enemy.

In the camp his followers overwhelmed him with reproaches: those who had hitherto praised his system of throwing down, entirely or in part, the fortifications of conquered towns, bitterly upbraided him because he had not defended Rome, or, in default of defending it, had not levelled it with the ground. Even in distant lands the misfortune of the Goths before the half-open Rome and the successful resistance of Belisarius excited astonishment. Some time later Totila was taunted on the subject by the King of the Franks, Theodebert, whose daughter he desired in marriage; the Frank made the cutting reply that he could not believe a man was King, or that he would ever become King, of Italy, when he did not know how to retain conquered Rome, but had allowed the partially destroyed city to fall again into the hands of the enemy.[1]

Totila left a measure of his military glory and a greater measure of his fortune before the fatal walls. Breaking down the bridges over the Anio, he now advanced with all his forces to Tibur, which he fortified.[2] Belisarius thus found leisure to provide Rome with gates bound with metal, and for the

[1] Procop., iii. 37.

[2] Procop., iii 24, it is true, speaks only of the bridges over the Tiber, saying that the Milvian, on account of its nearness to the city, alone remained. As, however, the Anio crosses the way to Tivoli, we are easily convinced that Totila must have destroyed the bridges over the latter stream. He broke down the Salarian and the Nomentan, perhaps also the Ponte Mammolo, but naturally refrained from destroying the Pons Lucanus below Tivoli.

second time could proudly send the keys of the city as trophies to Constantinople. Procopius here closes the winter and the twelfth year of the Gothic War. It must, therefore, have been the spring of 548 when Totila raised the siege of Rome; but it would appear that the historian somewhat hastens the course of time. It is possible, however, that the siege only lasted a month.

In the meantime the King had sustained another severe loss and one which considerably added to the moral weight of his misfortunes. John, who indefatigably prosecuted the little war in Southern Italy, had led a cavalry expedition into Campania. There, perhaps in Capua, the Roman Senators, with their wives and children, were detained in prison. Letters forced from the Senators had already served Totila to call the inhabitants of the provinces to obedience. John attacked Capua, cut down the Gothic sentries, released the Senators, and successfully carried off his prey to Calabria. Few of the Patrician Fathers, it is true, had fallen into his hands, the greater number having been dispersed by Totila after the fall of Rome. Many of the Patrician women, however, fell into the power of the Greek, and were sent by him to Sicily, where they remained as hostages to the Emperor.

Totila in Southern Italy.

On receiving the news of this unexpected stroke, Totila hastened from Perugia, to which he was laying siege, to Southern Italy; crossed the mountains of Lucania, fell on John's camp, and scattered the Greeks among the woods and mountains of the district; then, advancing to Brundusium, he annihilated a newly-arrived body of Greek troops. In thus removing the seat of war to Southern Italy, he forced Belisarius again to leave Rome and resort in person to Calabria, the Emperor himself commanding the general to repair to the scene of action. Leaving Conon in

Belisarius leaves Rome, 547.

defence of the city, Belisarius departed by sea, and taking only 700 cavalry and 200 infantry with him, quitted Rome for ever in the winter of 547 to pursue, without glory and without success, his wanderings round the southern shores of Italy.

The walls of Rome form the chief memorial of his sojourn in Italy. By them his name has been immortalised; not so much because he restored them, as because, with unexampled genius, he twice defended them against a numerous and powerful enemy. The belief was current for a time that he had repaired the aqueducts and restored to Rome the use of the baths. Enquiry, however, seems to show that the Baths of Trajan alone were rebuilt by him, and rebuilt only because indispensable to the mills.[1] The great expense of the restoration of the remaining aqueducts could no longer be defrayed, and, if we except the Trajana and some later insignificant restorations, from the time of their destruction by the Goths in 537 the aqueducts ceased to supply Rome; and the city, hitherto more

[1] Alberto Cassio, who, with great industry, has compiled a history of the Roman aqueducts (*Corso delle acque antiche,* Rome, 1756, t. i. n. 28, p. 260), is of this opinion. The mutilated inscription bearing the words: *Belisarius. Adquisivit. Anno D...,* was found on an arch of the aqueduct at the Sabbatine Lake (Lago di Bracciano) near Vicarello; and this is supported by a passage in the *Lib. Pont.,* "Vita Honor.," to which we shall refer later.

copiously supplied with water than any in the world, was reduced for centuries to the Tiber and a few cisterns and fountains, as in the earliest period of her existence.

The *Liber Pontificalis* informs us that Belisarius had founded a House for the Poor in the Via Lata, and had presented two great candelabra and a gold cross of a hundred pounds weight, set with jewels, on which his victories were engraved, to the Apostle Peter. Apparently this work of art was enriched with scenic engravings, and its loss is therefore the more to be regretted.[1] Since we are told that these offerings were placed in the hands of Pope Vigilius, it follows that the gifts must have been made after the victory over Vitiges. The wealth accruing to the conqueror from the spoils of Vandals and Goths must have been incalculable; and Rome would doubtless have experienced many benefits at the hands of Belisarius, and would have been adorned with many monuments of his glory, had his short residence in the city and the strife and confusion of the time permitted.

[1] *Lib. Pont.*, "Vita Vigilii," n. 102: *crucem auream cum gemnis, pens. lib. C., scribens victorias suas.* The Greek γράφειν and not *scribere* is to be understood here. Some epitaphs belonging to the time of Belisarius' sojourn in Rome, and now in the New Museum of Christian Inscriptions in the Lateran, are of value. Muratori, *Nov. Thes. Vet. Inscr.,* p. 1852, n. 12, quotes one of a *Spatharius domini Patricii Belisar.,* and I was shown the fragments of a sepulchral inscription of a dyer by the monks of S. Pancrazio on the Aurelian Way, which Marini gives in the notes to *Pap. Dipl.,* p. 251, n. 28. Roman tradition designates the present church of S. Maria dei Crociferi in the neighbourhood of the Fontana di Trevi as the house for the poor founded by Belisarius in the Via Lata. An inscription over the door of the church, belonging to the time of Gregory XIII., names Belisarius as the builder.

2. Belisarius's Wanderings in Southern Italy; His Return to Constantinople—Totila advances to Rome for the Third Time, 549—Condition of the City—Entrance of the Goths—The Greeks in Hadrian's Mausoleum—Rome Repopulated—The last Games in the Circus—Totila leaves the City—The Goths at Sea—Narses takes Command of the War—A Roman Omen—Contemporary Remarks on some of the Monuments—The Forum of Peace—Myron's Cow—The Statue of Domitian—The Ship of Aeneas—Narses advances to the Foot of the Apennines—Fall of Totila at Taginas, 552.

On leaving the harbour of the Tiber, Belisarius directed his course to ancient Tarentum, but a storm driving him into Croton, he was obliged with his infantry to remain in the unfortified town, while his cavalry advanced along the celebrated shores of that gulf where the Greek colonies were already beginning to fall to decay. Here at Ruscia (the present Rossano), the ancient anchorage of the Thurians, he was overtaken and routed by Totila, who forced him again to take ship and withdraw to Messina. According to the account of Procopius, it was now the end of the thirteenth year of the Gothic war, or the spring of 548.

The whole of the following year was filled with struggles in Southern Italy; struggles which always ended to the disadvantage of the Greeks. The unfortunate Belisarius looked on in sorrowful inactivity—the reinforcements from Byzantium were scanty and useless—until at last he happily received from Justinian his recall to the East. His ignominious return to Constantinople, after having spent five unfortunate years in Italy and left the country in the power of the victorious enemy, was the greatest grief of his life. After deeds worthy of a hero of antiquity, the great general died in disgrace, and in oblivion so utter, that he lives in tradition a type of the uncertainty of human fate. His removal simplified the schemes of Totila. This indefatigable general, in truth a second Hannibal, having subdued several towns in Calabria, after the fall of Perugia (the siege of which had been continued by the Goths), set forth for Rome, for the third time, in the early months of 549.

Totila appears before Rome, 549.

The city was no longer commanded by Conon. Irritated by his avarice, the mutinous garrison had murdered the general, and Justinian had been obliged to promise pardon for the crime to their messengers, the Roman priests, as otherwise the soldiers would have surrendered Rome to the Goths. Diogenes, a brave and experienced general who gave hope of a successful defence, now remained in the city with 3000 men. Providing for the necessities of a siege, he had the granaries filled, and every available space within the walls sown with corn, the unfortunate Romans being forced to look on the scenes of their former greatness, perhaps the very Circus itself, covered like the Campagna with fields of waving grain.[1] Totila already stood before Rome, and already from their camp (apparently the old

[1] Καὶ πανταχόθι τῆς πόλεως σῖτον ἐντὸς τοῦ περιβόλου σπείρας—a valuable trait in the picture of the Rome of that date. Procop., iii. 36.

camp below the gate of S. Paul on the river) the Goths made frequent attack upon the walls.[1] They were, however, repulsed with energy, and even the capture of important Portus would scarcely have hastened the conquest, had treason not on this occasion again opened the gates to Totila. Isaurians stationed in the gate of S. Paolo, indignant at their long arrears of pay, and allured by the hope of rewards, such as their countrymen had previously received for having allowed the Gothic King to enter, imitated the example of their predecessors, and offered their treacherous services to Totila. One night he stationed his followers in the neighbourhood of the gate; caused musicians to be placed on two boats on the Tiber, and commanded them to sound a blast from the trumpets at a distant spot. While the troops in the city, startled at the sudden sounds of war, hastened to the place apparently threatened, the gates of S. Paul were opened, and the Goths entered. All whom they encountered were ruthlessly slain. The Greeks fled along the Aurelian Way to Centumcellae, and there fell into the ambush prepared for them, the wounded Diogenes escaping with but a few followers.

He enters the city.

Rome, as far as the tomb of Hadrian, was for the second time in the hands of Totila. A brave officer, however, the Cilician Paulus, had thrown himself

[1] The site and recollection of this camp must have been long preserved. We discover it in ecclesiastical deeds of tenure of the eighth century, where a *massa* is spoken of, *juxta campum Barbaricum ex corpore patrimonii Appiae.* Collect. Deusdedit in Borgia, *Breve Istor. del dom. Temp.,* p. 12 of the documents.

with 400 cavalry into the mausoleum. Attacked in the morning by the Goths, he drove them back with great loss. They determined to starve him out, and for two days Paulus and his followers endured the pangs of hunger; then, ashamed to devour their horses, they determined to die like heroes. Embracing each other in a last farewell, they seized their arms to rush out and sell their lives as dearly as they could. But Totila, who had heard of their project, and feared or honoured their desperate resolve, offered them a free retreat. The brave horsemen, however, their weapons in their hands, preferring to serve under the banner of a generous conqueror rather than expose themselves to poverty and derision in Byzantium, allowed themselves, with the exception of their two leaders, to be enrolled amongst the Goths.

Totila, now in possession of Rome, thought no more of abandoning, still less of destroying, the city. It is on this occasion that Procopius relates that the Goth was confirmed in his change of purpose by the scoffing reproach of the Frankish King. He found the city a lifeless waste, sparsely inhabited by miserable people, and poor as the most needy provincial town. To repopulate it he recalled Goths as well as Romans, even Senators from Campania; and, providing for their needs, gave orders that everything which had been destroyed in his first conquest should now be restored. He then invited the people to the Circus Maximus, and the last chariot races which the Romans saw were those given in farewell by a Gothic King. As the scanty files of the citizens

Revives the sports in the Circus.

and the few remaining Senators took their place on the timeworn steps of the Circus, Rome must have shuddered at this assemblage of shades, perhaps even at the games themselves, as at the sight of some mocking spirit.

But the war did not long permit of Totila's sojourn in the city. In vain had he hoped that the fall of the capital and so many victories in the provinces would have made an impression on Justinian. The Roman messengers, who were to have brought before the throne of the Emperor the representations of the sincere desire of the Goth for a peaceful settlement of affairs in Italy, had not even been admitted to Byzantium; on the contrary, the pressing entreaties of Pope Vigilius, who had been in Constantinople since January 547, united to the exhortations of the patrician Cethegus (both the Bishop and the head of the Senate were representatives of the national party in Rome), decided the Emperor to make yet greater efforts for the reconquest of Italy.

Totila, unwearied and inexhaustible in resources, again left Rome in 549; and while he held the neighbouring Centumcellae besieged by part of his troops, with four hundred vessels, which he had built or collected, he appeared as ruler of the seas. He sailed from the coast of Latium again to the Southern shores to punish hated Sicily, and to destroy any enemy that he might find in her waters. He thus appears before us in a new and appalling character. We are, however, obliged to renounce the task of following his brilliant and extraordinary achievements, neither the conquest of Sicily, Corsica, or Sardinia, nor the bold expeditions of the Goths, mariners, and forerunners of the Normans, belonging to the scope of our history.

Narses takes the command in Italy, 551.

In the seventeenth year of the war, towards the end of 551 or the beginning of 552, Narses appeared in Italy; and with his arrival the course of events suddenly changed. The struggle of a hero with a eunuch presents a strange spectacle. Fortune, which seemed to have wearied of Totila, abandoned him in favour of his adversary, and the virtues of the victor were not unworthy of his success.

A Roman omen.

An omen, as quoted by Procopius on the authority of a Roman Senator, had long previously announced his victory. The historian relates that, during the reign of Athalaric, as a herd of oxen was one day being driven across the Forum, a steer suddenly mounted the bronze statue of a cow which stood upon a fountain, an occurrence which a Tuscan peasant, who accidentally passed by, interpreted as an omen that a eunuch was destined to subdue the ruler of Rome.[1] The anecdote would scarcely have arrested our attention, had not the casual observations of the historian on the works of art existing in the city in his day served to recall it to our minds.

Some works of art in Rome.

Procopius saw the Forum of Peace and the adjacent Temple (struck by lightning, and never afterwards restored), the traces of which have since so completely disappeared. He saw the Fountain, and the bronze cow which he esteemed a work of Phidias or Lysippus, and informs us that in his time many statues from

[1] Procop., iv. 21.

the hands of both artists still remained in Rome. Without, however, specifying these works, he mentions another statue bearing the signature of Phidias. "There also," said he, "stands the cow of Myron." It is possible that the celebrated statue may either have been brought to Rome by Augustus; or that the Byzantines may have confounded this work of Myron's hands, which Cicero had seen in Athens, with some of the other bronze statues of cows then existing in the city. The Romans had an especial liking for representations of animals, and the most precious work in the city was the bronze dog licking his wounds, which stood in the Capitoline Temple. The Forum Boarium derived its name from the statue of an ox; Augustus had adorned the Vestibule of the Temple of Apollo Palatinus with four bulls from the hand of Myron.[1] Statues of animals also stood around and on the confines of the Roman Forum, the elephant Herbarius on the side of the Capitol next the Tiber, and the bronze elephants on the Via Sacra. On these, as they had only a short time before been restored by Theodatus, the eyes of Pro-

[1] That the Forum Boarium derived its name from this source is beyond a doubt: *area quae posito de bove nomen habet,* says Ovid, *Fastor.,* 6, v. 478; Tacit., *Annal.,* 12, c. 24; Plin., ii. 34; Nardini, *Roma Ant.,* ii. p. 257. Of the eleven epigrams of Ausonius on Myron's cow, I only quote No. 66:—

Quid me, taure, paras, specie deceptus, inire?
Non sum ego Minoae machina Pasiphaae.

Winckelmann, *Gesch. der Kunst des Alltert.,* iv. B. 9, c. 2, note 372, followed by his translator Fea, concludes, from the above passage of Procopius, that Myron's cow was actually in Rome at the time in question.

copius must have also rested.[1] The historian further mentions a bronze statue of Domitian standing on the Clivus Capitolinum to the left of the entrance to the Forum, and since he remarks that this is the only statue of Domitian, it is clear that the celebrated equestrian statue of the Emperor, described so minutely by Statius in the first poem of his *Silvae,* is not taken into account. This renowned work stood, according to Statius, on the Forum itself, but at the time of Procopius was no longer in existence. The bronze statue, therefore, of which the historian speaks, must have been that which stood before the Senate house built by Domitian.[2]

Had the historian of the Gothic war been able to describe some of the works of art which belonged to his period in Rome, he would have rendered an inestimable service. The Romans of his time, in their ignorance, doubtless attributed many statues on insufficient grounds to the most celebrated of Greek masters, and perhaps the pedestals of the two Colossi in front of the Baths of Constantine may even at this period have borne the

[1] Cassiodorus (*Var.,* x. 30) takes occasion to discourse of the nature of the elephant with childish garrulity.

[2] Procop., *Histor. Arcana,* c. 8: ἐπὶ τῆς εἰς τὸ Καπετώλιον φερούσης ἀνόδου ἐν δεξιᾷ ἐκ τῆς ἀγορᾶς ἐνταῦθα ἰόντι. According to Statius (*Silv.,* i. v. 66), the equestrian statue stood between the Basilicae Julia and Aemilia, and had the Temples of Vespasian and Concordia behind and the Lacus Curtius before it. It may with safety be assumed that it occupied the spot in front of the column of Phocas. Nibby supposes that at the date of the *Notitia* the equestrian statue of Domitian was popularly held to be the Caballus Constantini (*Rom. Ant.,* p. 138). Had the statue, however, been still in existence, it is hard to believe that it could have escaped the notice of Procopius.

names of Phidias and Praxiteles. Procopius, while applauding the love of the Romans for their monuments, which, in spite of the long period of barbarian rule, they had jealously preserved,[1] describes one work of alleged antiquity with especial minuteness. This was the fabulous Boat of Aeneas preserved in the Arsenal on the shores of the Tiber.[2] He describes it as a vessel with one bank of oars, 120 feet long, and 25 feet broad; the planks of it were skilfully joined together without clamps; the keel consisted of one immense trunk slightly curved. The credulous Greek has recorded his admiration of this work, "surpassing all conception," assuring his readers at the same time that the vessel looks as if just fashioned by a carpenter, and betrays no traces of decay.[3]

After this cursory survey of the works of art in the fallen city, we return to Totila and Narses. The new general, furnished with full power over the imperial treasury, generous, skilful, and eloquent, collected a large army in Dalmatia, the motley nature of which presented the varied aspect of a

[1] I have already quoted the passage in Procop., iv. 21.

[2] Νεώσοικος means *navale*. I have already indicated the probable site of the Navalia. But the expression of Procopius, ἐν μέσῃ τῇ πόλει, causes some difficulty.

[3] Procopius had seen in Corcyra the marble vessel in which Ulysses had sailed to Ithaca; but he noticed, with regard to the inscription, that it was a votive gift of Jupiter Casius. In Euboea he saw the dedicated ship of Agamemnon, of which he gives the mutilated inscription. (*De bello Goth.*, iv. 22.) He must also have seen like votive ships in Rome itself; one such—although only a copy due to the time of Leo X.—still stands in front of S. Maria in Navicella on the Coelian.

crusade. Huns, Langobards and Heruli, Greeks Gepidae, even Persians, entirely differing in outward form, in language, weapons, and customs, but all moved with a like desire for the treasures of Italy, were assembled by Narses at Salona. Along the marshy coasts of the Adriatic he skilfully led these troops to Ravenna, and Totila was startled by the unexpected news that his adversary was already advancing towards the Apennines.

The Gothic King was at the time in Rome. Soon after leaving Sicily he had returned to the city, there to await the arrival of Narses. Summoning some of the Senators, he committed to them the care of the restoration of the city; the rest of the patricians he left in custody in Campania. The Fathers thus summoned to Rome were entirely destitute of means to provide for public affairs, and were themselves treated as slaves of war by the suspicious Goths. It appears that Totila lingered a considerable time in the city, whence he may, on a previous occasion, have directed the enterprise against the Greek coasts. He was at least in Rome when Narses advanced from Ravenna, and there remained to await those Goths who had hitherto been stationed under Tejas at Verona to bar the passage of the Po against the enemy. After receiving these reinforcements, with the exception of 2000 horse, he left Rome, and, advancing through Tuscany, pitched his camp in the Apennines, at a spot named Taginas. Narses arrived soon after, and took up his station, at a distance of only a hundred stadia, at the graves of the Gauls (Busta Gallorum), where, according to legend, this people had been conquered by Camillus. It is the plain near Gualdo Tadino.

Here was seen for the last time the heroic form of Totila. Procopius describes him to us the morning before the beginning of the fight, between the two armies placed in order of battle, and we seem to see before us the ideal knight of the Middle Ages. Clad in armour glittering with gold, helmet and lance adorned with the plumes of royal purple, he sat his magnificent charger, and gave both armies a spectacle of his skill in the arts of horsemanship. He made his horse prance, wheeling in circle upon circle on the field, bending from side to side with youthful dexterity, or hurling his spear in the air to seize it again in full gallop. Night found him dead, his lines of battle broken, and his followers scattered in flight. As, wounded by an arrow, he had turned to leave the field, a Gepidan struck him through the body with a lance; his companions bore him with difficulty to a spot called Capras. Here he died and was hurriedly buried. It was now the summer of 552.

Death of Totila, 552.

The Greek historian has honoured with his lament the unworthy fate of so glorious an enemy, and others have ranked Totila beside the heroes of antiquity. If the greatness of the hero be set against the crowd of hindrances which he has overcome, or against the perversity of fate, in the face of which he has to struggle, then is Totila more deserving of immortality than Theodoric. Not only in his youth, amid unexampled struggles, did he restore his shattered kingdom; he defended and maintained it for eleven years against Belisarius and the army of Justinian. Further if nobility of character be accepted as the test of human worth, neither amongst the heroes of antiquity, nor those of succeeding times, can we discover many to equal the great Goth in magnanimity, justice, and moderation.

3. TEJAS LAST KING OF THE GOTHS—NARSES TAKES ROME BY STORM—CAPITULATION OF HADRIAN'S MAUSOLEUM—RUIN OF THE ROMAN SENATE—CAPTURE OF THE GOTHIC FORTRESSES—NARSES ADVANCES TO CAMPANIA—HEROIC DEATH OF TEJAS IN THE SPRING OF 553— CAPITULATION OF THE GOTHS ON THE BATTLEFIELD OF VESUVIUS—RETREAT OF THE THOUSAND GOTHS UNDER INDULFUS—SURVEY OF GOTHIC RULE IN ITALY—IGNORANCE OF THE ROMANS WITH RESPECT TO THE GOTHS AND THE HISTORY OF ROMAN ANTIQUITIES.

Six thousand Goths covered the field of Taginas; the remainder had been scattered. The greater part of the fugitives hastened across the Po, and at Pavia chose Tejas, the bravest of their warriors, as King. Narses meanwhile, after having richly rewarded and dismissed his wild Lombard auxiliaries, had withdrawn from the field of battle towards Tuscany, and taking Perugia, Spoleto, and Narni by assault, appeared before Rome.

Tejus last King of the Goths.

The little Gothic garrison here prepared for stout resistance, but, relinquishing the idea of defending the whole extent of the walls, they confined themselves to the mausoleum of Hadrian. Totila had made this building the centre of new fortifications, had enclosed the space surrounding it with a wall, and united it with the city walls by means of Hadrian's Bridge.[1] Here the Goths had deposited their most valuable possessions. Narses, equally recognising the impossibility of surrounding the entire city, placed portions of his troops at different points, and caused the walls to be stormed where he thought best, while the Goths, assembling at the threatened spots, were obliged to leave the remainder unheeded. After several unsuccessful attacks led by Narses, John, and the Herulian Philemuth, the Greeks, under the leadership of Dagisthaeus, at last scaled the walls at an entirely unprotected spot and sprang into the city. Resistance was too late. The Goths fled, some hastening to Portus, others thrusting themselves into Hadrian's mausoleum, where, however, Narses did not long allow them to remain. They capitulated on condition of retaining their lives and freedom.

Narses enters Rome, 552.

Thus in 552, in the six and twentieth year of the reign of Justinian, in whose time the city, as Procopius remarks, was conquered no less than five times,[2] Rome fell again into the power of the Byzantines. Once more the victor sent the keys to the Emperor at Constantinople, and the Emperor

[1] Procop., iv. 33: τειχίσματι βραχεῖ ὀλίγην τινὰ τῆς πόλεως μοῖραν ἀμφὶ τὸν 'Αδριανοῦ περιβαλὼν τάφον καὶ αὐτὸ τῷ προτέρῳ τείχει ἐνάψας φρουρίου κατεστήσατο σχῆμα.

[2] In 536 by Belisarius; in 546 by Totila; in 547 by Belisarius; in 549 by Totila; and in 552 by Narses.

accepted them with a like degree of satisfaction as he had shortly before shown on receiving the bloody robe and royal helmet of Totila.

Extinction of the Senate.

The Greek historian on this occasion relates in prosaic words the downfall of the oldest and most celebrated of Roman institutions, the recollection of its great past failing to evoke the faintest expression of sympathy. This victory, he says, was to the Roman people, as well as to the Senate, the cause of a great misfortune. The retreating Goths, despairing of being any longer able to retain Italy, in their revenge pitilessly slew all Romans whom they chanced to meet, and their example was followed by the barbarians who served under the flag of Narses. Instigated by love of their native city, many Romans hastened back on the news that it was liberated. Many of those Senators who had been exiled by Totila to Campania still remained in banishment, only a few having been taken by John to Sicily.[1] Some of these men now hurried back to Rome, but the Goths, hearing of their flight or their intention, immediately put to death any who still remained in the fortresses of Campania. Among these victims Procopius only mentions by name the Anician Maximus. With the downfall of so many patricians was further at the same time associated the murder of three hundred noble Italian youths. Before setting forth to meet Narses, Totila had chosen these youths (sons of the most illustrious families) from various cities, and had them sent as hostages

[1] Πολλοὶ τῶν ἀπὸ τῆς ξυγκλήτου βουλῆς, expressly says Procopius, iv. 34, .

beyond the Po; and here, by the orders of Tejas, they were now put to death.[1]

The senatorial families were thus reduced to a very few representatives; to the few, in fact, who had either succeeded in escaping to Constantinople or Sicily, or who, having returned at the end of the war with the other fugitives, were now to be found in Rome. A scanty remnant of the ancient nobility again represented for a time a shadow of the Senate until in the beginning of the seventh century this phantom also disappeared, together with the once glorious names of Senator and Consul. These names were, however, revived in later times and borne as titles by the wealthy and distinguished.[2]

Narses had meanwhile snatched Portus from the Goths, and, with the fall of Nepi and of Petra Pertusa,

[1] Procop., *ibid.*, speaks of 300 youths belonging to provincial towns: τῶν ἐκ πόλεως ἑκάστης δοκίμων Ῥωμαίων τοὺς παῖδας ἀγείρας. Curtius, *De Senatu Rom.*, p. 142, misunderstands the passage, supposing the hostages to have been the children of Roman Senators. Roger Willmanns, in his treatise, "Rom vom 5 bis zum 8 Jahrhundert," in Schmidt's *Zeitschrift für Geschichtswissenschaft*, ii. Heft 2, p. 141, allows himself to be betrayed into the same error. He is also mistaken in the assertion that Totila had formerly suppressed, and later reinstated, the Senate; Procopius says not a word of this. Totila merely led the Senators into imprisonment and later twice summoned some of them back to the city.

[2] I find confirmation of my views in Karl Hegel's *Geschichte der Städteverfassung von Italien*, Bd. i. v. To put it shortly, the Roman Senate expired after the overthrow of the Goths: *deinde paulatim Romanus defecit senatus, et post Romanorum libertas cum triumpho sublata est. A Basilii namque tempore Consulatum agentis usque ad Narsetem Patricium provinciales Romani usque ad nihilum redacti sunt.* So Agnellus, the biographer of the Bishops of Ravenna, tom. ii., *Vita S. Petri Senior.*, c. 3.

had made himself master of all the fortresses in the Tuscan district as far as Centumcellae, to which the Greeks now laid siege.[1] Narses himself lingered in Rome, occupied with the disposal of affairs in the city;[2] a part of his army he shipped to Cumae in Campania, where Aligern, the heroic brother of Tejas, defended the Gothic treasure; another body of troops he sent under the command of John into Etruria to harass the progress of Tejas. The last King of the Goths, deceived in the hope of receiving assistance from the Franks, directed his march to Campania to save the important stronghold of Cumae. By tedious and difficult paths, he boldly advanced southwards along the Adriatic coast, and suddenly appeared in Campania. On hearing of his arrival, Narses collected his troops, and hastened to Naples by the Appian or Latin Way.

For two months Greeks and Goths remained opposite each other in the lovely fields of the lower slopes of Vesuvius, separated by the river Draco or Sarnus, where it falls into the sea by Nocera; until at length the treacherous surrender of the fleet compelled Tejas to break up his camp. The dismayed Goths assembled on the slopes of Mons Lactarius, until, driven down by hunger, they

[1] The ancient Roman colony, Nepi or Nepet (Νέπα in Procopius), is a little place near Civita Castellana. Sir William Gell (*The Topography of Rome and its Vicinity*) there claims to recognise remains of Gothic fortifications. Pietra Pertusa lies ten miles from Rome along the Flaminian Way. The name survived in a farm long after the place itself had been destroyed by the Lombards. Westphal, &c., p. 135. With regard both to name and place, see Cluver, *Ital. ant.,* ii. p. 529.

[2] Procop., iv. 34: αὐτὸς δὲ Ῥώμην διακοσμῶν αὐτοῦ ἔμεινε.

determined to perish like heroes. The glorious struggle of the last Goths on the most beautiful scene on earth, at the foot of Vesuvius, over the grave of the vanished cities of antiquity, and in sight of the lovely bay of Naples, closes the history of the heroic German race. The thought of their overthrow, mitigated though it be with the recollection of the greatness by which it was accompanied, fills us even now with pain. The Goths fought with unexampled courage, Procopius himself acknowledging that no hero of ancient history had excelled Tejas in bravery. In inferior numbers they strove in closely serried lines from daybreak until night, their King, surrounded by a chosen band of heroes, at their head. In the thickest of the battle, a hailstorm of arrows and lances falling on his buckler, stood Tejas furiously felling his assailants. As soon as one shield became overweighted by the arrows which pierced it, he took another from the hand of his armour-bearer, and fought steadily on. Thus he struggled until midday, when, unable any longer to support the burthen of his shield, weighted as it was with twelve lances yielding not a foot nor pausing in the fight, he loudly called for his armour-bearer. But, as he now stood exchanging his shield, he staggered, thrust through by a spear, and fell backwards.

The Greeks bore the bloody head of the last King of the Goths in triumph on a lance between the ranks of battle, but although the sight struck dismay into the hearts of his followers they soon rallied and continued to fight with unabated energy until night concealed the enemy and themselves. After a brief repose they arose in the early morning to renew the combat, which raged without interruption until night fell for the second time. As, worn out with fatigue, they now counted their diminished ranks, they held a council of war, and decided to negotiate with the enemy. The same night some of their leaders appearing before Narses said that: "The Goths recognised that it was useless to fight against the will of God; they scorned flight and desired a free retreat, to leave Italy to live, not as subjects of the Emperor but as free men, in some foreign land. They further demanded permission to take with them their possessions scattered in various towns." Narses hesitated, but John, who had experienced the determination of the Goths in a hundred fields, advised him to accept the proposals of heroes resolved to die. While the treaty was in progress, a thousand Goths, led by the brave Indulfus, scorning every stipulation as dishonourable, quitted the camp; and, as the Greeks yielded to the resolution of desperate men and allowed them to pass, they boldly effected their retreat to Pavia. The remainder promised by a solemn oath to fulfil the provisions of the treaty and leave Italy. With these events, which took place in March 553, ended the eighteenth year of this disastrous war.[1]

Where the last remnant of the Goths wandered at

[1] Here Procopius, after having briefly told us that the Greeks took Cumae and all the other fortresses, closes his invaluable history of the Gothic war. Aligern, however, defended Cumae and the Cave of the Sibyl for fully a year with conspicuous bravery.

length from the battlefield of Vesuvius, we do not know; their sorrowful exit from the beautiful country for which their fathers had fought, and where innumerable scenes reminded them of glorious deeds in the past, remains shrouded in mystery.

Retrospect of Gothic rule in Italy.

The kingdom established by Theodoric had lasted only sixty years. During this period the transition from Antiquity to Mediaevalism had been accomplished in Italy, and to the Goths, who stood on the confines of the two ages, belongs the imperishable glory of having been the protectors of the ancient culture of Europe in the dying hours of the Roman world.[1] The Goths themselves remained strangers in Italy on account of the innate opposition which they offered to the nationality and religion of the Latins; further, because they were powerless to infuse a fresh vitality into the land which they had conquered. It is idle to speculate in the face of the facts of history as to what form Italy and the West might have assumed had the Goths been allowed to settle permanently in the conquered land, had opportunities been granted them of self development, of peaceful intercourse, and of fusion with the Italian race. Under their sceptre the country was united for the last time, and in the premature overthrow of the Goths the national unity of Italy perished.

The Goths represented in outward form, customs, and language that primitive race of Zamolxis or

[1] *Gothorum laus est civilitas custodita.* This admission of Cassiodorus (*Var.*, ix. 14) forms the epitaph on the Goths, and ought to be borne in mind by the Italians.

Ulfilas, of whom, according to the testimony of Jordanes, Dio said, in his lost history of the Goths that they were wiser than all barbarians, and in genius closely resembled the Greeks.[1] To the great facility for culture, which the shortness of their tenure in Italy had not given time to develop, they united the gentleness and also the manliness of the Teutonic character, and, if we but compare the period of Gothic rule with any later foreign government in Italy, further comment is unnecessary.

We may, however, add the sentence of the greatest of Italian historians on the Ostrogoths: "If we mention the name of Goth in Italy," says Muratori, "some of the people shudder, chiefly the half-educated, as if we spoke of inhuman barbarians, destitute of laws and taste. Old buildings of bad style are called Gothic architecture, and Gothic is the rude character of print at the end of the fifteenth or the beginning of the following century.[2] These are the judgments of ignorance. Theodoric and Totila, both Kings of the Gothic nation, were certainly not free from many faults, but

[1]Jordan., *De reb. Get.,* c. 5: *unde et pene omnibus barbaris Gothi sapientiores semper extiterunt, Graecisque pene consimiles.* Compare with this statement the memorable letter of the Visigothic King Sisebut to Adelwald, King of the Lombards, where the German character is depicted: *genus inclitum, inclita forma, ingenita virtus, naturalis prudentia, elegantia morum.* Troya, *Cod. Dipl. Long.,* i. p. 571, according to Florez, *España Sagrada,* vii. 321–328.

[2] In the age of Humanism the so-called Gothic character was exchanged for the Antiqua. Valla expressly designates the pre-humanistic characters as Gothic: *codices Gothice scripti,* and bewails the *depravatio* of the Roman handwriting (*Elegant.,* lib. iii. praef.).

each possessed the love of justice, moderation, wisdom in the choice of his officials, abstemiousness, sincerity in his treaties, and other notable virtues to such a degree as to render him a model in the art of good government. It is sufficient to read the letters of Cassiodorus and the history of Procopius, himself an enemy of the Goths. Moreover, these rulers did not in any wise change the magistrates, the laws or the customs of the Romans, and the legends of their bad taste are but childish folly. The Emperor Justinian was more fortunate than the Gothic Kings, but if only half related by Procopius be true, he was excelled in virtue by these very Goths."[1] "The Romans," Muratori further says, "longed for a change of masters; they changed them indeed, but they paid for the fulfilment of their desires by the incalculable losses inseparable from a long and tedious war; and, what is worse, the change involved the utter ruin of Italy in a few years, and plunged the country into an abyss of misery."[2] The best apology for Gothic rule is to be found in the state of tedious and utter misery into which Italy sank, when, after the overthrow of the Goths, the wild Lombard race had settled on the ruins of the kingdom of Theodoric.

Throughout the entire course of the Middle Ages,

[1] Procopius, in the *Historia Arcana,* c. 6, &c., brands Justinian as a foolish and malicious impostor, greedy alike for gold and blood, and portrays him as a second Domitian. The notorious description of Theodora, which almost taxes the belief of the most wanton libertine, follows in c. 9. Compare the learned comments of Alemannus on these passages.

[2] *Annal. d'Italia ad Ann.* 555; and the enlightened opinion of La Farina, *Storia d'Italia,* i. p. 61, &c.

Ignorance of the Romans and Italians concerning the Goths.

down to later times and even in the age of Humanism, the Romans retained the absurd belief that the Goths had destroyed their city.[1] Of the wonderful fables that were in circulation we are informed by the memoirs of Flaminius Vacca, a Roman sculptor, bearing the date of 1594, and the history of the city exhibits proofs of the ignorance of the Romans concerning their monuments.[2] While the inhabitants surveyed the remains of their ancient city, and knew not that, more even than time, the rude barons of the Middle Ages and even popes had destroyed the monuments of antiquity, they recollected from tradition that the Goths had long ruled Rome, frequently stormed, conquered, and plundered her. They saw the greater part of the ancient buildings, the triumphal arches, and the huge walls of the

[1] This belief was greatly strengthened by the national sentiment fostered in Italy by the Humanists. Nevertheless, Flav. Blondus was sufficiently impartial to acquit the Goths of the reproach of Vandalism. In his *Roma Instaur.,* n. 99, f., he says: *ut per annos septuaginta quibus Ostrogothi regno Romae et Italiae sunt potiti, Octaviani Augusti Trajani Hadriani Antonini Pii aut Alexandri Severi amorem in Romanam rem desiderari non oportuit.* In the face of the popular ignorance he shows that the destruction of the aqueducts was not the work of the Goths, but of the Romans, who were in search of building materials. In the *Italia Illustrata* (Etruria) Blondus has also exonerated Totila from the charge of having reduced Florence to ruins. Leon Battista Alberti also diverts the reproach from the heads of the barbarians to that of the Romans themselves (*De re aedif.,* x. 1).

[2] Flaminio Vacca, collecting material for the antiquary, Anastasius Simonetti of Perugia, makes notes of various objects which he had seen discovered or dug up. See Fea in the *Miscellan.,* t. i., and Nibby in the Appendix to Nardini's *Roma Antica*: "Memorie di varie antichità trovate in diversi luoghi della città di Roma, scritte da Flaminio Vacca nell' anno 1594."

Colosseum as we see them now, pierced with innumerable holes; and not being able to explain these holes, came to the conclusion that they had been made by the Goths, either in order to break out the stones with levers, or to (which was more sensible) tear away the bronze clamps.[1] In Vacca's time were shown the so-called hatchets of the Goths, hatchets with which they had broken the statues; the naïve sculptor relating that one day two hatchets had been found in the "vigna" where the so-called temple of Caius and Lucius (called by the people "Galluzi") stood, and that they bore on one side a club and on the other a halberd. "I believe," he adds, "that these were the weapons of the Goths, that the edge served in battle to cleave the shield, the club to destroy the antiquities."[2]

The imagination of the Romans even discovered

[1] The learned Suares, Bishop of Vaisson, writing his *Diatriba de foraminibus lapidum in priscis aedificiis,* in 1651, puts forward seven suggestions to account for these holes, without being able to decide on any. 1. Envy of the barbarians, who, since they were not able to destroy the monuments, disfigured them. 2. That the holes had originated in the preparations for constructing dwellings. 3. Through barricades in the times of revolution. 4. Through the removal of concealed metal clamps. 5. In the search for hidden treasures. 6. That they had been formed in the original building for the purpose of construction 7. That they had arisen in the Colosseum when the arches were converted into booths. See also Marangoni, *Delle Memorie sacre e profane dell' Amfiteatro Romano,* Rome, 1746, p. 46 &c. Fea, *Sulle rov.,* pp. 276, 277, speaks with reason of the improbability of the damage having been the work of the barbarian. Vacca naïvely says: *tutti bucati all' usanza de' Goti, per rubarne le sprange.* I myself am of opinion that the holes arose in great part from the removal of the clamps in times when there was a great scarcity of metal.

[2] Fl. Vacca, n. 17.

the funeral urns of the Goths who had fallen at the siege of Vitiges. When, at the gate of San Lorenzo, several sarcophagi of granite and marble were one day found, they were held to be Gothic on account of their workmanship, and "I believe," the same sculptor says, "they belong to the time when poor Italy was ruled by the Goths, and I remember to have read that the Goths received a repulse at this very gate. Perhaps they were funeral urns of the officers who perished in the assault, and who wished to be buried on the spot where they fell."

It is amusing to discover fables such as these current in Rome at so late a date; to find that people still believed that the Goths had not only buried their treasures in the city, but had marked the spots where these treasures lay concealed, and that their descendants knew of these hiding places. So great was the popular ignorance that, down to the end of the sixteenth century, it was commonly believed that Goths, living in some unknown quarter, came by stealth to the city in search of the spoils of their forefathers, and prosecuted their excavations with an even greater ardour than many cardinals, without a like knowledge, had already prosecuted theirs. Flaminio Vacca, with naïve simplicity, gives us the following anecdote:—

"Many years ago I went to see the antiquities. I found myself beyond the gate of San Bastian at the Capo di Bove (the mausoleum of Cecilia Metella), and, as it was raining, I stepped into a little Osteria below. While waiting there, I talked with the host, who told me that a few months before a man had come for some fuel, and had returned in the evening with three companions for supper. After supper they all went away, the three companions never exchanging a word. The same thing happened three evenings in succession. My host, suspected that something wrong and resolved to accuse them. One evening when they had supped as usual, he watched them by moonlight, and saw them enter some caverns in the Circus of Caracalla (Maxentius). On the following morning, having informed the authorities of what had taken place, search was made in the caverns, when a quantity of loose earth and a deep hole were discovered, and amid the earth numerous recently broken fragments of earthenware vases and iron instruments which had been used in digging. Wishing to convince myself of these facts, and being near the spot, I entered and saw the excavations and the fragments of vases, which resembled tubes. It is supposed that these men were Goths, who, following the same old clues, had here unearthed a treasure."[1]

Another tale is as follows:—"I recollect that in the time of Pius IV. a Goth came to Rome having in his possession a very ancient book, dealing with a hidden treasure, with a serpent and a figure in bas-relief; on one side of it was a Cornucopiae, and on the other it pointed to the earth. The Goth sought until he found the described bas-relief on the side of an arch; then, going to the Pope, begged for permission to dig for the treasure, which, as he said, belonged to the Romans. After going to the people

[1] Fl. Vacca, n. 81.

he received the required permission, set to work with a chisel at the side of the arch, and laboured until he had made a opening. The Romans, suspicious of the enmity of the Goths, believing that they still harboured the desire to destroy the monuments of antiquity, and fearing that the man might undermine the arch, attacked him, in the prosecution of his work, with such violence that, thankful to make his escape, he left his design unfulfilled.[1]

Fables such as these were the only associations retained by the Romans of the glorious period of Gothic rule, and the care displayed by the barbarians for the monuments of antiquity. We shall, however, see hereafter that, during the Middle Ages, the ignorance of the people reached such a depth that even Caesar, Augustus, and Virgil disappeared from the sight of their descendants in the mists of fable.

[1] Fl. Vacca, n. 103. The arch itself is not specified, but may have been that of Septimius Severus. The ancient myth concerning buried treasures ever and anon reappears in Rome. I came across it in December 1864, when, with the sanction of the Pope, excavations were made in search of a treasure in the Colosseum. A man feigned to have discovered an old parchment which gave an accurate description of the spot where this treasure lay hid. For fourteen days they dug under the arch of entrance on the side of the Lateran and an engine was incessantly engaged in pumping out the water, which rushed like a stream about the amphitheatre. The search, however, brought to light nothing but the bones of some animals.

CHAPTER VII.

1. Descent into Italy of Barbarian Hordes under Bucelin and Leutharis and their Overthrow—Triumph of Narses in Rome—The Goths Capitulate in Compsa—Condition of Rome and Italy after the War—Justinian's Pragmatic Sanction— Increased Importance of the Roman Bishop—The Senate—Public Buildings—Death of Vigilius—Pelagius Pope, 555—Oath of Purgation.

Invasion of Leutharis and Bucelin.

The victory of Narses was not yet complete. A frightful horde of barbarians suddenly descended upon the unhappy country and threatened to overwhelm Rome. Tejas had already sought, by promises of booty and of the treasures of Totila, to induce the Franks to invade Italy, and the Goths of Upper Italy had sent them a still more urgent summons. The overthrow of the well-ordered kingdom of the Goths again set in motion the current of wandering barbarism which had been held in check by the vigilance of Theodoric. Italy, torn asunder by long wars and a thousand ills, appeared defenceless and an easy prey. More than 70,000 Alemanni and Franks crossed the Alps under the leadership of two brothers, Leutharis and Bucelin, and advancing through the northern provinces spread devastation indescribable. The feeble Greek garrisons made but trifling resistance. The general himself hastened from Ravenna to Rome, where he spent the winter of 553–4, and it was owing to the threatening attitude which he there assumed that the barbarians did not attack the city. Avoiding Roman territory, they entered Samnium, and there separated into two divisions. Leutharis advanced along the Adriatic as far as Otranto, Bucelin laying waste Campania, Lucania and Bruttium to the Straits of Messina.

The greedy hordes of robbers wandered through Southern Italy with the speed and destructive force of the elements, their aspect terrifying the historian and lowering his conception of humanity. In truth this phenomenon, one of the most terrible in the history of Italy, resembled only too nearly some dreadful visitation of nature. Leutharis and his followers, laden with spoil, had already returned to the Po at the end of the summer of 554, when pestilence seized on the leader and his hordes. Bucelin, on the contrary, having turned northwards by Reggio, had reached the Capuan territory. Here, at a spot named Tannetus, on the banks of the river Casilinus or Vulturnus, he encountered Narses. After a battle as terrible as those of Marius against the Cimbri or Teutons, the half-naked barbarians succumbed before the military skill of the Greek veterans. Cut down like cattle, barely five were left to save themselves by flight.[1]

Defeated by Narses.

[1] Agathias, the tedious and lifeless continuator of Procopius, describes the battle minutely: *Historiar.,* ii. c. 4, &c. (ed. Bonn.). See also

Narses had thus become the liberator of Italy; and the annihilation of these hordes had given him a greater claim to the gratitude of his contemporaries than even his victories over the Goths. Laden with the plunder of the slain, the spoils of Italy, the Greek army entered with rejoicings the city they had saved, and the streets of deserted Rome glittered with the last triumphal pomp which her people were to witness. The triumphal procession of Narses signified the subjugation of the German race in Italy, under whose rule the country had become free; it signified the restoration of the unity of the Roman Empire under the sceptre of the Byzantine Emperor, and it further signified the victory which the Catholic Church had gained over Arianism. Narses may well have been deemed worthy to follow the path of the Roman conquerors of old, the path which led to the Capitol; but the venerable Capitol was now nothing more than a pile of ruin haunted by great memories. And in harmony with the scene was the aspect of the Senate, a small band of nobles in purple-bordered togas, who, like a shade of the past, greeted the victor at the city gate. The triumfator, a pious eunuch, proceeded to the Basilica of S. Peter, where he was received on the steps by the clergy with hymns, and where he prostrated himself in prayer at the grave of the Apostle. His soldiers, richly rewarded and laden with spoils, gave themselves up to sensual enjoyments, "exchanging the helmet and

Paul. Diacon., *De gest. Langob.*, ii. c. 2. The *Chronicle* of Marius Aventicensis marvellously places an interval of seven years between the times of Bucelin and Leutharis.

shield for the wine-cup and lyre." But Narses, who, as at least reported by the priests, was accustomed to ascribe all his conquests to prayer, assembled his troops and, exhorting them to moderation and humility, required them to subdue sensual instincts by constant military exercises. A last struggle still awaited them; 7000 Goths, companions of the Alemanni, had thrown themselves into the fort Compsa, or Campsa, and, under the leadership of the Hun Ragnaris, here offered an obstinate resistance. They were, however, at length overcome by Narses in 555.[1]

Consequences of the Gothic war in Rome and Italy.

Having reached the close of this long and terrible war for the possession of Italy, let us try to ascertain its consequences on the condition of Rome. The city had, within a short space of time, been five times devastated by war and five times conquered. Famine, pestilence, and the sword had mown down the inhabitants by thousands. At one time driven forth one and all by the Goths, they had returned again, although not in like numbers, to be exposed afresh to all the vicissitudes of war. We cannot give the number of the population with any certainty, but according to the highest reckoning, it may have

[1] Agathias, ii. c. 13 : ἐς Κάμψας τὸ φρούριον. Muratori believes that the fortress was Compsa, now Consa; an ancient site in Hirpinian territory (Cluver, *Ital. ant.,* iv. p. 1204). Agathias is silent with regard to the Goths after the fall of Compsa. That Narses, however, did not succeed in driving them out of Italy, but that they continued dwelling on the banks of the Po, is evident from various authors. We hear of a Goth named Guidin, who, with the aid of the Franks in Verona and Brescia, revolted against Narses. Paul Diaconus, ii. 2; Theophan., *Chronogr.,* p. 201; Menander, *Excerpta,* p. 133 (he only speaks, however, of Franks). Muratori is at pains to prove that this insurrection took place in 563.

amounted to from 30,000 to 40,000 souls. The exhaustion and the misery of Rome could not at any time, even at that of the so-called exile of the Popes to Avignon, have been greater than at the end of the Gothic war. All characteristics of civil life were utterly destroyed. Private property, with the remains of such precious relics of antiquity as had escaped the Vandals and Goths, had disappeared, owing to the necessities of the siege and the extortions of the Greeks. The Romans who still remained were reduced to utter beggary, inheriting from their ancestors scarcely anything beyond bare and desolate dwellings or the right of possession over distant estates and farms on the Campagna, which, deserted as early as the third century, had now become an uninhabited desert. All traces of agriculture must long since have disappeared and every colony have been destroyed. Entire tracts were now reduced to swamps by the destruction of the aqueducts.

The condition of Rome at this time was reflected throughout the whole of Italy. In despair of being able to depict the universal desolation, we may confirm what a historian says concerning the period, that "the human mind is unable to conceive so many changes of fortune, so many cities destroyed, so many men driven into exile, so many peoples slaughtered, far less adequately to describe them."[1] Italy, from

[1] Sigon., *De Occid. Imp.*, p. 536. The words under the text in the *Breviary* of Zacharias apply to the destruction inflicted on Rome under Totila and during the Gothic war: *Haec autem descripsit scriptor urbem deplorans, cum barbari eam intrassent, diripuissent et vastassent* (Jordan., *Topogr. d. St. R.*, ii. 577).

the Alps to Tarentum, was strewn with corpses and ruins; famine and pestilence, following on the track of war, had reduced whole districts to deserts. Procopius undertook to reckon the numbers of those slain in the Greek war, but despaired of reckoning the sands of the sea. For Africa he reckons five millions, and, since Italy was three times greater than the Vandal province, he assumes that her loss was proportionately greater. The estimate, although probably somewhat exaggerated, since the Italy of that time could scarcely have numbered a population of five millions altogether, must have amounted at least to a third part of the population.[1] Amid the frightful storms of the Gothic war classical civilisation perished for ever in Rome and throughout Italy. In cities burnt, desolated and mutilated, ruins remained the sole evidences of former splendour. The prophecy of the Sibyls was fulfilled. The night of barbarism had descended on the Latin world, a darkness in which no light was visible, other than that of the tapers of the Church, and the lonely student-lamp of the monk brooding in his cloister.

Justinian regulated the affairs of Italy in his Pragmatic Sanction of August 13, 554—a celebrated edict in twenty-seven articles, called forth by the entreaties of Pope Vigilius.[2] Uniting Italy again with the Eastern Empire, Justinian confirmed all the

The Pragmatic Saction, Aug. 13, 554.

[1] Procop., *Hist. Arcan.,* c. 18.

[2] "Pragmatica Sanctio Justiniani Imper." in the *Corpus Jur. civ.* of Gothofred, t. ii., Paris, 1628, under the *Novell. Constit.* in the Appendix, p. 684, &c. It was promulgated on the Ides of August, in the twenty-eighth year of the reign of Justinian, and addressed to Antiochus, Prefect of Italy.

decrees of Athalaric, of his mother Amalasuntha, and even the appointments of Theodatus (thus recognising the dynasty of the Amal), but declared void the acts of Totila. He sought to remedy the confusion with regard to property, while he protected the property of fugitives against seizure by claimants, and established the fixity of contract from the time of the siege. In the 19th article of the Sanction the appointment of weights and measures for all provinces of Italy was made over to the Pope and Senate, which not only shows the increased municipal importance of the bishop, but also bears witness to the fact that the Senate still existed in Rome.[1] Henceforth the Pope began to exercise the influence over the administration and jurisdiction of the city which the legislation of Justinian accorded to bishops in other cities. Bishops henceforward possessed not only jurisdiction over the clergy, but the right of supervision of all Imperial officials, even the Judex of the province. They interfered in the government of the cities, and the election of the *Defensores* and of the *Patres Civitatis* depended more upon the bishops than upon the "Primates" of the cities themselves.[2] Justinian invested the Italian bishops with legal authority; and from the influence which they exercised on all branches of secular administration, the dominion of the Pope within the city by degrees arose.

[1] *Quae beatissimo Papae vel amplissimo senatui nostra pietas in praesenti contradidit.*

[2] Section 12 expressly determines the election of the provincial judges themselves *ab episcopis et primatibus uniuscujusque regionis idoneos eligendos.* These important matters are dealt with by Hegel, &c., p. 126.

The Senate.

With regard to the Senate we know nothing. Historians, however, who have sought to prove the continued existence of the Senate through the succeeding centuries, have assumed that Justinian restored this august body, replacing the loss of its most illustrious members by new creations from plebeian families.[1] Undoubtedly the ancient Roman race with its aristocracy must have been reduced to very small proportions during the Gothic wars. In the meantime, however, a new population had arisen, owing to the influx of natives of other districts. In the city, it is true, there remained behind a remnant of the State authorities, who continued to direct the administration and jurisdiction under the leadership of the Praefectis Urbi, until these authorities made way for the Imperial magistrates. Justinian gave the Senators full freedom to go and settle where and when they willed, did they wish to withdraw to their devastated estates in the Italian provinces, or to migrate to the court at Constantinople, an alternative which many naturally preferred.[2]

The same Pragmatic Sanction contained resolutions in favour of Rome, apparently however to be regarded as nothing more than benevolent wishes. Under the 22nd head it is enjoined that the public distributions (*annona*) given to the people by Theodoric, and which Justinian boasted to have revived—although the assertions of Procopius go to prove quite the

[1] The passage in John Lydus, *De Magistr.*, iii. c. 55, τῇ δὲ Ῥώμῃ τὰ Ῥώμης ἀπέσωσεν, appears to me mere verbiage.

[2] *Viros etiam gloriosissimos ac magnificos Senatores ad nostrum accedere comitatum volentibus,* &c. Sanct. Prag., c. 27.

contrary—should for the future be administered. It further decrees that even the grammarians and rhetoricians, the physicians and the learned in law, should continue to be paid the customary salaries, "in order that youth, trained in the liberal sciences, may flourish in the Roman Empire."

By this regulation was revived an edict of Athalaric, which had ordered that the salaries of the professors of grammar, eloquence, and law should be paid out of the State coffers. These payments, which had been introduced by the Emperor Hadrian, were discontinued when the Empire fell into confusion. We have reason, however, for doubting whether these good intentions of Justinian were ever carried into effect. In the utter overthrow of all public and private relations, the schools, which had again flourished under Theodoric, had perished, and rarely was a rhetorician or grammarian heard in the ancient Athenaeum or the halls of the Capitol. Latin learning died. The Roman aristocracy who, in the time of the last Emperor worthy of the name, and under the first Gothic King, eagerly, if perhaps unprofitably, had cherished literature, was now destroyed. The supporters of classic culture, the last Maecenas of Rome, had perished or had disappeared without leaving a trace. We look with grief on the dark or bloody fate of the last cultured Romans of ancient and illustrious houses, with whom the associations and traditions of Latin civilisation come to an end; on Faustus and Avienus, Festus, Probus and Cethegus, Agapitus and Turcius Rufius, on Symmachus, Boethius and Cassiodorus. The last of these great men retired to a cloister, a witness that henceforth the Church should be the only asylum where the remains of Pagan literature could hope for preservation. Moreover, the fall of the Gothic kingdom involved not merely the overthrow of schools, teachers and knowledge, but likewise the destruction of libraries, since it was utterly impossible that, in the terrible catastrophe which had overtaken the city, the splendid collections of books given in the *Notitia Urbis,* namely the Palatine and Ulpian libraries, or the libraries belonging to princely houses, could have been preserved. And as in Rome, so throughout Italy, the war of annihilation between Goths and Byzantines swallowed up the priceless treasures of ancient literature, with the exception of such remnants as had happily been collected and saved in the rising monasteries of the Benedictines.

The public buildings lastly were taken into account in a paragraph. "We command," it says, "that the accustomed privileges and grants to the city of Rome be continued henceforward, be they for the restoration of public buildings, for the channel of the Tiber, for the market, for the harbour of Rome, or the restoration of the aqueducts, in such manner that the costs shall be provided only out of such revenues as have been set apart for the purpose."[1]

Growing importance of the Pope.

Justinian now turned his attention to ecclesiastical affairs. These he hoped to establish on a permanent basis, and ecclesiastical matters constituted hencefor-

[1] *Vel foro aut portui Romano*—that by *forum* the market for bread and provisions is alone to be understood seems evident from its connection with *portus.*

ward the question of gravest import in the relations between East and West, between Rome and Byzantium. The fall of the Gothic kingdom had redounded to the advantage of the Bishop of Rome; the Arian heresy was now completely overcome; the independent kingdom in Italy was removed; his own importance in the city was increased by Justinian's ordinances; and lastly, the ruin of the old Roman nobility left bishop and priesthood masters of the field in Rome. The decay of all political virtue and manliness, and the decline of learning were the chief causes that contributed to raise the priesthood to power; and we may observe, that only in periods of exhaustion of thought and demoralisation of literature such as this does the priesthood ever attain supremacy. The Church stood in the midst of the ruin of the ancient State alone upright, alone vigorous, alone conscious of an end and aim; around her desolation reigned. She had to mourn but as a momentary loss that independence which she had enjoyed under the uncertain rule of the Arian stranger. She had been free under the Goths, but during the war she had already discovered the position which the Emperor had decided to adopt towards her, and when the clash of weapons was stilled and Rome sank into a provincial town under the military yoke of Byzantium, the Papacy had to face a doubtful and troublous future. On one side these troubles were of a theological nature, on account of the restless and sophistical spirit of the East, where Greek philosophy, not yet entirely extinguished, was indefatigable in contending against existing dogmas and in nourishing new theorems. Others had to do with her relations towards the State. The Byzantine Emperors interfered in theological matters, not so much out of inclination for such controversies as because their interference gave them an opportunity of keeping the Church subject to the State. In Justinian, whose only greatness consisted in having, through his jurists, completed the Roman Code, the policy of Imperial despotism rose again to a fearful pitch; and after him succeeding centuries offered the remarkable spectacle of the struggle of the Church of the West, represented by Rome, against the Pagan absolutism of the State, embodied in Byzantium.

Vigilius meanwhile had remained in Constantinople, engaged in a dogmatic contest with the Emperor concerning the dispute of the Three Chapters. After many difficulties, and after enduring some hard usage, Vigilius, by shameles recantation of his earlier opinions, acceded to the desire of the Emperor, and accepted the decisions of the Fifth Council (the second held in Constantinople). Justinian now yielded to the entreaties of the Roman clergy, who through Narses had implored the release of their bishop, and allowed Vigilius, and the presbyters or cardinals who accompanied him, to return to Rome. The Pope, however, was taken ill on the way, and died at Syracuse, June 555.[1] The pontificate of a Roman, who had reached the sacred chair by means of intrigue and crime, is memorable in history as being contemporary with the disruption

[1] *Lib. Pont.,* life of Vigilius. The continuator of Marcell. Comes gives 554 as the year of the Pope's death; Pagi more correctly 555; Jaffé, June 7, 555.

of ancient Rome. The city preserves no memorial of his reign, beyond a metrical inscription lamenting the sack of the churches and cemeteries by the Goths.[1]

Pelagius I., 555–560.

Some months later the archdeacon Pelagius, a Roman of noble birth, and the most influential man who had appeared among the Roman clergy since the terrible days of Totila, was elected to S. Peter's chair. He had returned a second time to Constantinople, having, by the desire of the Emperor, in whose favour he stood, accompanied Vigilius thither.

Justinian, who, since the subjection of Vigilius to the dogmas of Byzantium, had become ruler of the Western Church, now commanded the election of Pelagius, and Pelagius therefore hastened to return to Rome. A great part of the clergy and nobility, however (the *Liber Pontificalis* no longer mentions the Senate), hesitated to have any communion with the newly-elected Pope, on account of the suspicion which rested upon him of having been accessory to the sudden death of Vigilius.[2] To free himself from

[1] Vigilius restored the tombs of the martyrs, which had been destroyed by the Goths, in the cemetery of the Gordani, and repaired the broken inscriptions of Pope Damasus. See the already noted inscription in Gruter, 1171, 4, and in De Rossi's *Roma sotter.,* i. 217, 218. It ends:—

Diruta Vigilius nam mox haec papa gemiscens
Hostibus expulsis omne novavit opus.

Also another inscription in Gruter, 1170, 13:—

Hic furor hostilis templum violavit iniquus
Cum premeret vallo moenia septa Getes.

[2] *Multitudo religiosorum et sapientium nobilium. Lib. Pont.*

this suspicion, he ordered a solemn procession, and by the side of the Patrician Narses, and accompanied by the chanting of hymns, walked from the church of S. Pancrazio to S. Peter's, where, ascending the chancel, the Gospels in his hands and the cross of Christ laid upon his head, he took the oath of purgation and asserted his innocence before all the people.

Pelagius succeeded to the Papacy and the care of the unfortunate and almost annihilated city at one of the most terrible periods in her history. The distress was so great that the Pope turned to Sapaudus, Bishop of Arles, with the entreaty that he would send him money and clothes, writing that "poverty in the city has so increased, that not without pain and grief of heart can we now behold our nobly born and prosperous acquaintance of former days."[1]

2. PELAGIUS AND JOHN III. BUILD THE CHURCH OF SS. APOSTOLI IN THE REGION VIA LATA—RUIN OF THE CITY—TWO INSCRIPTIONS AS MEMORIALS OF NARSES.

The Basilica of SS. Apostoli.

In spite of the misery that universally prevailed, Pelagius began to build the beautiful church of the Apostles Philip and James, but, as he died on March 3, 560, the completion of the basilica was left to his successor, the Roman Catelinus, known as John III.

[1] *Tanta egestas et nuditas in civitate ista est, ut sine dolore et angustia cordis nostri homines, quos honesto loco natos idoneos noveramus non possimus adspicere,* Rome, April 13, 556. Jaffé, *Reg. Pont.,* 2 ed., n. 947, p. 126. See also n. 943.

The church of Pelagius is that which is now called after the Twelve Apostles, or rather the site of which is occupied by the building of Clement XI. of the year 1702, since of the original church nothing remains but six antique columns. The early basilica was of considerable size and decorated with mosaics and paintings.[1] The fact of its standing below the Baths of Constantine in the Via Lata gave rise to the opinion that it had been originally founded by Constantine and restored by Pelagius.[2] It is probable that materials from the Baths of Constantine may have been used in its construction, since in the time of Pelagius the baths must have fallen into decay, and Narses would the less have hesitated to adopt such material, from the fact that, after the destruction of the aqueducts, the baths had ceased to be of any service. A basilica could not have been

[1] A letter of Adrian I. (*Acts of the Second Council of Nicea,* Labbé, tom. viii. p. 1591) enumerates the Roman churches which were more especially decorated with mosaics, such as S. Silvestro, S. Marco, the Basilica of Julius, S. Lorenzo in Damaso, S. Maria (Maggiore), and S. Paul; he there says: *mirae magnitudinis ecclesiam Apostolorum a solo aedificantes historias diversas tam in musivo quam in variis coloribus cum sacris pingentes imaginibus.*

[2] Such is the opinion of Andr. Fulvius, *Ant. Rom.,* v., where he speaks of the Christian churches. Volaterranus, Protonotary and Vicar of the Basilica of the SS. Apostoli, described this church about the year 1454, and his words are quoted by Martinelli, *Roma ex eth.,* &c., p. 64, from the Vat. Cod., 5560. Volaterranus saw the ancient church, and read the following lines on the apse :—

Pelagius coepit, complevit Papa Joannes
Unum opus amborum par micat et meritum.

Malvasia, *Comp. storico della B. de' dodici Ap. di Roma,* Rome, 1665; Bonelli, *Mem. stor. della Basil. Constantiniana dei SS. XII. Apostoli,* Rome, 1879.

erected at this period without the aid of stones and columns from ancient buildings, and only on such an assumption is a building intelligible at all in an age of such complete exhaustion. The statement that Narses gave columns and marbles from the Forum of Trajan, and bestowed the column of Trajan with its district in perpetual right on the new basilica, is, however, a fable of later date.[1] The immediate neighbourhood of Trajan's Forum probably gave rise to the legend; but donations of this nature— making the celebrated works of antiquity over to the Church—were not customary at the period. Both the great Imperial columns, it is true, in the course of time became, like many other splendid monuments, the property of the city churches. In the year 955 Agapitus II. conferred the column of Marcus Aurelius on the convent of S. Silvestro in Capite, and we have evidence to show that before the year 1162 the column of Trajan belonged to the church *S. Nicolai ad Columpnam Trajanum* which had arisen beside it, after the splendid forum had already fallen into ruin.[2] This chapel was one of the eight churches which belonged to the basilica built by Pelagius.

The Basilica of the Apostles must be regarded as built under the auspices of Narses as a monument to the emancipation of Italy from the Goths and their Arian heresies. John III. probably raised it to

[1] Volaterranus in Martinelli.

[2] Galletti, *Del Primicerio,* n. lvi. p. 323, gives the document belonging to the year 1162, from the archives of S. Maria in Via Lata, to which I shall later have occasion to refer.

the dignity of a titular church, and to him is ascribed the settlement of its territorial property in a Bull, ratified by Honorius II. in 1127. The document, however, bears every trace of belonging to the twelfth or thirteenth century.[1]

The ardour displayed in the building of churches found no counterpart in any other sphere of public activity, and to the occupation it afforded, a great number of the poorer classes owed their means of subsistence. The houses of men and the establishments of civic life fell to decay, but the sumptuous dwellings of the saints grew and multiplied. They arose solely out of the spoils and plunder of ancient splendour, no new structure, or even the necessary restorations of public buildings or private dwellings, being any longer possible, otherwise than at the expense of the deserted and ruined monuments.

Ancient Rome fell with ever increasing rapidity to decay. The city, as well as the State, had been held upright for the last time by the Goths. With the fall of the Gothic kingdom Rome also fell. The last remains of the ancient Roman pride and of the ancient reverence for the monuments of their great forefathers disappeared with that generation, with which also the illustrious name of Patrician became almost entirely extinct. Constantinople felt no reverence for Rome, whose bishop soon excited the jealousy of the Eastern Church. In vain we seek any evidence for the fulfilment of such

[1] Printed in full in Marini, *Papir. Dipl.,* n. i. The topographical designations undoubtedly belong to the period of the *Mirabilia* and of the *Ordo Romanus Benedicti.*

promises as Justinian had given the unhappy city in the Pragmatic Sanction. To facilitate its restoration, he had allotted to each individual express permission to restore ruins out of his own private means.[1] But who was forthcoming to defray the expenses of temples, baths or theatres? and where were the authorities who, as in the time of Majorian or Theodoric, jealously watched over the monuments of antiquity to see that theywere not misused as quarries of building material?[2] The history of the city is veiled in impenetrable darkness immediately after the Gothic war and during the whole time of Narses' governorship. Nowhere do we find mention of any single building which owed its restoration to the Greek governor. Only two inscriptions remain as memorials of the so-called deliverance of Rome, both on the Salarian bridge of the Anio, destroyed by Totila and restored by Narses in 565. The pompous ostentation of these inscriptions, viewed in regard to the insignificance of the work—a little bridge over a little stream—is characteristic of the period.

Inscriptions to the honour of Narses.

"Under the reign of our Lord, the most pious and ever-triumphant Justinian, the Father of the country and Augustus, in the thirty-ninth year of his reign.

[1] Pragm. Sanct., 25.

[2] Since Justinian laid Ephesus, Cyzicus, Troy, Athens, and the Cyclades under contributions for the building of S. Sophia, it is probable that he may have also despoiled Rome for the same purpose. *Incerti Auctoris de Structura Templi—S. Sophiae* in Combefis Origin. Constant. Here and in the *Codinus,* p. 65, we are told that Maria, a Roman widow, sent eight columns, which she herself had received as dowry, to the Emperor Justinian at Byzantium: *Fuerant hae in Solis Delubro a Valeriano Imp.* (read *Aureliano*) *extructo.* It is thus evident that the Temple of the Sun was already in ruins.

Narses, the most glorious, late Praepositus of the holy palace, Ex-consul and Patrician, after the victory over the Goths, after he had overcome and laid low with marvellous rapidity their kings in open battle, and had restored freedom to the city and to the whole of Italy, restored the bridge on the Salarian Way (which had been destroyed to the level of the water by the atrocious tyrant Totila), cleansing the bed of the river and placing the bridge in better than its former condition."[1]

Eulogistic distichs, for which some poet of the time still found inspiration, arrested the attention of the traveller on the same bridge:—

Lo! where the stream erst sundered the highway, straight as an arrow
 Over the archèd bridge leads the unbroken path;
High o'er the angry stream we pass, and the sound of the waters
 Murmuring under our feet fills the delighted ear.
Go then, Romans, in joy unhindered; ever resounding
 Let your applause ring forth, echoing Narses' name.
Narses the stubborn hearts of the Goths did conquer, and Narses
Set the unbridled streams under a yoke of stone.[2]

[1] *Imperante D.N. Piisimo Ac Triumphali Semper Justiniano P. P. Aug. Ann. XXXVIIII. Narses Vir Gloriosissimus Ex Praeposito Sacri Palatii Ex Cons. Atque Patricius Post Victoriam Gothicam Ipsis Eorum Regibus Celeritate Mirabili Conflictu Publico Superatis Atque Prostratis Libertate Urbis Romae Ac Totius Italiae Restituta Pontem Viae Salariae Usque Ad Aquam A Nefandissimo Totila Tyranno Destructum Purgato Fluminis Alveo In Meliorem Statum Quam Quondam Fuerat Renovavit.*

—*C. I. L.*, vi. 1199.

[2] *Quam bene curvati directa est semita pontis*
Atque interruptum continuatur iter.

3. NARSES FALLS INTO DISGRACE—HE GOES TO NAPLES AND IS BROUGHT BACK BY POPE JOHN—HIS DEATH IN 567—OPINIONS CONCERNING THE CAUSE OF THE LOMBARD INVASION—ALBOIN FOUNDS THE LOMBARD KINGDOM, 568—ORIGIN OF THE EXARCHATE—THE GREEK PROVINCES OF ITALY—THE ADMINISTRATION OF ROME.

Narses spent the last years of his life in Rome, dwelling in the Palace of the Caesars; but the annals of his sojourn in Italy, as Patrician and Lieutenant of the Empire, are limited to some accounts of his continued wars against the Franks and the remnant of the Goths. Pestilence meanwhile, which had made its appearance in June 542, has since continued its ravages in the West. The utter darkness in which, for some decades after the fall of the Goths, history is shrouded, is rendered yet more sinister by the awful destruction worked by the forces of Nature. Rome

Calcamus rapidas subjecti gurgitis undas
Et lubet iratae cernere murmur aquae.
Ite igitur faciles per gaudia vestra Quirites
Et Narsim resonans, plausus ubique canat.
Qui potuit rigidas Gothorum subdere mentes
Hic docuit durum flumina ferre jugum.
—*Corp. I. L.*, vi. 1199a.

Even these solitary monuments to the memory of Narses have perished; they were destroyed when the Neapolitans broke down the bridge on their retreat from Rome in 1798. A bridge erected in its place was blown up by the papal soldiers on the approach of Garibaldi's troops in 1866, but has since been entirely rebuilt. Padre Eschinardi, *Dell' Agro Roman.*, p. 324, is of opinion that Narses also restored the Ponte Nomentana over the Anio. Marius Avent. mentions under Narses' restorations especially: *Mediolanum,* and adds *vel reliquas civitates, quas Gothi destruxerant, laudabiliter reparatas,* &c.

and the whole of Italy were visited suddenly by pestilence, earthquakes, storms and inundations. Even the last years of the renowned conqueror of the Goths are lighted only by uncertain gleams, and at the end, like those of Belisarius, are lost in legend.

Disgrace of Narses.

Tradition relates that the victor of Rome and Italy, a prey to avarice, the vice of old age, spent the remainder of his declining years in the accumulation of wealth; it asserts that he amassed piles of gold, and buried treasures so vast in a fountain in some town of Italy, that after his death it took several days to bring them to light.[1] His wealth, it was said, excited the envy of the Romans;[2] but it is probable that, more than his wealth, the people found the military despotism of Byzantium, the burthen of taxation, the rapacity of the Greek vampires, the invasion of their churches, and the ill-usage to which Latin nationality was subjected, difficult to bear, and looking back with longing regret to the times of Gothic rule. Incapable of shaking the position of Narses so long as Justinian lived, the Romans sought to overthrow the favourite as soon as Justin the Younger succeeded to the throne (565). The fall of Narses is perfectly in accordance with the nature of the rule of favourites in Byzantium, more especially when the dread which his power in Italy had awakened is taken into consideration. The Romans accused him to Justin and to Justin's wife Sophia,

[1] Paul. Diacon., iii. c. 12, and the *Histor. Misc.,* xvii. p. 112, give Constantinople as the place where his wealth was found. Both authorities took the legend from Gregory of Tours, v. 20.

[2] Paul. Diacon., ii. c. 5.

writing with audacious candour: "It were better for us to serve the Goths than the Greeks where the Eunuch Narses reigns and oppresses us with slavery. Our most pious prince knows nothing of his oppressions; but deliver us out of his hands, or we shall give ourselves and the city up to the barbarians."[1] In 567, after having been rector of Italy for sixteen years, Narses received his recall from the Emperor Justin.[2] It is said that he fled from Rome to Campania on hearing that Longinus had been sent to fill his place in Italy.[3] He either did not venture to return to Constantinople, or he defied the command on being informed of the threat of the Empress Sophia that she "would make the eunuch spin wool with the women." Legend relates that Narses replied that he "would weave her such a web as would take all her lifetime to unravel," and that forthwith he sent messengers from Naples summoning the Lombards from Pannonia to Italy, sending, as evidences of the wealth of the country, choice fruits as well as other valuable things.[4]

His recall.

[1] Paul. Diacon. derives his information from the *Lib. Pont.*, life of John, where we find: *Tunc Romani invidia ducti suggesserunt Justino Augusto et Sophiae Augustae, dicentes: Quia expedierat Romanis, Gothis potius servire, quam Graecis; ubi Narses eunuchus nobis fortiter imperat, et servitio male nos subjicit.*

[2] This is evident from Agnellus, *Lib. Pont.* (*seu vitae Pontif. Ravennatium*), tom. ii., "Vita S. Agnelli," p. 127: *Tertio vero anno Justini minoris Imperatoris Narsis Patricius de Ravenna evocitatus, egressus est cum divitiis omnibus Italiae, et fuit Rector XVI. annis,* &c. This is, however, *Ann. II. cons. Justini Jun. Aug. Indict. I.* of Marius Aventicensis, and synonymous with *Ann. I. post Cons.*

[3] These are the statements of Paul. Diaconus.

[4] The fruits of Salerno (*multimoda pomorum genera*) were sent 500 years later by the earliest Norman adventurers to their brethren in

The fear of the Romans, who dreaded his revenge, was aroused by the departure of the irate governor for Naples, and Pope John was immediately despatched to try and prevail on him to return. "What harm have I done to the Romans, Most Holy Father?" cried Narses. "I will go and throw myself at the feet of him who has sent me, and all Italy shall acknowledge how with all my might I have striven for the country." The Pope soothed the aged governor and brought him back to Rome. John took up his abode in a house in the churchyard of SS. Tiburtius and Valerianus, and there remained to consecrate bishops;[1] while Narses returned to the Palace of the Caesars, where, sunk in grief and dejection, he soon afterwards died. His body, enclosed in a leaden coffin, was taken to Constantinople.[2] The assertion that he died in his 95th year is clearly an exaggeration, since it is utterly incredible that a veteran of nearly eighty could have conquered Italy in the face of such difficulties, and since, moreover, the date of his death must be fixed in 567.[3] Neither is it probable

His death in Rome.

Normandy, in order to show them that the land was a paradise. Great numbers of the Lombards, however, having served under Narses in Italy were already acquainted from their own experience with the fruits of the country.

[1] A part of the Coemeterium of Praetextus on the Via Appia. *Roma Sotterranea,* iii. c. 17, p. 190.

[2] *Lib. Pont.,* life of John; Paul. Diacon., ii. c. 11: *Narses vero de Campania Romam regressus, ibidem non post multum tempus, ex hac luce subtractus est. Cujus corpus positum in locello plumbeo, cum omnibus ejus divitiis Constantinopolim est portatum.*

[3] Agnellus, *Vita S. Petri Senioris,* ii. p. 178, places his age at 95, and says: *Italiae palatio quievit*; it was the Palace of the Caesars in

that the dismissed governor lived six years quietly in Rome, nor that the Romans, already harassed by the Lombards, could oppose the commands of the Emperor and the new Exarch, whilst they retained Narses and his treasures.[1]

Did he summon the Lombards?

The statements of the Latin chroniclers that Narses had summoned the Lombards into Italy admits of grave doubt. Favourable circumstances assuredly invited Duke Alboin to the depopulated country, the climate and fertility of which were known to all barbarians. Further, the Lombard hordes had already served under Narses himself against the Goths, and had become acquainted not only with the weakness of Italy, but also with that of the Byzantine Empire. Were it, however, true that the Greek general himself had summoned the invaders, the fact that such an act of high treason was not without parallel is shown by the history of Bonifacius, who, in a similar case, invited the Vandals to Africa. Narses found himself at the end of his life rewarded with the hatred of the Romans and the ingratitude of Constantinople; he already stood in friendly relations with the Lombards, and

Rome. Horatius Blancus, in the note to lib. ii. c. 11 of P. Diacon., thinks that *Constantinopoli* should be read instead of *Italiae*.

[1] The *Lib. Pont.* says that John was dead at the time of the death of Narses. This would then be in 573, according to the reckoning of Pagi and Muratori, and is at variance with the foregoing passages. The opinion of Baronias that Narses died in Constantinople is explained by the confusion between the general and another Narses whose praises have been sung by Corippus, an indifferent poet (*De laudibus Justini II.*), as is shown by Pagi. Cedrenus also confuses the two with regard to the subject, see Benedict., Bacchini *Dissert.*, ii. ad cap. 3 *Vitae S. Agnelli* in Agnellus, ii. 146.

the revengeful thought of bringing a fresh barbarian horde into Italy would not, in a Byzantine, have been counteracted by any feeling of patriotism. We might, however, have supposed that the pride of the conqueror of Italy, or the sense of religion ascribed to Narses, would have deterred him from such a step.[1] It was undoubtedly the latter motive which prompted him to yield to the Pope's entreaties and return to Rome. He nevertheless died at tragic variance with himself and with his past, after the Lombards, following the progress which invariably impelled barbarians from inland countries to press towards Mediterranean shores and the centre of civilisation, had already forsaken their Pannonian homes. If, at the time of the Gothic invasion, Italy had become depopulated, the country, in consequence of the prolonged wars, was now reduced to a desert, and the Lombards encountered as little resistance in settling down and replacing the void left in the population as did the Slavs when, at the end of the sixth century, they invaded Greece and covered her provinces with a fresh stratum of inhabitants.

[1] The grounds on which Baronius founds his opinion are opposed by Pagi and Muratori. The latter authority is the more cautious. Sigonius resolutely maintains the treason of Narses, *De Regno Ital.*, i. p. 6. The celebrated *Chronicon* before the edict of King Rothar, c. 7, asserts it in plain terms (*Edicta Reg. Langob.*, ed. Baudi a Vesme, Turin, 1855); also Herm., *Contract. Chron. ad Ann.* 567; further Adonis' *Chron. ad Ann.* 564. St. Marc, i. 157, rejects the account as a legend, and Zanetti, *Del Regno dei Langobardi,* i. c. 12, repudiates it in like manner. Schlosser, *Weltgesch.*, i. 81, has doubts on the subject. Finlay, *"Greece under the Romans,"* p. 278, rejects it as a fable.

Alboin, the leader of the horde, appeared in the beginning of April 568 in North Italy.[1] His numerous followers, and with them greedy swarms of Gepidae, Saxons, Sueves, and Bulgarians, descended on the rich plains of the Po, where, in the fresh vigour of their powers, they defeated the army of the Greek Emperor. During three years the barbarian King besieged Pavia, and there at length established the capital of his new Lombard kingdom; whilst the strong Ravenna, where the first German Kings, as successors of the last Roman Emperors, had dwelt, still remained the capital of Greek Italy and the seat of its regents, the Exarchs. Thus, immediately after the fall of the Goths, a second Teutonic kingdom was founded in Northern Italy. This kingdom endured for several centuries, and even now the territory watered by the Po bears the name of the invaders.

Invasion of the Lombards under Alboin, 568.

Before continuing the history of the city, we may close our present volume with a glance at the position to which Rome had attained under the new institution of the Exarchate.

Longinus, the successor of Narses, had already assumed the government of Italy in Ravenna before the appearance of the Lombards, and, following the precedent set in Africa, where the government of the province had been administered by an Exarch, had adopted that title. A complete change in the government of the country has been ascribed to Longinus; it being asserted that he gave an entirely new form to the government, removing the Consuls,

Longinus Exarch in Ravenna.

[1] "Origo gentis Langobardorum," c. 5 (*Script Langob., Mon. Germ.*).

Correctors and Presidents of provinces.[1] Our knowledge, however, of the new order of things is very imperfect. After the time of Constantine the country had been divided into seventeen provinces, thus enumerated by the *Notitia*: Venetia, Aemilia, Liguria, Flaminia and Picenum Annonarium, Tuscia and Umbria, Picenum Suburbicarium, Campania, Sicilia, Apulia and Calabria, Lucania and Bruttium, the Cottian Alps, Rhetia Prima, Rhetia Secunda, Samnium, Valerium, Sardinia, Corsica.[2]

The government of these provinces had been administered by Consulars, Correctors and Praesides while, at the same time, the seven northern remained under the jurisdiction of the Vicar of Italy, and the ten southern under that of the Vicar of Rome, and all under the Prefect of the Praetorium of Italy. The Gothic Kings had not altered this disposition of provinces, nor, although with Longinus the titles of governors disappeared, whilst the provinces remained, was any modification of existing arrangements introduced. His administrative changes first acquired importance under the advance of the Lombards.

[1] Giannone, iii. c. 5.

[2] Panciroli, *Comm. in Notit. Imp. Occid.,* p. 116. The *Catalogus provinciar. Italiae,* Appendix to the *History of the Lombards,* by Paul. Diaconus, enumerates: Venetia, Liguria and the two Rhaetias, the Cottian Alps, Tuscia, Campania, Lucania; the seventh province is defined as that of the Apennines, and is severed from the Cottian Alps; then Aemilia, Flaminia, Picenum, Valeria and Nursia and Samnium; Apulia and Calabria form the thirteenth, Sicily the fourteenth, Corsica the fifteenth, and Sardinia the sixteenth (*Mon. Germ. Script. Langob.,* ed. Bethmann, Waitz and Holder-Egger, p. 188). On the other hand, the catalogue in lib. ii. c. 14 of Paul. Diacon. enumerates eighteen provinces, the two Rhaetias being counted separately.

These newcomers pushed their conquests here and there in Greek Italy; rent the union of provinces and the unity of Italy, and even gave to the possessions of the Emperor the form of separate dukedoms or "ducates," such, for example, as Venetia, the Exarchate in a narrower sense, and Rome and Naples became.

Institution of the Exarchate.

Having stepped into the place of the Prefect of Italy, the Exarch succeeded to the chief power in all civil and military affairs. Under Constantine the civil had been separated from the military power; the Goths had maintained the system of Constantine, and the Exarch rigorously adhered to the example of his predecessors in the government.[1] Judges or "judices" were appointed in the provinces. These judges were under the supervision of the bishops; and military commanders, named in the chief cities "Duces" or "Magistri Militum," in the smaller "Tribuni," were also appointed. Notwithstanding these appointments, it cannot be shown that the provincial centralisation was overthrown by Longinus, or that the provinces henceforth were split in consequence into "ducates," that is to say, greater and smaller towns with their territories, which received such titles from their military chiefs (*duces*).[2] We may, however, conclude that through the weakening of the central power mainly, though also in a some-

[1] Savigny, *Gesch. des röm. Rechts im Mittelalter,* i, c. 6, p. 339, accepts this separation as a proof "that the internal institutions of Italy still remained unaltered."

[2] Giannone, who is by no means profound, here adopts the opinion of the superficial Blondus, *Historiar. dec.,* i. 1, 8, p, 102.

what less degree through the dismemberment of the provinces in consequence of the Lombard conquests, the cities became isolated and restricted to a political life within themselves, while their bishops by degrees acquired increased authority.[1]

Rome and the Roman duchy.

With regard to Rome, we find that the traditional chief civil authority remained unaltered under Longinus, the Prefect of the City continuing to retain his office as before. The assertion that the Exarch did away with the Consuls and the Senate, which had subsisted in name until his time, is an utter fabrication, since the ancient Imperial Consuls had already disappeared, and the title ex-Consul remained in Rome, as in Ravenna, throughout the whole of the sixth century common and even attainable by purchase.[2] The Senate endured in name as late as 579, when an embassy of Roman Senators is mentioned as going to solicit help from the Emperor Tiberius against the Lombards.[3] It is generally believed that Rome was politically governed by a Dux appointed by the Exarch, and that from the Dux was derived the Ducatus Romanus.[4] Neither can it be doubted

[1] Cesare Balbo, *Storia d'Italia,* i. c. 3, p. 18.

[2] S. Gregory, Ep. 27, lib. xii. Ind. 7, gives proof of this, speaking of Venantius, nephew of the Patricius Opilio, who, possessing no title of honour, desired to buy the *chartae ex consulatus* for thirty pounds of gold, and sued for the papal recommendation to the Byzantine court.

[3] Menander, *Excerpt.,* p. 126: διὸ δὴ καὶ ἐκ τῆς συγκλήτου βουλῆς τῆς πρεσβυτέρας Ῥώμης—πεμφθέντων τινῶν.

[3] Blond., *Histor Dec.,* i. 1, 8, p. 102: *sed a Duce Graeculo homine, quem Exarchus ex Ravenna mittebat, res Romana per multa tempora administrata est.* We have, on the other hand, the objections of the judicious Joh. Barretta, *Tabula chronogr. medii aevi: Ducatus Rom.,* n. 105.

that, as a rule, the Exarch, and at times the Emperor himself, appointed a supreme official who also possessed military authority in the city. The extent of the jurisdiction of this official is, however, unknown, but, from the universal use of the title in cities and districts, we conclude that he was known as Dux in Rome also.

No Dux of Rome is, however, mentioned during the whole of the seventh century, though Duces of Sardinia, Naples, Rimini, Narni, Nepi, &c., often appear; even in the *Liber Diurnus*—the celebrated book of Formulae of the Roman chancery—where we might reasonably expect to hear of such an official, no mention is made of a Dux of Rome.[1] In 708, however, the *Liber Pontificalis* suddenly names a Dux, and the Ducatus Romanus.[2] The same authority has, however, already spoken of "judices" or officials before this period; officials appointed by the Exarch for the administration of the affairs of the city. In the life of Pope Conon (686–687) it is related that his archdeacon hoped to ascend the papal throne through the influence of the "judices" who had been

[1] *Liber Diurnus Rom. Pont.*, ed. J. Garnerius in Hoffmann's *N. Coll.*, ii., latest edition by E. de Rozière, Paris, 1869. The compilation of this formulary is due to some date between 685 and 752. Under the formulae addressed to the Emperor, Empress, Patricius, Exarch, Consul, King, Patriarch, not a single one is found directed to the Dux of Rome, as Roger Willmanns has already remarked in his treatise.

[2] For the earliest passage which deals with the Dux, see *Vita Constantini*, n. 176: *Petrus quidam pro ducatu Romanae urbis.* Throughout the whole of the seventh century there is complete silence regarding the title Senatus or Senator.

sent by John, the new Exarch, to Rome.[1] It therefore follows that the Exarch, and apparently yearly, appointed more than one official for Rome; moreover, that these Imperial judices, amongst whom we may understand the Dux or Magister Militum, must have conducted the administration of military and fiscal affairs. The date, however, at which the idea of a "Ducatus Romanus" arose, is altogether uncertain.

[1] *Lib. Pont.*, life of Conon: *quod et demandavit suis judicibus, quos Romæ ordinavit, et direxit ad disponendam civitatem.* Willmanns is justly censured by Karl Hegel (i. p. 226) for having overlooked this passage, when he allows himself to be misled into saying that the Exarch apparently did not think it worth while to send an official to a place so insignificant as Rome.

INDEX.

This Book Was Reset to Match, Page-for-Page, the Second Revised Edition. It was Completed on June 25, 2000 at Italica Press, New York, New York. It Was Set in Times and Printed on 60 lb Natural Paper by BookMobile, St. Paul, MN U. S. A.

* *

*